SUSPECT IDENTITIES

SIMON A. COLE

Suspect Identities

A History of Fingerprinting and
Criminal Identification

HARVARD UNIVERSITY PRESS

Cambridge, Massachusetts

London, England

2001

Library of Congress Cataloging-in-Publication Data

Cole, Simon A., 1967–
  Suspect identities : a history of criminal identification and fingerprinting /
Simon A. Cole.
    p. cm.
  Includes bibliographical references and index.
  ISBN 0-674-00455-8 (alk. paper)
    1. Fingerprints—Identification.   2. Fingerprints—Classification.
3. Criminals—Identification.   I. Title.

HV6074 .C557 2001
363.25′8—dc21   00-054054

To the memory of my father
David Anthony Cole
whose boundless love and
unshakeable faith in me
made it possible

CONTENTS

Before you read this book, take a close look at your own fingertips under a good strong light. You may see that the patterns of their ridges are different on different fingers. Some ridges may simply curve across your fingertip. Some may loop around the center of your finger and return the way they came. And some may swirl around the center in concentric circles like a whirlpool. If you look more closely, you may be able to see even more intricate details. Ridges may occasionally fork into two divergent paths, and some may simply end in the middle of your finger, their way blocked by other ridges. The mesmerizing convolutions of these tiny ridges are sometimes called upon to determine people's fates.

SUSPECT IDENTITIES

Jekylls and Hydes

In Robert Louis Stevenson's world-famous 1886 horror story *The Strange Case of Dr. Jekyll and Mr. Hyde,* the respectable yet slightly licentious Dr. Jekyll discovers the dreadful "truth . . . that man is not truly one, but truly two": in his case, Henry Jekyll, a man with a conscience but tempted by earthly pleasures, and an inner demon, Edward Hyde, an amoral, savage beast devoted only to his own interest and pleasure. Through his chemical experiments, Jekyll discovers "certain agents" which "have the power to" separate his two selves. Drinking this concoction removes the veneer of Jekyll, exposing the hideous form of Hyde.

In one sense, the Jekyll-Hyde story is a familiar one, touching on recurring themes of the duality of all people, the coexistence of good and evil, and our shared vague dread of Doppelgängers. But Stevenson's tale is also very much a reflection of his time and its effort to visually identify criminals. Cesare Lombroso's Italian School of criminal anthropology, which arose in the late 1870s in Turin, where Lombroso was a professor of psychology, held that criminality was not simply a matter of individual choice and free will but often had a biological cause. Since criminality had an organic origin, it must be physically manifested in the body. Criminality should be visible to the trained eye in certain bodily stigmata, such as "sugar-loaf" skull shapes, pointy heads, heavy jaws, and receding brows. The influence of the Italian School is evident in Stevenson's portrayal of the murderer Hyde as a man whose evil nature is visible in his face.

Yet, though the criminality of Hyde is clearly visible, it becomes invisible when the aptly named Hyde disappears behind the respectable cloak of Dr. Jekyll. Here Stevenson draws on a contradictory contemporary concern: that criminals, far from exhibiting their villainy on their faces, were invisible, concealed beneath an inconspicuous facade. Criminals, it was said, exploited the anonymity of modern society, melting into the urban crowd, and this made them all the more dangerous. While the criminal body could be a biological manifestation of depravity, it might also be a mask which hid the criminality that lay within.

In the Jekyll-Hyde character, Stevenson drew attention to a problem that was much on the minds of contemporary jurists and criminal anthropologists alike. In modern, anonymous, socially mobile societies, distinctive dress, appearance, and accent were losing their power to convey social status at a glance. These emerging societies were brimming with people who were strangers, both to one another and to the state. The most heinous criminal could appear in the most innocent guise. How, then, were those rapidly growing arms of the state—the police, the prisons, the courts—to detect the invisible danger hidden beneath the social fabric, behind what Dr. Jekyll called the "fleshy vestment" of respectable bodies?

Even as Stevenson wrote, even as Lombroso and his followers scrutinized their collection of criminals' skulls for some sign of criminality, a motley assortment of police clerks, detectives, amateur anthropologists, photographers, and petty bureaucrats were struggling to devise practical solutions to the very problem Jekyll and Hyde highlighted. To these thinkers, the criminal body, with its capacity to house different selves, was not the problem but the solution. Both good and evil, criminality and respectability, might inhabit a single body, but the body itself was stable and inescapable. These pioneers devised identification techniques of the body, technologies of skin and bone: in the early 1880s several different experimenters began using the corrugated patterns on the skin of the fingertips to record unique identities, while the French police official Alphonse Bertillon's anthropometric system of identification used the lengths of bones to track individualized identities.

"Jekyll's finger patterns remain the same when he transforms himself into Hyde," boasted Henry Faulds, one of the pioneers of the new science of "dactyloscopy," or fingerprint identification, in a short-lived magazine called *Dactylography* he published in 1922. Individuals might be two, or even more, but the body was truly one. In fact, all bodies changed slightly over time, but the new identification techniques were able to accommodate these changes, to link bodies to themselves across time and space. With these techniques in place, the authorities could relax their efforts to find physical signs of potential criminality. Instead, they could track the bodies of proven criminals. The new identification techniques mastered the criminal body by marking it and making its criminal history visible to the state. In so doing, the authorities had found a new way to manage potential dangers to the body politic—by controlling dangerous bodies.

And yet, the search for a way to identify criminals retrospectively, by reading their criminal histories in state records, remained closely bound up with the search for a way to identify criminal potentiality, by finding some visible biological marker of latent criminality. Although identification technologies made criminal histories visible to the eyes of the state, the search for a method of rendering potential criminality visible, using the very same technologies, persisted. Indeed, these twin conceptions of "identifying criminals" remain closely entangled today, as genetic identification technologies have stimulated hopes of finding a genetic method for targeting potential criminality, a so-called crime gene.

Such entanglements inevitably raise suspicions that identification technologies can be used to stigmatize marginalized groups of people. And indeed, identification technologies were developed, not for society's respectable Jekylls, but for its suspicious-looking Hydes. Not just criminal suspects, but also a wide range of people considered "suspect" and alien for other reasons: the natives of Europe's colonies; recent immigrants; people of color; poor, mobile "vagrants"; "degenerates"; and prostitutes. The desire to identify, and therefore control, these "suspect" bodies is what fueled the demand for identification technologies.

In our own time, however, even "respectable" citizens, today's Dr. Jekylls, can feel the web of surveillance tightening around them. Fingerprinting and new identification technologies like retina scanning, voice spectrometry, face recognition, and DNA typing are extending identification from criminal justice into "civilian" areas like welfare and Medicaid disbursement, immigration, banking, and workplace security, as biologically defined identities play an increasing role in everyday social and governmental interactions.

Early pioneers of identification did something extraordinary: they created a link between an individual body and a paper record held by the state. It was a link, moreover, that everyone believed in: judges, bureaucrats, scientists, and the general public alike. Fingerprint examiners, as is well known, went even further. In addition to linking bodies to the inked finger impressions contained on the identification cards archived by the state, they also managed to link finger impressions left at crime scenes to those same inked cards. These impressions, it was said, could be matched with one and only one source finger out of all the possible fingers in the world—living, dead, or not-yet-living.

Dactyloscopers had created one of the most seemingly powerful and unshakeable forms of truth around. Fingerprint identification became without question the most trusted type of forensic evidence in criminal trials. Judges and juries have shown themselves readily willing to believe that no two fingerprints are alike and that fingerprint examiners can reliably trace "latent prints," fragments of fingerprint patterns found at crime scenes, to one and only one person. Aside from a few cases early in this century when the technique was new and unfamiliar, there are no recorded cases of juries choosing to ignore fingerprint evidence. Since those early trials, there have been minor quarrels over fingerprint evidence, but there have been no successful challenges to its fundamental reliability. Juries have convicted—and appeals courts have upheld these convictions—even when a latent fingerprint stood as the only evidence against a defendant. Fingerprint evidence can literally decide matters of life and death.

In 1993 when the O. J. Simpson trial began to turn "DNA fingerprinting" into a household term, the aura of infallibility surrounding fingerprinting stood in marked contrast to the reputation of DNA typing. Geneticists and lawyers were hotly contesting the reliability of genetic evidence, but there was no such debate about fingerprint evidence. How had fingerprint identification been transformed from a subject of debate into something that everyone took for granted? How had fingerprint identification become a virtually incontestable form of truth?

The search for answers to these questions has led far beyond the source of the ironclad courtroom credibility of fingerprinting to the historical origins and impacts of technologies of criminal identification. The power of the fingerprint to convey who we are goes far deeper than its place in the courtroom. Fingerprint records determine who gets what kind of punishment. Fingerprints are used to resolve cases of mistaken identity and to give names to the unidentified dead. But more fundamentally, fingerprinting has embedded firmly within our culture the notion that personhood is biological. The idea that our individuality is vouched for by our biological uniqueness—this is the legacy of fingerprinting that affects all of us, criminals and citizens, Hydes and Jekylls.

At the turn of the twenty-first century, the relative positions of fingerprinting and DNA seem to have reversed. DNA typing has become much more widely trusted than it was a few short years ago. Meanwhile, longstanding fissures in the reliability of fingerprint identification have become visible cracks. The identities bestowed upon us by expert readings of our fingerprint patterns, it turns out, are "suspect" in yet another way. It may well be that we are approaching the end of the century-long period in which our fingerprint patterns told the state who we were and even defined our individuality, our very personhood. And yet, as DNA technology promises to create a whole new set of biologically defined, seemingly unquestionable identities for all of us, we would do well to reflect upon the ways in which previous methods of criminal identification have been suspect.

In village after village in two dioceses, people were asking themselves how you could tell who a man was—a man snatched from the
known context of fields and family and now on display in the court
chambers of Rieux . . . How, in a time without photographs, with
few portraits, without tape recorders, without fingerprinting, without identity cards, without birth certificates—how did one establish
a person's identity beyond doubt?

—Natalie Zemon Davis, *The Return of Martin Guerre* (1983)

CHAPTER 1

Impostors and
Incorrigible Rogues

In the Martin Guerre case in sixteenth-century France, made famous
by Natalie Zemon Davis's book and the subsequent film, two different
courts charged with determining whether the individual calling himself Martin Guerre was an impostor were faced with the difficult task
of determining who a man was. The closest the courts could come to a
physical record of Martin Guerre was a pair of wooden shoe lasts submitted by the village cobbler. Although these molds did not appear to
fit the feet of the purported Martin, the courts did not regard this as
definitive proof, and they relied more heavily on tests of memory, eval-
uations of dialect, and the confused and divided recollections of eyewitnesses. Around 150 people testified as to the prisoner's identity.
Some forty-five testified that Martin Guerre was taller, thinner, darker,
with a flatter nose and a more projecting lower lip than the prisoner,
and had a scar on his eyebrow that the prisoner lacked. On the other
side, around thirty-five people who had known Martin since birth
swore that the prisoner was he, pointing for confirmation to a scar on
his forehead, three warts on his right hand, and extra teeth. At the
same time, around sixty witnesses testified that they could not be certain whether or not the accused impostor was indeed their old neighbor
Martin Guerre.[1]

The Martin Guerre case forces us to imagine identification as a problem without a solution, transporting us back to a time before the development of the identification techniques so familiar today: photographs, fingerprints, birth certificates, voice recordings, passports, and ID cards. From a modern perspective, it is tempting to assume that premodern courts lacked a method of identification because they lacked know-how: because photography had not yet been invented and fingerprinting had not yet been "discovered." But, in fact, early modern societies were not desperately seeking some means of identifying people because, for the most part, it was unnecessary. Most people *were* known in their small local communities. Many lived their whole lives without ever leaving the vicinity of their village, and so were enmeshed in the memories and perceptions of their families and neighbors. Martin Guerre posed a problem of identification precisely because he had been "snatched from the known context of fields and family" for eight years.

Crude forms of criminal identification had existed in ancient, medieval, and early modern Europe. The famous "mark of Cain" testifies to the idea of marking criminals in biblical times. The Goths, Lombards, and Visigoths reportedly used *décalvation* (baldening) to mark convicts. In medieval Europe some courts used branding or mutilation. Early modern European and American courts also occasionally branded—or, more rarely, mutilated—convicts, and courts in Amsterdam even, presciently, branded convicts on the ball of the thumb. In some cases a rudimentary system of symbolic brands even communicated the type or severity of the offense, as, for example, in the colonial East Jersey codes of 1668 and 1675, which mandated a letter "T" branded on the hand for burglary and an "R" on the forehead for the second offense, or in the famous scarlet letter "A" for adultery of Puritan New England.[2]

Branding was an effective, low-cost form of identification, but it had drawbacks: visibility and irreversibility. Some courts expressed concern that branding precluded true reintegration of the convict into society, since the criminal record was visibly inscribed on the body for all (potential employers, neighbors, and so on) to see. Courts, therefore, tended to reserve brands for seemingly incorrigible cases, but most criminals deemed so reprehensible were likely to be executed anyway. Other courts tried to brand discreetly, placing the brand on a private part of the body so that the record of past offenses would be invisible to the public but visible if the convict was stripped before the court. Nowhere, however, do brands appear to have been routinely applied to all convicts. The use of early forms of criminal identification were sporadic. Why didn't early modern societies make more strenuous efforts to mark criminals for future recognition? Why, alternatively, didn't they consider using fingerprints, which were already known in Europe by the sixteenth century, for identification?

In general, premodern societies already had an effective method of personal, and criminal, identification: the network of personal acquaintance through which persons were "known" in the memories and perceptions of their neighbors. Most people spent virtually their entire lives in the village, or region, in which they were born. Of course, many others did leave their village or region, and when they did they often needed to identify themselves using letters of introduction or tools of their trade (which "marked" them as itinerant artisans rather than vagrants or criminals). Those who did not identify themselves in these ways were considered "strangers," and they invited prejudice, suspicion, and even imprisonment. Premodern identity papers were used, by rich and poor alike, only for specific purposes, such as journeys. There was no centralized bureaucracy to coordinate identity documents. Drivers' licenses, social security numbers, passports, ID cards—all these were unknown. Business and social transactions could be based on acquaintance and trust. In village society, there was little need for a signature to verify the identity of a neighbor. If a signature was used, it was more as a gesture of good faith than as a test of identity.[3]

In addition, early modern states lacked the bureaucratic governmental institutions that today make up "criminal justice systems." Police did not exist in their modern form, prisons were more arenas of corporal punishment than bureaucracies governed by paperwork and procedure, and courts were concerned with meting out immediate justice, not maintaining lifetime criminal records. None of these institutions had the bureaucratic scope or ambition to covet the task of keeping track of large numbers of peripatetic individuals.[4]

All this began to change following the vast social changes of the industrial revolution and the birth of the modern era. In the wake of the industrial revolution, enormous numbers of people migrated from intimate rural villages to anonymous urban settings. Cities grew dramatically along with population density. The informal system of personal acquaintance and collective memory began to collapse. "In small old communities, everybody knew (or thought they knew) all the good-for-nothings, the violent people, the lopsided," notes the historian Lawrence Friedman. "This same knowledge was difficult to obtain in a city, or in a new community of whatever size." The industrial revolution accelerated not only physical but also social mobility. As the strict divisions between the classes broke down, the characteristics that had marked membership in a particular class—such as language, dialect or accent, clothing, bearing, demeanor, and manners—became more fungible. As it became easier for individuals to climb or fall from one class into another, class became a less reliable indicator of identity and of trustworthiness. "In modern, anonymous, anomic society, one cannot rely on appearance, on social markers, on accent, on anything, to tell good from evil, human from subhuman, saint from murderer," Friedman observes. But the changes were not just felt in regard to criminals. Business and social transactions, once based on trust, took on a new air of suspicion. People in modern cities might not be who they claimed to be. They could be anyone; they could come from anywhere. Nineteenth-century society shifted from a closely hierarchal society of ranks and orders, in which everyone knew his or her place and the place of others, into what the historian Michael Ignatieff has called a "society of strangers."[5]

While modern cities were certainly more congenial environments for strangers than early modern towns, their residents retained "a profound distrust of men without settled connections." There was an increasing formal criminalization of mobility itself, from the concept of "criminal vagabondage" in France, where mobility *was* the crime, to a series of vagrancy panics in Britain, to increasing legal hostility to vagrants and anxiety about "crimes of mobility" in the United States. Expanding cities were faced with the formidable task of identifying hordes of newcomers pouring into urban centers. In addition, especially in the Americas, they faced large-scale immigration of millions of strangers from other countries, speaking other languages, immersed in other cultures, yet not always visually conspicuous.[6]

Meanwhile, early modern institutions were evolving into modern bureaucratic governmental institutions, which increasingly saw their mission as generating and archiving knowledge about individuals, especially stigmatized individuals like criminals. For the first time, governments considered it their business to collect and store information about ordinary people. Bureaucracies arose whose mission was *know-*

ing individual citizens. For the first time, governments thought it important that some people, notably criminals, have an identity that existed outside the physical body, in the files and paper records of some government bureaucracy.

One mechanism implemented by the state bureaucracies to cope with both internal and external migration was the passport. The modern passport traces its origin to post-Revolutionary France, the first European state composed of citizens, not subjects, who were considered equal rather than being ordered by rank. In 1792 France issued regulations requiring both foreign and domestic travelers to carry state-issued identity documents. The goal was to stymie the assembly of antigovernment forces, prevent infiltration by foreign agents, and suppress vagrancy and crime. Other European states, while not sharing France's conception of an equal citizenry, did embrace the passport as a way of suppressing dissent and controlling crime. No longer a letter of recommendation for noble travelers, the passport became a humble marker of ordinary citizenship, the earliest expression of the idea that all citizens should have some kind of identity document.

But attempts to use passports to control mobility were poorly executed. Blank identity documents were often stolen, allowing the thief to complete the forms at will. Although some passports included space for physical descriptions, the descriptive terms were generic, subjective, and uninformative, noting features like a "normal" nose or a "healthy" complexion. Moreover, outside France, middle- and upperclass people were not described at all, since the better sorts of people found abhorrent the idea of subjecting their physical person to the descriptive gaze of some petty bureaucrat. On the other hand, most nineteenth-century passports were issued for travel between specific dates and over specific routes, thus limiting their usefulness if they were stolen or altered. While it was quite possible and common for enterprising revolutionaries and impostors to forge or doctor identity documents, passports did achieve some control over the large-scale migration of such undesirable people as foreign workers and vagrants.[7]

If the descriptive efforts devoted to passports were meager, convicts, understandably, attracted more strenuous efforts at identification. The register of Newgate Prison, located in Greenwich Village in New York City, offers an illuminating glance at criminal identification at the turn of the nineteenth century: convicts were entered into the register in the order in which they were received into the prison. In addition to name, place of origin, date of birth, complexion, hair, stature, and county and judge of conviction, the register included a single column for "marks." The brief descriptors that filled this space—from 1797 until 1803, when jailers, for reasons that are unknown, stopped recording descriptions—ranged from the commonplace ("blue eyes," "freckled," "pockmarked," "bald") to the detailed ("small mole in left cheek," "scar over his left eye") to the imprecise ("small eyes," "large head," "long nose," "very broad nose," "round head," "corpulent," "very corpulent") to the vague ("high forehead") to the impermanent ("broken foot," "long hair") to the ethnically stereotyped ("aquiline nose," "Indian") to the judgmental ("bad forehead") to the oddly distinctive ("long neck," "red nose," "cross eyed," "stammers") to the slightly gory ("lost one eye," "pitted with small pox," "rupture in the groin") to the colorful ("shot in right arm," "purple spots in face") to the easily disguised ("speaks low") to the oblique ("very gross habit") to the downright poetic ("tender eyed").[8]

The situation was similar at one of the world's most famous penal institutions, the Pennsylvania Penitentiary in Philadelphia. There the Convict Sentence Docket also allowed only a single space for "description," which included anything from physical descriptions to miscellaneous remarks like "born in England." The growth of the Penitentiary was accompanied by a greater effort to recognize repeat offenders upon entry to the prison. This was primarily accomplished by recording better descriptions upon departure. Although the logbooks still left only a single space for description, the average number of words used to describe each individual grew from a terse three in 1797 to five in 1809 to ten in 1822. The vocabulary was also increasingly standardized so that clerks chose from a common set of descriptive terms. In 1808 an alphabetical index was added to the Convict Sentence Docket, and in the 1820s the prison introduced a Convict Description Docket with separate entries for birthplace, age, occupation, complexion ("sallow," "fresh," or a racial classification), hair color, eye color, and stature, plus a space to describe marks, scars, or tattoos. But even these more detailed descriptions were of limited value because the docket books were arranged in chronological or alphabetical order. Since there was no way for a prison clerk to use a physical feature to look up a prisoner's name, a prisoner using an alias, unless actually recognized by a prison official, was shielded from identification.[9]

It did occur to some "medico-legalists," as nineteenth-century experts on the intersection between law and medicine were called, that the body's natural markings might serve to identify a person in extraordinary cases. One treatise on medical jurisprudence concluded that "peculiar marks upon the body are a very important, perhaps much the most reliable means of identification." Occasionally, eyewitnesses might recollect scars or other peculiar bodily attributes belonging to a person whose identity was disputed. In the Thomas Hoag imposture case in New York City in 1797, for example, the absence of a pronounced scar on the bottom of Joseph Parker's foot conclusively proved that he was not Hoag. Sometimes, however, scars could be misleading. In the 1849 impersonation case of Luther Hause in Bangor, Maine, a man, later proved to be an impostor, was able to show scars on his knee, breast, and neck—all of which corresponded to those remembered by the true Hause's parents.[10]

If even scars could mislead, then what could be a more reliable method of identification? One method, proposed by the French medico-legalist Barruel in 1829, was the use of "smell" prints, a supposedly scientific method of identifying individual odors. (A variation of this theory, dubbed the "armpit effect," has recently been promoted by the geneticist Richard Dawkins.) In 1865 the French physician Ernest Morillon listed sex, age, size, hair, teeth, scars, deformities, particularities, blemishes, and tattoos as the best indicators of personal identity. As a supplement to these, Morillon advocated the reading of "professional signs": scars, nicks, cuts, and abrasions characteristic of certain professions, such as knife grinding, laundering, butchering, and shoemaking.[11]

By the mid-nineteenth century, seemingly permanent natural bodily markings, such as "cicatrices [scars], fractures, and natural deformities," were generally recognized as better indicators of identity than, say, handwriting, voice, or memory, but they were not considered absolutely reliable. Jurists envisioned, or perhaps hoped for, a truly unique body mark which might provide proof of identity, but what that mark might be they could not yet imagine. "If it were true," said the British legal scholar John Hubback wistfully in 1845, "that every individual had any peculiar mark or designation, natural or imposed, which once impressed was adherent and indelible, the possession of that peculiarity by the person in the case and the person in the evidence would conclusively prove them to be the same." Such a mark, however, remained elusive.[12]

In the 1870s a particularly sensational case of imposture shocked Europe. A British heir, Roger Tichborne, had been lost at sea in 1854. Lady Tichborne, convinced that her eldest son was alive, advertised for his return, and in 1866 a man from Wagga Wagga, Australia, appeared and claimed to be her lost son. Although Lady Tichborne believed "the Claimant" was indeed her son, relatives countered that he was Arthur Orton, a butcher. Seemingly endless legal wrangling ensued from 1871 through 1874. Orton was ultimately found guilty of perjury, his claim rejected, but many legal scholars of the time were incensed that the case dragged on for so long, paralyzing the courts, scandalizing the public, and stirring up working-class resentment, even though Orton apparently bore scant physical resemblance to Tichborne. Struggling to evaluate the conflicting testimony of family and friends regarding Orton's similarity to Tichborne in appearance, diction, accent, handwriting, manner, and knowledge of family lore, the courts ended up thoroughly confused. Advocates of fingerprinting would later cite the Tichborne case to illustrate the need for a reliable system of identification. The law seemed to require some quicker, surer method of determining identity, so that it could act confidently and decisively in such matters. By the final decade of the nineteenth century, the American legal scholar George Harris declared that the identification of persons and things "has become a question of growing importance and one that is daily before the courts."[13]

Beyond the odd case of imposture or mistaken identity, a more substantial need arose for a uniform means of positive identification. As social and political concern about crime intensified, jurists became more concerned with establishing the identity of the ever larger numbers of people who passed through their criminal justice systems. Government officials began to focus more on crime as a social problem and an "epidemic" disease afflicting the social body. Moreover, jurists became increasingly convinced that this "crime problem" could be traced to repeat offenders, "habitual offenders," or "recidivists." These habitual criminals were conceived of as deviant, fundamentally—in fact, biologically—different from "normal," law-abiding citizens.

Special penalties for second, third, or fourth offenses had already appeared in Roman, Gothic, medieval, and early modern law. In North America, colonial and early state laws mandated special penalties for second and third offenses. In the late eighteenth century, however, re-peat offenses had become largely irrelevant under the influence of the Milanese jurist Cesare Beccaria. He aimed to bring consistency and rigor to criminal sentencing by rationalizing it. Justice, according to this enlightened view, could only be effected through strict sentencing guidelines based upon the specific offense committed rather than the criminal history of the offender; that is, the punishment must fit the crime. Beccaria, who later would devise the standard decimal weights and measures which eventually evolved into the metric system, simi-larly sought to calibrate punishments and crimes. Judicial discretion had produced what he condemned as the ultimate injustice: "the same crimes differently punished at different times." Believing that consis-tent severity was both fairer and a better deterrent than fickle leniency, the "classical school" of jurists who followed Beccaria imposed severe mandatory sentences in the name of reform, regardless of the individ-ual's history. Beccarian sentences were harsh, and their application was inflexible, but in a basic sense they were fair. By the nineteenth century, offenders across Europe were punished proportionately to the crime; past misdeeds or good conduct was rarely considered.[14]

By the middle of the century, however, a new generation of reformers began to question the strictures of classical jurisprudence. Crucial to their critique was the notion that a small number of repeat offenders were responsible for a large proportion of the crimes committed. If this was true, then the state could combat crime by giving repeat offenders longer sentences or even exiling them. The increasing availability of criminal records and statistics supported the notion of a pattern of habitual crime among certain offenders. Crime statistics, including rough estimates of the number of repeat offenses, began to appear in continental Europe in the 1820s. In Britain the Constabulary Force Commissioners calculated the first estimate of the number of "habit-ual depredators and other criminals" in 1839. Understood statistically, crime became less a series of isolated acts of individual will than an organized social phenomenon, an epidemic. This new conception of crime was most famously articulated in the 1840s by the Belgian stat-istician and social scientist Adolphe Quetelet, whose "social physics" treated crime, like other social phenomena such as birth, death, and suicide, as determined by statistical laws. "Criminal statistics," Quetelet asserted, "becomes as positive as the other observational sci-ences . . . We are forced to recognize that the *facts of the moral order* are subject, *like those of the physical order,* to invariable laws." Although the accuracy of these statistics could not have been very great, their availability allowed the idea of habitual criminality to enter into legal and penological discourse.[15]

The "repeat offender" emerged somewhat changed from the obscurity of the classical period. No longer a merely legal category, the repeat offender had become an object of scientific knowledge. Scientists began to search for a physical cause of habitual criminality, a search that began, intuitively, with the head. In 1840 Carl Gustav Carus published *Principles of a New and Scientific Craniometry,* in which he measured the skull sizes of "delinquents." In 1844 Hubert Lauvergne published a study of Toulon convicts which correlated criminality with skull abnormalities. Lauvergne was a pupil of Franz Josef Gall, a founder of phrenology, a technique that adduced personality and character from the size and prominence of various regions of the skull supposedly responsible for specific personality traits. In 1846 Marmaduke B. Sampson used phrenological evidence to support a medical model of criminality. Phrenological and craniometric approaches to criminology thrived in the 1860s, especially in France under the leadership of the craniometrist Paul Broca.[16]

Repeat offenders were even given a new, appropriately scientific name. The French term *récidiviste* was coined in 1844 by Arnould Bonneville de Marsangy, whose seminal treatise, *De la récidive,* was probably the earliest European text to focus on the repeat offender. Medieval French had offered the nouns *récidivation* and *récidive* to refer to the second offense, but it had named neither the recidivist, denoting a creature distinct from other criminals, nor the social phenomenon of recidivism. In English, meanwhile, one might recidivate, be recidivous, or even suffer from recidivity, but there were no such things as "recidivists" until the late nineteenth century.[17]

Changes in ideas about the causes of crime, the nature of criminals, and the purpose of punishment created a new demand for criminal identification. If habitual criminals were born, not made, and destined inevitably to repeat their crimes, then it was urgently necessary to link convicts to their past crimes in order to identify which of them were, indeed, habitual criminals or recidivists. The shift from classical to reformist jurisprudence demanded technologies of criminal identification.

In *De la récidive* Bonneville launched a counterattack on the classical jurists. He argued, against Beccaria, that punishment should be tailored to what he called "the perversity of the delinquent" rather than the criminal act. The criminal's "perversity," for Bonneville, was indicated by the criminal record. "One can not justly and effectively proportion the punishment to the crime," he declared, "without knowing all the aggravating circumstances of the criminality, most importantly the state of recidivism."[18]

Bonneville was frustrated to find the application of appropriate punishment stymied by the courts' inability to keep track of individuals' convictions. The problem was that court records were kept only for cases, not for individuals. Therefore, he noted, "the degree of recidivism of the accused is almost never known exactly." In 1808 the French Courts of Assizes had begun keeping alphabetical registers of convicts. These constituted the first step in the transfer of criminal recordkeeping from the body of the criminal himself to paper records archived by the state. Along with changing attitudes toward corporal punishment stimulated by Enlightenment liberalism and changing notions of free will and the sources of evil, the emergence of written criminal records helped convince the French to abolish branding in 1832. The marking of the criminal record replaced the marking of the criminal body.[19]

Ordering the registers by name, however, left the system vulnerable to the use of aliases. Moreover, the annual registers pertained to a given year and a given jurisdiction, but they were compiled neither geographically nor temporally. Finally, the registers made no effort to distinguish even among individuals with the same name. All this meant that a search for the previous convictions of "Martin Pierre," would, as Bonneville pointed out, require searching all the registers of different jurisdictions for different years for all 300-odd Martin Pierres listed. The nondistinctiveness of names was a particular problem in countries like France with religiously shaped nomenclature. What was needed was some way of linking the various court records generated by a single individual to one another, across both space and time. Otherwise, Bonneville lamented, "all these innumerable documents, collected with a great deal of care and effort, lie in the judicial registers, as in catacombs, whence it is almost impossible to extract information needed from them in a timely manner." The problem was not collecting information but accessing it. The registers were useful for compiling crime statistics, he observed, but not for identifying the record of any individual criminal: "The criminal antecedents of suspects, presumed to be recidivists, are scarcely better known than in the past, and the courts have been reduced, on this point, to chance." Shoddy recordkeeping would not have been a problem, Bonneville noted, in a society where everyone stayed put, but "cosmopolitanism" and "continual peregrination from one country to another" made it all the more difficult to recognize criminals' antecedents.[20]

This was an even greater problem in the United States, which had a rapidly growing immigrant population and where the states, for criminal justice purposes, operated almost as separate nations. In his report on the American penal system, written during his celebrated visit to the United States in 1833, Alexis de Tocqueville reported:

> Where passports do not exist, nothing is easier than to change one's name. If, therefore, a delivered convict commits a new crime under a fictitious name, he can very easily conceal his relapse, providing he is not brought back to the prison where he underwent his first punishment. There are, besides, a thousand means of avoiding the chances of being recognized. Nothing is easier than to pass from one state to another, the ties between the various states being strictly political, there is no central power to which the police officers might refer to obtain information respecting the previous life of an indicted person: so that the courts condemn, almost always, without knowing the true name of the criminal, and still less his previous life.

The United States was already a place where people with checkered pasts could begin anew. The lack of any sort of a centralized or coordinated identification system, furthermore, ensured that a criminal could essentially start over by traveling even within the country, from state to state. This hampered the application of the sort of reformist jurisprudence with which Tocqueville had become enamored during his visit. Under reformist jurisprudence, it was necessary to know each individual criminal's past history, so that criminals might be punished in a manner suitable to their individual character. In sharp rebuke to Beccarian principles, Tocqueville asserted, "There are similar punishments and crimes called by the same name, but there are no two beings equal in regard to their morals."[21]

As an improvement on alphabetical registers, Bonneville, in *De la récidive*, developed a new method of criminal identification by adopting technologies of recordkeeping, treating criminal bodies as merchants treated consignments or librarians treated books. He had discovered the index card file, which "one can incessantly increase or decrease . . . without upsetting the alphabetical order indispensable to the speed and ease of the searches." This offered a solution to the problem of annual registers. All records, from all years and even possibly from many jurisdictions, could be kept together in a single, alphabetically ordered file. Cards could be added or removed without disrupting the overall order.[22]

Although the index card file exponentially enhanced the mobility and utility of bureaucratic knowledge and marked yet another step toward a modern identification system, problems remained. There was as yet no means of indexing the information, no means of ordering it, other than the alphabet. A criminal still had only to adopt an alias when arrested, and, barring the unlikely event that his face was recognized, he could prevent the sentencing judge from knowing about his past crimes. Alphabetical filing systems were even vulnerable to something as innocuous as variations in the spelling of names, a problem the French were forced to remedy by developing a phonetic classification system which enabled "identification of the man despite variations in orthography or pronunciation."[23]

The British took the first steps toward solving the indexing problem. Both France and Britain were plagued by growing concern about crime, and particularly repeat offenders, in the mid-nineteenth century. While France responded to the "burgeoning fear of recidivism" in 1851 by mandating the deportation of parole violators to penal colonies in New Caledonia and Guyana, the British began winding down deportation in the 1840s because the eastern colonies of Australia were refusing to accept any more British convicts. With deportation being phased out, reformist British jurists became increasingly concerned about the "habitual offender." In 1846 Matthew Davenport Hill called for "indefinite" sentencing, in which the convict would remain in custody, potentially forever, until rehabilitated, and in 1857 W. Barwick Baker demanded "cumulative" penalties for each additional offense. In 1868 the author, playwright, and civil servant Sir Henry Taylor, in his *Letter to Mr. Gladstone*, advocated a "dual-track" scheme. First-time offenders would be sentenced to a severe prison regimen aimed at deterring them from choosing a life of crime. Those who did not get the message and after release were convicted again, Taylor concluded, could never be weaned from crime and therefore should be placed on the second "track": confined for life in austere but humane conditions for the protection of society and to spare the criminals themselves a "wretched life" at large.[24]

The final cessation of "transportation" to Australia in 1868 put increased pressure on the British judicial system to do something about habitual criminals. The following year Parliament passed the Habitual Criminals Bill, the first modern law that used past offenses to guide sentencing. The Bill mandated seven years' penal servitude (served in Britain) for a third offense, but the problem was how to determine whether the convict had committed previous offenses. Jurists could do little more than recommend that "where there is any reason to believe that the prisoner is living a life of habitual crime, or that the ends of justice might be promoted by a more accurate knowledge of his previous history, a remand should take place for the purpose of affording time to procure farther information."[25]

But what if the prisoner used an alias? What means did the British authorities have to link him to his past crimes? Identification was achieved primarily through personal recognition. In London, wardens and detectives from Scotland Yard, the various divisions, and the City of London Police gathered three times a week at Holloway Prison to view and identify prisoners. Supplementing personal recognition were daily "informations," a biweekly *Police Gazette* containing descriptions and photographs of unknown prisoners, and a circular issued thrice yearly featuring photographs of "the more eminent criminals known by the Metropolitan Police to be at large." Outlying cities used "route forms" to circulate descriptions through neighboring jurisdictions.

To facilitate identification, the Bill established an annually published Alphabetical Register of Habitual Criminals. Once again, the terse physical descriptions and peculiar marks recorded in this volume were of little use because the contents were listed alphabetically, and a convict could evade official knowledge of his prior convictions simply by giving a false name. British jurists believed visual identification was the solution to the problem, since "it is by faces that persons are chiefly known; and no two faces are perfectly alike." In order to achieve that solution, however, officials would have to turn away from written descriptions and adopt a new technology for capturing and storing images of people's faces: photography.[26]

Police had been using photography to capture the faces of criminals almost since its invention. As early as 1841 the French had begun taking daguerreotypes of prisoners. The British police employed a photographer in the 1840s, and ambrotypes (an early method of photography developed by the inventor James Ambrose Cutting, which employed a glass negative) of Birmingham prisoners date from the 1850s. In 1854 Lausanne authorities began circulating photographs of suspected criminals. The first reported use of a "rogues' gallery," in which notorious criminals were displayed so the police became acquainted with their faces, was at the New York Police Department (NYPD), which held a collection of 450 ambrotypes by 1858. From New York the practice spread across the United States. In Albany, for example, police constables instituted a rogues' gallery in 1859 "at their own expense"; it included photographs they took themselves along with duplicates they received from cities like Philadelphia and New York, and the public was "invited to call and examine this . . . attraction." By 1861 the Albany gallery contained some seventy photographs. The rogues' gallery soon spread to Europe as well. Danzig introduced one in 1864, Moscow followed in 1867, and the practice had spread to London by 1870. The Prevention of Crimes Act of 1871 added photographs to the British Register of Habitual Criminals.[27]

To the police of the late nineteenth century, the greatest advantage of the photograph was its superiority to the written word as a means of communicating a representation of the human body. George Walling, New York police chief in the 1870s, doubted "that over ten rogues in a hundred are ever caught by the printed descriptions of them, which may be sent broadcast all over the country without result . . . But when the authorities are furnished with a photograph of the suspected criminal, the case is different." Although faces certainly underwent superficial changes, some underlying structure was permanent. The eyes, the police thought, were truly windows to the soul: "A man cannot change the expression in his eyes," said Walling, "which is, after all, the main point."[28]

The ostensible rationale for rogues' galleries was that police and, in some cases, members of the public would memorize the faces of known criminals and then be able to recognize them on the street. Detectives were expected to "familiarize themselves with the appearance and names of persons known to have criminal records or to be of bad character." A good detective "should have a considerable collection of faces in his mind's eye in order to render efficient service." In 1897 the Boston Police Department claimed that all its detectives "know hundreds of criminals by sight; and some with remarkably retentive memories could recognize and name over a thousand rascals"—but in spite of such boasts, recognitions based on archived photographs were actually quite rare.[29]

In the United States the most prominent exploiter of photographic technology was the legendary Thomas Byrnes, who headed the detective bureau of the NYPD and then served as police chief from 1880 until 1895. Byrnes's publication of a photo album of known criminals, *Professional Criminals of America* (1886)—a rogues' gallery in coffee-table-book format—demonstrated his enthusiasm for photography. His conception of photographic identification was partly revealed by the title: photography targeted the "professional" criminal, the repeat offender who made a living from crime, not the occasional more violent criminal. Who were these "professional criminals"? Browsing through *Professional Criminals of America*, one finds not murderers, rapists, kidnappers, but mostly forgers and confidence artists. These were the "poster criminals" of the era of photographic identification.

The "confidence man," an American term coined around 1849, was a criminal suited to the highly mobile, anonymous social milieu of nineteenth-century America, where people could abuse the trust of strangers, disappear, and reappear in another city with a new identity. "Swindling and fraud," Friedman notes, "were very much crimes of mobility; these crimes depended on anonymity, ambiguity of identity, and the fluidity of lines that separated strata and classes in the population." Along with fraud, the other emblematic crime of the photographic era was forgery and counterfeiting. "The forger," says Tamara Plakins Thornton, "loomed as an object of horrified fascination . . . in the popular literature on crime. What made him so dangerous was his ability to counterfeit not only bank notes or documents but entire identities"—an earlier version of today's "identity theft." There was violent crime, too, but it was less culturally resonant than fraud and forgery because it was rarer and because under draconian sentencing laws violent criminals, once caught, were unlikely to find themselves at large again. Violent criminals, therefore, were less objects of fear and fascination than con men and counterfeiters. The representative crimes of the late nineteenth century were crimes of identity and authenticity, in which the swapping or abuse of identity itself constituted the crime. No wonder, then, that the identification techniques of the time focused on rendering identities stable, on the processes of capturing and fixing identity, for which the freeze-frame served as such an appropriate metaphor. The shutter of the camera, as Byrnes said, "imprisoned the lines of the profile and the features."[30]

It was no accident, then, that photography focused on the face, the tool of the trade of the confidence game. The rogues' gallery sought to expose this face, to strip it of all pretense under the cold light of the camera, to render it familiar to members of the public, so they would not be suckered by it in the future. Photography, in Byrnes's conception, exposed as criminal those faces which looked most respectable; Byrnes was obsessed with notorious con artists who looked like respectable bankers, family men, or devoted wives. Considering nineteenth-century attitudes toward gender and ethnicity, historians have noted the surprisingly high representation of both women and Anglo-Saxons among Byrnes's "professional criminals." It seems that Byrnes was most interested in displaying the faces of confidence artists who—because of gender, ethnicity, attire, demeanor, or manners—were particularly likely to "pass" as trustworthy. He was less interested in exhibiting those criminals who—for the same reasons—would already be regarded with suspicion by the public.[31]

There were others who were less interested in criminals who could pass for respectable than in criminals who "looked like" criminals. The idea of using physiognomy, the study of facial features, as a guide to criminality dated back to the eighteenth-century research of the Swiss cleric Johann Kaspar Lavater. Medical researchers had been employing photography to capture criminality for as long as police officials had been using it to capture criminals. The idea that criminality might be visible in the face or the head began gaining currency in the 1840s. As early as 1846 Matthew Brady, best known for his Civil War photographs, took daguerreotypes of mental patients and criminals at the Blackwell's Island Penitentiary in New York City for Marmaduke Sampson's phrenological treatise on criminality, *The Rationale of Crime and its Appropriate Treatment*.[32]

Photography rejuvenated the search for a criminal physiognomy. The era of photographic identification coincided with the rise of "criminal anthropology," the earliest fully articulated attempt to turn the study of the criminal into a "scientific" discipline, complete with theories, skills, and methodologies, and the prototype for the field of criminology. The guiding spirit behind criminal anthropology was Cesare Lombroso, a professor of psychiatry at the University of Turin, whose book *Criminal Man* (1876) was the seminal text of the new discipline. The most prominent feature of the theories of crime espoused by Lombroso and followers like Enrico Ferri and Raffaele Garofalo, who became known collectively as the Italian School, was their relentless positivism—their belief that every criminal act could be traced back to some original cause. Although the Lombrosians allowed for both social and biological causes of criminality, their emphasis was decidedly on biological, or "organic," causes, and in most cases they sought the explanation for criminality in the criminal body itself rather than in the criminal's environment. The original cause of the vast majority of criminal acts, they believed, could be discovered through the scientific study of the criminal—perhaps his or her past history, but more likely his or her body.

The Italian School popularized the notion of the "born criminal"—that criminals were born of bad heredity rather than made by poor social conditions. Criminals and other deviants were biologically different from "normal," law-abiding citizens. On the basis of the Darwinian theory of evolution, which was then gaining in popularity, the Italian School posited that criminals were products of bad stock—individuals who were less evolved than the rest of the population, in much the same way that "savages" and other indigenous peoples were less evolved than Europeans. The chief causes of this poor development were "atavism," the reversion to a primitive evolutionary state, and "degeneration," the tendency of some subcultures to "evolve backwards," weakening, rather than improving, their evolutionary fitness.[33]

In the search for a biological cause of criminality, the Italian School turned naturally to the "science of man," anthropology, which offered a variety of tools for indirectly measuring the supposed evolutionary state of individuals and cultures. These tools included the analysis of skull size and shape, body proportions, physiognomy, tattoos, and other bodily attributes—in short, the close reading of the savage body. As anthropologists did for the savage, the Italian School did for the criminal—indeed, the Italian School drew explicit links between the savage and the criminal—hence the new discipline of "criminal anthropology."

On the basis of this reading of the criminal body, the Italian School identified a long list of "stigmata" that might indicate an inherited criminal propensity, such as "sugar-loaf" skull shapes, pointy heads, heavy jaws, receding brows, and scanty beards. Unfortunately, while any of these stigmata might indicate criminality, criminal anthropologists had yet to find a single, unmistakable sign of criminality. Despite the goal of devising a method of predicting criminal behavior before it occurred, in practice criminal anthropologists tended to examine the bodies of criminals after they had been apprehended, only then to find the damning stigmata that had presaged their inevitable fall into crime. Undeterred, with supposed scientific precision, criminal anthropologists fashioned precise taxonomies of a motley assortment of "criminal types" ranging from "born criminals" to only slightly dangerous "criminaloids."[34]

It was only natural to try to incorporate the new technology of photography into this "scientific" search for visible markers of criminality. Since the camera offered a way of capturing a seemingly "objective" representation of the human body, it might help reveal the elusive visible mark of criminality. In the 1880s the British statistician Francis Galton devised a technique called "composite photography," which he hoped would help isolate the criminal physiognomy. Galton layered multiple exposures of a group of criminals onto a single photographic plate. The resulting ghostly "composite" image revealed the physiognomic attributes common to that set of criminals, thus allowing authorities and researchers to "see" the criminal type. Galton and others who adopted the technique assembled composites of criminals with certain specialties, such as forgers, burglars, "bank-sneaks," "hotel thieves," and pickpockets. By rendering visible the common physiognomic features of criminals, it was hoped, photography might also render visible the face of criminality itself.[35]

Some police departments even claimed to put this theory into practice, training their detectives to arrest "criminal types"—who had not to their knowledge committed any crime—on sight. "Keen observers have over and over again marked and arrested apparently inoffensive rogues, whom they had never seen before in person or in pictures," Boston Superintendent of Police Benjamin Eldridge boasted in another rogues' gallery book, *Our Rival the Rascal: A Faithful Portrayal of the*

COMPOSITE OF
6 BANK SNEAKS.

COMPOSITE OF
5 FORGERS.

COMPOSITE OF
4 BURGLARS.

COMPOSITE OF
5 CRIMINALS.

COMPOSITE OF
4 CRIMINALS.

COMPOSITE OF
9 CRIMINALS.

CO-COMPOSITE
OF ALL.

COMPOSITE OF
6 HOTEL THIEVES.

COMPOSITE OF
7 PICKPOCKETS.

CO-COMPOSITE OF
28 CRIMINALS.

1. Composite photographs after the method of Sir Francis Galton. Multiple exposures of several different criminals onto single photographic plates yielded ghostly images of criminal types.

Conflict Between the Criminals of this Age and the Defenders of Society—The Police (1897). "Often some impression made by the appearance of rogues, which is beyond exact definition and explanation, will assure the trained detective that he is warranted in making arrests."[36] What Eldridge described was essentially a form of "physiognomic profiling" akin to the racial profiling we hear about today. In late-nineteenth-century America, the targets of such profiles were persons with strong Eastern and Southern European features, suspected of being recent immigrants and hence likely to be "criminal types."

Thus, as soon as photography emerged as a method for recording the identities of known criminals, an irresistible temptation arose to use the same technology for something much more ambitious: to home in on the common physiognomic attributes of known criminals in order to have a picture of what criminals in general might look like and thus to identify criminals prospectively, even before they committed crimes. Criminal behavior, at least in most cases, was believed to be biologically based, and physiognomy was the state-of-the-art way of differentiating bodies: savage from civilized, black from white, pathological from normal, degenerate from evolved. It made sense, then, to use physiognomy, aided by the mechanical objectivity of the camera, to try to distinguish the criminal as well.

These experiments in composite photography, however, never succeeded in discovering any unequivocal physiognomic marker of the criminal type. Instead, criminal physiognomy became a crude pretext for prejudices, such as the association of criminality with "swarthy" Eastern and Southern Europeans, Jews, Gypsies, and others who simply looked lower class. Nor did the rogues' gallery develop into a full-fledged criminal identification system. The chief obstacle to creating a photographic system for identifying criminals was arranging photographs in some order from which they could be retrieved. Deriving some sort of indexing mechanism from the face or the photographic image itself would have been extremely difficult. Instead, collections of photographs were simply arranged alphabetically, according to the name given by the offender, which brought the authorities back to the problem of the use of aliases.

When a suspect refused to give a name or provided a false name, British jurists found, "such a vast list of names . . . such a vast mound of photographs . . . became useless as a means of identification." Unable to find a way to index photographs, the British in the 1870s devised the first criminal identification register indexed, not according to names, but according to the criminal body itself: the Register of Distinctive Marks, an ambitious if cumbersome attempt to describe systematically the vagaries of the human body. An annual bound volume like the Alphabetical Register, the Distinctive Marks Register divided the body into nine general areas: head and face; throat and neck; chest; belly and groin; back and loins; arms; hands and fingers; thighs and legs; feet and ankles. It then subdivided each area by type of mark or physical peculiarity, and in some cases there were further subdivisions. An unknown prisoner would be stripped and examined for his most distinctive mark. For example, if a prisoner was found to have a prominent and seemingly permanent burn scar on the inside of his right arm, the clerk would refer to the Distinctive Marks Register, look under the heading "right arm," then consult the subheading "scars from wounds or burns," and then the sub-subheading "inside." There he would find a list of names of convicts with prominent burns on the insides of their right arms. He would then refer to the Alphabetical Register, look up each of these names, and study the complete physical descriptions found there to see if any of them matched the prisoner before him. Similarly, if an unknown prisoner bore a tattoo of an anchor on his right arm, the clerk would look under the heading "right arm," the subheading "tattoo marks," and the sub-subheading "anchor or cross." There he would find names of convicts with anchors tattooed on their right arms, and he would look these names up in the Alphabetical Register (Table 1). This was a laborious process, and it is perhaps not surprising that a Home Office report on the Registers of Distinctive Marks concluded that "the evidence we have received as to their use conveys an impression that even those police forces who frequently consult them do not by this means make a large number of identifications."[37]

The first Register of Distinctive Marks proved "far too large a scale . . . the results attained were altogether disproportionate to the labour involved—a large part of the persons registered not being habitual criminals in any ordinary sense of the term." In 1877, therefore, the Secretary of State decreed that Registers include only "every person convicted on indictment of a crime, a previous conviction of crime being proved against him." In other words, a criminal had to be determined to be habitual by some other means, such as personal recognition, before he could be entered into the system for identifying habitual criminals.[38]

TABLE 1

A sample of the form of the Register of Distinctive Marks kept by the Convict
Supervision Office, London, ca. 1877

			RIGHT ARM.						
		Limb deficient, malformed, injured, or	Tattoo Marks.						Moles
Name.	No.	diseased.	Anchor or Cross.	Man or Woman.	Ship or Flag.	Heart or Star.	Other Marks.	or Warts.	Other Marks

Source: C. E. Troup, A. Griffiths, and M. L. Macnaghten, *Report of a Committee Appointed by
the Secretary of State to Inquire into the Best Means Available for Identifying Habitual
Criminals,* British Sessional Papers, House of Commons, Command Paper, C.-7263 (London,
1894).

Still, the police found even the abridged Register system tedious and
awkward to use. "No one . . . would venture to say that the recognitions are obtained easily and without the expenditure of much labour,"
the Home Office committee grumbled. "In using the Habitual Criminals' Register, when a prisoner has some special and unique mark, his
identity may perhaps be discovered easily; but according to all the evidence we have received, the use of this register in ordinary cases is extremely laborious and it appears to be mainly on account of the time
and labour which the searches involve, that it is generally so little used
by the police." In addition, the Register produced occasional errors,
"false positives" in today's parlance, in which someone was wrongly
accused of being a repeat offender. David Callaghan, who was convicted of begging in May 1889, was identified through the Register of
Distinctive Marks as William Minson, who had eleven begging convictions. On the basis of these previous convictions, Callaghan was convicted under the Vagrancy Act as an incorrigible rogue and sentenced
to six months. It was later established that Callaghan had been in
prison when Minson was convicted. Although this incident displayed
the weakness of the Register, the authorities hastened to add that
"Callaghan was subsequently convicted as an incorrigible rogue" on
his own merits. The British Register was also notable for its creators'
failure to heed Bonneville's suggestion to use index cards. By recording
descriptions in annual bound volumes, the British created just the kind
of register Bonneville had criticized thirty years earlier: a source of in-

formation that became obsolete as soon it was published because of a format that did not allow information to be compiled over time.[39]

The very fact that the British instituted a scheme as labor-intensive as the Register of Distinctive Marks signaled their desperate need for any kind of identification system. Clumsy though it may have been, the Register was the earliest attempt to arrange individual records not according to names but according to physical descriptions—to use the criminal body itself as an index to a set of criminal records. Rather than marking the criminal body (as in branding), the Register treated the criminal body as already carrying its own identifying marks, which merely needed to be recorded.

Distinctive marks, the Home Office report concluded, were useful identifiers, but they proved awkward to classify. Although the diversity of forms of the human body made individualization possible, this same stubborn uniqueness made indexing human bodies very difficult. What was needed was some way of characterizing the body that would make it easy to sort records of large numbers of bodies into some order from which individual bodies might be easily retrieved. The most acute problem facing the nineteenth-century police and penal bureaucracies was not *recording* information, but *ordering* it. Methods of indexing, filing, classification, archiving were the crucial techniques needed to make criminal identification possible. "What is wanted," the Home Office committee declared, "is a means of classifying the records of habitual criminals such that, as soon as the particulars of the personality of any prisoner (whether description, measurements, marks or photographs) are received, it may be possible to ascertain readily and with certainty whether his case is already in the register, and, if so, who he is." But this would require an entirely new approach to the use of written inscriptions to represent the criminal body.[40]

These early visual and textual identification techniques did succeed in linking some suspects to their criminal records. In Britain, all methods together resulted in the identification of between 1,500 and 2,000 prisoners a year from 1883 until 1893, although at great cost in labor. Scotland Yard calculated that each successful identification using the Register of Distinctive Marks required more than eight man-hours, while officials at Holloway Prison estimated a whopping ninety man-hours for each successful identification. Improvements in identification had the predictable effect of raising recorded recidivism rates. In 1895 the British Prisons Committee observed that "it is difficult . . . to avoid the belief that the proportion of reconvictions during the last 20 years has increased." Government officials were well aware that such increases reflected a rise in the effectiveness of identification at least as much as a rise in recidivism itself. The British Prisons Committee, for example, was inclined to attribute the apparent statistical increase in the number of "reconvictions" both to an actual rise in recidivism and to "the fact that since 1873 the methods of identification, though far from complete, have continued to improve." Nonetheless, nineteenth-century jurists also believed they were seeing only the tip of the iceberg of habitual crime. The little they did know about habitual offenders heightened their awareness of how many habitual criminals might be passing undetected. The Prisons Committee concluded that "it is not possible to make an estimate of any value of the number of habitual criminals in the country."[41]

To a certain extent, this caveat was beside the point. If "recidivism" only existed to the extent that criminal justice bureaucracies knew about it, then recidivism *was* rising. Identification techniques were making recidivism a more concrete, measurable category—and thus a more pressing social problem. Early identification techniques literally gave a face to habitual criminality, exposing some criminals as "habitual offenders," but at the same time they hinted at a much more widespread phenomenon that remained hidden. Thus early criminal identification techniques, which developed in response to a perceived need to identify the repeat offender, ended up helping to turn the habitual offender into a prominent social problem. In this way, the criminological idea of recidivism and the early technologies of criminal identification arose in concert, each justifying the other.

Before the nineteenth century the demand for criminal identification had been rather sparse. The seemingly quaint techniques of identification detailed in this chapter—the colorful descriptions, the "mounds of photographs," the laborious Register of Distinctive Marks—all illustrate the desperation with which criminal justice bureaucracies sought a method of criminal identification as crime became at once more visible and more anonymous in modern, urban environments. This desperation was fueled by the new science of criminology, which, more than anything, sought some form of knowledge that would allow it to sort and classify criminal bodies.

The simultaneous rise of these new technologies and ideologies had very practical consequences in law enforcement and the administration of punishment. If identification techniques could pick out some habitual offenders, even if it was understood that others were going undetected, then certain actions could be taken. First, as in the British Habitual Offenders Act, harsher sentences could be given to repeat offenders. Second, separate penal regimes, and in some cases separate prisons, could be created for habitual and "first-time" offenders with the intent of protecting redeemable first-timers from the corrupting influence of prison. The late nineteenth century saw increasing efforts to separate habitual and first-time offenders in the United States, in Britain, and across Europe. In part this was due to the growing realization that prisons were breeding criminals, but it also owed a great deal to the nascent technical ability to distinguish habitual offenders.[42]

Still, measures based on the isolation of first offenders were marred by the uncertainty of the "habitual criminal" designation. The category "first offender," the British Prisons Committee cautioned,

> is open to much misconception. Presumably it is intended to mean those persons whose offence is the first known to be proved against them. While it is desirable to devote special treatment to them as a class, it should be recognised that many "first offenders" have probably been convicted more than once . . . A certain discretion should be allowed to the prison authorities when the evidence is sufficient to distinguish between the *bona fide* first offender and the more dangerous criminals who technically rank in the same class.[43]

In other words, the reach of identification techniques was still not broad enough to assure penologists that people for whom criminal records could not be located were in fact first-time offenders. Until they gained this assurance, until criminals could more reliably be sorted into their various "states of recidivism," reformist criminologists, penologists, and judges hesitated to act decisively in applying individualized or differentiated criminological diagnoses, penal regimens, and criminal sentences. Decisive action would require some more confidence-inspiring method of criminal identification.

CHAPTER 2

Measuring the Criminal Body

By the late nineteenth century, two new technologies appeared which
promised to streamline the process of criminal identification. One,
fingerprinting, is familiar to us. The other, an identification system
based on anthropometry, the physical measurement of the size and
proportions of the human body, has become a historical curiosity. Yet
the two techniques were once well-matched rivals, which vied for
ascendancy for forty years. Although fingerprinting is now generally
viewed as a successor to anthropometry, the two actually arose around
the same time. Theoretical discussions of using fingerprints for criminal identification began in the late 1870s, even as the French police
official Alphonse Bertillon began work on his anthropometric identification system. Although Bertillon's system was implemented first,
fingerprinting was not far behind. They were two different approaches
to solving the same problem, but they developed in quite different social and political contexts. Anthropometry emerged in the cities of Europe, while fingerprinting developed in the colonies and on the fron-
tiers of the Western imperial states. Each system made sense within
the context in which it was developed.

The Bertillon system, or "Bertillonage," as it was called, became the
first modern system of criminal identification. That is, any unknown
persons entering the Paris police station could be identified, and their

criminal records retrieved, if they had been "Bertillonaged" before. If Bertillon could not match a criminal body with a previous criminal record, that meant the person had never been arrested in Paris before. Until Bertillon's system was implemented, criminal identification in France had been based on photography, personal recognition, and the annual alphabetical registers described by Bonneville. Police officials were paid bounties for recognizing known criminals, and they were known to share the proceeds with convicts who identified their cell-mates.[1]

Even with such uncertain methods, the proportion of *récidivistes* among those arrested rose alarmingly from 10 percent to 40 percent between 1828 and 1869. In another accounting the increase was even greater: from 28 percent in 1850 to 50 percent in 1881. Meanwhile, the public, noted the French Minister of the Interior, "has not done the statistics, but nonetheless it has arrived at a conclusion absolutely identical to that of scholars"—that France was being swept by an "epidemic" *(contagion du mal)* of crime. A small explosion of legal treatises published in the early 1880s drew attention to the growing problem of *récidivistes*, who were becoming a "true social wound." In the face of popular demand that something be done, in the early 1880s French legislators proposed the very policy Britain had just abandoned: *relégation*, or exile, of *récidivistes* to the colonies. French jurists were especially alarmed about "incurable vagrants," rural poor who migrated to the cities after bad harvests. People arrested for vagrancy in Paris were commonly expelled from the city and warned not to return, but city officials were well aware that many promptly did return.[2]

One police official who was particularly concerned about recidivist vagrants was Alphonse Bertillon. While legislators debated the merits of the relégation law, Bertillon raised a practical question. "It is not enough to make a law against recidivists," he pointed out. "It is then necessary to enforce it. In order to condemn a recidivist to relégation, the first requirement is the recognition of his identity." Here the French justice system was sorely lacking. "Unless we find a solution," Bertillon cautioned, "make no mistake, the law against recidivists will be difficult and limited in application."[3]

It so happened that Bertillon thought he had a solution, based on the application of anthropometry to the problem of criminal identification. This idea was in large part the result of Bertillon's unusual upbringing. Alphonse was the son of Louis-Adolphe Bertillon, one of the pioneers of the nineteenth-century social sciences, including demography and anthropology, that sought to apply the methods of science to human beings. In this work, Louis-Adolphe was closely associated with such luminaries as Adolphe Quetelet and the anthropologist and craniometrist Paul Broca. The Bertillon children grew up in a home filled with anthropometric measuring tools, such as calipers and gauges, and a fervent belief in the importance of Quetelet's "social physics," which called for measuring anything and everything about people in order to collect sufficient data to derive the statistical laws that governed them. In this positivistic environment, Alphonse's brothers Jacques and Georges became prominent demographers.[4]

Alphonse, however, did not initially seem to fit the mold. He floated around France and England, showing little inclination to fulfill the destiny his father surely had planned for him. Solely in an effort to settle his son, Louis-Adolphe secured Alphonse a relatively menial position as a clerk at the Paris prefecture of police. Underachiever though he may have been, Alphonse had enough of his father's meticulous mind to be appalled by the chaotic state of police recordkeeping in Paris. Sometime in the late 1870s he realized that the solution to the problem of identification—and his own route to professional success—lay in the fusion of the two halves of his own life: the application of the tools of his father's scientific approach to the mundane problem of filing and retrieving criminal records. While European anthropologists scattered around the globe were using anthropometry to quantify the physical differences between the "savage" and "civilized" races, he applied anthropometry at home. Moreover, he used anthropometry, not to delineate group identity—races—but for the novel purpose of individualization.

A prisoner being Bertillonaged was first subjected to eleven different anthropometric measurements taken with specially designed calipers, gauges, and rulers by one of Bertillon's rigorously trained clerks, or "Bertillon operators." Each measurement was a meticulously choreographed set of gestures in which the exact positioning and movement of both bodies—prisoner and operator—were dictated by Bertillon's precise instructions. Here, for example, is an excerpt from among the twenty movements Bertillon prescribed for measuring the left foot:

2. Measuring the foot according to the Bertillon system.

The operator gives the order: "Place your left foot on the tracing," and when this is done, "Lean your body forward;" then: "Put your right hand on the handle of the table;" and then only does he add: "Stand on the footstool on one foot only." These commands, announced rigorously in the order given above, will in a few seconds make the most stupid individual place himself in the proper position . . .

The object of this position is to force the weight of the body to rest entirely on the left foot . . . By making the subject lean his right hand on a point of support a little in front of him, the operator causes him to displace his centre of gravity in the same direction; a movement which produces an automatic extension of the toes.

Before placing the instrument, the operator should ensure himself that the toes are well in place and particularly that the great toe does not rest sideways on the stool, which would cause a deviation in its direction, and consequently a small diminution in the length of the foot . . .

After having verified the natural position of the body, of the foot, and particularly of the big toes, place the caliper-rule squarely, so that the fixed branch of the instrument may be exactly applied, with a very light pressure, against the back of the subject's heel and that the inner side of the heel and the joint of the big toe touch the stem . . .

Bring down the movable branch gradually until it is in contact with the great toe. Exert a pressure with the *right thumb* on the first and second joints of the great toe, if there is reason to fear that the too brutal pushing of the slide has bent the toe anew or that the subject himself has voluntarily drawn up his toes . . .

To facilitate the recoil movement of the slide, impart to the instrument a slight trepidation by gently shaking the extremity of the graduated stem with the right hand . . .

Before reading, replace and slightly tighten the instrument, which the bending of the knee or the shaking may have disarranged, and finally dictate the figure indicated.[5]

The recording of anthropometric measurements was an elaborate dance, in which the movements of both operator and prisoner had been strictly choreographed by Bertillon himself. All this rigorous discipline was aimed at preventing inconsistent positioning of the body from producing discrepancies in measurement. The reason for putting the prisoner into such an awkward position in the foot measurement, for example, was to prevent discrepancies caused by either intentional or unintentional curling of the toes. Anthropometric measurements were intended to be scientific; they had nothing to do with casual measurements taken by amateurs. As Bertillon acerbically remarked, "It is needless to say that the anthropological length of the foot is different from the *measure* taken by the shoemaker . . . The aim in this case is not to make a pair of shoes, but to obtain a constant length that will be unalterable and that may at any time be taken over again with as much precision as at the time and place of the operation."[6]

The prisoner would undergo eleven similarly precise measurements: height, head length, head breadth, arm span, sitting height, left middle finger length, left little finger length, left foot length, left forearm length, right ear length, and cheek width. Bertillon selected these specific "osseus lengths" because they were the proportions least likely to be affected by weight change or aging over time. The operator would record each of the eleven measurements on a special identification card devised by Bertillon.

Bertillonage is generally known as an anthropometric system, but it was in fact a tripartite system, embracing three means of description. After measuring the prisoner, the operator would record the prisoner's physical description. Bertillon brought his characteristic rigor to this task. Rather than merely providing a blank space for physical description, the "Bertillon card" included spaces for descriptions of the prisoner's eyes, ears, lips, beard, hair color, skin color, ethnicity, forehead, nose, build, chin, general contour of head, hair growth pattern, eyebrows, eyeball and orbit, mouth, physiognomic expression, neck, inclination of shoulders, attitude, general demeanor, voice and language, and habiliments.

Although descriptive documents with such categories had existed since the early eighteenth century, they tended to be filled with bland terms like "normal," "regular," "average," and "medium." Ordinary language did not provide enough nuance to describe all these features adequately. As Bertillon noted, vernaculars had devised words for the extremities of human appearance—for harelips, protruding ears, or hooked noses—but lacked vocabularies for the "normal." "Is it not astonishing," Bertillon exclaimed, "that while there have existed from time immemorial, under the name of *Hippology*, special marks for the precise description of the shape and color of the horse, there has never existed until the present time, so far as we know, a methodical treatise on human description?" The absence of a systematic language for describing the human body, Bertillon felt, was what caused the police to be so poor at identification.[7]

Bertillon single-handedly undertook the ambitious project of developing a precise, "scientific" language, which he called a "morphological vocabulary," to describe human features in all their variety. Eye color, for instance, was typically, as Bertillon observed, given by only

3. A "Bertillon card" from the National Bureau of Criminal Identification (Washington, D.C.), ca. 1908.

three generic descriptors, with no clear rule about where the divisions lay between "blue," "brown," "green," and various intermediate shades. Upon close analysis, Bertillon concluded that eye color was the product of an "orange-yellow pigmentation" superimposed over a blue base. He therefore divided the iris into two distinct segments: first, the "ground tint," which ranged from azure blue to slate blue; second, the intensity of orange-yellow pigmentation, of which there were seven classes, ranging from unpigmented to a "maroon" (meaning brown) areola covering the whole iris. He defined more than fifty types of eye color, each with a standard abbreviation.[8]

FROM RECORDS OF NATIONAL BUREAU OF CRIMINAL IDENTIFICATION, WASHINGTON, D. C.

Bertillon went on to develop a morphological vocabulary for every aspect of the human visage. Lips might be "pouting," "thick" or "thin," "upper" or "lower prominent," with "naso-labial height great" or "little," with or without a "border"; some faces might even be "blubber lipped." The hair of the beard might be "straight," "stiff," "supple," "slightly curly," "frizzly," or "very frizzly." Eyelids were on occasion observed to be "red," "bleared," "weeping," or "drooping." Facial wrinkles were described precisely by phrases such as "horizontal wrinkles of the forehead," "vertical interciliary wrinkles," "horizontal fold at the root of the nose," or "crow's feet."[9]

But the jewel of Bertillon's morphological vocabulary was the ear. Bertillon cards devoted a large section to a detailed description of the ear, with separate entries for four aspects: border, lobe, antitragus, and folds. Each of these general areas included four specific features, for which there were between three and five officially sanctioned descriptive terms, complete with standardized abbreviations. For the antitragus, for example, the operator noted the inclination, profile, reversion, and dimension. For each of these categories Bertillon had developed a standardized nomenclature with abbreviations. The inclination might be "horizontal," "intermediate," or "oblique"; the profile might be "concave," "rectilinear," "intermediate," or "projecting," and so on. Bertillon operators had to memorize all these descriptive terms, their definitions, and the differences between them. The operators would complete the Bertillon card by recording the description of each aspect of the physiognomy (Table 2).[10]

The final stage of identification was the recording of "peculiar marks." Again, Bertillon found that the practice of describing scars and tattoos had been haphazard and unsystematic, producing generic descriptions that gave the location, size, and orientation of a mark only generally. The records of Sing Sing Prison illustrate the state of the art of describing peculiar marks at the time. A typical description of a prisoner's "marks" might read:

Small scar on top of forehead near center and another small one on forehead over left eye. Has scar in left eyebrow.[11]

Such a description, Bertillon noted, might be vaguely useful in suggesting the identity of a prisoner. But it was practically valueless for *proving* identity in a court of law. Since neither the precise dimensions of the scars nor their descriptions nor their precise locations were noted, even a prisoner bearing scars corresponding to these descriptions could plausibly claim that the descriptions referred to other scars borne by someone else.

This was also one of the principal weaknesses of the British Register of Distinctive Marks, whose own administrator complained "that there should be greater precision in the taking of descriptive marks, and that their distance from fixed points in the body should be measured and recorded." Bertillon insisted upon giving the location of peculiar marks as a measured distance from a recognizable reference point. He also demanded that his clerks describe marks precisely: not-

TABLE 2

Abbreviations of the morphological qualifications of each part of the ear

Border

Origin	Superior	Posterior 1st. Its dimension	2nd. its degree of openings
Nil....... nl	Flat (Fr. plate).. flat	Flat........... flat	Open........ o
Small....... p	Small........... p	Small........... p	Intermediate... i
Medium..... m	Medium...... m	Medium...... m	Adhering...... a
Large........ g	Large........ g	Large........ g	
Very large... tg	Very large.... tg		

Lobe

Contour	Adherence	Model	Dimension
Descending.. d	Blending...... f	Traversed..... t	Very small.... tp
Square...... q	Intermediate... i	Intermediate... i	Small........ p
Intermediate. i	Separated...... s	Smooth........ n	Medium...... m
Gulfed..... gf		Eminent....... e	Large........ g
			Very large..... tg

Antitragus

Inclination	Profile	Reversion	Dimension
Horizontal.. h	[Con]cave..... c	Turned...... v	Nil......... nl
Intermediate. i	Rectilinear..... r	Intermediate... i	Small........ p
Oblique..... b	Intermediate... i	Erect......... d	Medium...... m
	Projecting...... s		Large........ g

Folds

Inferior	Superior	General form	Separation
[Con]cave... c	Nil......... nl	Triangular.... tri	Superior....... sup
Intermediate. i	Effaced....... ef	Rectangular... rec	Posterior..... post
Convex.... v	Intermediate... i	Oval......... ov	Inferior...... inf
	Accentuated... ac	Round........ rnd	Total........ total
			Medium...... m

Source: Alphonse Bertillon, *Signaletic Instructions: Including the Theory and Practice of Anthropometrical Identification*, trans. R. W. McClaughry (Chicago, 1896).

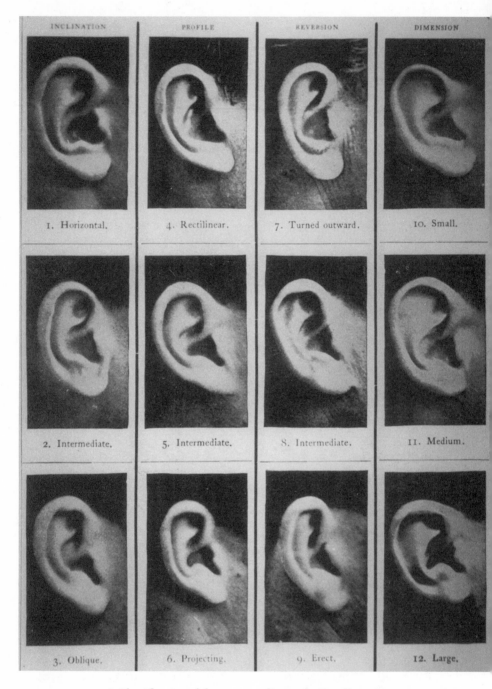

4. Classification of the ear according to the Bertillon system.

ing their shape, measuring them carefully. Finally, he devised a specialized idiom for recording peculiarities. The resulting descriptions he called "cicatrical sentences." A typical "sentence" might read:

cicatrix, rectilinear, of a dimension of one centimetre, oblique external, on middle second phalanx of middle finger, left side, posterior face.

But Bertillon did not stop there. He also devised a system of standardized abbreviations and symbols, which he called "abridged writing." The above sentence could then be reduced to:

$$\text{cic. r. of 1b } \varepsilon, \text{ ml. } 2^{\text{d}} \text{ f. M. g.}$$

On the front of the Bertillon card the operator would use abridged writing to describe two, three, or four of the most prominent peculiar marks. Compared with longhand descriptions of either facial appearance or marks and scars, Bertillonage allowed more descriptive information to be compressed into the scarce space available for individual description. Instead of writing out a description in complete sentences, choosing which features to record, the identification clerk needed only complete the Bertillon card, which provided dedicated spaces for each aspect of the face and body.[12]

Finally, the Bertillon card included two photographs, one full-face and one profile, like today's standard mug shots. Once the operator had completed the card, he took it to the criminal records archive. Bertillon records were indexed according to anthropometric measurements. Peculiar marks, though more "identifying" than anthropometric measurements, were not suited to indexing because of what Bertillon called "the inextricable difficulties which a classification based on these peculiarities would present." The British method of cataloging individuals according to "distinctive marks" had already proven how unwieldy and clumsy this could be.[13]

Photographs, similarly, offered no obvious basis for classification. Bertillon was no opponent of photography. To the contrary, he pioneered many techniques in legal photography, including standardizing the pose and lighting of mug shots. (It is because of Bertillon's belief in the identifying potential of the ear that today's mug shots include the profile.) But photographs did not lend themselves readily to indexing either. By 1880 the Paris police had a collection of 75,000 photographs of criminals, but it was ordered alphabetically. "Would you like to examine these 75,000 cards successively for each suspect that turns up?"

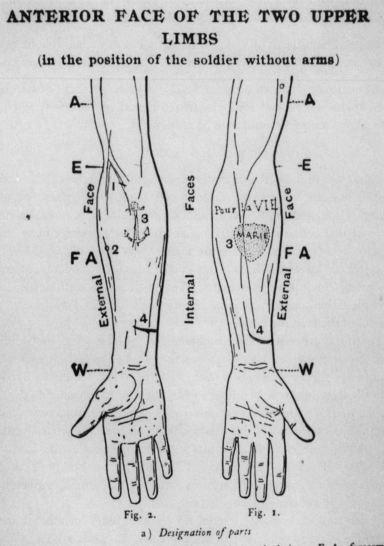

ANTERIOR FACE OF THE TWO UPPER LIMBS
(in the position of the soldier without arms)

Fig. 2. Fig. 1.

a) *Designation of parts*

A, humerus or upper arm ; E, humero-cubital articulation ; F A, forearm ; W, fold of the wrist.
Left side of drawing, external face of right upper limb; *right side*, external face of left upper limb; *in the middle*, internal faces of the two members turned towards each other.

5. An example of the notation of peculiar marks according to the Bertillon system, with descriptions of the scars in Bertillon's special shorthand, called "abridged writing."

Bertillon asked sarcastically. He was the first to grasp what would become the essential principle of criminal identification: "The solution to the problem of judicial identification consists less in the search for new characteristic elements of individuality than in the discovery of a method of classification." The problem was how to organize and access the information that had been collected.[14]

The answer, Bertillon decided, lay in anthropometric measurements, which, unlike photographs or peculiar marks, could be represented quantitatively. Therefore his system of indexing was based entirely on anthropometric measurements. After separating the identification cards by sex, he classified them according to whether the head length was "small," "medium," or "large." He defined these three categories empirically, on the basis of statistical studies of their frequency in the population of Parisian prisoners. The three categories were equally populated: the "medium" category occupied a narrow range under the apex of the bell curve, which, as Bertillon had expected, formed the distribution for all measurements, and "small" and "large" were broad categories at the curve's extremes. The cards were then subclassified by head breadth, subclassified again by middle finger length, and so on through foot, forearm, height, and little finger. These groups were further subdivided by eye color (of which Bertillon defined more than fifty varieties). Each of the resulting groups was then assigned to a separate file drawer and arranged according to ear length. This method of classification broke a file of 120,000 cards down into groups of around twelve cards each (Table 3).[15]

The Bertillon operator would take a newly obtained identification card into the archive, an enormous room full of criminal records indexed according to Bertillon's system, and look for a card with matching anthropometric values. If he found a tentative match, he would confirm it by reference to the physical description and peculiar marks. "Anthropometry, which is a mechanism for elimination, chiefly demonstrates *non-identity*," Bertillon noted, "while the direct *identity* is established by the peculiar marks, which alone can produce *judicial certitude*." Each of the three forms of identifying information thus functioned as a check on the others.[16]

Precise descriptions and standardized abbreviations formed the basis for Bertillon's famous *portrait parlé* (spoken portrait). By describing the most prominent aspects of a suspect's visage or peculiar marks, Bertillon hoped, one operator fluent in his special idiom might transmit a us-

TABLE 3

A sample overview of an anthropometrical system for filing identification cards modeled on the Bertillon system but using both English and metric measurements

I.—Length of Head. Medium 18.55 to 18.1

II.—Width of Head. Long 14.35 and upwards. Med. 14.3 to 13.95. Short 13.9 and downwards.

III.—Left Middle Finger.

Long 11.05 and upwards.	Medium 11.0 to 10.55.	Short 10.5 and downwards.
IV.—Left forearm— Long 47.45 and upwards. Med. 47.4 to 46.35. Short 46.3 and downwards.	IV.—Left forearm— Long 45.7 and upwards. Med. 45.65 to 44.8. Short 44.75 and downwards.	IV.—Left forearm— Long 43.9 and upwards. Med. 43.85 to 42.9. Short 42.85 and downwards.
V.—Left foot— Long 26.4 and upwards. Med. 26.35 to 25.7. Short 25.65 and downwards.	V.—Left foot— Long 25.35 and upwards. Med. 25.3 to 24.7. Short 24.65 and downwards.	V.—Left foot— Long 24.5 and upwards. Med. 24.45 to 23.9. Short 23.85 and downwards.
VI.—Height— Long 5'-7½" and upwards. Med. 5'-7½" to 5'-6¼". Short 5'-6⅛" and downwards.	VI.—Height— Long 5'-5¾" and upwards. Med. 5'-5⅝" to 5'-4¾". Short 5'-4⅝" and downwards.	VI.—Height— Long 5'-4½" and upwards. Med. 5'-4⅜" to 5'-3¼". Short 5'-3⅛" and downwards.
Long left forearm.	Long left forearm.	Long left forearm.

	Medium left forearm.	Short left forearm.
Medium left forearm.	V.—Left foot— Long 25.85 and upwards. Med. 25.8 to 25.25. Short 25.2 and downwards. VI.—Height— Long 5'-6¼" and upwards. Med. 5'-6⅛" to 5'-4¾". Short 5'-4⅜" and downwards.	V.—Left foot— Long 24.8 and upwards. Med. 24.74 to 24.3. Short 24.25 and downwards. VI.—Height— Long 5'-4⅝" and upwards. Med. 5'-4½" to 5'-3½". Short 5'-3½" and downwards.	V.—Left foot— Long 24.0 and upwards. Med. 23.95 to 23.5. Short 23.45 and downwards. VI.—Height— Long 5'-3" and upwards. Med. 5'-2⅞" to 5'-2". Short 5'-1⅝" and downwards.
Short left forearm.	V.—Left foot— Long 25.4 and upwards. Med. 25.35 to 24.7. Short 24.65 and downwards. VI.—Height— Long 5'-5⅛" and upwards. Med. 5'-5" to 5'-3¾". Short 5'-3⅜" and downwards.	V.—Left foot— Long 24.8 and upwards. Med. 24.75 to 24.3. Short 24.24 and downwards. VI.—Height— Long 5'-3½" and upwards. Med. 5'-3⅜" to 5'-2⅛". Short 5'-2" and downwards.	V.—Left foot— Long 23.4 and upwards. Med. 23.35 to 22.8. Short 22.75 and downwards. VI.—Height— Long 5'-1¾" and upwards. Med. 5'-1⅝" to 5'-0½". Short 5'-0⅜" and downwards.

Source: E. R. Henry, *Classification and Uses of Finger Prints,* 3rd ed. (London, 1905).

able physical description to another entirely in words, numbers, and coded abbreviations, without the use of a photograph, sketch, or Bertillon card. Translating bodily features into a universal language allowed the transmission of physical descriptions by telegraph. "The ideal to be attained," Bertillon wrote, "would be for it to be made possible for a person operating in another place, when he reads a statement of this kind, to reproduce on his own body designs imitating exactly, as to general aspect, form, dimension and position, the marks of the individual described." Eventually, police officers on the beat, trained in human morphology and Bertillon's terminology for describing it, would supposedly be able to apprehend suspects they had never seen before solely on the basis of verbal descriptions. The criminal body became, in the words of the historian Matt Matsuda, "an electric body of speed, transmitted telegraphically. This was a body to be read in many cities, provinces, across borders and regions, a body sent and received as transmitted numbers, then transcribed, translated, and reconstructed, a body whose materiality was print, wire, electricity, and transcription."[17]

With the *portrait parlé*, Bertillon sought to replace the photograph with a systematized language as the medium of police communication and surveillance. Although he did incorporate photography into his system, Bertillon, unlike many of his contemporaries, was not impressed by the supposed objectivity of the camera. "No one in the history of photography," asserts the historian Harris Tuttle, "did more to destroy the fallacy that the camera never lied than Bertillon." Widely different images, Bertillon pointed out, could be obtained from the same visage. Moreover, a photograph became obsolete the instant the shutter snapped. While the face aged, the photographic image remained frozen in time. (To be sure, many features recorded in Bertillon records also changed with age. But the amalgam of numerical and verbal descriptions on a Bertillon card could still serve to identify a prisoner even years later.) Bertillonage was an attempt to track the criminal body across time in a way that photography could not.[18]

Instead of the visual image, Bertillon put his faith in words and numbers. Even the visual analysis of a photograph or the first-hand assessment of a prisoner's face, he argued, passed through language, since "we only think that which we can express in words. It is the same with sight: we only can again mentally see that which we can describe. A detective charged with a mission so difficult as that of seeking and arresting a criminal by the aid of a photograph, must be able to repeat and describe from memory the face of the individual of whom he is in pursuit."[19]

Bertillon envisioned nothing less than the complete reduction of human identity to a language of notations which could be organized and accessed at will. It is the same quest that has guided the technology of criminal identification through the present day. What, after all, is DNA identification, if not the reduction of complete human identities to sentences expressed in the specialized four-letter language (A,G,T,C) of genetics? Bertillon reduced the body to language and then to code—turning the criminal body into pure information. In this way, he was able to link criminal bodies to themselves across both time (from one arrest to another) and space (from one locale to another), responding to the intensifying desire of communities to apprehend the stranger, the vagrant, and the deviant.

Bertillon submitted his first proposal for employing anthropometry to identify recidivists to his superiors on October 1, 1879. It was summarily dismissed. Not until four years later, following a change in leadership, did the Paris prefecture consent to test Bertillon's proposed system. In February 1883 Bertillon identified his first recidivist. In 1884, the first full year of his system's operation, he identified 241 recidivists. Slowly, Bertillon demonstrated the value of his identification system. His superiors were so pleased that in 1888 the Paris police created a Department of Judicial Identity with Bertillon at its head, and the number of "recognitions" grew to 680 by 1892. Now Bertillon had his own department, with his own subordinates, whom he drilled mercilessly on the details of his system. Several hundred times a year, Bertillon's clerks located the prior records of offenders whose "state of recidivism" would have otherwise gone undetected. Moreover, Bertillon's identifications were confirmed, not by the testimony of potentially corrupt or mistaken witnesses, but by the body of the criminal himself. The new technique was met with an enthusiasm that had never greeted photographic or descriptive identification systems. Bertillonage, it was thought, might be more than a provisional solution to the problem of identification. With patriotic fervor, one Paris newspaper gushed: "Bertillonage is the greatest and most brilliant invention the nineteenth century has produced in the field of criminology. Thanks to a French genius, errors of identification will soon cease to

6. Teaching Bertillon's *portrait parlé* at New York Police Headquarters, ca. 1918. Note the types of noses, ears, and eyes on the blackboards. The date of the photograph is evidence that the *portrait parlé* was still considered an important method of identification well into the 1910s.

exist not only in France but also in the entire world. Hence judicial errors based upon false identification will likewise disappear. Long live Bertillonage! Long live Bertillon!"[20]

Suddenly the authorities could think, behave, legislate, and sentence with confidence in their ability to know who most recidivists were. This encouraged them to pass laws targeting recidivists, without fearing that those laws would be enforced so arbitrarily as to make a mockery of their intent. The early success of Bertillonage in France must be credited—at least in part—for the passage, in 1885, of the *relégation* law proposed since 1880, which established recidivism as what the historian Patricia O'Brien has called "a new criminally punishable category." *Récidivistes,* designated "according to a careful formula based on the number of convictions within a given period," were exiled to New Caledonia or Guyana for life. At the same time, the liberal Parole Law for first-time offenders signaled the advent in France of widely divergent treatments for offenders depending upon their "state of recidivism." The new laws mandated "both greater leniency toward new offenders and greater repression of habitual criminals."[21]

Thus Bertillonage facilitated the realization of a new penal philosophy that had been fermenting for some time: that criminals should be sorted, perhaps even separated, and differentially punished according to their "state of recidivism." Bertillonage, O'Brien says, "made it easier to detect and prosecute the multiple offender . . . The criminal record and case history replaced branding and mutilation as a means of identification and control." The Bertillon system of identification had been motivated by popular and political belief in recidivism and its critical role in the growth of the crime problem. Once in place, however, Bertillonage operated like a feedback mechanism, confirming the belief in recidivism by exposing real flesh-and-blood recidivists. In this way, Bertillonage supported the very criminological philosophy that had created it: the belief in habitual criminality as a primary cause of crime.[22]

Bertillon's instruction manual was translated into several languages, and it spread rapidly through the world's police departments and penal institutions. Anthropometric identification was instituted in the United States and Canada in 1887, Argentina in 1891, colonial Bengal in 1893, and Great Britain in 1894. Fear of political radicalism and the anarchist movement helped stimulate the diffusion of the Bertillon system. At the International Anti-Anarchist Conference of 1898 in

Rome, which had been convened in response to a wave of political as-
sassinations and terrorist acts culminating in the assassination of Em-
press Elizabeth of Austria, "a highly secret committee of police chiefs
and representatives" endorsed Bertillonage "for criminals and anar-
chists alike" in an effort to create a standardized identification system
across Europe in order to track international terrorists and radicals. By
1899 Germany, Belgium, the Netherlands, Spain, Italy, Russia, Sweden
and Norway, Turkey, Monaco, Luxembourg, Romania, and Switzerland
had all adopted some form of anthropometric identification. Outside
Europe, most of South America and Tunisia adopted anthropometry as
well.[23]

It was precisely in the diffusion abroad, however, that the Bertillon
system suffered its greatest weakness. Learning the system from translated books, far from the exacting presence of Bertillon himself, identification clerks seldom replicated the rigor that characterized operations in Paris. Instead, they skimped on learning the morphological
vocabulary, glossed over the precise movements in the measuring process, and contented themselves with sloppily recording a few measurements. Worse, most identification bureaus, too proud to simply adopt
Bertillon's system wholesale, took it upon themselves to modify various aspects of the system. Foreign bureaus modified the number and
type of measurements to be taken, added and deleted categories from
the physical description, switched the measuring scale from metric to
English, and even altered the design of the instruments themselves.
Not surprisingly, the accuracy of anthropometric identification decreased proportionally with the distance from Paris.

Bertillon was well aware of such shenanigans: his later books were
laden with exhortations and pleas to readers not to deviate from the
procedures he had established. "The arrangement of these instruments
was the subject of many experiments and numberless improvements
before they reached their present shape, which we consider as final,"
he huffed. "So we reject in advance every modification, every further
change, however slight, either in their form or in the manner of using
them. That is a great temptation to beginners, to whom numerous new
ideas occur, but who are not aware that all these ideas, even those that
they believe to be the most original, the most personal, have already
been proposed by others, tried and finally rejected for divers reasons."[24]

These deviations stymied one of Bertillon's ultimate aims: that his *portrait parlé* would become a sort of international language that could transcend national and linguistic boundaries. Whereas Bertillon had envisioned an internationally standardized system controlled and calibrated, like the metric system, in Paris, instead an international patchwork of incompatible anthropometric systems developed. Even worse, sloppy practice decreased the accuracy of anthropometric identification outside France, eventually damaging the reputation even of his own carefully controlled system.

In the earliest years, however, an identification system that functioned at all was such a novelty that there was little criticism. Bertillon operators, with their rulers, calipers, and index cards, could—almost magically—compel the body to incriminate itself. "Of over 1,400 photographs now classified and filed in the Joliet collection or placed in its index," marveled Gallus Muller, a warden at the Illinois Penitentiary, "*any one* can be found in a minute's time, from the subject's anthropometrical description, a fact which by itself creates astonishment among those witnessing the proceeding, and speaks volumes for the reliability and exactness of everything that has been claimed for the method."[25]

No longer a name or a position in society, the individual became biological, defined simply, crudely, as a unique body, distinguishable, in the eyes of science, from all others. No name change, no change in personality could elude Bertillon's classification system, which ensnared the body in a textual net made of its own naked corporeality. The individual, perhaps for the first time, began and ended at its skin and bones. In short, Bertillon created a definition of the individual that the body could not escape. Even as the notion of identity was becoming more fluid—as class boundaries became more porous, as global migration increased, as the notion of "multiple personality" became more widely accepted—Bertillon was able to keep the individual identity stable over an adult lifetime. The criminal body betrayed itself. "To fix the human personality, to give each human being an identity, a positive, lasting and invariable individuality, always recognizable and easily demonstratable," a Belgian prosecutor commented, "such seems to be the broadest aim of this new method."[26]

As in France, anthropometric identification systems had a profound effect on the practice of criminal justice in other countries. While habitual criminality had been a concern for several decades and earlier

identification methods had turned up a handful of actual habitual offenders, Bertillonage provided a growing cadre of proven recidivists.
Bertillonage made recidivism real, concrete, palpable, even utterable:
the term "recidivism" entered the English language in 1886, three
years after the introduction of Bertillonage in France. By 1894 the idea
of the habitual offender had become so robust in Britain that the Prison
Committee thought it "remarkable that previous inquiries have almost altogether overlooked this all important matter." By applying
new penological measures to this group, jurists and legislators could at
last claim to be addressing "the crime problem" at what they saw as its
root cause: recidivism.[27]

These new measures took several forms. One was the special punishment of recidivists. But, useful as knowledge about a criminal's history might be during sentencing, penologists thought it might have
even greater applications within the prison itself. Knowledge of a prisoner's history would at last allow wardens to begin fulfilling the ideal
set forth by the reformatory movement: to tailor the punishment to
the criminal and effect a cure. Progressive penologists had been trying
to gather such information even without Bertillonage, but the new
identification technique promised increases in both the volume and
the accuracy of information about criminal histories.[28]

Progressive penologists were hungry for information. Without
knowledge about their inmates, they felt helpless to escape the de-
pressing prison cycle: wardens were becoming increasingly convinced
that prisons were breeding criminals instead of rehabilitating them.
More information about individual prisoners would allow them to provide "individualized treatment." In 1887 North American penological
reformers founded the Wardens' Association for the Registration of
Criminals, whose object was "to secure the registration, in a central office, of the criminal record of prisoners . . . with a view to distinguishing between habitual and occasional offenders, and as an aid to reformatory work in prisons." The original by-laws of the Association
called for the collection of criminal histories and photographs of convicts "who are known or presumed to belong to the criminal class."
The wardens aimed to assemble "a full description of the physical,
mental, and moral characteristics of prisoners."[29]

Bertillonage promised to improve the process of assembling criminal histories. Six months after its formation, the Wardens' Associa-

tion endorsed Bertillonage. Identification, the wardens argued, might be used to facilitate the "sifting process prior to the administration of punishment." As in France, this separation allowed wardens to impose "sterner and more repressive measures" for habitual criminals, while simultaneously applying "gentler and more reformatory discipline to novices in crime." Similarly, the New York Superintendent of Prisons welcomed the introduction of Bertillonage in 1896, predicting that "in addition to supplying a means for identification of criminals generally, it will be a great aid . . . in the proper classification of prisoners in the prisons in relation to their criminal records; and thus will have a marked tendency to decrease the number of recommitments in this State."[30]

The wardens explicitly invoked the power of knowledge for controlling and molding the prisoner. "By seeking to know the real desert of every criminal brought up for sentence, by knowing his parentage, his moral perceptibilities, physical structure, habits of life when not in confinement, the temptations he failed to resist, and the causes that have driven him into criminal pursuits," progressive wardens hoped to be able to reform, rather than merely confine, prisoners. "Half the battle has been won," wrote Charles Felton, superintendent of the Chicago House of Correction, "when the criminal realizes that the warden is not in ignorance; that, in fact, he knows all about him, and about his life." Felton, like many of his peers, viewed knowledge of the prisoner as a progressive alternative to corporal punishment. "The deterrent power of fear has its place in reformation," acknowledged Joseph Nicolson, superintendent of the Detroit House of Correction, "but fear of brutalizing punishment has proven a failure, and we are now seeking to make the deterrent power of fear more potent by practically wise and humane treatment."[31]

In 1898 George Porteus, a proponent of Bertillonage, articulated the positive role that a criminal history could play in reformation:

If a warden could begin his talk by saying: "Your name is not Jones, but——; you are not from——, but from——; this is not your first term in prison but you were convicted of such and such offenses in the past," what would be the result in the difference in the feeling of the prisoner to the warden who is advising him! He is then talking to a man whose character he knows, whose past is no secret, and the natural result of such a talk can easily be realized. This is one feature of the necessity of identification in prisons.[32]

The reaction against classical jurisprudence and the rise of modern criminology marked a new emphasis on the individual criminal body rather than on the generic criminal act. Bertillonage, and later finger-printing, compelled the criminal body to answer criminologists' and penologists' most pressing question: Who are you? In this way, Bertil-lonage fit into a broader emphasis on individualization that was taking root in every facet of modern criminal justice systems. Just as penolo-gists were seeking to know the prisoner as an individual, criminolo-gists were making individual criminals their unit of analysis, and au-thorities and institutions were seeking to treat convicts as individuals. Bertillonage helped strengthen this tendency by offering these disci-plines and institutions seemingly reliable knowledge about individual criminals in a systematic and accessible form.[33]

The great irony of anthropometry, however, was that the individual-ization of criminal records was not accompanied by the promised in-dividualization of penology and criminology. The goals of reformist penology and criminal anthropology were to institute individualized penal treatments and cures modeled on medical treatment. But while anthropometry provided access to individualized criminal histories, penologists and criminologists were not able to follow through on the individualizing project. Criminal anthropology, for all its supposed at-tention to individuals, could only shuffle individuals into a bestiary of deviant "types": idiots, imbeciles, morons, lunatics, epileptics, moral imbeciles, degenerates, defective delinquents, born criminals, crim-inaloids, prostitutes, and so on. "The criminal would thus be studied much as the botanist studies plants," wrote the French jurist Raymond Saleilles in 1898, "classifying and subclassifying them as soon as a new variety is discovered."[34]

Penology too failed to deliver what the reformatory movement had promised: the "individualization of punishment, which consists in ap-plying special methods of repression and occupation to each individ-ual, as a physician does in prescribing dietary rules and special reme-dies according to the temperament of each patient." Prison wardens simply did not command the resources to administer such individual-ized treatment. Instead, they fell back on crude methods of separating prisoners into types: assigning first-timers and habitual offenders, young and old, to separate prisons, and creating graded hierarchies within each prison. Thus they achieved "individualized" treatment by sorting inmates back into general types.[35]

Just as Bertillon had been born of an anthropologist, Bertillonage was born of anthropology. Nineteenth-century anthropology was most concerned with "scientific" observations of "savages" and people of "other" races. The assumption underlying these inquiries was that human nature—intelligence, savagery, race, ethnicity, heredity, evolutionary history, and so on—would be manifest in the body. Hence anthropologists' careful study of skull sizes and shapes, anthropometric measurements, tattoos, scars, and other somatic signs. The new discipline of criminal anthropology had extended the anthropological gaze to "savages" within Europe. Although Bertillon was more interested in the practical exigencies of criminal recordkeeping than in using anthropometry to plumb the physical basis of criminality, criminal anthropologists saw him as a natural ally.

Bertillon helped legitimate the use of anthropological tools—such as anthropometry and physiognomy—in the realm of criminal justice. To criminal anthropologists, the distinction between *using* the criminal body as a link to a criminal record and simply reading criminality directly from the body was not entirely clear. As with photography, the use of a new technique for identifying criminals stimulated interest in using the same technique for diagnosing criminality. Thus Cesare Lombroso hailed Bertillon's carefully calibrated quantitative measurements as "an ark of salvation." Here at last was a rigorous application of anthropometry, physiognomy, and even tattoo reading. The same anthropometric data used to assemble the criminal record could also sustain "scientific" studies of the criminal body. At the New York State Reformatory in Elmira, for instance, anthropometry was used not just for identification but also for scientific research into the proportions of the criminal body. In 1898 the Elmira medical staff compared their data with measurements taken of Amherst College undergraduates, whom they found to be more brachycephalic (broad-headed) and otherwise larger and heavier than their inmate population. Their conclusion was that criminals tended to be naturally scrawny, not that they were underfeeding their charges.[36]

The line between criminal identification and criminal anthropology was blurry indeed. While Bertillon carefully recorded the location, size, and description of prisoners' tattoos, Lombroso was arguing that the tattoo, which he called "a specific and entirely new anatomico-legal characteristic," was the most significant attribute of the "born criminal." Among the pieces of evidence Lombroso marshaled in support of this argument was the fact that a "recidivistic thief" had a tattoo that read "Woe to me! What will be my end?" (Criminal anthropologists did not distinguish sharply between innate signs of criminality, such as skull shape, and acquired ones, such as tattoos.) While Bertillon was measuring and describing ears for identification purposes, Louis Frigerio, superintendent of the Royal Asylum for the Insane in Alessandria, Italy, was designing an "otometer" to measure the "criminal" ear type.[37]

Criminal anthropologists were not very successful at finding a reliable physical indicator of criminality. Although Bertillonage served to support criminal anthropology in the short run, over time it tended to substitute the recidivist, defined by the criminal record, for the anthropological "born criminal," defined by physical stigmata or anthropometric measurements. But, far from undermining deterministic criminology, Bertillonage played into the same categories: for all practical purposes, Bertillon's recidivist *was* the criminal anthropologists' elusive "born criminal," and the special penal regimens designed for the born criminal were simply applied to the recidivist. What emerged, then, was a new way of visualizing criminality: the authorities did not read criminality in the body itself, but rather used the body as an index to a written criminal record.

Bertillon himself was wary of attempts to use his anthropometric data for any purpose other than identification. "Without entering into the discussions of aesthetic philosophy," he cautioned, "we may yet say in passing that it would be temerarious to seek from this source [physiognomy] a moral prognosis of the individual." At the same time, Bertillonage undermined the project of visually diagnosing criminality by offering a simpler, if less ambitious, alternative. Perhaps *potential* habitual criminality was visible in the shape of the skull, the proportions of the body, or the contours of the face. Perhaps not. But one thing was becoming clear. Using Bertillon's method, *proven* habitual criminality could be made visible through the paper records held by police and penal bureaucracies. Bertillon made it possible to visualize criminality in a ploddingly bureaucratic yet devastatingly effective way. The criminality of the body could be made visible, but only by virtue of the link Bertillon had constructed between it and the written inscriptions on the criminal record. Nonetheless, Bertillon raised criminologists' hopes that all sorts of information might eventually be read from the criminal body. From this point of view, it would be only a small conceptual leap to imagine that the body bore upon it another inscription, one less apparent but more informative, in which might be encoded not only the individual's unique mark but also all the diagnostic information the state sought.[38]

If any one will but take the pains, with an indifferent *Glass*, to survey the *Palm* of his *Hand* very well washed with a Ball; he may perceive innumerable *little Ridges*, of equal bigness and distance, and everywhere running parallel one with another.

—Nehemiah Grew, *Philosophical Transactions of the Royal Society of London* (1684)

CHAPTER 3

Native Prints

There is something a bit overblown about claiming to "discover" fingerprint patterns, since they have always been right at everyone's fingertips. Since ancient times, plenty of people must have looked at their own fingers and noticed the complex patterns of the papillary ridges. As the seventeenth-century anatomist Nehemiah Grew pointed out, all the discovery of fingerprints required was "taking the pains" to look closely at one's own fingertips. However, just noticing papillary ridges is not the same as conceiving of what we now know as fingerprint identification.

It is impossible to pinpoint exactly when the idea of authenticating personal identity through papillary ridges first emerged. Fingerprints appear on ancient pottery and cave paintings in Asia, Europe, and North America, where they may have denoted authorship or identity. Archaeological evidence from seventh-century China shows fingerprints embossed in clay seals which were used to sign documents, and the practice may have been as old as the Former Han dynasty (202 BCE—220 CE). From China the practice spread to Japan, Tibet, and India, where fingerprints were used as signatures or seals. The use of fingerprints as signatures suggests that fingerprint patterns were believed to be unique. In 1303 the Persian historian Rashid-eddin, reporting the use of fingerprints as signatures in China, declared: "Experience shows that no two individuals have fingers precisely alike."[1]

Europeans did not describe fingerprints in writing until the late seventeenth century. At almost exactly the same time that Grew reported his observations, two other microscopists noticed papillary ridges. The Dutch anatomist Govard Bidloo published an illustration of the papillary ridges of the thumb in his *Anatomy of the Human Body* (1685), and Marcello Malpighi, one of the founders of embryology, described papillary ridges in his *Concerning the External Tactile Organs* (1687). Malpighi concluded that papillary ridges were organs of touch, in contrast to Grew who argued that their function was to facilitate sweating in order to release the "more noxious" wastes of the blood.[2]

These classical microscopists did not posit the idea of uniqueness in their discussions of papillary ridges. In 1788, however, the German anatomist J. C. A. Mayer, whose *Anatomical Copper-plates with Appropriate Explanations* (1788) contained an illustration of papillary ridges, stated that "the arrangement of skin ridges is never duplicated in two persons." In 1804 and again in 1818 the British engraver Thomas Bewick published woodcuts of his own thumbprints on the frontispiece of his ornithology texts, apparently as a sort of signature. In 1823 the Czech physician Jan Evangelista Purkyně, who later numbered among the founders of histology and contributed to the understanding of sight, discussed papillary ridges in a dissertation given in Breslau. Purkyně noted the presence of papillary ridges on human hands, simian paws, and prehensile tails, and, in the earliest attempt to develop a taxonomy of fingerprint patterns, he classified the patterns into nine basic types. In the first two types, which Purkyně called the "transverse curves" and the "central longitudinal stria," the ridges cross the fingertip, bulging upward at the center of the fingertip, slightly in the first type, more in the second. In the second two types, the "oblique stria" and "the oblique loop," the central ridges, instead of passing through the center, loop around in the center of the fingertip and then exit from the same side they entered. In the next four types, the "almond," the "spiral," the "ellipse," and the "circle," the ridges form a circular pattern in the center of the fingertip. In the almond the circular pattern is enclosed by a loop and takes the shape of an almond, "blunt above, pointed below." In the ellipse the pattern is more elliptical than circular. In the final pattern the ridges form an S-curve. This idea of classifying fingerprint patterns into types laid the foundation for future fingerprint identification systems. In modern parlance, the first two patterns would be described as "arches" (the first a "plain arch," the second a "tented arch"), the second two as "loops," and the next four as "whorls." Purkyně's last type is a rare pattern known today as a "double" or "twinned" loop. Purkyně, who had studied philosophy in Prague, adopted Leibniz's assertion that every natural object is identical only to itself and concluded that no two individuals had identical fingerprint patterns.[3]

In the twentieth century two British gentlemen, along with their protégés and descendants, would spend more than fifty years feuding over which of them had "invented" fingerprinting despite the microscopic and taxonomic work that preceded them. The invention these disputants referred to was not the discovery of papillary ridges themselves but rather the creation of an identification system, along the lines of the Bertillon system, whereby an unknown person's prints

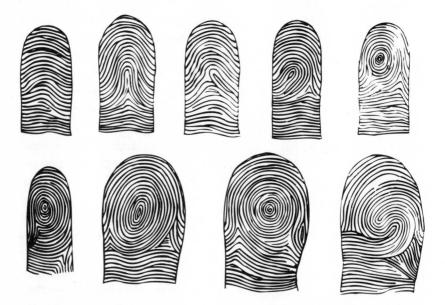

7. Nine fingerprint pattern types, denoted by Jan Evangelista Purkyně, ca. 1823. Top row, from left to right: transverse curves (plain arch, in modern terms), central longitudinal stria (tented arch), oblique stria, oblique loop (loops), almond (whorl). Bottom row, from left to right: spiral (whorl), ellipse (elliptical whorl), circle (whorl), S-curve (twinned loop).

could be compared with a file of criminal records indexed according to fingerprint patterns. Using a fingerprint to verify that someone really is who he or she claims to be requires only checking that person's fingerprint against some other recorded fingerprint. Using a fingerprint to identify an unknown person—to determine whether a person has been arrested before under some alias or to identify a corpse—requires something far more complex: a system for cataloging fingerprint records that is somehow based on the fingerprint patterns themselves. Such a system, in turn, requires some way of classifying fingerprint patterns into a recognizable order. This was a far more ambitious undertaking, and the two gentlemen, William Herschel and Henry Faulds, do each deserve some credit for setting in motion the events that eventually led to such a system.

Although most people associate fingerprinting with that bastion of modern policing, Scotland Yard, the British system of fingerprint identification actually emerged in the colonies rather than in England, in response to the problem of administering a vast empire with a small corps of civil servants outnumbered by hostile natives. Specifically, fingerprinting emerged in India, "the jewel in the crown," Britain's most cherished colonial possession but also its largest and the most daunting to govern. The agents of the East India Company, and later of the foreign service, charged with governing India were overwhelmed by the size of the country, in terms of both area and population, and by the variety of its religions, ethnic groups, languages, and terrains. As one administrator complained, it was "almost ludicrous to observe . . . how often the same things are called by different names, and different things by the same names." This was thought to be true of everything from grains to races, tribes, and, significantly, people. Crucial to the enormous project of governing India was the rule of law, which, in British eyes, was at once the justification for British hegemony and the stick with which it was enforced. In this endeavor, the police served a vital function: "to strengthen administrative control over the countryside and, in the contemporaneous phrase to be the 'eyes and ears' of an alien government ruling over a vast indigenous population."[4]

The birth of modern fingerprint identification came, not coincidentally, at one of the tensest moments in the history of British India. In 1857 Indian conscripts, known as "sepoys," spurred by rumors that the grease that lubricated their rifle cartridges contained beef and pork fat—thus violating the dietary laws of both Hindus and Muslims—rebelled against their British officers and, for a time, took control of Delhi. After British troops crushed the Sepoy Mutiny in 1858, the East India Company ceded all administrative functions to the British government. The Mutiny heightened "the need to enforce law and order in the unruly colonies more severely," and, at the same time, "the need to reinforce a sense of Britain's proper role in history as a beacon of order and civilization in a world of darkness and barbarism." Colonial administrators on the ground, meanwhile, knew it was vital to reassert both their own authority and the rule of law. One of these men was William Herschel, the chief administrator of the Hooghly district of Bengal. Herschel, though demonstrating few talents of his own, came from a distinguished scientific lineage. His grandfather, William, discovered the planet Uranus and became Astronomer Royal, the highest achievement for a British astronomer, and his polymath father, John, a chemist and astronomer, helped Henry Talbot invent photography and Charles Babbage invent the "difference engine"—often called the earliest computer—and made numerous astronomical discoveries of his own. William had served five years as an assistant for the East India Company before being given his post in Hooghly.[5]

Herschel later recalled that the 1857 "disturbances had given rise to a great deal" of not only "violence" but also "litigation and fraud; forgery and perjury were rampant." "Things were so bad in this and other ways that administration of Civil Justice had unusual difficulty in preserving its dignity." In these circumstances, Herschel "was driven to take up finger-prints." One particularly acute example of the interlocked problems of fraud and impersonation lay in the area of pension disbursement. There were pensioners "whose vitality," as Herschel delicately put it, "has been a distracting problem to government in all countries." Herschel, like many other colonial officials, believed natives were collecting government pensions by impersonating deceased pensioners. They succeeded in this deception because the British officials responsible for disbursing pensions could not tell one Indian from another. The rudimentary written descriptions of the pensioners helped little. "The marks of identification noted in the pension roll," one member of the Indian Staff Corps commented, "were usually variations of:—'Hair black—Eyes brown—Complexion wheat colour—Marks of tattooing on fore-arm'—terms which are equally appropriate to a large number of the pensioners." Because of the vague terms of physical description, a pension could be collected by almost any body that presented itself. Only a technique that linked the pension to a single, unique body could distinguish the rightful claimant from the false one.[6]

In 1858 Herschel asked Rajyadhar Kōnāi, a road contractor, to impress his handprint in ink on a deed. Herschel's intention was to deter Kōnāi from trying to repudiate the contract at a later date. He believed he had found a way to reduce the fraud and misrepresentation he suspected among the natives. While he always staunchly insisted that the inspiration for fingerprinting was his alone, some contend that Herschel learned about fingerprints from the Bengalis themselves, pointing out that *tip sahi*, or signature by finger impression, had been in use in Bengal "from a time not known to us," possibly after being imported from China. Though Herschel would later tout Kōnāi's handprint as the point of origin of modern fingerprinting, it is actually a handprint, not a fingerprint, and the details of the papillary ridges of the fingertips are barely visible. Only several years later did Herschel begin taking inked impressions of the tips of the fingers.[7]

Fingerprinting in India, then, began as a technique for civil, not criminal, identification. (Thus recent initiatives in the United States to fingerprint welfare recipients are not a new application of the technique at all, but rather a return to its original application.) The "invention" of fingerprinting by British colonial officials had as much to do with perpetuating the state's authority as arbiter of legal disputes as with the suppression of criminal activity. Yet the civil application was in a colonial context in which the assumed inferiority of the ruled and their attendant deceptions and frauds provoked the search for greater and more efficient social control and identification. It is not surprising, therefore, that the most important application of Herschel's idea was the identification of criminals, who similarly required control and containment.

By the 1870s Herschel was using "sign-manuals," as he called them, to register prisoners. He also took new impressions of his own fingerprints. The patterns had not changed, thus demonstrating, anecdotally at least, the permanence of papillary ridge arrangements. In an 1877 letter to the Inspector of Jails and Registrar-General, Sir James Bourdillon, Herschel proposed that fingerprinting be adopted for the identification of criminals across India. "Here," he declared, "is the means of

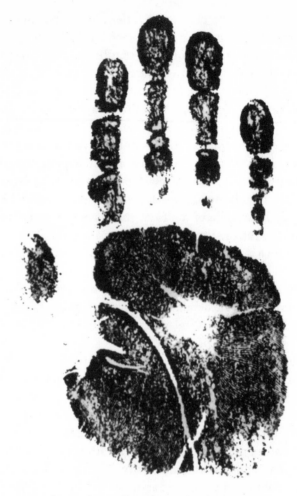

8. Handprint of Rajyadhar Kōnāi taken by Sir William Herschel and used as proof of identity for a construction contract, Hooghly District, Bengal, India, 1858.

verifying the identity of every man in jail with the man sentenced by the court, at any moment, day or night." But Bourdillon was not impressed, and by the 1880s Herschel's idea remained largely untested.[8]

Nineteenth-century British conceptions of criminality in colonial India were inextricably bound up with contemporary evolutionary ideas about race. Although European jurists had already posited the existence of "habitual" or "professional" criminals, this concept took on new meaning in India. British amateur ethnographers believed that Indian castes, because of their strictures against intermarriage, represented "pure" racial types, and they concocted the notion of racially inferior criminal castes or "criminal tribes," inbred ethnic groups predisposed to criminal behavior by both cultural tradition and hereditary disposition. Some members of some of the supposed "criminal tribes" were doubtless involved in a great deal of criminal activity, but most of those labeled "criminal tribes," as the historian David Arnold points out, were simply lower-caste, nomadic peoples: "wandering gangs, nomadic petty traders and pastoralists, gypsy types, hill- and forest-dwelling tribals, in short . . . a wide variety of marginals who did not conform to the colonial pattern of settled agriculture and wage labor." Others were groups that participated in *kaval*, a system of watchmen who would protect a village's property, which the British interpreted as an extortion racket. Put in terms of caste, the habitual criminal became a "hereditary criminal," a member of a genetically determined criminal group. Criminality became ethnic. This was most chillingly expressed by the eminent jurist James Fitzjames Stephen, who arrived in India in 1869 to help write the Indian Code of Criminal Procedure. "When we speak of 'professional criminals,'" Stephen told the colonial legislature in 1871, we should "realize what the term really does mean. It means a tribe whose ancestors were criminals from time immemorial, who are themselves destined by the usages of caste to commit crime, and whose descendants will be offenders against the law, until the whole tribe is exterminated or accounted for."[9]

In 1871, at Stephen's urging, the colonial legislature passed the Criminal Tribes Act, which called for the "registration, surveillance, and control of certain criminal tribes." The Act allowed local officials to designate as a "criminal tribe" any group of people "addicted to the systematic commission of non-bailable offences," such as theft. Since the British equated unpredictable mobility with criminality, both at home and abroad, and nomadism was an essential characteristic of the criminal tribe, the Act restricted the movement of members of criminal tribes, forcing them to obtain passes for travel and to report periodically to local officials. Violations were punished with prison terms. This "made it possible to proclaim entire social groups criminal, on the basis of their ostensibly inherent criminality," and "hundreds of communities were brought under the Criminal Tribes Act" (Table 4).[10]

TABLE 4

Indian castes and British characterizations of them in official correspondence, ca. 1870

Caste	Criminal habits
Aheers or Gowallas	adroit cattle stealers and burglars, whilst, ostensibly engaged in other pursuits, they are ready at all times to join in any marauding expeditions . . . troublesome lot
Sunnyassees	religious mendicants who wander about the country . . . live by begging, cheating, and pilfering
Nutts	professional jugglers of gipsy habits, and sometimes given to pilfering
Bowreahs	low caste . . . given to thieving
Sonareahs	wandering class of professional thieves
Binds	commit organized dacoities
Budducks	notorious dacoit tribes
Bedyas or Shikarees	a very low caste and have no particular religion . . . the word "Budh," of which their name is a corruption, means a "hunter"
Mughya Domes or Dormas	lowest of outcasts . . . their presence in any district or part of a district is always marked by a decided increase in thefts, robberies, dacoities
Bembodyahs	gipsies . . . subsist by fishing and snaring birds
Keechuks	gipsies of up-country origin
Dosads	a low caste of people
Koneriahs	regular thieves . . . have no particular profession
Moosaheers	a thieving caste
Rajwars	thievish, neglected, half-starved, and utterly degraded set of beings.
Gahsees	professional thieves
Banjors	workers in bamboo . . . cheats and thieves
Boayas	low caste . . . great thieves
Dharees	worst thieves
Sowakhyas or Kowakhyas	gipsy origin . . . snare and eat crow

Source: Anand A. Yang, "Dangerous Castes and Tribes: The Criminal Tribes Act and the Magahiya Doms of Northeast India," in Yang, ed., Crime and Criminality in British India (Ann Arbor: Association for Asian Studies, 1985).

Stephen's ominous pronouncement alludes to the intimate relationship between evolutionary theory, criminal anthropology, and surveillance technologies like fingerprinting. Stephen used the theory of heredity to cast entire ethnic groups as irredeemably prone to crime.
From this it followed that a responsible government could take only
two courses of action: one genocidal (Stephen's "extermination"), the
other techno-bureaucratic (Stephen's "accounting for"). Colonial jurists' and anthropologists' corruption of evolutionary theory in the service of British racism demanded the development of new methods of
tracking, monitoring, and controlling suspect populations. The colonial official who most prominently responded to this demand, Edward
Henry, was well familiar with the supposed problem of criminal tribes.
In 1883, even as Bertillon was introducing his identification system in
France, Henry, the magistrate of Champaran, a district in northeast India, devised a plan to settle one "criminal tribe," the Magahiya Doms,
on waste lands, in the hope of turning "criminal" nomads into settled
agriculturalists. As this ultimately unsuccessful plan demonstrates,
Henry, like most colonial officials, viewed mobility as the criminal
tribes' most threatening characteristic. A decade later Henry would
devise another remedy for the mobility of suspect people—a remedy
based not on resettlement but on surveillance.[11]

In the 1880s criminal identification methods in India, which consisted of "parades" at local jails and "descriptive rolls" in the *Police
Gazette,* were considered to be "of the feeblest." Magistrates had no
way to tell whether strangers from other districts were "habitual criminals" or not. "Thieves have frequently been brought before me who I
am convinced must have been many times previously convicted, who
are wanderers and decline to give a true account of their antecedents,"
complained one magistrate. "What is the use of multiplying law as to
surveillance of habituals if when a habitual offender runs away from
surveillance no one away from his home can identify him even if he
is caught?" Identification registers in the British style, consisting of
verbal physical descriptions, railed another cantankerous magistrate,
"were filled with wooden imbecilities." Still another magistrate could
"see no way out of the difficulty except branding this class *on the face*
in such a manner as to defy concealment."[12]

In the late 1880s colonial officials began discussing the implementation of a new criminal identification system in India. "What is
wanted," commented a magistrate, "is a plain useful classification of

habitual criminals, to which, when an unknown offender is caught, a reference can be made, and it can be at once, or almost at once, ascertained if he is included in it. It is no use trusting to recognition or general description or description of dress, stoutness, and the like things which are variable." An anthropometric identification system similar to Bertillon's seemed the obvious solution. "The French system of anthropometry is believed to be singularly effective," wrote one judge, with "a few simple measurements of the unchanging bones in the body enabling the police to decide whether a given prisoner is one of some hundreds or thousands entered in a register or not."[13]

Edgar Thurston, curator of the Indian Museum in Calcutta, had introduced anthropometry to India in 1885 as an anthropological tool for investigating the physical basis of castes and races. Ethnographers like Thurston showed a "heavy reliance on anthropometric measurements for the classification of various tribes into a hierarchical pyramid." Thurston reportedly "pursued his special interest in anthropometry rather unusually; he kept his calipers and other measuring instruments handy, using them on native visitors to the museum—sometimes paying them, sometimes not." The police recruited Thurston to teach anthropometry in Madras, and from him they gained an appreciation for the anthropological side of the technique. "There was . . . a vigorous correspondence between police reformatory officials, missionaries and amateur anthropometrists, through journals and personal correspondence, on the 'nature' of the Indian criminal." Thus anthropometry in India, as in Europe, was at once an identification technique and a research tool. It was used both to identify individuals and "for the collection of anthropometric data on the physiognomy and physiology of criminal 'types.'"[14]

In 1892 the Bengal government, joining a global trend, adopted a modified version of the Bertillon system. Colonial officials were initially enthusiastic about anthropometry, which Edward Henry called "a scientific solution of what had long been deemed an insoluble problem, and . . . an enormous improvement upon all rough-and-ready means previously adopted." From Bengal the system spread across India, and by 1898 the police records offices of the various provinces had collected nearly 200,000 Bertillon cards. But anthropometry enjoyed less acclaim in the colonies than it had in Europe. In the colonial context, anthropometric identification suffered from two crucial drawbacks. From the outset, colonial officials were skeptical of the ability of Bertillonage to distinguish individuals within the Indian population. Bertillon's morphological vocabulary might work fine for Frenchmen, but could it really distinguish people who, in British eyes, looked bewilderingly homogeneous? One official complained that "uniformity in the colour of hair, eyes, and complexion of the Indian races renders identification far from easy, and the difficulty of recording the description of an individual, so that he may be afterwards recognised, is very great." In fact, the British modified the Bertillon system according to their perception of intraracial physiognomic variety. Most notably, British officials decided to dispense with recording eye color, "there being little variation in the pigment of the iris amongst orientals." In France there had been an implicit faith in the physiognomic heterogeneity of Frenchmen. Brown eyes, for example, were rather prevalent in Europe too, but where colonial officials saw "uniformity" in India, Bertillon saw immense diversity in France. The number of different irises, Bertillon rhapsodized, "is almost infinite, and it is impossible to meet with any two alike." The Bertillon system enumerated more than twenty different shades of "brown" eyes.[15]

The second problem with anthropometry was inconsistency between operators. Bertillon had managed to keep measurements relatively consistent by exercising strict discipline over his operators, ensuring that they followed his procedures for recording measurements exactly. In India, however, with operators, most of them natives—and therefore not well trusted by the British—dispersed across the vast reaches of the subcontinent, such discipline proved elusive. Edward Henry, who as Inspector General of Police was put in charge of administering anthropometric identification in Bengal, noted, "There must be a residuum of error attributable to what may be termed the personal equation of the measurer, however well devised the checks may be, or however good the instruments used." The term "personal equation," which Henry borrowed from astronomy, referred to the inevitable subtle differences between observers in reading precise scientific instruments.[16]

Bertillon himself was aware of measuring discrepancies between operators. Some operators tended to round up, while others tended to round down. Some fit the calipers as snugly as possible, while others applied them loosely. Indeed, Bertillon did not expect measurements to come out exactly the same when measured on different occasions or by different operators. He even viewed an exact correspondence of results as a sign of error: "*An ABSOLUTE similarity in the figures, under such circumstances, far from proving the successive transit of one same individuality through the lock-up of a prison would be an infallible indication of a mistake.*" Variations between measurements were signs of authenticity. "The minute differences in question should then be interpreted as being the incontrovertible and precious evidence that two signalments have been taken independently of each other, at different times, and are not duplicates of one same original." To account for what he called "human frailty," as well as small natural variations over time in the bone lengths being measured (bone lengths were known to vary slightly over both a day and a lifetime), Bertillon had used "scrupulously compiled statistics" to calculate a "maximum of tolerable deviation" for each measurement. For two different measurements to correspond to the same individual, Bertillon stipulated, they "*may reach,* but *cannot exceed*" these standard deviations. In this way, Bertillon argued, he had contained the personal equation problem.[17]

But, as Henry pointed out, this margin of error could sometimes cross the boundaries between the "small," "medium," and "large" categories that governed the classification of anthropometric cards. For example, suppose an operator measured a head length of 18.4 centimeters. Since the "maximum tolerable deviation" for the head length measurement was 2 millimeters, it would be necessary to assume that prior measurements of the same person's head might have yielded readings anywhere between 18.2 and 18.6 centimeters. Now suppose "large" had been defined as anything above 18.5 centimeters, and "medium" as between 18.1 and 18.5 centimeters. The operator, when searching for a match for this subject, would have to do *two* searches, instead of one: one assuming that the head length was large, the other treating it as medium. This problem could conceivably multiply with each successive measurement, greatly extending the searching time. The result, Henry complained, was "that the process of search with a record of 30,000 cards may occupy an hour or longer."[18]

Police officials in Bengal tried to skirt the personal equation problem by devising new, "automatic . . . self-registering" instruments. In other words, they sought to eliminate operator judgment by mechanizing the measuring process. They put their faith in mechanism instead of disciplined observation. Bertillon, of course, explicitly forbade this sort of tinkering with his measuring instruments. Far from improving matters, he insisted, "every change introduced into the anthropometrical manual of operation can only result in augmenting the amount of the possible and inevitable error with which human observations are always more or less marred."[19]

"In Bengal," Henry later recalled, these "weaknesses in the system showed themselves so detrimental to successful working that attention was directed to the feasibility of substituting a system of identification by finger prints only, not supplemented by measurements." If, however, fingerprinting was ever to compete successfully with Bertillonage, it would require something that did not yet exist: a classification system capable of subdividing fingerprint patterns with precision equal to that of Bertillon's plan for subdividing identification cards according to anthropometric measurements.[20]

The chief obstacle to the use of fingerprinting for criminal identification was the problem of how to index a set of records according to fingerprint patterns. Purkyně had sorted all fingerprint patterns into nine classes, but, not intending to devise an identification system, had progressed no further. One could, as Herschel did, simply compare a new fingerprint with one's whole collection of fingerprints, but this was obviously impractical for a collection of any size.

The earliest attempt at a classification system was proposed by yet another British colonial, Henry Faulds, a physician who, while serving at Tsukiji Hospital in Tokyo during the late 1870s, had noticed fingerprints on ancient Japanese ceramics. Faulds published his observations in a letter to *Nature* in 1880, in which he suggested that "fingermarks" might be used to identify criminals. Faulds, like Herschel, recorded fingerprints by pressing the fingertip first into printer's ink, spread thinly and evenly, and then onto a sheet of slightly damp paper. He had even used "greasy finger-marks" to solve a minor crime: the mysterious disappearance of "some rectified spirit." The publication of Faulds's letter prompted a hasty response from Herschel asserting his own prior claim on the technique. Faulds bitterly disputed Herschel's claim; the dispute over priority would last well into the 1950s.[21]

A year later John S. Billings, a U.S. Army physician who abstracted Faulds's article for *Index Medicus*, told the International Medical Congress in London: "Just as each individual is in some respects peculiar and unique, . . . even the minute ridges and furrows at the end of his forefingers differ from that of all other forefingers and is sufficient to identify." The Western scientific community had accepted the premise of uniqueness immediately upon the "discovery" of fingerprints. But, as Faulds himself would later point out, the simple assertion that all fingerprint patterns are, in some absolute sense, unique does not address the question of whether it is possible for two fingerprint *impressions* from different fingers—especially if those impressions are smudged, indistinct, or incomplete—to be mistaken for each other.[22]

Faulds presented his ideas about fingerprint identification to an Inspector Tunbridge of Scotland Yard sometime during the 1880s, but the Yard declined to follow up. Faulds outlined a "syllabic" classification scheme in which consonants represented fingerprint pattern types, such as bows, hooks, sinuous patterns, loops, "pear-shaped or battledore-like figures," spirals, and "mountain peaks." He modulated the consonants with vowels which described the character of the "core" (the center of the print): empty, simple, three rods, one rod, bifurcation, and so on. He further subclassified using long and short vowels. Each fingerprint pattern could then be described as a syllable consisting of one or two consonants modified by a long or short vowel, as in the following examples:

bra, spo, art prīd, prĭd, nut, nŭt

Each person's set of ten prints could be represented by a "word," which might then be kept in "a syllabic index arranged in alphabetical order" like a dictionary. Faulds was the first to envision a criminal identification register, catalogued solely according to fingerprint patterns, which *"needs no other index than its own essential structure."* His curious insistence upon vocalizing identity recalls Bertillon's strenuous efforts, through the *portrait parlé,* to create identities that could be spoken.[23]

In 1880 Faulds wrote to Charles Darwin about his fingerprint research. Since it concerned "a queer subject," Darwin forwarded the letter to his perpetually inquisitive cousin Francis Galton, one of Britain's most eclectic scientists. Galton's most cherished interest was in heredity, a project that would eventually flourish into the field of eugenics. In Galton, eugenics and evolutionary theory again intersected with the development of fingerprint identification. He was fascinated by fingerprint patterns, which he hoped might be the elusive visible markers of heredity for which he had long been searching. The purpose of papillary ridges, he believed, was to raise the mouths of pores so sweat could be released more easily. He also thought that nerve endings were concentrated in ridges, and this might "assist the sense of touch." But Galton was less interested in the function of fingerprint patterns than in how those patterns might be exploited: both to identify individuals and to provide a physical marker of heredity, ethnicity, and race.[24]

First Galton taught himself to record serviceable fingerprint impressions. After experimenting with many types of ink, he settled upon a particular brand of printer's ink made of lampblack, which he obtained in small, collapsible quarter-ounce tubes from Messrs. Reeve and Sons in London. Galton spread the ink very thinly upon a copper or glass slab using a printer's roller. Like anthropometry and photography, the recording of fingerprints required a certain degree of cooperation from the subject: the subject would have to relinquish control of his body, or at least his hand, to the identification clerk, who, as with anthropometry, was called an "operator." The operator would take the subject's right hand and press the tips of all four fingers onto the inked slab, then onto a designated place on an index card measuring eleven and a half by five inches. The operator would then repeat this process for the left hand. These prints, in which four fingers were taken together, were known as "plain impressions."

Next the operator would take "rolled impressions," in which each finger was printed individually. The operator would take hold of the finger or thumb and roll it gently from left to right in the ink, then similarly roll it on a designated spot on the index card. A rolled impression made it possible to record a larger area of the fingerprint pattern; it essentially transformed the curved surface of the fingertip into a flat image. The plain impression served as check on the rolled impression, especially against the common error of mistakenly rolling a finger in the wrong box either through negligence by the operator or sleight of hand by the subject. Today's fingerprint cards retain this form devised by Galton: ten rolled impressions complemented by plain impressions.

Galton did not conceive of fingerprinting as a replacement for Bertillonage. In fact, he strongly believed that Britain should adopt the Bertillon system. Instead, he viewed fingerprinting as a tool for colonial governance. Galton had heard complaints from colonial officials that the Indian natives' "features are not readily distinguished by Europeans," and he agreed that this constituted a significant drawback for anthropometric identification in the colonies, where the need for individualized identification was, if anything, greater than at home. Finger-

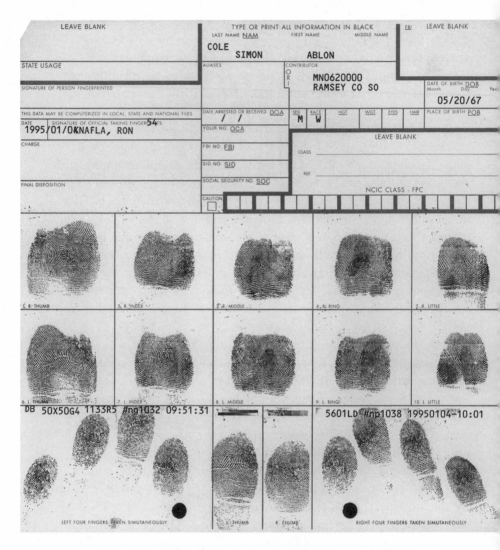

9. The author's fingerprints on a typical modern fingerprint card, 1995. Finger-prints are not inked but taken by "Livescan," an inkless optical scanner. The author has whorls on all fingers except the left thumb and the two little fingers. The "plain impressions" on the bottom of the card are used as a check on the "rolled impressions" above.

prints offered a way to identify individuals by the abstract whorls of the papillary ridges rather than subjectively perceived physical features. Galton saw application for the technology all over the Empire. In an address before the Anthropological Institute in 1889 he suggested that fingerprinting might avoid "the great difficulty in identifying coolies either by their photographs or measurements." "Whatever difficulty may be felt in the identification of Hindoos," he said, "is experienced in at least an equal degree in that of the Chinese residents in our Colonies and Settlements, who to European eyes are still more alike than the Hindoos, and in whose names there is still less variety."[25]

Still, fingerprinting lacked a classification system. In 1889 Galton set out to devise one. Bertillon had solved the problem of classification by reducing the body to numbers. Galton, however, was faced with the problem of classifying not quantitative but qualitative data. He needed a way to sort complex visual images into defined categories. He first tried using Purkyně's nine fingerprint pattern types, but he kept coming across "transitional" patterns that blurred divisions between classes. "On trying to sort them according to Purkenje's [sic] standards," Galton "failed completely," and, he lamented, "many analogous plans were attempted without success" as well. The individuality of fingerprint patterns, the very quality that rendered them so useful for identification, also muddled any classification scheme. "A complex pattern" like a fingerprint, Galton sighed in his book *Finger Prints* (1892), "is capable of suggesting various readings, as the figuring on a wall-paper may suggest a variety of forms and faces to those who have such fancies."[26]

In his next effort Galton "endeavoured to sort the patterns into groups so that the central pattern of each group should differ by a unit of 'equally discernible difference' from the central patterns of the adjacent groups, proposing to adopt those central patterns as standards of reference. After tedious re-sortings, some sixty standards were provisionally selected, and the whole laid by for a few days." But fingerprint patterns can play tricks even on a mind as orderly as Galton's: "On returning to the work with a fresh mind, it was painful to find how greatly my judgment had changed in the interim, and how faulty a classification that seemed tolerably good a week before, looked then. Moreover, I suffered the shame and humiliation of discovering that the identity of certain duplicates had been overlooked, and that one print had been mistaken for another." Frustrated, Galton conceded that "re-

10. (Top) Basic fingerprint pattern types: plain arch, tented arch, loop, and whorl. (Bottom) Delta and core, ridge counting and tracing under the Henry system of fingerprint classification. The delta is a point where the transverse ridges split to form the central pattern. Loops have one delta; whorls have two. The core is a point at the center of the pattern. A ridge count (for loops) is the number of intervening ridges between the delta and the core. A ridge trace (for whorls) follows a ridge emanating from one delta and determines whether it passes inside, outside, or meets the other delta.

peated trials of the same kind made it certain that finality would never be reached by the path hitherto pursued."[27]

Eventually Galton retreated from his sixty patterns, and even from Purkyně's nine, deciding that all fingerprints could essentially be characterized as one of three patterns, "arches," "loops," and "whorls," a tripartite division that would form the basis for most subsequent classification schemes. Henry Faulds would later mock Galton's simplistic tripartite scheme "of having them done up in similar bundles, like chocolate cakes" as "decidedly amazing on the part of a mind really of high scientific power"—but in fact Galton had finally recognized that the key to classification lay in lumping, not splitting, in categorizing, not differentiating.[28]

Galton's three pattern types were not evenly distributed. Approximately 60 percent of all fingerprints were loops, around 30 percent were whorls, and the remaining 10 percent were arches. Since loops were the most common pattern, Galton further subdivided them into "inner," or "radial," loops (which open toward the thumb) and "outer," or "ulnar," loops (which open toward the little finger). This brought the number of patterns to four. For purposes of criminal identification, Galton proposed to classify all ten fingers, in a specified order, expressing the full complement of an individual's fingerprints as a ten-letter word expressed in a four-letter alphabet consisting of the letters A (arch), I (inner loop), O (outer loop), and W (whorl). For example, Galton's own prints would be represented as "WOWOOOWOWO," meaning that he had only whorls and outer loops. Identification cards might then be indexed alphabetically according to this ten-letter word. One cannot help noticing the parallel with DNA and its expression of identity as "the book of life," an enormously long word in a four-letter language. Like Bertillon and Faulds before him, Galton translated identity from a visual image into language.

Galton also considered the question of using fingerprints as legal proof of identity. He suggested that two fingerprints might be matched by comparing features he called "minutiae," which later became known variously as "ridge characteristics," "ridge details," "points of similarity," or "Galton details." These were points along a papillary ridge where the ridge ended abruptly, split in two, or split and then rejoined. By matching minutiae, Galton could establish a common source for two different fingerprints. The question was how much matching detail was needed to ensure that two different, yet similar, fingerprints would not be mistaken for each other. Galton, ever the statistician, calculated the statistical probability of two whole fingerprints matching, which he estimated as one in 64 billion. Given a human population of 16 billion, this meant that the chance that two different matching fingerprints existed was approximately one in four.[29]

In 1893 the British Home Office appointed a committee, chaired by Charles Troup, to recommend whether to implement Bertillonage or fingerprinting in Britain. The Troup Committee heard a report on the functioning of the Bertillon system in Paris, and it visited Galton's laboratory, where he demonstrated his classification scheme. Classifying all ten fingers as one of four pattern types yielded 104,976 possible permutations. But Galton, much to his chagrin, had already discovered that human fingerprints were not at all evenly distributed among these combinations but tended to cluster in certain classifications. For example, the classification "OOOOOOOOOO," meaning all ten fingers showed outer loops, was very common, appearing in more than 6 percent of the population. In Galton's modest collection of 2,645 fingerprint cards, 12 ten-letter "formulas" occurred more than 26 times, and one formula occurred 164 times. What was needed, therefore, was a method of subdividing the people with outer loops on all ten fingers into finer groups. But Galton had not yet devised a working method of subclassification. The Committee reckoned this lack would begin pre-

RIDGE TERMINATION	
BIFURCATION	
INDEPENDENT RIDGE	
DOT OR ISLAND	
LAKE	
SPUR	
CROSSOVER	

11. Ridge characteristics, also known as minutiae, ridge details, or Galton details. Although there are disagreements about terminology (such as whether a "lake" should really be considered two "bifurcations"), for most of this century fingerprint identifications were made by matching corresponding ridge characteristics between two prints.

senting problems when the collection exceeded 1,000 identification cards.[30]

"On the other hand," the Committee noted, "the strongest point in favour of M. Bertillon's system is the method of classification." Galton himself conceded that Bertillon had developed a better method for indexing a large collection of criminal identification cards, and he advised the Committee to stick with anthropometry. The Committee finally recommended adopting a modified anthropometric system. The Home Office's preference for the French system, despite national pride in the Astronomer Royal's grandson's supposed "discovery" of the fingerprint, illustrates the prevailing wisdom in Europe in the 1890s: that anthropometry was a reliable, scientific method of identification and, though it had certain drawbacks, there was no reason to resort to an unproven technology like fingerprinting.[31]

Colonial police officials like Edward Henry were less enthusiastic about anthropometry because of the twin problems of supposed racial homogeneity and the difficulty of disciplining operators across India. Henry and his assistants, Azizul Haque and Chandra Bose, therefore attacked the problem of devising a workable fingerprint classification with greater vigor. Their crucial contribution was a scheme for using "ridge counting" and "ridge tracing" to sort loops and whorls into smaller groups, thus subdividing Galton's general patterns into finer categories. Although Henry later claimed that he scribbled the outline of his classification idea on his cuff after conceiving it in a burst of inspiration on a train, there is evidence that the most of the credit belongs to Haque and Bose. There is even a report that they had considerable difficulty explaining the system to their boss. Henry estimated that this new method, which became known as the "Henry system," could comfortably accommodate a collection of up to 100,000 prints.[32]

When someone suspected of theft was brought to a police station in Bengal, a police clerk would record the suspect's fingerprints on a card similar to that described by Galton. The card would then be forwarded to central headquarters for classification, which would be performed by a skilled clerk trained in the Henry system. The rules of fingerprint classification under the Henry system are quite complex, but a brief summary may be instructive.

The first two steps in the Henry system were based on Galton's three basic pattern types: arch, loop, and whorl. To these Henry added a fourth group, called "composites," which consisted of rare hybrid patterns that fit into no known type, including "central pocket loops," "lateral pocket loops," "twinned loops," and "accidentals." The "primary classification" involved examining each finger and noting where whorls appeared. The fingers were numbered 1 through 10, beginning with the left little finger and proceeding from left to right across both hands. The primary classification was expressed as a fraction with odd-numbered fingers over even-numbered fingers. A certain value was added to the numerator if a whorl appeared in a odd-numbered finger, and a certain value added to the denominator if a whorl appeared in an even-numbered finger. These values were determined by the finger. The values were squares of one another: 1, 2, 4, 8, 16 (Table 5). Henry then added 1 to both the numerator and the denominator in order to avoid having zeroes. The primary classification could, therefore, range from 1/1 (zero whorls) to 32/32 (ten whorls). My prints, for example, would have a primary classification of 27/28, since I have whorls on seven fingers. With a range between 1/1 and 32/32, there were 32^2, or 1,024, possible primary classifications. The fingerprint cards were stored in a filing cabinet with 32 rows and 32 columns of pigeonholes. A fingerprint card with a primary classification 20/11, for instance, would be found in the twentieth pigeonhole on the eleventh horizontal row.

The secondary classification went on to characterize the fingers of the right hand (in the numerator) and the left hand (in the denominator). Since whorls had already been described in the primary classification, they were omitted in the secondary classification. Uppercase letters were used for the index fingers only. The patterns of the fingers were characterized as arches (A or a), tented arches (T or t), radial loops (R or r), or ulnar loops (U or u).

Further subclassification of whorls was performed by *ridge tracing*. Whorl patterns originate in two *deltas*, where the transverse ridges divide (like a river delta) to form the whorl. Examiners would trace the lower ridge of the left delta and see whether it passed inside, outside, or met the right delta. If the ridge passed inside the right delta, the pattern was classified as an "inner" whorl, designated by I. If it passed outside, the pattern was classified as an "outer" whorl, designated by O, and if it met the right delta it was classified as a "meeting" whorl, designated by M. These letters were then added to the secondary classification.

Loops were subclassified by *ridge counting*. The examiner counted the number of ridges between the delta and the *core*, and these values

TABLE 5

Basis for primary classification under the Henry system of fingerprint classification

The numbering of the fingers for the Henry system. Fingers are numbered, left hand first, beginning with the little fingers.

	1	2	3	4	5	6	7	8	9	10
	Left little	Left ring	Left middle	Left index	Left thumb	Right little	Right ring	Right middle	Right index	Right thumb
Numerator	Left little 1		Left middle 2		Left thumb 4		Right ring 8		Right index 16	
Denominator		Left ring 1		Left index 2		Right little 4		Right middle 8		Right thumb 16

Schematic for determining primary Henry classification. Odd-numbered fingers count for the numerator. Even-numbered fingers count for the denominator. If a whorl appears on a finger, the given value is added to either the numerator or the denominator. The primary classification is calculated using these values and then adding 1 to both numerator and denominator. The values for the primary classification may then range from 1/1 (zero whorls) to 32/32 (10 whorls).

Source: E. R. Henry, *Classification and Uses of Finger Prints,* 3rd ed. (London, 1905).

were appended to the secondary classification. Ridge counts from one to nine in the index finger (one to ten in the middle finger) were characterized by I, counts above these thresholds by O. The third term of the equation was the actual numerical ridge count of each little finger, if it was a loop. An example of a Henry classification might look as follows:

$$\frac{5}{17} \quad \frac{R}{U} \quad \frac{OO}{II} \quad \frac{19}{8}$$

(Whorls in both thumbs, high-ridge-count radial loops in the right index and middle fingers, low-ridge-count ulnar loops in the left index and middle fingers. Nineteen-ridge-count loop in the right little finger. Eight-ridge-count loop in the left little finger.)

After this there were even more subclassifications. With all this subclassification, the Henry system was able to sort fingerprint cards into finer groups than Galton's rudimentary system. Even common primary classifications, like 1/1, could be subdivided using ridge tracing and counting. So a properly classified fingerprint card would have to be searched against only a small number of cards bearing exactly the same classification. Henry's finer-grained classification system, therefore, greatly speeded up the process of checking whether a suspect's fingerprint had already been registered with the police, perhaps under an alias.

Here, in Henry's own words, is an example of the working of the Henry system of fingerprint identification:

A man charged with housebreaking and theft is convicted under the name of John Smith, sentenced to a term of imprisonment and sent to jail, where his finger prints, together with the finger prints of other prisoners received, are taken by a prison warder. On the back of each slip is recorded the prisoner's name, with dates and full particulars of the case, and the slip thus filled up is forwarded to the Central Office. On receipt there, they are classified by one officer, and his work is tested by another, before they are filed in their respective collections and groups . . .

After the lapse of a year or two, the Central Office receives from police or Governor of a jail a slip, containing the finger prints of man on trial for theft, who has given the name of William Jones, and other information concerning himself, which the inquiries locally made show to be false . . .

On receipt of the slip one officer draws up the search form containing the full formula, viz. 13/18 U/U (IO/IO) 14, and makes over the slip and the search form to the searcher, who first verifies the correctness of the formula, and then proceeds to search. The type in all the impressions is unmistakable, so there can be no doubt as to the correctness of the Primary Classification number 13/18—the subclassification U/U (IO/IO) of index and middle of the two hands is also obviously correct—but there may be divergence of opinion as to there being exactly 14 *counts* in the right little finger. To eliminate the possibility of error arising from this, he decides to search through the subgroups of 13/18 U/U (IO/IO), which have from 12 to 16 *counts* in the right little finger . . . If the slip he is looking for is in the Criminal Record, he knows it must be among subgroups 12 to 16 of 13/18 U/U (IO/IO), which file he picks out, and he concerns himself no further with ridge *counts*, but concentrates attention upon the salient features of the slip. The right thumb is a Lateral Pocket, the left thumb a Twinned Loop. He turns the slips of subgroups 12 to 16 over rapidly, much in the same way as a pile of bank notes are looked through, and delays only when he comes to a slip the right thumb impression of which is a Lateral Pocket, and his eye then glances at the left thumb. If it is not a Twinned Loop, he passes on to the next slip, and finally stops at one which has the right thumb a Lateral Pocket, the left thumb a Twinned Loop, and the two ring fingers Central Pockets. He then compares the ridge *characteristics* of one or two impressions on the slip in his hand with the corresponding impressions of the slip in the Record, and if they agree he knows that his search has been successful. The Central Office then inform the requisitioning police that the so called John Smith was, on a specified date, convicted under the name of Wm. Jones, of housebreaking with theft, and give all information concerning him recorded on the back of their slip, which is sufficient to enable the local police to prove, in the manner prescribed by law, the previous criminality of the *soi-disant* Wm. Jones.[33]

Around 1895 Henry introduced his system in the police department in Bengal. When new criminals were apprehended, the police fingerprinted them instead of taking their anthropometric measurements. In 1897 the colonial government appointed a committee, chaired by General Strahan, the Surveyor-General of India, to evaluate the new sys-

12. The Fingerprint Bureau, Police Headquarters, Dresden, Germany, ca. 1907. The man on the far left is having rolled inked fingerprint impressions taken by the man next to him. The men in the background are classifying fingerprint cards. The fingerprint cabinet, where the cards are filed according to their classification, is at the far right.

tem. The committee's report was critical of anthropometry. It worried that "skilled persons are required to take the measurements and they must have sufficient education to enable them to read the instruments and to use the decimal notation. This is more particularly a serious objection in India, where warders and policemen are frequently far from well-educated men." Moreover, errors in recording anthropometric measurements were irreparable—they went into the record as gospel. In contrast, "Finger prints are absolute impressions taken from the body itself under conditions which eliminate error as regards transcription or recording. The subject impresses his own prints"—and even misfiled prints still contained the information which would allow them to be filed correctly at some later date. Furthermore, the committee warned that "carefully made and delicate instruments are necessary to take the measurements with sufficient accuracy," and that "the actual anthropometric record of one person occupies the measurer between half an hour and one hour," a very long time indeed if one anticipated registering large numbers of people. A search of the Bertillon file, meanwhile, "exceed[ed] one hour," not least because of the need to do double searches.[34]

"Such complications," Henry declared, "do not trammel the fingerprint system." Fingerprinting was "simplicity itself." Most important, fingerprints could be taken "without skilled labour, and without instruments." For the purposes of maintaining administrative control over the vast expanses of India, the committee found particularly advantageous "the fact that all skilled work required is transferred to the central or classification bureau." Moreover, taking a full set of fingerprints "occupies only five minutes or less," and, with Henry's new classification system, a search in a file of more than 8,000 cards required less than five minutes. The Governor-General of India decided to switch to fingerprinting on June 12, 1897. Henry's new classification system was crucial in making the difference between the Troup and Strahan reports. "Mr. Henry's classification and subclassification," the committee concluded, "has, we consider, effectually got over the objections raised" to Galton's system.[35]

The Henry system soon spread to the other provinces. Although the ten-print system remained confined to police departments and prisons, other branches of government in India adopted the practice of using single fingerprints to *verify* identity. The Opium Department used fingerprints to authenticate the identity of those cultivators to whom it paid advances for their crops. The Emigration Department recorded the left thumbprints of emigrants. The Survey of India and the Post Office registered the thumbprints of all employees in order to avoid rehiring undesirable workers. The Medical Department used thumb impressions to prevent candidates taking the medical boards from hiring stand-ins to take their examinations. And the Registration Office used a left thumbprint to authenticate deeds and other legal documents. All these examples anticipated later uses of fingerprinting for civil identification.[36]

In 1897 the Indian police got an opportunity to try using fingerprints, not just for recordkeeping, but for criminal investigation. On the night of August 15, 1897, the manager of a tea garden in Julpaiguri district of Bhutan was stabbed to death in his bungalow with a *kukri*, a Nepalese knife. A wooden box belonging to the deceased had been opened and money removed from it. There were a number of suspects, including the manager's employees, the cook, the relatives of a woman with whom the manger had been romantically involved, "a wandering gang of Kabulis of criminal propensities" (another of the "criminal tribes"), and an ex-servant who had been imprisoned because the manager had accused him of theft and recently released. A bloody fingerprint was found on an almanac that had been removed from the wooden box. The ex-servant, a Bengali named Kangali Charan, had been seen spending unusually large amounts of money. Since Charan's fingerprints had been taken upon his imprisonment, the police were able to retrieve them and compare them with the bloody fingerprint found on the almanac. Here the police used the method of comparison outlined—but never actually practiced—by Galton: they matched ridge characteristics between the bloody print and the inked print from their records. Having matched eighteen such characteristics, the police concluded the print belonged to Charan, who was apprehended in Birbhum, hundreds of miles away. In 1898 the first criminal trial based on forensic fingerprint evidence began.

In this murder trial, the scientific foundation of fingerprint identification faced a much more stringent test than it did in Henry's recordkeeping system. Fingerprint records consisted of *all ten* fingerprints and were indexed according to all ten. When a magistrate interpreted a match between a prisoner and a fingerprint record as proof that the prisoner was guilty of prior crimes, he based this conclusion on the premise that no two individuals had identical *sets of ten* fingerprints. When fingerprints are used for forensic purposes, however, the question is quite different, because investigators rarely find a complete set of ten fingerprints at the scene of a crime. Usually they find the impressions of one or two fingers. Often these impressions are fragmentary, so that detectives are not even working with whole fingerprints but with *partial* prints. Forensic fingerprint identification, therefore, rests in part upon the far more ambitious premise that there are no two identical *single* fingerprints anywhere in the world. And ultimately it rests upon the still more ambitious premise that no two *partial* prints are alike, or that fragmentary areas of papillary ridge detail of a certain size (exactly what size is unclear) can be matched to one and only one finger, to the exclusion of all other fingers in the world. Moreover, the impressions are often blurred, smudged, overlaid upon on another, and distorted by foreign matter. The detective must match this distorted crime scene print to an inked print, taken under pristine "laboratory" conditions, to the exclusion of all other fingerprints in the world.

In the Charan case, it was the eighteen matching ridge characteristics that convinced detectives that the bloody print must have come from the finger of Kangali Charan. There was nothing magical about the number eighteen, nor any proof or demonstration that there could not be some other fingerprint that resembled the fragmentary impression found on the almanac. Whether this was convincing or not was a question for the judge and assessors, who presided over the trial under British law. Unlike later fingerprint trials, there was no expert witness for fingerprint evidence in this case. Instead, the judge and assessors performed their own examination of the evidence, with varying degrees of competence: "The Judge recorded that, although he had no personal difficulty as a layman in finding complete similarity in the finger-impressions of [the defendant] with those on the almanac, it took him 'several hours' to explain matters to the Assessors and obtain their acquiescence in his opinion!" Although the judge and assessors were convinced that the bloody print belonged to Charan, they hesitated to convict him of murder. The judge declared:

No doubt the brown finger-impressions on the Bengali almanac are strong presumptive evidence, if believed, to consider the defendant to be present in the room, and he having touched the blood had stained his fingers with it; but, beyond that, I do not see how that can connect the defendant with the actual murder, or even of its abetment. It will not only be unsafe to hold the defendant guilty of such a crime, but it will be unfair and unjust to presume him to have murdered the deceased without any direct evidence, or even indirect evidence, to connect him with the commission of murder.

The bloody fingerprint, the judge concluded, was "good and sufficient evidence to hold that the defendant was the man who trespassed into the room of the deceased on the night of the 15th August and handled the papers and the calendar in the wooden box. At the same time I do not hold that it proves that he murdered the man or that he was an actual abetter in the crime of murder." Therefore, the judge and assessors convicted Charan of burglary but acquitted him of the murder.[37]

Nonetheless, the ability of fingerprints to convict had been established. In 1899 the colonial legislature passed the Indian Evidence Act, the world's earliest endorsement of fingerprints as legal evidence. In a 1904 case, *Emperor v. Sahdeo,* an Indian court found that a fingerprint record constituted legitimate evidence that an offender had committed previous offenses. The government used a fingerprint record to prove that a convicted thief had five previous convictions and should therefore be subjected to a more "rigorous imprisonment" as a repeat offender. The court hailed fingerprinting as a significant advance over previous "rough and ready" methods of identification: "hand-writing may be a deliberate forgery or an innocent or accidental imitation; the photograph may present a deceptive likeness," but "finger impressions . . . afford a surer criterion of identity than any other comparable bodily feature."[38]

The court also ratified the still unproven assumption that no two fingerprints were alike. The court did not cite any proof of its assertion that "there are no two human beings in the world who exactly resemble one another in every single detail." Instead, it alluded to the "well established fact" that "the absence of absolute repetition seems to be a universal law of nature." In a pattern that would be repeated throughout the history of fingerprint identification, the court simply noted that there had "never yet been found any case in which the pattern made by one finger exactly resembled the pattern made by any other finger of the same or of any other hand." The absence of disproof was taken as proof.[39]

The success of fingerprint identification in the colonial laboratory of India helped establish both the feasibility of the Henry system as a legitimate rival to the Bertillon system and the credibility of its underlying premise: that no two fingerprints were alike. This helped prepare the ground for the triumphant return of fingerprinting to Britain. Henry published his system in *The Classification and Uses of Finger Prints* in 1900. That same year, encouraged by the success of "the Indian system," the British Home Secretary convened yet another committee, chaired by Lord Henry Belper, to resolve the competing claims of anthropometry and fingerprinting. By this time Britain included fingerprints on its anthropometric identification cards, as was rapidly becoming the practice around the world. Even Bertillon himself had added space for four fingerprints to his identification cards, although the cards were still classified according to anthropometric measurements. The debate, therefore, was not over whether to *record* measurements or fingerprints, but over how identification cards should be *filed:* according to anthropometric measurements or fingerprint patterns.

For the Belper Committee, as for the Strahan Committee, the "chief disadvantage" of the anthropometric system was "the labour involved in obtaining accurate measurements and the variations that must frequently occur between measurements of the same man made by different people at different times." Again, skill could not be concentrated at the center but had to be distributed throughout the country: "For its successful working it is necessary to have properly trained and careful officers in every district where the measurements have to be taken and constant supervision is needed for the purpose of keeping the work up to the mark, and of checking any tendency to inaccuracy in any individual measurer." "The labour involved in training and supervising the measurers" was viewed as a heavy burden on the state, and several witnesses testified that fingerprinting promised to reduce that labor. A chief allure of fingerprinting was that the bulk of identification work, the recording of inked fingerprints, could be performed by unskilled labor. Officials could train people to *record* legible fingerprints in a manner of minutes. Learning to *classify* sets of fingerprints according to the Henry system was a far more ambitious undertaking, requiring weeks if not months of study or instruction. These skilled classifiers, however, could be concentrated at a central headquarters, where their productivity would be greatest.[40]

But the Bertillon system had a proven ability to handle a large volume of data. Could Henry's system match that? "The question," the committee noted, "is whether finger prints can be so classified that when those of an old offender are sent up to the Central Office his re-cord could be found readily and with certainty in a collection that may amount to 100,000 sets or more." The committee was duly impressed by the Indian collection, which boasted between 40,000 and 50,000 prints, but fingerprint identification still had its critics. Significantly, the defenders of anthropometry were men of science to whom the an-thropological technique appeared more scientific. Dr. John Garson, the former head of the Anthropometric Office, remained skeptical of the Henry system, citing the tendency of fingerprint patterns to cluster in certain classification groups and transitional patterns, which might be classified differently by different operators. Moreover, uncooperative prisoners and poor training and sloppiness on the part of operators could undermine fingerprinting just as well as anthropometry by fill-ing the system with poor-quality, "defective," or smudged prints.

Dashing the committee's hopes of using fingerprinting to economize on labor, Garson predicted an *increase* in staff if fingerprinting was adopted, because fingerprinting "is very trying work for the eyes, and takes considerable time to do, the work being done through a glass. Ev-ery record would have to be checked before being finally disposed of, so that we could neither classify nor arrange the cards nearly so quickly in the central office as we can now. In making search for previous records, more time would be required in determining where to search than we now take." Even Francis Galton, the man now known as a founder of fingerprinting, felt more comfortable with anthropometry, declaring that "finger prints alone are less certain than measurements and finger prints combined." "I am timid of making so great a change without more knowledge," he quavered. The perception of fingerprinting as un-proven continued to militate against introducing it in Europe. Among scientists like Galton and Garson, anthropometry remained more sci-entific than fingerprinting.[41]

Crucial to the committee's decision, then, was the unresolved issue of whether criminal identification was properly a scientific or a bu-reaucratic matter. Advocates of anthropometry like Garson testified that criminal identification was a scientific process and should be per-formed by trained, credentialed scientists:

GARSON: This work is really that of a scientific laboratory, and unless this is admitted we will get into no end of trouble. The whole sys-tem must be conducted on scientific lines—it is absolutely neces-sary to do so.

CHAIRMAN: I don't quite understand your definition of it as a "laboratory"?

GARSON: This system of identification is a scientific system, and all
things connected with it have to be worked out according to scientific principles; the whole work of the office should be conducted on
the lines of an anthropometric laboratory, and not as an ordinary
Government or police office.[42]

Proponents of fingerprinting, meanwhile, thought "an ordinary Government or police office" was precisely where criminal identification
should occur. They viewed criminal identification as routine clerical
work, which should be streamlined according to the latest principles
of industrial management. "My view of it," commented Sir Robert
Anderson, the new head of the Anthropometric Office, "is that this
scheme can be administered on the same lines as any other Government work, the assistance of experts being obtained to any extent necessary . . . It should be administered on the ordinary principles of any
ordinary work." He admitted that "there probably is a certain element
of truth" in Garson's claim that measuring accuracy had suffered since
Garson's removal as head of the Anthropometric Office, but, he contended, "the work is done more expeditiously than it was, and things
run more easily—that is to say, I get more work out of the office than I
did before."[43]

The Belper Committee decided to adopt fingerprinting on a trial basis in Britain. Assuming that the Henry system proved satisfactory, the
committee was prepared to recommend a complete switch to fingerprinting, primarily because "the ease with which the finger prints can
be taken in any place, at any time, and by untrained officers, inclines
the balance of advantage decisively in its favour." The perceived advantages of fingerprinting were, in a certain sense, industrial: unskilled
workers, higher productivity and processing speeds, and the seemingly
automatic working of the system. The crucial advantage of anthropometry, meanwhile, was its greater scientific credibility: the technique had a longer track record, it was more trusted, and it was used in
other fields, such as anthropology. Thus the choice of fingerprinting
over anthropometry implied a preference for quantity over perceived
quality and for industrial-style speed, efficiency, productivity, and
economy over what was seen as scientific accuracy and precision.[44]

Scotland Yard soon boasted of the savings in labor and the enormous
increase in "identifications"—that is, matching an arrestee with his or

her previous record—achieved by the switch to fingerprinting. By discontinuing anthropometry, the Yard reduced its staff significantly. Fingerprint officers made a total of 1,722 identifications in 1902, the first full year of the system's implementation. This well exceeded the peak of 462 identifications effected by anthropometry in 1900. Identifications continued to accelerate, more than doubling in 1903. By 1904 the Yard was processing 350 fingerprint cards each week. "The results obtained," the Yard crowed, "appear to fully demonstrate the greater effectiveness as a means of establishing recognitions of the new system," which "brought about a marked saving of the time of police officers." From Scotland Yard the Henry system would soon spread across the world.[45]

The Henry system was not the only criminological import from the Indian colonies. The link that British jurists in India forged between habitual and hereditary criminality likewise found its way back to Britain. James Fitzjames Stephen retained his eugenic conception of criminality when he returned to Britain, where he declared flatly that habitual criminals "should die." And, in a seminal 1870 article, J. Bruce Thomson, a prison surgeon at Perth Prison in Scotland, in the earliest European mention of *hereditary* criminality, announced that he had arrived at "the conviction that in by far the greatest proportion of offences, *Crime is Hereditary.*" The influence of the colonial experience was clear in Thomson's argument, which was peppered with references to caste as a way of delineating types of persons within races. "We all admit the distinctive characteristics of mankind, as seen in the black and white, the red and yellow, and other less marked varieties of mankind," Thomson noted. "But even among the civilized men of Europe there are *castes* and characteristics which cannot escape the eye of the natural historian and medical observer; and constitute here and there, in the midst of even cities and populous districts, human varieties."[46]

Caste served as a way of applying a fine-grained racial typology even to the native population of Europe. This opened up the possibility of the hidden existence of criminal castes at home. Criminality was perpetuated, Thomson posited, because the criminal class was inbred by choice, just as Indian castes supposedly were inbred by religious stricture. "Only connecting themselves with those of their own nature and habits," Thomson argued, criminals "must beget a depraved and criminal class hereditarily disposed to crime. Their moral disease comes *ab ovo*. They are born into crime, as well as reared, nurtured, and instructed in it." The idea of inbreeding was crucial to constructing a racial conception of criminality. It allowed criminal anthropologists to attach the stigma of criminality to supposedly inbred groups, such as gypsies, Jews, or the lower classes in general. It also allowed criminologists to provide a Darwinian explanation of the criminality of certain groups: inbreeding produced evolutionary degeneration, which in turn resulted in criminal propensity.[47]

Thomson's idea proved more influential on the continent than in Britain. Caste also figured prominently in the writing of Cesare Lombroso, who acknowledged his debt to Thomson. "There exist whole tribes and races more or less given to crime, such as the tribe Zakka Khel in India," Lombroso wrote. "At birth" in this tribe, he soberly reported, "every male child is consecrated to thievish practices by a peculiar ceremony, in which the new-born infant is passed through a breach in the wall of his father's house, whilst the words 'Become a thief' are chanted three times in chorus." Gypsies also provided an example of "an entire race of criminals." The belief in hereditary criminality became a central tenet of the Italian School of criminology, and it eventually returned to Britain in the work of Havelock Ellis.[48]

Although overt hereditarianism was never popular in Britain, concern over *habitual* criminals did not abate there. The Henry system made it "possible to refer to 'known habitual criminals' with some approximation to accuracy." British officials used criminal records to segregate habitual offenders in much the same way as criminal anthropologists had wanted to segregate hereditary criminals. In 1901, the year the fingerprint system was introduced at Scotland Yard, several jurists issued new calls for special measures targeting habitual criminals. The Judges of the King's Bench called for a separate "habitual offender's division" of the prison system. Meanwhile, Robert Anderson described Britain as besieged by "a gang of habitual criminals" and called for eugenic "asylum prisons," which would prevent persistent offenders, "begotten and born and bred in crime," from reproducing. Clearly the British habitual criminal was not far removed conceptually from the Indian hereditary criminal. After much public and parliamentary debate, these proposals eventually resulted in the passage of the Prevention of Crime Act of 1908, which targeted "professional" criminals.[49]

"The discipline of criminal anthropology and the theory of finger-printing," according to the literary scholar Ronald R. Thomas, "alike spring from" Darwinian evolutionary theory "and may be understood as direct applications of the principles of evolutionary biology to the study of social behavior." The importation of both the Henry system and the Indian "born criminal" into Britain illustrate, Thomas says, how "the theory and practice of criminology and the history of imperi-alism consistently intersected one another in the latter part of the nineteenth century. The empire served as the laboratory in which criminological theories and techniques were discovered, developed, and tested for eventual application on the common criminal back home." The replacement of anthropometry by fingerprinting in Britain was more than merely a technical decision in favor of a "better" sys-tem. Like so many aspects of British policing, the Henry system was rooted in colonial governance. The Belper Committee's decision to switch to fingerprinting, with its greater ability to measure "habitu-ality," presaged the transformation of the English criminal into some-thing more like the Indian criminal—"a physiological foreigner in need of domestication."[50]

This colonial mentality, moreover, spread throughout the world along with the Henry system itself. The adoption of the Henry system around the world, the decision by states that it was necessary to moni-tor and track, not only colonial subjects, but their own citizens as well, signaled a shift at home to almost colonial models of government, a transformation of the relationship between the state and its citizens, who became less like French citizens, those paragons of *égalité*, and more like colonial subjects: a mass of strangers, alien, dangerously mobile, and predisposed by heredity to crime, whose identities were batch-processed by the fingerprint system.

One of the inducements to making these inquiries into personal identification has been to discover independent features suitable for hereditary investigation . . . it is not improbable, and worth taking pains to inquire whether each person may not carry visibly about his body undeniable evidence of his parentage and near kinships.

—Sir Francis Galton, "Personal Identification" (1888)

CHAPTER 4

Degenerate Fingerprints

When Henry Faulds stumbled across fingerprint patterns in Japan in 1880, the first person to whom he wrote describing his "discovery" was Charles Darwin. Faulds's choice of correspondent tells us a great deal about how late-nineteenth-century European scientists conceived of fingerprints. At the time, Western science was in the throes of the Darwinian revolution wrought by the publication of *Origin of Species* in 1859. The most burning issue surrounding Darwinian theory was, not surprisingly, the evolutionary history of the human species, which Darwin had begun to address in *The Descent of Man* (1871). Western scientists were obsessed with tracing the relationship between humans and other primates, using evolutionary theory to delineate the various racial and ethnic groups that made up the human species, and exploring the role of heredity in shaping human intelligence, personality, and other attributes. Evolutionary theory ushered in the era of "biological determinism," the belief that the character, abilities, and even destiny of each individual were strongly influenced, if not absolutely mandated, by biological inheritance. European scientists interested in fingerprint patterns, like Faulds, assumed that evolutionary theory would be crucial for explaining their origin and significance. At the same time, they thought fingerprint patterns might have something to contribute to the scientific understanding of evolutionary history. Indeed, they hoped that fingerprints might function something like a fossil record, providing clues about the evolutionary history of the species, the races, and individuals.

It was only natural therefore that, in addition to proposing that "finger-marks" be used to identify criminals, in his 1880 letter to *Nature* Faulds reported that he had recorded the fingerprints of different ethnic groups—English and Japanese—and of different species. He had taken the fingerprint of a Gibraltar monkey, and he recommended "to others more favourably located the careful study of the lemurs, &c., in this connection, as an additional means of throwing light on their interesting genetic relations." Faulds predicted that "these analogies may admit of further analysis, and may assist, when better understood, in ethnological classifications." He also speculated that it might be possible to use a hereditary understanding of fingerprint patterns to resolve cases of disputed paternity like the Tichborne case: "There might be a recognisable Tichborne type, and there might be an Orton type, to one or the other of which experts might relate the case."[1]

While William Herschel, a bureaucrat, had thought only of authenticating individuals' identities for legal purposes, Faulds, a scientist, saw in fingerprint patterns something far more profound. Fingerprint patterns might be a visible trace of evolution, a code in which each individual's genealogy, racial and ethnic background, and even character traits might be encrypted. While the colonial bureaucrats in India were most interested in the individuality of fingerprints, for Faulds the most intriguing thing about fingerprints was not that they were so individual but that they were so alike, that they fell into such regular patterns. These patterns, it stood to reason, had to have some evolutionary meaning. "Why should those lines run into patterns, often of much complexity, and sometimes even assuming the aspect of curiously complex artistic designs?" Faulds asked about papillary ridges. The ridges, furrows, branchings, and bifurcations that composed fingerprint patterns, moreover, were not unique to fingerprints but recurred throughout nature:

> You meet them in the stripes of the tiger and of the zebra, in the spots of the leopard and of the ocelot, and on the eggs of many birds. There are similar markings in the grain of woods, in the veining of leaves, and

in the spots and stripes of flowers. The barks of some trees often display the very patterns that are so useful and interesting in finger prints. You see similar figures on the skins of scarlet-runner beans and on the backs of mackerel. So with sand under the sway of tidal waters, the ripples of which seem to repeat themselves in the ridges of the sand, as we find too, in the desert under the sweep of arid winds; or powdery snow on a frozen lake under a dry East wind. Photography shows furrows exactly like those of finger prints in the overflowing lava of a volcano.

In Faulds's view, fingerprint patterns were codes that contained secret information about the history of the species, race, individual character, and even nature itself. Plumbing their mystery, he thought, might "lead us close to the very centre of nature's great forge."[2]

Evolutionary theorists like Herbert Spencer, meanwhile, believed that the overall fingerprint pattern type was genetically influenced, but that minute variations in the embryonic environment made the details of each individual's fingerprints unique. This evolutionary approach to fingerprint patterns was taken up most fully by Darwin's cousin Francis Galton, to whom Darwin had forwarded Faulds's original letter. For Galton, fingerprint patterns had two potential uses. First, as Faulds had suggested, they might be used to identify criminals. Second, and for Galton more important, they might be used to trace heredity. At the time, Galton had already published several books arguing that virtually every human attribute could be traced to heredity. Galton's strong belief in the power of heredity would later blossom into the eugenics movement, which sought to control mating practices in order to improve the human race through directed evolution. One of the main obstacles to Galton's study of heredity lay in finding a reliable somatic indicator of inheritance—that is, a hereditary marker in the body itself. Galton thought fingerprint patterns might prove to be visible markers of heredity, that in fingerprints each person might "carry visibly about his body undeniable evidence of his parentage and near kinships." The key to this code, Galton hoped, would allow all sorts of information to be derived from fingerprint patterns—genealogy, intelligence, personality, disease propensity, criminality, and so on—information that would play a vital role in his eugenic program. In short, Galton saw fingerprint patterns much in the way we now see DNA: as both an identifier and a hereditary marker. Just as DNA is used today for both criminal identification and paternity testing, a century ago Galton thought fingerprinting would have those same applications.[3]

In trying to find a way to use fingerprint patterns to trace heredity, Galton had stumbled upon a classification scheme—arch, loop, whorl—that laid the foundation for the use of fingerprints to index criminal records. Although this would later be viewed as Galton's primary contribution to the development of fingerprint identification, his heart really lay with his eugenic fingerprint research. The very success of Galton's work in using fingerprints for criminal identification, however, by turning fingerprints into solely an individual identifier, ultimately undermined the legitimacy of using fingerprints to predict heredity, race, and character—research that Galton, as the "founding father" of the eugenics movement, would have found far more important.

Although the attempts to use other identification techniques, such as anthropometry and photography, to trace heredity, delineate differences between the "races," and predict criminality and disease propensity are fairly well known to historians of the nineteenth-century human sciences, the use of fingerprinting for the same purpose has largely been forgotten. Today we think of fingerprinting solely as an identification technique. This selective amnesia is not accidental; rather, it played a crucial role in establishing the legitimacy of fingerprinting in criminal identification. Fingerprint examiners strengthened their authority by disassociating themselves from their colleagues who speculated about the predictive powers of fingerprints to tell, not only the past, but also the future. By turning the fingerprint into an empty signifier—a sign devoid of information about a body's race, ethnicity, heredity, character, or criminal propensity—fingerprint examiners made fingerprint identification seem less value-laden, more factual.

Consider the problem of forensic fingerprint identification in criminal cases. Fingerprint examiners today testify with an air of detached neutrality. They can claim to have looked at no evidence from the case other than the fingerprints. Ideally, they should know nothing about why the suspect was charged with the crime, the suspect's criminal record, the suspect's race, or anything else about the suspect. In other words, they do not see the suspect; they see only fingerprints. This insularity enables them to play the role of neutral scientist. If they knew the suspect's race, criminal record, and so on, this might potentially prejudice their testimony. While such testimony would not necessarily be legally inadmissible or improper, it would not be as convincing as testimony given from a more impartial vantage point.

Now suppose it was widely believed that fingerprints do contain information about the suspect's race, heredity, or criminal propensity. The purity of the fingerprint examiner would be irreparably compromised because the evidence itself would contain potentially prejudicial information. For instance, if some fingerprint patterns were thought to correlate with criminality, then the examiner, upon seeing such a pattern, might be more inclined to declare a match. Alternatively, if some fingerprint patterns were thought to correlate with race, then an examiner could tell detectives to look for someone of a certain race. Similarly, if an examiner knew that an eyewitness had identified someone of a certain race, the examiner might be more inclined to match a fingerprint that was characteristic of that race. This is already being discussed as a potential problem with DNA.[4]

A related problem arose around the vexing question of the inheritance of fingerprints. By 1892 Galton was convinced that fingerprint patterns were inherited, but the French legal physician René Forgeot had come to the opposite conclusion. The issue was important because the assertion that identical twins had different fingerprints was one of the items of "proof" of the uniqueness of fingerprint patterns. Indeed, in some early criminal trials the prosecution actually took identical twins into court to demonstrate that their fingerprints were different. In the two decades following the publication of his book, Galton and other anatomical researchers came to the general conclusion that fingerprint patterns were indeed inherited. This did not mean that a child inherited an entire fingerprint pattern from a parent or relative, nor even that the fingerprint patterns of identical twins were identical. It simply meant that the fingerprint patterns of identical twins were more similar than those of fraternal twins, the patterns of relatives more similar than those of unrelated persons, and the patterns of persons of the same race more similar than those of persons of different races. Discussions of inheritance, while vital to academic researchers like Galton, were downright dangerous to dactyloscopers who worked in law enforcement. The popular press often interpreted assertions that the fingerprint patterns of identical twins were "similar" to mean that they were "identical." This undermined the fundamental assertion of the uniqueness of all human fingerprint patterns which was crucial to the judicial application of fingerprinting. Moreover, if fingerprints were inherited, then the chance of an accidental match between the fingerprints of two different people would be highest among family members, who are often either suspects for the same crimes or suspects for crimes against one another.[5]

This conflict came to a head around the issue of paternity disputes. If, as academic researchers believed, fingerprint patterns showed signs of inheritance, then paternity cases would be a logical application for the technique, just as they are for DNA today. In one 1912 case in Germany, one of the parties called a fingerprint expert to testify that the similarity of fingerprint patterns pointed toward a relationship between the child and the purported father. The expert, whose name has not been preserved, testified that "not only the prints of father but those of the grandfather may appear in the child . . . In twins equivalent patterns of ridges may occur, and they agree so well that a differentiation is impossible." An account of this testimony, published in the *Archiv für Kriminologie*, outraged mainstream dactyloscopers, one of whom denounced the testimony in a rival journal, the *Archiv für Kriminal-Anthropologie und Kriminalistik*. Not only was such testimony erroneous, it also threatened to destroy the entire field of fingerprint identification:

> What should we say . . . when friends appear with the best intentions to further our work and are not aware that they shake our position at the very foundation? . . . How can we show that the finger prints found at the scene of the serious crime belong to a certain person—when we would be confronted with statements printed in our most outstanding professional journal, statements from a disciple of finger-print procedure affirming the possibility even though conditionally that parents and their children or siblings can have the same prints? . . . When even the possibility that finger prints are inherited is stated, then the basis of all dactyloscopy, namely that two different fingers can never furnish the same prints, is shattered.[6]

Thus any correlation of fingerprint patterns with race, heredity, or criminal propensity would have been dangerous to the credibility of forensic fingerprint identification. The enormous credibility that fingerprint examiners enjoy in the courtroom today derives in part from the fact that any reference to hereditary and racial fingerprint research has been buried in the catacombs of history. This serves fingerprint examiners' purpose by disassociating fingerprint patterns from race, heredity, and criminal propensity. Again, we encounter Galton's bitter irony: in order for fingerprinting to attain legitimacy as a criminal identification technique, his cherished research program into the heredity of fingerprint patterns had to be sacrificed, and his burning question— "whether each person may not carry visibly about his body undeniable evidence of his parentage and near kinships"—would remain forever unanswered.

In the heady 1890s, Galton called fingerprints "the most important of anthropological data." Twenty years later, however, Galton would be profoundly disappointed that his fingerprint research had not provided a reliable way of tracing hereditary relationships, assessing character, determining racial or ethnic background, or predicting criminality. Although biometricians like Galton, who believed that the key to heredity lay in the measurement of the body, did find differences in the distribution of fingerprint patterns among different races and did believe they could arrange fingerprint patterns into an evolutionary hierarchy, these findings were hardly convincing enough—even to them— to warrant judicial, or even actuarial, decisionmaking. The effort to read criminality, heredity, and race in the fingertips ultimately failed as a research program. But in its place a new way of visualizing criminality arose. Fingerprint patterns might not contain the secret code of criminality, but, properly indexed to a file of criminal records, they could tell the authorities about an individual's past convictions. If a prisoner had offended before, that knowledge could be read in the criminal record—accessed by the patterns in the fingertips. In a certain sense, it did at last become possible to read habitual criminality directly from the body, although the procedure was far more literal than the elaborate prophetic map of individual destiny Galton had first envisioned.[7]

The idea of using papillary ridges to discern character had a long history. "Palmistry" or "chiromancy" (palm-reading) long predated the modern "discovery" of fingerprint patterns. Although in 1823 Jan Purkyně, the first scientist to classify fingerprint patterns into types, remained "convinced that there is hardly any truth in palmistry," neither could he convince himself that fingerprint patterns were merely

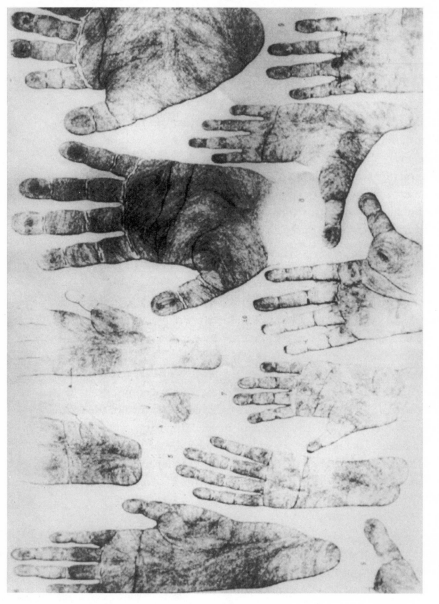

13. Illustration of papillary ridges of palmar and solar surfaces on a variety of nonhuman primate species, ca. 1868. Researchers believed that primate palm and sole patterns would correlate with less evolved, "degenerate" human individuals and races.

random. Purkyně suspected that some sort of biological structure underlay the patterns. "The differences between individuals did not arise by mere chance nor were they formed by accidental influences of the outer world," he wrote. "We must acknowledge that there is some law and some kind of essential, definite, recurring type which lays down the pattern for the variations of organic bodies within boundaries for each deviation. The discovery of this could uncover the way for the most penetrating understanding of the minds of individuals." At this early date Purkyně expressed a tension that would plague the practice of fingerprint analysis for more than a century thereafter: a tension between the conception of fingerprints as signs of every body's unique individuality and the conception of fingerprints as markers signaling membership in some human "type."[8]

If scientists were to make a connection between fingerprint pattern types and human types, it would be necessary to do primate studies, racial studies, and character studies of fingerprint patterns. As early as 1867 the French anatomist Alix, with no inkling of the future use of fingerprints for identification, had published a study of palm print patterns among a large number of primate species. He concluded that, though there was great variety even within a given species, the frequency of pattern types was characteristic for each species. Alix also found that humans shared patterns with the monkeys of the Americas, carnivorous apes, and rodents, but not with the African monkeys. In light of Darwin's theory, these findings suggested that papillary ridge patterns might reflect evolutionary history—that evolutionary lineages might be traced using fingerprint patterns and that some patterns might be "more evolved" than others.[9]

In 1883 the German anatomist Arthur Kollmann examined epidermal cross-sections and papillary patterns of several primate species and small samples of various human races. Kollmann thought his data insufficient to make any conclusions about the racial characteristics of fingerprints. He did, however, define a "simian" fingerprint pattern, suggesting that it might be worthwhile, from an evolutionary standpoint, to trace the frequency of this pattern among races. Kollmann thus laid the groundwork for the idea of a stigmatized fingerprint pattern, one that signaled a lower state of evolution.[10]

In 1892 Galton published the initial results of his fingerprint research in his landmark book *Finger Prints*. He compared the frequency of his three basic pattern types—arches, loops, and whorls—among several ethnic groups: English, Scotch, Welsh, Germans, Basques, Arabs, "Hindoos," American Indians, Chinese, Negroes, Irish, Jews, and Eastern Europeans. To his dismay, he found only a single statistical correlation between race and fingerprint pattern: fewer arches among Jews. This was what the anthropologist Paul Rabinow calls "Galton's regret," since Galton wanted desperately to correlate fingerprint patterns and race. In fact, Galton's disappointing early results did not prevent the development of a robust research program aimed at correlating fingerprint patterns with race, criminality, insanity, and propensity to disease. Galton himself continued until his death to search for ways to use fingerprint patterns to trace heredity. The imagined correlations between fingerprint patterns and race, ethnicity, or criminality were never disproved. Indeed, researchers consistently found different pattern frequencies among different races, found what they considered indisputable evidence that patterns were inherited, and believed they had identified certain pattern types that indicated evolutionary "degeneration" and hence a greater propensity toward both criminal behavior and insanity. Our current cultural assumption that fingerprint patterns tell us "nothing about individual character or group affiliation" derives, not from some natural fact, but rather from the decline of a specific scientific research program that sought to derive predictive information from fingerprint patterns. Although this research program failed to produce correlations that were either interesting to the scientific community or useful to the state, it did flourish for at least three decades beginning in the 1890s.[11]

French medico-legalists, for example, produced more promising results than Galton. French researchers were heavily influenced by degeneration theory, which held that the diseased, the insane, the criminal, and the lower classes in general were "degenerating," or evolving backward toward a more primitive state. In the 1890s French intellectuals of all kinds were preoccupied by the supposed threat of evolutionary "degeneration" to the reproductive health of the French people and the body politic. Degeneration was closely associated with crime. In *Degeneration and Criminality* (1888), the psychiatrist Charles Féré, one of France's leading degeneration theorists, blamed widespread degeneration of French human stock for the nation's perceived crime wave. A morphological analysis of fingerprint patterns potentially offered a way to make this insidious degeneration visible. Not only would a correlation between fingerprint patterns and degenerate persons help probe the evolutionary basis of degeneracy, but it would also provide the means for preemptively identifying potential criminals. Degeneration theory also offered a clear way to interpret the morphology of Galton's arch-loop-whorl classification scheme: fingerprint patterns evolved from the simple to the complex, from the arch through the loop to the whorl.[12]

In 1892 René Forgeot published a study of the fingerprints of criminals at the Bologne penal colony. Although he acknowledged the "philosophical" difficulties of correlating fingerprint patterns with criminality, he found that the prisoners showed arches more frequently than the general population. The next year Féré supported Forgeot's conclusions about the "degenerate" class with his study of the fingerprints of 182 epileptics (physicians frequently associated epilepsy with degeneracy) and a handful of monkeys. Féré found a tendency toward arches among both the epileptics and the monkeys. The prevalence of arches among these populations provided visual corroboration that the epileptics had reverted to a more primitive state. The arch was a stigma of degeneration and therefore also of criminality, insanity, epilepsy, and so on. The more complex patterns, the whorls and loops, Féré argued, represented a higher stage of evolutionary development adapted to the sophisticated manipulations required by the human species. He supported this conclusion by observing that the patterns of the thumb and index finger, the most frequently used digits, showed the most complex patterns. Féré also noted higher "asymmetry," by which he meant the presence of different pattern types on different fingers of a single individual, among "degenerates." This asymmetry supposedly reflected, at a fundamental level, the disorder that plagued the degenerate organism as a whole.[13]

David Hepburn, a professor at the Anthropological Laboratory at Trinity College in Dublin, agreed with Féré that the arch was the most primitive pattern, but for different reasons. Hepburn argued in 1895 that complexity of fingerprint pattern signified *decreased* functionality. Human fingers, relieved of the ancestral task of swinging from tree branches, were free, in an evolutionary sense, to indulge in fancy pattern-making which was practically ornamental. Whorls represented the triumph of form over function. Hepburn supported his argument by appealing to the primate hierarchy. The "higher" primates, chimpanzees and orangutans, showed some loops and whorls, he asserted, but "the lower monkeys do not."[14]

In the United States the most prominent morphological researchers were Harris Hawthorne Wilder, an anatomy professor at Smith College, and his research assistant (and later wife) Inez Whipple. Following Hepburn, they argued in the early 1900s that papillary ridges were vestigial remnants of humans' tree-dwelling days. "Individual variations, no longer discouraged," Wilder wrote, "tend to increase, and that which was once a necessary and vital arrangement of the papillary ridges becomes of little importance." In other words, fingerprint patterns were so varied precisely because they no longer served any purpose. This argument followed Darwin's, articulated in *Origin of Species*, that "rudimentary organs, from being useless, are not regulated by natural selection, and hence are variable." Thus, Wilder concluded that "only useful and important parts retain a certain normal form in the various individuals of a given species, and that, as they become of less importance, they tend more and more to vary individually, the range of variations increasing with time and degree of uselessness, if such an expression may be allowed."[15]

While Wilder churned out popular science articles, Whipple published the most sophisticated morphological study of papillary ridges to date in 1904. She argued that there was a homology between mammalian paw pads, known as "volar pads," and the balls of primate fingers, palms, and soles. "Scales and warts" on mammalian pads fused to become papillary ridges, which at first ran transversely across the pad, acting as tread to prevent slipping. These evolved into the concentric whorl pattern, which functioned as a better tread. In humans, the vestigial whorl gradually "degenerated" into loops, tented arches, and finally plain arches. Thus Whipple flipped the European morphologists' hierarchy on its head: now the arch, not the whorl, was the "most evolved" pattern. Whipple agreed with Hepburn that human fingerprints were vestigial, but she argued that the civilizing process caused them to lose complexity rather than gain it. Although she concluded, like Féré, that arches were the most "degenerated" pattern, for Whipple, less encumbered than Féré by the impulse to graft a moral philosophy onto human evolution, "degeneration" was not a pejorative term. Instead, the plain arch was, in fact, the most human, or most evolved, pattern because it represented the decreased functionality of the walking pad. In *fingerprints* especially, less functional patterns symbolized the evolution of quadrupedal walking pads into the elevated forepaws of bipedal *Homo erectus*. For Whipple fingerprint "degeneration" was a sign of civilizing, while for Féré it was a sign of atavism. As one adherent of the "Wilder/Whipple theory" later put it, the "Age of Whorls" was waning, modern man was living in the "Age of Loops" (as indicated by the overall predominance of that pattern), and the "Age of Arches" was dawning.[16]

Wilder and Whipple's theory applied an almost modernist aesthetic to fingerprint morphology, viewing simpler, less ornamental patterns as more highly evolved. In this way, it echoed the broader culture of the modernist movement, which found its most famous expression in the Viennese architect Adolph Loos's manifesto "Ornament and Crime" (1908). Loos declared that excessive ornament was an unmistakable sign of degeneracy and even criminality. He compared tattoos, the identifying marks of the "savage," to "degenerate" rococo flourishes of neoclassicism, calling instead for a spare, austere, modern aesthetic. "In a highly productive nation," Loos argued, "ornament is no longer a natural product of its culture, and therefore represents backwardness or even a degenerative tendency." Loos would have considered the ornate whorl the more potentially criminal pattern, and he would have found the plain arch a suitable fingerprint pattern for a modern, civilized person whose "individuality is so strong that it can no longer be expressed in terms of items of clothing." "The lack of ornament," he added, "is a sign of intellectual power."[17]

Meanwhile, Galton's hereditary research continued at his Biometric Laboratory, but his attempts to establish the heredity of fingerprint patterns were frustrated by the very factor that made fingerprints such a success at criminal identification: uniqueness. Since all fingerprints were unique, it was not clear when it was appropriate to say that any one fingerprint was inherited from another (similar, but nonetheless different) fingerprint. The solution clearly lay in patterns. One might plausibly claim that a whorl was inherited from another whorl. Statistically, one might be able to show more whorls in the children of parents with whorls than in children of parents without. Galton's tripartite classification scheme, however, was plagued by borderline cases. Certain "transitional cases" could be interpreted as more than one pattern type. Galton dealt with transitional cases by creating more pattern types, gradually extending his classification system to employ fifty-three different types. But the more pattern types he added, the more difficult it became to distinguish between them. Galton could not even reconcile his own classification decisions with those of his colleague Howard Collins, forcing him to keep their data separate. Eventually a frustrated Galton "put the problem on one side," turning it over to his assistants, but "the inheritance of finger-print types" always remained "in his thoughts and activities."[18]

Others at Galton's laboratory continued his work. In 1920 Ethel Elderton, who had been "set to work on fingerprint data and family records" in 1905, published a study that incorporated all of Galton's abandoned data, a total of 2,300 prints. Like Galton, Elderton was hampered by her inability to devise a "natural order" for fingerprint patterns. Another difficulty she confronted was determining exactly what kind of transmission to look for. Were fingerprint patterns transmitted from a specific finger of an individual to the corresponding finger of a descendant, or should the researcher just look at the sum total of fingerprint patterns on all ten fingers? Elderton could conclude only that inheritance was likely to occur but that patterns might pass to any finger of the offspring.[19]

Amateur and professional researchers all over the world pursued ways of using fingerprint patterns to understand race, ethnicity, and character. In 1919 L. W. LaChard, a British police official in the Niger Province of West Africa, completed a study of the fingerprint patterns of the various tribes in West Africa and some primates. LaChard confirmed his suspicion that the more "civilized" Fulanis and Hausas had more of the supposedly evolved patterns than the "ethnologically inferior" Yorubas and Pagans. He predicted that greater understanding of fingerprint patterns would allow "character divination, reviving a science which has been discredited and obscured by the charlatanism surrounding modern palmistry." In 1922 Professor Heinrich Poll of Berlin reported "that the future of all persons is written on their finger tips," not, as commonly believed, on their palms. Poll, the *New York Times* reported, "even predicts that this idea will soon be recognized as an accurate science whereby life insurance companies can tell from finger prints what will be the insured's career." Poll based "his assertions on the study of the finger tips of six thousand individuals, two thousand of whom were insane."[20]

In 1924 the Norwegian researcher Kristine Bonnevie published the largest study of heredity to date in the *Journal of Genetics*, using the entire collection of the Kristiania (now Oslo) Office of Identification, a total of 25,000 sets of convict prints. In order to solve the problem of pattern definition that had stymied the Galton school, Bonnevie quantified fingerprint patterns by ridge counting, a procedure she borrowed from the Henry system. She further subdivided patterns according to their "shape-index" and their "twisting tendency." This method left Bonnevie with a bell curve of quantitative values for her collection of fingerprint patterns. She concluded that there were hereditary tendencies in overall pattern types: pattern types were not transmitted directly to the corresponding finger of an offspring; rather, what was transmitted was a general tendency toward certain patterns. On the evolutionary morphology issue, Bonnevie agreed with Whipple that whorls "reduced" into arches, but she thought loops were too numerous to be a transitional form between the two. Instead, she argued that loops too were ancient forms, having followed a separate line of descent from another group of primates. Then both loops and whorls reduced into the arch, the truly modern form. Bonnevie also made racial inquiries based on both secondary sources and her own data, which sampled "the several races composing the Norwegian population." She found that Asians had relatively more whorls and Europeans had more arches and loops. For a European, this finding accorded well with Whipple's contention that arches were "more evolved" since it suggested that Europeans were more evolved than Asians.[21]

These studies were finding evidence of hereditary transmission, slight racial variations, and potentially criminal or "degenerate" patterns—the arch or the whorl, depending on which version of evolutionary morphology the researcher adhered to—and they had sophisticated morphological theories to explain the evolution of human fingerprint patterns. But their findings were not significant enough to maintain the momentum of a scientific research program. None of these researchers was prepared to advocate actually making judicial decisions on the basis of fingerprint pattern types. One clear sign of the diminishing scientific prestige of morphological fingerprint research was the gender of the researchers. After the turn of the century, it was women—Inez Whipple, Ethel Elderton, and Kristine Bonnevie—who performed the most sophisticated studies.

There were several reasons for this. One was that Galton's Biometric Laboratory was run by the statistician Karl Pearson, an early advocate of women's liberation. More important, hereditary and morphological fingerprint research was closely tied to the eugenics movement, which, with its implications for reproductive freedom, was in some ways a women's movement. In the early twentieth century, eugenics, far from having the negative connotations it has today, was considered a liberal, progressive movement allied with some forms of feminism because it implied reproductive control. Finally, female scientists, struggling against prejudice, hostility, and professional obstacles within the male-dominated world of science, sought out "women's work"—low-prestige areas of science considered feminine and therefore appropriate for female investigators (and undesirable for men). Hereditary research was one area where female researchers—properly supervised, of course, by men like Pearson and Whipple's husband Harris Wilder—could pursue scientific research without ruffling too many feathers. This "feminization" of hereditary and morphological fingerprint research after 1900 was the first step in its banishment to the margins of science. The beginning of the downturn in fingerprint morphology also coincided almost exactly with the rediscovery of the gene in 1900. In the twentieth century, biologists increasingly turned their attention to genes rather than fingerprints as mechanisms of heredity and of a predictive science.[22]

At the same time, another occupational group working with fingerprints was proving extremely useful to criminal justice systems. These people were not scientists; they were police and prison officials, who saw in fingerprints, not a key to nature's secret code, but rather a convenient method of identifying the criminal bodies passing in rapidly increasingly numbers through their institutions. The law enforcement officials who began to take over the practice of fingerprinting showed little interest in morphological research, and for good reason. As fingerprinting became increasingly important as an individualizing identification technique, morphological research became irrelevant and, even worse, a hindrance. Morphological research sounded too much like the disreputable "scientific palmistry," and it soon became a potential embarrassment to those who were trying to define themselves as "fingerprint experts." In 1925 T. G. Cooke, head of the Institute for Applied Science, a fingerprint school in Chicago, commented that, though research into the character of fingerprint patterns was promising, "these attempts smack too much of phrenology, character reading, and all such black arts to be taken seriously." "It is not to the finger-print expert's advantage," he warned, "to be associated, in the minds of the public, with fortune tellers and palm-readers. The science of finger print identification is a real science and should not be dragged to the level of the pseudo sciences." By the 1920s, therefore, anatomical researchers found themselves marginalized from two sides. Morphological fingerprint research began to seem outdated to biologists increasingly enamored with genes. Meanwhile, law enforcement officials were rapidly outnumbering scientists among the group of people who took a professional interest in fingerprinting.[23]

The decline of a research program does not imply the cessation of all research. Indeed, small pockets of research seeking to correlate fingerprint patterns with race, ethnicity, character, and criminality persisted, even down to the present day. Rather, when a research program declines, the research becomes increasingly marginalized: it takes place further outside what is considered mainstream science; its practitioners become less well credentialed and more likely to be regarded as "crackpots"; its findings appear in less prestigious journals. This is what happened gradually to morphological fingerprint research as the use of fingerprinting for identification grew exponentially in the 1920s.

By the late 1930s diagnostic fingerprint research was in serious decline. In *The Disturbing Revelations of Finger and Palm Prints* (1937), H. Mutrux-Bornoz, a professor and police captain in Lausanne, Switzerland, lamented the fact that, despite the work of Bonnevie, Féré, Forgeot, the Wilders, and others, what he called "clinical" research into the ethnology, anatomy, and histology of fingerprint patterns had ceased. Though he hailed fingerprinting as an excellent method of identification, he declared that dactyloscopy, the *scientific* study of fingerprint patterns, had, regrettably, come to a halt. Although it was not possible to determine any individual's race through fingerprint patterns, Mutrux-Bornoz claimed that different races did show "very marked" differences in the distribution of pattern types, a fact he attributed to "unequal evolution." Like Bonnevie, Mutrux-Bornoz found that Asians had around 10 percent more whorls than the overall mean and Northern Europeans had around 4 percent more arches. Again, this corresponded nicely with the Whipple theory that the arch was the "most evolved" pattern type. For all races, he found that the distribution of patterns among "degenerates" was the same as that among "the normal." It was, however, possible to identify degenerates through "stigmata"—essentially unusual patterns and deformities like electrodactyly (the fusion of digits) and polydactyly (extra digits). Calling criminal psychiatry an inexact and unconvincing science, Mutrux-Bornoz suggested that primitive fingerprint patterns could better identify degenerates.[24]

Research into the morphological basis of fingerprint patterns and their associations with race, ethnicity, and heredity continued in the 1930s and 1940s under the name "dermatoglyphics." In the United States the most active researcher was the Tulane University anatomy professor Harold Cummins, who elaborated Whipple's explanation of the embryological development of papillary ridges. During fetal development, the volar pads, those vestigial remnants of mammalian paw pads, "regressed" into fingertip bulbs, and nascent ridges formed around sweat glands. These ridges proliferated, making the fingertip area dense with ridges, and branched because of environmental changes in pressure, temperature, and so on in the embryonic environment. Cummins concluded that "some characteristics of finger prints . . . are inherited," that fingerprint patterns varied with race, and that individuals suffering from certain diseases like schizophrenia, psoriasis, or epilepsy showed different frequencies of pattern types—but that no credible research had yet demonstrated any way to predict criminality or character from fingerprint patterns.[25]

The findings of Cummins and other anatomical researchers were published in anatomy and biology journals unlikely to find their way into police stations and prisons, and their work became increasingly remote from that of fingerprint examiners, who by now numbered in the thousands, virtually all of whom worked in law enforcement. Since fingerprint examiners believed that the scientific foundation for the uniqueness of all human fingerprints was based on their collective practical experience, and since this assertion encountered minimal opposition in the courts, they saw little reason to study the anatomical basis of the formation of papillary ridges. Although the findings of anatomical researchers were occasionally reported in the pages of the fingerprint examiners' professional journal *Finger Print and Identification Magazine,* they became a mere curiosity rather than something fundamental to fingerprint work. Rank-and-file fingerprint examiners saw no reason to master the questions of evolutionary morphology underlying the individuality of fingerprint patterns. Thus fingerprint examiners created a separate realm of identification in which morphological research was irrelevant.

Only a few examiners saw any merit in bridging the gap between identification and morphology. The professional organization of fingerprint examiners, the International Association for Identification (IAI), had a science committee, which lobbied in vain for greater familiarity with the "Wilder/Whipple theory" of the evolution of fingerprints and related matters. In the 1930s one member of the committee, the Brooklyn fingerprint examiner G. Tyler Mairs, devised a new classification system, dubbed "Identakey," which sought to unite morphology and judicial identification. Mairs described Identakey as "Universal Numerical Classification by Nature's Sequences." Based on the "Wilder/Whipple theory" of fingerprint evolution, Identakey purported to create a "natural" taxonomy of fingerprint patterns, ranging from the primitive concentric whorl "to the ultimate Patternless Configuration," the "omega arch," or plain arch. Arches, loops, and whorls defined "classes." These were subdivided into "families" and "orders." The direction of the flow of ridges placed the print into a "genus," and Mairs devised ways of further subdividing these into "species" and "subspecies," "so we have a consecutive series of form variations which can be graded under the same divisional names or categories that zoologists and botonists [sic] use for grading animals and plants." Unlike the Henry system, which defined its various subclassifications solely for the convenience of the classifier, Identakey aimed to be true to the evolutionary "natural order." In this way, Identakey resembled attempts by nineteenth-century taxonomists to devise "natural systems" for the classification of plants and animals. Although Mairs thought his system made "indexing lots more accurate," his proposals fell on deaf ears. Outside of a few practitioners, the rift between morphology and identification remained intact.[26]

Although the idea of "criminal" fingerprint patterns may seem quaint today, the dream of a predictive signifier never died out. In 1971, when the XYY chromosome was the reigning biological explanation for criminal behavior, David O'Farrell, a sociologist, found more arches among XYY criminals, and Ogden Glasow, a professor of education at Western Illinois University, also correlated "criminal" fingerprint patterns with the XYY chromosome. At the same time, some dermatoglyphic research persisted within mainstream science and medicine. As late as 1972 a panel convened by the IAI recommended that "an attempt

14. Overview of Identakey system of fingerprint classification "by Nature's sequences" devised by G. Tyler Mairs, ca. 1925. The patterns were arranged in a supposed evolutionary hierarchy from the "primitive concentric whorl" (alpha) on the left through the "ultimate patternless configuration" (omega) on the right.

should be made to pre-determine the size of a data base which could be used as a quantitative and qualitative base for possibly determining gross pattern types, sex, predominance of patterns for criminals, ethnic origin, and so forth" through fingerprint patterns. In general, however, the identification community thought such studies "should not be allowed into the courtrooms" because "they are simply not related to our work."[27]

Even as recently as 1991 Paul Gabriel Tesla published a system of dermatoglyphics, with which he claims to be able to identify race and diagnose criminal tendencies by interpreting finger and palm patterns. In the introduction to Tesla's book, *Crime and Mental Disease in the Hand*, David Brooks, supervisor of the Identification and Crime Scene Division in Bartow, Florida, concludes that "for all its strangeness and complexity, the system does work." Even Tesla concedes that "the fact that interpretive dermatoglyphics is a scientific refinement of classical palmistry can guarantee it a certain amount of bad press," but he believes it will ultimately prevail, as did acupuncture, Kirlian photography (a method of "photographing" nonmaterial energy and force fields), and Cleve Backster's research on the emotional lives of plants.[28]

Today genetics is poised to fall into the same pattern set by earlier identification techniques. Again, "criminal identification" has a double meaning, as behavioral geneticists search for a "crime gene" even as their colleagues build DNA databases for criminal recordkeeping. Those who oppose these databases often claim that genetic databases threaten privacy because, unlike fingerprint databases, they contain important information about the individual, such as disease propensity, race, ethnicity, heredity, and possibly even criminal propensity. What these critics seldom realize is that we thought the same thing about fingerprint patterns a century ago. How did the fingerprint, which in the heady days of Galton's initial research promised to be rich in meaning—"the most important of anthropological data"—end up being treated as empty of meaning?

It is certainly not that researchers discovered that fingerprints are *not* hereditary or that they do *not* correlate with "race." Indeed, all the evidence suggests that fingerprint patterns are influenced by inheritance and that different "races" show different frequencies of certain pattern types. In 1982 a study published in the *Journal of Forensic Sciences*, a reputable journal, concluded that fingerprint patterns may, indeed, be hereditary, and researchers have consistently found a higher percentage of whorls among Asians and a higher percentage of arches among Europeans. Neither of these conclusions has been refuted, although the interpretations attributed to them may have been.[29]

Fingerprint patterns came to be viewed as empty of meaning because fingerprint examiners were so successful at disassociating the identification project from the diagnostic project. As fingerprinting beat out anthropometry as the world's dominant identification system in the 1920s, fingerprint examiners were able to marginalize and silence the morphologists who, however inadvertently, cast a shadow of doubt on their efforts. What emerged, then, was a new way of visualizing criminality: criminality, rather than being indicated by the body itself, through the stigma of a supposedly "criminal" fingerprint, was "proven" by using the fingerprint as a link between the criminal body and the criminal record. The fingerprint was no longer a stigma, a sign containing its own meanings and indications about the character of the bearer. Instead, the fingerprint had become merely an indexical sign which referred the eyes of the authorities to another message—the text contained in the criminal record.

I am invisible, understand, simply because people refuse to see me.

—Ralph Ellison, *Invisible Man* (1947)

CHAPTER 5

Fingerprinting Foreigners

Much of the English-language literature on the history of scientific detection tends to treat fingerprint identification as a purely British invention which was then exported to the Americas and the rest of the world. This version of history has Scotland Yard delivering the Henry system to the New World shortly after the turn of the twentieth century. Although the British did play an important role in developing modern fingerprint identification, Americans had begun to think about—and in Argentina actually implement—fingerprint identification even before the British began promoting the Henry system.[1]

North and South America proved fertile ground for innovation in fingerprint identification. The expanding nations of the Americas were "societies of strangers" to a much greater extent than Europe, where many people could still be identified by familial and geographic ties. The Americas were on the receiving end of the great waves of immigration in the late nineteenth and early twentieth centuries. Immigrant cultures mingled the promise of the chance to start anew with a fresh identity—unfettered by the mistakes or status one left behind in the Old World—with a profound suspicion of strangers. Many immigrants were viewed as racially "other," with all the biases and blinders that conceptualization entailed, by immigrants who had arrived a generation or more earlier. Thus, as in the British Empire, innovation in fingerprint identification in the Americas was stimulated by a perceived need to identify "faceless," racially unfamiliar "hordes" of people who came in successive waves to their shores.

While the early-twentieth-century development of fingerprint identification in the United States is fairly well documented, there were nineteenth-century forays into fingerprint identification that have largely been lost to history. The first reported mention of fingerprint identification in the United States dates to the 1850s, thus predating even the work of William Herschel. Sometime in the late 1850s John Maloy, a police constable in Albany, New York, reportedly secured the conviction of a burglar in the following manner: "The burglar broke a pane of glass on entering the building and accidentally left an impression of his blood-besmeared thumb on a piece of paper. A second impression of his thumb was taken and the two were identified. This was considered a remarkable piece of detective work and the case caused much excitement in Albany."[2]

Unfortunately, this account is based on a second-hand report written almost thirty years later, and it has not been possible to confirm the story by reference to Albany newspapers. We do know, however, that Maloy served as a constable in Albany from 1856 until sometime during the Civil War, when he became a U.S. Marshall. Newspapers from this period describe Maloy as a particularly energetic law enforcement officer who displayed "that degree of shrewdness and tact which is an essential qualification of a first class detective," possessed a remarkable ability to pick wanted men out of the crowd, and frequently "took the boat" down to New York City to collar escaped fugitives. After the war Maloy was appointed chief of detectives back in Albany in the newly organized Capital Police Department. Shortly thereafter he took a post with the U.S. Secret Service, which he held until 1870, when he was appointed the first chief of the Albany Police Department. He served as chief until his death in 1884, when he was remembered as a skilled policeman whose "detective sagacity and instinct" were "displayed in several notable cases." If the thumbprint story is true, then Maloy deserves credit for making the earliest known use of fingerprints to solve a crime, predating what historians had previously believed to be the earliest such instance by around twenty years.[3]

In 1877 Thomas Taylor, a scientist who founded the division of microscopy at the U.S. Department of Agriculture, delivered a lecture with lantern slides on "the markings on the palms of the hands and the tips of the fingers." Taylor went so far as to discuss "the possibility of identifying criminals, especially murderers, by comparing the marks of the hands left upon any object with impressions in wax taken from the hands of suspected persons." A report on the lecture appeared in the *American Journal of Microscopy and Popular Science*. This was the earliest published mention of the idea of using traces of fingerprints to investigate crimes. However, while Taylor beat both Herschel and Faulds to publication, no one followed up on his suggestion. His work was forgotten until 1972, when the fingerprint examiner Duayne Dillon rediscovered it.[4]

These stillborn efforts of the 1850s, 1860s, and 1870s illustrate that an identification system required far more than merely casually observing the uniqueness of friction skin ridges. Francis Galton had not yet taken the first steps toward developing a classification system for fingerprints, nor had he advanced the first arguments, however tenuous and anecdotal, toward their uniqueness and permanence. American police, penal, and judicial institutions, moreover, were still too weak to support an identification system. In fact, the government agency that first showed an interest in fingerprint technology was not part of the criminal justice system at all: it was the U.S. Customs Service, which was in charge of controlling immigration. Fingerprinting was first considered for application in controlling Chinese immigration into the country through Western ports. As in the British Empire, the need for identification in the United States did not concern criminality so much as it did the control of a highly—even threateningly—mobile population of racial "others."

During the 1848 gold rush and the transcontinental railroad construction boom, thousands of Chinese immigrants poured into the United States, and the influx continued for the next several decades. By 1880 there were more than 100,000 Chinese in the United States, 75,000 of them in California. Although the immigrants tended to work in different industries from whites and at lower wage levels, white laborers found them convenient scapegoats for their financial troubles during the depression of the 1870s. Anti-Chinese sentiment ran high. By 1879 California "nativists"—people hostile to immigrants—had coalesced around Denis Kearney's Workingman's Party, and San Francisco had elected Isaac Kalloch mayor on an explicitly nativist platform which demanded that the "Chinese must go and good men stay."[5]

In response to nativist political pressure, Congress passed the first federal immigration law, the Page Act, in 1875, directed at restricting Chinese immigration. In 1882 it passed the Chinese Exclusion Act, which barred the immigration of all Chinese "laborers," who were distinguished from an "exempted class" of diplomats, merchants, and students. The Exclusion Act contained a loophole, though: Chinese already residing in the United States would be permitted to visit China without giving up their right to return to the United States. In order to facilitate reentry, the Customs Service instituted a system of "return certificates." Departing Chinese nationals would apply at the Custom House, where they had their "height, physical marks, and peculiarities" recorded and were issued a "white tag." This could be exchanged aboard ship for a "red certificate," which would authorize reentry.[6]

The situation was ripe, officials believed, for the sale of surplus certificates abroad. "I presume many Chinese obtain certificates upon the occasion of their departure from the United States, who do not intend to return, and upon their arrival in Hong Kong they sell them!" San Francisco Collector of Customs W. H. Sears wrote in 1885 to Charles Denby, the Minister to China. "Others die upon the voyage or after reaching China, and their certificates are stolen and pass into other hands."[7]

Customs officials encountered difficulties with physical descriptions. The certificate and register book of the Custom House, much like the early American prison registers, allowed only a single blank space for "description," leaving it up to the clerk to choose which aspect of the visage to record for each particular person. Clerks often squandered this single space by recording information of little descriptive value, such as "flat nose," "large features," "small features," or "hole in right ear" (for an earring). Such an arbitrary system, subject to individual whim, gave little hope of accurately identifying returning Chinese.[8]

In 1887 Deputy Collector E. E. Penn of Port Townsend, Washington, complained to his supervisor Quincy A. Brooks about the "meager descriptions on Chinese Laborers Certificates issued at the Ports of New York and San Francisco." Penn noted that "the descriptions of the Chinese are very vague, and it is almost impossible for this office to tell with any degree of certainty whether the Chinese who hold the certificates are the persons described therein." "Mole on left wrist," he dryly observed, is "rather an indefinite means of identification." Another representative description was limited to "mark on each eyelid." "No mention," Penn pointed out, was "made of the character or extent of these marks," and no other description was given. Penn included a sampling of descriptions that appeared on more than twelve different certificates. These included "scar on right temple," "mole left side of neck," "scar below left ear," "scar on right wrist," "small features, thick lips," "long neck, and high cheek bones," "high cheek bones and narrow forehead," "round features and scars on chin," "pitmarked, and large mouth," and "mark on point of fore finger of right hand." In some cases "no description whatever" was recorded, and weight and height measurements were taken only sporadically. Penn's observations were reinforced by Special Agent O. L. Spaulding, whom the Treasury Department had dispatched in 1885 to investigate allegations of corruption at the custom houses in San Francisco and other Western ports. He noted that "some certificates have been issued here omitting physical marks or peculiarities of the person receiving it."[9]

In 1886 U.S. Representative William Morrow of California criticized the certificate system in a speech before the House. "The return certificate provided by the present law, although intended to identify the person to whom it is issued, is really a much more useful document," he sarcastically remarked, "since it may be used to identify any one of many thousands with equal certainty." Morrow contrasted the Customs Service's certificates unfavorably with passports issued by China, "containing a description of the person to whom it was issued with the most elaborate detail. Compared with that document our own certificate designed for our protection is utterly worthless." But Morrow did not blame the problem solely on lazy customs clerks and a poorly designed certificate. He doubted whether even the most diligent clerks would be able to compose truly distinguishing descriptions of an ethnic group so physically homogeneous, in Western eyes, as the Chinese: "There is a remarkable similarity in the size, complexion, color of eyes and hair, and general appearance of all Chinamen coming to this country. It therefore happens that the present certificate of identification issued to a departing Chinaman will do equally as good service as a certificate of admission into the country for a thousand other Chinamen."[10]

Although many customs inspectors complained about "the great similarity among Chinese in the color of their hair, eyes, and skin," others thought that marks and scars might serve to distinguish them. "The Chinese race are the most marked or scarred race in my knowledge, and I have always found it easy to find some distinguishing marks on them," one inspector commented. But the identifying potential of "peculiar marks" remained unexploited. "In a personal examination of these Chinese," wrote Penn, "I found nearly all of them bearing numerous, and plain marks by which they might have been identified with a considerable degree of certainty, but as no mention of these marks was made in the certificate, the question of identification resolved itself into mere guess work."[11]

Even the height measurement suffered from inconsistency, because many inspectors were allowing their subjects to be measured in shoes or with "their pigtails curled on top of their heads." "They say that it is impossible to obtain the same height for a Chinaman in two consecutive measurements," the *San Francisco Daily Report* noted in 1885. It was uncertain, however, whether the fault lay with the measurer or the measured: "Surveyor of Port Morton says that the same Chinaman varies in height an inch or two on consecutive measurements." These problems in the custom houses illustrated the futility of verbal identification systems, especially when descriptive terms were not standardized but left to each inspector's subjective perception. At that very moment in France, Bertillon was developing just such a standardized vocabulary, but this was not yet known in the United States.[12]

In the early 1880s, just as the French were refining a technology of identification based on the physical description and measurement of the body, Americans were abandoning the project as futile and searching for a new solution. Again the relative appeal of anthropometry or fingerprinting was shaped by the cultural perceptions of the government officials implementing the system. U.S. customs officials' firm conviction that the Chinese were physically indistinguishable encouraged them to abandon as hopeless their attempts to refine an identification system based on physical measurement and verbal description. Bertillon, in contrast, believed in the measurable and discernable physical uniqueness of all individuals. Hence it was the Americans, rather than the Europeans, who were willing to take a chance on a less reputable, less tested identification technique: thumb marks.

In 1883 Detective Harry Morse suggested that customs officials use thumb marks to identify immigrants. Morse, a legendary California law enforcement figure who had corralled several notorious desperadoes while serving as Alameda County Sheriff, had been retained by the Treasury Department to help investigate the allegations of fraud at the San Francisco Custom House. It is not clear where Morse got the idea of thumbprinting. He might have picked it up from Thomas Taylor, from Herschel and Faulds's 1880 correspondence in *Nature*, or perhaps from the Chinese themselves. Fingerprints had been used as signatures in China for centuries, and Chinese prostitutes' indenture contracts found in the United States dating from as early as 1886—and perhaps earlier—were signed with thumbprints.[13]

Morse proposed that thumbprints be used for the identification of Chinese immigrants. "The test is certain and cheap," he declared in a letter to Special Treasury Agent J. F. Evans, and "better than a photograph—mens [*sic*] features change, but the creases of the skin, never." He enclosed right and left thumb marks from ten unidentified persons in his letter. Evans forwarded Morse's letter to Treasury Secretary Charles J. Folger with a covering letter indicating that he was "inclined to think the suggestion a good one, and that the certificates of all Chinamen in transit through the United States, and those departing with the expectation of returning, would be marked with the thumb impression on arrival and departure, or vice versa, as the case may be." "The test is made by using india ink," Evans added, "and is believed to afford a positive means of identification and is simple in its application." Folger referred Evans's letter to the Commissioner of Customs, H. B. James, who tersely responded that "the regulations we have already issued are sufficient," and there the matter rested.[14]

By August 1, 1885, Special Agent Spaulding reported, 35,235 certificates had been issued from all Pacific ports, but only 14,726 had been used in returning. The 20,509 certificates that remained unaccounted for gave Spaulding cause for alarm. "With this number outstanding," he averred, "some will find their way back in the hands of the wrong persons." In San Francisco nativists continued to clamor for immediate action. In a report by a special committee of the city's Board of Supervisors in 1885, officials voiced their displeasure with the lax enforcement of the Chinese exclusion acts: "We cannot shut our eyes to the fact that the Treaty and the Restriction Act constitute no effectual barrier as yet against Chinese immigration. The tide may not be flowing in upon us as rapidly nor with the same volume as before, but 'the cry is still they come,' and the problem of Chinese immigration is not yet solved."[15]

In 1885 Spaulding was consulted by Franklin Lawton, superintendent of the San Francisco Mint, concerning thumbprints. Lawton had heard about fingerprinting from John Maloy during his days as a district attorney back east in Albany. He pitched the idea to Isaiah West Taber, a prominent Western landscape photographer, suggesting that Taber photograph the thumbs directly (which indicates that he was probably unaware of Morse's proposal to use india ink). Taber quickly found that it was more effective to photograph inked impressions of the thumb, and he took several sets of thumbprints from whites and Chinese alike. The prints were reproduced in a newspaper, the *San Francisco Daily Report*, and Taber planned to display an enlarged thumbprint in the window of his Montgomery Street studio so "that every one might study the matter at leisure." The press viewed thumb-printing as a descriptive technology that, unlike photography, averted the supposed problem of racially homogenous facial features. "The thumb marks of Mon Shing, a Chinese laundryman," commented the *Daily Report* "are more easily recognizable than his face." In the United States, as in India, fingerprint identification developed in response to the problem of identifying Asian individuals whose faces were supposedly too similar for officials to distinguish. The myth of racial homogeneity proved crucial to the cultivation of fingerprinting identification.[16]

Customs officials praised thumbprinting, but they hesitated to fully endorse it. In his final report Spaulding recommended that "more space should be given in the blank forms for entering physical peculiarities." More complete written descriptions of Chinese laborers should suffice to solve the identification problem experienced at the Custom House, Spaulding argued, and the costly option of photographing all certificate holders was "unnecessary." "If other means of identification than those now employed are thought necessary," he wrote, the Treasury Department should consider "further experiments with the thumb marks. This means of identification is said to have been employed in eastern countries for hundreds of years, and to be infallible. While I am not prepared to recommend its adoption, I believe it worthy of consideration before resorting to the doubtful and expensive expedient of the photograph."[17]

In 1888 the question became moot when Congress, under still more nativist pressure, put an end to the certificate system by banning entry to all Chinese laborers. This effectively stranded laborers who were outside the country when the law was passed, a consequence that the U.S. Supreme Court endorsed in the *Chinese Exclusion Case* (1889). In 1892 the Geary Act renewed the ban on Chinese immigration for another ten years and required the registration of all Chinese residing in the United States. These draconian measures rendered thumbprints irrelevant for Chinese immigration since return certificates were no longer used.[18]

With identification no longer focused on the supposedly homogeneous Chinese, enthusiasm for the new technique waned. In response to an inquiry about thumbprinting from Professor Otis T. Mason, an anthropologist at the Smithsonian Institution, in 1888, Congressman Morrow replied: "Upon investigation it was discovered that such an identification was impracticable on account of many difficulties that would arise in comparing the thumb with the photograph, and besides it was found that any injury to the face or ball of the thumb would destroy the identification. After a careful examination of the whole subject, it was determined that the best identification was by the whole photograph of the face, and this is the judgment of the best detectives in the country."[19]

Once again, the idea of fingerprint identification was quickly forgotten in the United States. News of Taber's photographs of thumbprints did reach Europe, and Francis Galton's brief account of Taber's work appeared in subsequent fingerprint textbooks. But the details of the story were eventually lost, and all that was left was Galton's elliptical account. In 1927 the German fingerprint authority Robert Heindl could do no more than refer to the "elusive" Taber. By 1938, when Harry Myers II began his survey of the history of fingerprinting in the United States, not enough evidence remained to even credit the story. "Neither Galton nor any other writer has ever identified Tabor [sic]," Myers wrote, "and I can find no evidence of Tabor's having ever done anything with finger prints . . . It is regrettable that we have not more documentary evidence concerning the work of Tabor."[20]

Although the problem of identifying Chinese immigrants stimulated thinking about thumbprinting in the United States, government officials clearly viewed the technique as somewhat exotic and felt more comfortable with familiar technologies like writing and photography. A serious attempt to implement an identification system based on fin-gerprinting would have required ambitious vision and stubborn deter-mination. Someone with these qualities did appear, not in the United States, but in Argentina: the young head of the statistical bureau of the La Plata police, Juan Vucetich.

Vucetich immigrated to Argentina from Croatia in 1884. In 1888 he took a position in the statistics office of the Central Police Department in La Plata. By 1891 he had become head of the Office of Identificat-ion, and his superiors ordered him to write a report evaluating current methods of criminal identification. Vucetich compared the Bertillon system with Galton's four-letter fingerprint scheme as he found it de-scribed in the *Revue Scientifique*. He judged fingerprinting more prom-ising, making him the first public official to back the new technique against the dominant anthropometric system. This bold decision earned Vucetich the eternal enmity of Bertillon, and it may have been responsible for Bertillon's reported physical assault on him when he visited Paris.[21]

Vucetich studied the classification schemes of various European re-searchers, including Galton and René Forgeot. He found these systems "inadequate" and took it upon himself to improve upon them. By Sep-tember 1891 Vucetich had devised a new classification system, for which he coined the Greek-derived name "icnofalangometrica" (fin-ger-sign measurement), which enumerated 101 different fingerprint patterns. This was the world's earliest criminal identification system classified according to fingerprints.[22]

Meanwhile, Vucetich had the opportunity to use fingerprints for fo-rensic identification. In 1892 the police in Necochea, a small coastal village in Buenos Aires Province, were investigating the murder of the two young children of a woman named Francesca Rojas. The police had initially suspected the mother's suitor, one Velasquez, but neither in-terrogation nor torture had yielded a confession. A bloody fingerprint had been found at the scene, and Inspector Eduardo Alvarez, the police official in charge, contacted Vucetich. Alvarez took the bloody finger-print, Velasquez, and Rojas to La Plata, where Vucetich matched the fingerprint to that of Rojas, not Velasquez. This evidence was never presented in court; rather, the fingerprint match was employed to in-timidate Rojas, and eventually it elicited a confession. (Rojas made the mistake of denying that she had touched the blood-stained corpses, thus depriving herself of what is today called a "legitimate access" defense. She could have contended that the blood on the fingerprint came from touching the corpses *after* finding them murdered rather than from committing the murders.) Maloy's fingerprint case forgotten, the Rojas case has been hailed around the world as the earliest crime solved by the use of fingerprinting.[23]

Despite Vucetich's success in forensics, it is not clear how effective icnofalangometrica was as an identification system. The 101 basic pattern types would inevitably produce confusion, as classifiers struggled to decide to which category a particular fingerprint belonged. Vucetich's innovation, therefore, evoked a mixed response. Some police officials called for police chiefs around the country to adopt icnofalangometrica, even as a replacement for Bertillonage. In 1893, however, the Argentine government, dissatisfied with Vucetich's scheme, ordered him to switch back to anthropometry. This decision reflected the general tendency at the time to view anthropometry, a known and respected anthropological technique, as the more scientifically credible identification method. Vucetich also encountered opposition from officials with an interest in the anthropometric system. Just as John Garson, the head of Britain's Anthropometric Office, had opposed the introduction of the Henry system, Agustín Drago, chief of the Anthropometric Office of the Buenos Aires police, declared in 1895 that Vucetich's system was inferior to anthropometry and even accused Vucetich of plagiarism. Vucetich went back to work, and by 1896 he had devised a new classification system which he called "dactyloscopy" (the science of looking at fingers). The name change was significant: it signaled the shift from a quantitative science of measurement, modeled on anthropometry, to a qualitative visual technique.[24]

Like Galton, Vucetich simplified his scheme to four basic pattern types: arch, loop with "internal inclination," loop with "external inclination," and whorl. For the thumbs, each of these patterns was designated with a letter: A, I, E, or V. For the fingers, they were indicated by the numbers 1–4. Vucetich's primary classification was given by the pattern types of the fingers in order, from thumb through little finger, expressed as a fraction with the right hand over the left. For example, the primary classification

$$\frac{\text{V1211}}{\text{E1311}}$$

indicated a whorl on the right thumb, an external loop on the left thumb, arches on both index fingers, an internal loop on the right middle finger, an external loop on the left middle finger, and arches on the remaining fingers.[25]

So far, Vucetich's system was no more discriminating than Galton's original four-letter alphabetical system. But Vucetich used a secondary classification to further subdivide sets of fingerprints. For the secondary classification, each of the primary pattern types was categorized, according to a complex set of rules, as one of five subtypes, denoted by the numbers 5–9. For example, loops were divided as follows:

5—loop with plain pattern
6—loop with adhering ridges (one in which the central ridges curved back toward themselves like a question mark)
7—internal loop approximating a central pocket (equivalent to Galton's inner or radial, loop)
8—external loop approximating a central pocket (equivalent to Galton's outer or ulnar, loop)
9—irregular loops like none of the above.

One of these numbers for each finger was then placed in an adjoining fraction in the same manner as the primary classification.

Like Henry, Vucetich further subdivided patterns by ridge counting. Ridge counts for the index and little fingers, rounded to increments of five, were added in parentheses following the secondary classification. Thus a complete Vucetich classification might look as follows:

$$\frac{A214285687(5)(15)}{V341376678(25)(25)}$$

Identification cards were then arranged according to these classifications, which allowed them to be retrieved quickly. Vucetich thus solved the problem that had stymied Galton: creating subclasses that were few enough to be clearly defined, yet sufficiently numerous to break the primary classes into groups small enough to be searched easily. Classification, as Vucetich himself testified, was "the secret of the good results attained in the employment of my system." Vucetich's system made fingerprint patterns a practical means of indexing a large criminal identification file, much in the way that anthropometric measurements indexed Bertillon files. Despite their initial resistance, police officials acclaimed Vucetich's system for its ability to combat the problem of recidivism.[26]

Argentine criminologists hailed Vucetich for another reason: by solving a problem that had stumped some of Europe's most eminent scientists, including Galton, Vucetich had shown that Argentines could contribute to the field of scientific criminology on equal terms with European countries. In the late nineteenth century Argentina prided itself on being the most scientifically advanced country in Latin America. Criminal anthropology, along the lines of Lombroso's Italian School, was an especially prominent research topic in Argentina. Argentines saw criminology as a scientific field in which they could excel. Vucetich's system, though more a practical innovation than a contribution to high criminological theory, nonetheless became a point of national pride. "Vucetich's accomplishments promised to provide evidence for the Argentine criminologists that their science was not purely derivative of Europe—in it they saw the first real signs of a 'national science,'" writes the historian Julia E. Rodriguez.[27]

At the same time, European racial theories were particularly influential in Argentina, although they were shaped by Argentina's unusual history. Earlier in the nineteenth century Argentine racial theory had been focused on drawing distinctions between the European-American immigrant population, Native Americans, and African Americans. European settlers in Argentina initially welcomed all European immigrants as a way of "whitening" the population. By the 1890s, however, Native and African Americans had been almost completely exterminated from Argentina, far more so than elsewhere in the Americas: blacks composed only 2 percent of Argentina's population by 1887, and by 1895 Native Americans, owing to ruthless genocidal campaigns, had been reduced to less than 1 percent of the population.[28]

Racial theory survived, but with a twist. Instead of distinguishing European immigrants from Native and African Americans, racial theory focused on the differences between groups of Europeans. Anglo-Saxons were viewed as the most desirable immigrants, with Spaniards ranking second. Italians, Jews, and other Eastern and Southern Europeans took on the despised position formerly reserved for Indians and blacks. Native-born Argentines favored Anglo-Saxon immigrants because of their supposed status at the apex of the racial hierarchy. Essentially, they wanted to "whiten" further an already white population. In Argentina racial categories, initially applied to blacks, whites, and Indians, were applied to European ethnic groups instead. "European scientific racism had laid the groundwork for a way of thinking about race that ended up being applied to ethnicity in the debate on European immigrants, Italians or Russian Jews," says the historian Aline Helg.[29]

By the late 1880s immigration had become a "major social issue" in Argentina, not least because of its sheer scale. Argentina's population skyrocketed from 1.7 million in 1869 to 7.9 million in 1914. In addition, the immigrant population was highly urbanized. By wiping out the Native American population, the government had hoped to clear the interior for settlement. Many more of the immigrants than expected remained in the cities, however. During this period Buenos Aires was one of the fastest-growing cities in the world. From a population of around 170,000 in 1869, the city expanded to 286,000 in 1880 and 526,000 in 1890. By 1895 it had swelled to 649,000. This was a far faster rate of growth than that of, say, New York City. As conditions became increasingly chaotic in a city scarcely able to cope with its burgeoning population, native-born Argentines concluded that "lawlessness and disorder were attributable to the city's large immigrant population."[30]

During the peak of immigration, between 1880 and 1930, 43 percent of immigrants to Argentina came from Italy and 34 percent came from Spain. Argentine nativists, though often of Spanish or Italian descent themselves, portrayed Southern and Eastern European immigrants not only as racially inferior but also as criminal. Through the 1880s, the 1890s, and into the early twentieth century, Argentine society became obsessed with crime and hostile to immigrants. Statistics showed soaring crime rates. They also showed a steadily increasing percentage of immigrants among those arrested, although this probably had more to do with selective enforcement of the law than with the actual criminality of immigrants.[31]

In Argentina criminal identification was more than a method for keeping track of a manageable number of particularly egregious habitual offenders. Rather, it was a desperate measure for identifying and tracking what was perceived as a veritable tide of criminals and otherwise socially undesirable individuals being dumped upon Argentina by Europe. "The officials charged with controlling this unruly, mobile, and highly foreign population welcomed Vucetich's system. Just as the perceived need to distinguish individuals from the amorphous mass reached its peak, fingerprinting seemed to offer a solution." With the classification system devised by Vucetich, fingerprinting was faster and cheaper than Bertillonage and therefore better suited for tracking individuals within a horde of foreigners. As in colonial India, the objects of fingerprint identification in Argentina were conceived as a racially "other," mobile, large criminal population. In both countries criminal identification took on a sense of urgency, which justified the search for an identification technique that would be faster, cheaper, and easier to implement than anthropometry.[32]

Vucetich's experience was somewhat similar to Bertillon's: after an initial period of resistance, police officials rallied round his system with nationalistic fervor. In 1900 the criminologist Ernesto Quesada declared anthropometry superior to dactyloscopy in his book *The Recidivist and the Anthropometric System*. It was not until 1903 that the Buenos Aires police switched from anthropometry to dactyloscopy. By that time, however, the tide had begun to turn decisively in Vucetich's favor. In 1902 the criminologist Nicolás Roveda predicted that dactyloscopy "is destined to be adopted in all the nations of the world." The fame of Vucetich's system of fingerprint classification spread across Latin America. Vucetich published his magnum opus, *Comparative Dactyloscopy: The New Argentine System*, in 1904, and the Argentine criminologist José Ingenieros called dactyloscopy "indisputably superior to all other systems of identification." Some resistance remained, though. Officials like the Uruguayan police scientist Alfredo Giribaldi continued to support Bertillonage as late as 1905. But this was a minority position, and the South American Police Convention that year voted to endorse dactyloscopy.[33]

Vucetich envisioned an even broader reach for his system, arguing that, unlike Bertillonage, dactyloscopy was a "truly universal language" that could cross national and linguistic boundaries. During the first decade of the twentieth century the Vucetich system did spread to Europe, where it was adopted by Spain and even some non-Spanish-speaking countries. Many experts viewed it as technically superior to the Henry system. But—surprisingly, considering his ambitions— Vucetich never had his system translated into English. His instruction manuals contained extremely complicated rules for classifying fingerprint patterns, so it was necessary to be able to read them completely. The two systems, therefore, ended up splitting the global identification market: the Henry system dominated the English-speaking world, the Vucetich system dominated the Spanish, and countries that spoke neither language were free to choose between them.[34]

While Vucetich was developing dactyloscopy in Argentina in the 1890s, in the United States the pioneering proposals of Taylor, Morse, Lawton, and Taber had been forgotten. Fingerprinting, indeed, had been relegated to the realm of science fiction, notably Mark Twain's 1894 novella *Pudd'nhead Wilson*. In that famous story the central character, the lawyer and dilettante David Wilson, collects "fingermarks" as an amusement. His pursuit of this "fad without a name" is one of the eccentricities that have earned him the nickname "Pudd'nhead." Wilson's hobby comes in handy, however, for resolving the story's babies-switched-at-birth plot. At the climactic murder trial, Wilson not only uses a bloody fingerprint to identify the murderer but also uses his fingerprint records to show that the murderer, the wealthy heir Tom Driscoll, is in fact the "pure-white slave" Chambers. (Thus Twain wove both the forensic and the recordkeeping applications of fingerprinting into his story.) In the trial scene Wilson performs a dramatic demonstration: "While I turn my back, now, I beg that several persons will be so good as to pass their fingers through their hair and then press them upon one of the panes of the window near the jury, and that among them the accused may set *their* finger-marks." After the witnesses in the case leave their fingerprints on the window pane, Wilson turns and, by comparing "the delicate lines or corrugations" on the fingertips, identifies them all correctly from another set he had previously obtained. "A deafening explosion of applause was the answer. The Bench said—'This certainly approaches the miraculous!'" Wilson goes on to use his fingerprint records to demonstrate that his clients, the twins Angelo and Luigi, did not commit the murder, and that Chambers, switched at birth with Tom Driscoll, murdered Judge Driscoll.[35]

What is most remarkable about this scene is that, although the Rojas case had just occurred, fingerprints had never been introduced *in a trial* before Twain wrote the story. Twain, one of the first people to own a typewriter (like fingerprinting a technology that substituted mechanically printed records for handwritten ones), was fascinated with exploring the implications of new technologies and writing what would to-

day be called science fiction. It is not clear whether Twain knew of the
Rojas case, but his knowledge of fingerprinting predated it: he had used
a bloody fingerprint as a plot device in "A Dying Man's Confession," a
short story published in his *Life on the Mississippi* (1883). There has
been some speculation over where Twain got this idea. Some suggest
that he noticed fingerprints during his apprenticeship as a printer. Several commentators have argued that his source was Herschel and
Faulds's correspondence in *Nature* in 1880. Another contends that
Twain read an article about the British engraver Thomas Bewick,
which appeared in *Century* magazine opposite an article by William
Dean Howells about Twain himself. Still others insist that he learned
about fingerprinting from Chinese workers he met in California, such
as the prostitutes whose labor contracts contained thumbprints. In any
case, Twain was prescient, and his projection of how fingerprinting
might be used in the courtroom proved startlingly accurate. Although
anthropometry had been comfortably ensconced as the identification
system of choice in the United States, within a decade fingerprinting
would have its first chance to prove itself—not in the realm of criminal
identification but in the realm of civil identification. Ironically, the
earliest actual use of fingerprints for recordkeeping in the United
States was aimed not at exposing the deceptions of criminals but at fer-
reting out the corruption of police officers.[36]

In 1902 the New York City Civil Service Commission decided to put a
stop to the apparently widespread practice of hiring stand-ins to take
civil service examinations for police and fire department jobs. The city
had just been scandalized by one Mannix, who revealed that he had
taken the examination for twelve different candidates. The scandal had
been exposed only when Mannix sued several of the candidates who
had failed to pay him. The Civil Service Commission asked Henry De-
Forest, a physician who had just been named its chief medical examiner, to institute an identification system to prevent similar frauds. De-
Forest's instinct was to turn to Bertillonage until he read a newspaper
report about the use of fingerprinting by Scotland Yard. "The more I
thought of it," DeForest later recalled, "the more I became convinced,
that, in this method of identification, I had found a plan which . . . was
far superior to the rather complicated system of Bertillon and would be
far more accurate and expeditious in the hands of an expert operator."

DeForest scheduled a visit to Scotland Yard into a planned bicycling vacation in the British Isles.[37]

In the fall DeForest returned to New York, and James Johnson, a candidate for fireman, became the first civil service applicant fingerprinted. (Decades later DeForest would publicly retake Johnson's print in order to demonstrate the immutability of fingerprint patterns.) There is no record that the candidates objected to the procedure; fingerprinting was so new that it had not yet acquired an association with criminality. DeForest's fingerprint system proved successful at rooting out impostors, but for reasons that are not clear it was discontinued the following year when DeForest went into private practice.

The first working fingerprint file in the United States was, therefore, used exclusively for civil identification, a low-cost and quick procedure for verifying identity for relatively mundane bureaucratic purposes. Anthropometry, meanwhile, was reserved for the far more serious task of identifying criminals. Prison officials remained cautious about using something as new and untested as fingerprinting, and they continued to rely on anthropometry.

At the time the principal advantage of fingerprinting, besides its lower cost, was its ability to individualize members of supposedly homogeneous races. In 1902 the identification expert Harris Hawthorne Wilder noted that "this system would be of great service . . . in the official identification of Chinese, negroes, and other races, the features of which, at least to the Caucasian eye, offer hardly sufficient individuality to be at all times trustworthy." Wilder also thought fingerprinting would be useful for controlling immigration: "Should the government collect and catalog all the Chinese of the country, there would be no possibility of evasions of the Geary law, and most of the expense assumed in establishing identity would be saved." Fear of the foreigner and of the racial and ethnic "other" remained, at the turn of the twentieth century, the primary application for fingerprint identification.[38]

Fear of the foreigner, however, quickly blended into fear of crime, since nativists increasingly stereotyped immigrants as inherently criminal. As the pace of immigration from Europe grew, so too did the belief that the European countries were dumping undesirables and criminals on the United States. This perception combined with the fact that many immigrants were crowded into dense, poverty-stricken, crime-ridden urban slums. The steady flow of new faces into the city, from both other countries and rural areas, compounded the problem of urban anonymity. Massive immigration made the United States even more a society of strangers and exacerbated the fear of "crimes of mobility."[39]

Progressive reformers saw increased judicial knowledge and discretion as solutions to the growing problems of crime and social disorder. It became increasingly important to classify the individuals brought before the criminal justice system, to distinguish those destined to remain criminals and become a drain on society from those who were simply making the difficult adjustment to life in a new country. Just as penal reformers in the late nineteenth century had introduced flexibility into the prison regime, Progressives introduced flexibility into sentencing practices, which "became most flexible just when immigration reached unprecedented proportions. Now judges could distinguish among criminals not in terms of what they had done but in terms of who they were—and they may have found this leeway necessary in dealing with a bewildering variety of aliens."[40]

The growing burden on criminal justice systems and the growing demand for judicial information put a strain on anthropometric identification systems. In 1903 the New York State Bureau of Prisons in Albany sent two representatives, Charles Baker, chief clerk of the Prison Bureau, and R. B. Lamb, superintendent of the Dannemora State Hospital, to Paris to study improvements in the Bertillon system with the master, Bertillon himself. Someone in Paris, undoubtedly not Bertillon himself, told them about the Henry system of fingerprint identification, and they decided to add London to their itinerary to gather more information about fingerprinting. Baker and Lamb, apparently not as well connected as DeForest, were not able to get admitted to the Yard. Instead, they returned home with Henry's book *Classification and Uses of Finger Prints*. The book was put in the hands of James Parke, an identification bureau clerk, with instructions that he evaluate the idea of using fingerprints to supplement the Bertillon system. Parke and his son Edward learned Henry's system from the book, and under Parke's supervision the Bureau of Prisons implemented fingerprinting "for the purpose of experimentation and test" on March 1, 1903.[41]

Proud of its new system, the Bureau of Prisons dispatched Parke to demonstrate fingerprinting as part of the Bureau's exhibit at the 1904 Louisiana Purchase Exposition in St. Louis. This gigantic World's Fair offered an excellent opportunity for New York to show off its advances in the field of criminal identification. "Few are familiar with the operations of the Bertillon system," the Prison Bureau boasted, "and the finger print system is as yet practically unknown. New York State is the pioneer State in the Union in putting into practical operation the finger print system for the identification of criminals, and it is the only State in which it is at present in use." Parke's fingerprint demonstration was a great success. The New York State Exposition Commission reported that "the exhibit of the State Department of Prisons probably received as much attention from the public as any single State exhibit prepared."[42]

The Prison Bureau's exhibit was upstaged, however, by Scotland Yard, which sent Detective John Kenneth Ferrier to the Exposition as part of the detail to guard the crown jewels. Ferrier spent little time with the royal treasure. Instead he took up residence near New York's exhibit and also began demonstrating fingerprint identification. Reports have it that the young, handsome Ferrier cut a rather dashing figure in contrast to the middle-aged, dour Parke. Ferrier was a master showman, performing dramatic demonstrations, along the lines of the courtroom scene in *Pudd'nhead Wilson*, in which he left the room and returned to identify which one of a group of spectators had left a fingerprint on a test surface. For those who wanted more serious instruction, Ferrier stayed in the United States and trained identification clerks in the Henry system. He taught proper procedure for recording inked fingerprints, the niceties of pattern analysis and classification under the Henry system, how to file fingerprint cards, how to use powder to develop latent prints from crime scenes, and how to search for matches in the fingerprint file. His trainees included the Evans brothers, Edward, Emmett, and William, sons of Michael Evans, the identification bureau chief of the Chicago Police Department; R. W. McClaughry of the Federal Penitentiary at Leavenworth; Edward Foster of the Canada Dominion Police; and Mary Holland, wife of Philip Holland, editor of *The Detective*. Ferrier also trained detectives in other cities, including New York, during his visit, disseminating the Henry system across North America.[43]

Although the New York State Prison Bureau would later brag about its pioneering role in introducing fingerprinting for criminal identification, at the time it viewed fingerprinting as an experimental supplement, not a replacement for anthropometric identification. In 1903 Superintendent of Prisons Cornelius Collins fully expected Bertillonage to "continue to be the approved system of criminal identification for

America." "There are, however," Collins noted, "classes of persons, other than criminals, whose identity it is necessary to fix more fully and positively than by name or signature. For this purpose the Superintendent does not hesitate to recommend the finger print system, as it requires no expensive apparatus and makes positive identifications; only five minutes of instruction enables anyone to take the prints properly. Its scheme of classification is so comprehensive that the labor of research is reduced to a minimum."[44]

In other words, Collins ranked fingerprinting somewhere above handwriting and below anthropometry. He recommended its use, not for convicts, but for persons not worth the expense of anthropometric identification, such as immigrants, civil servants, military personnel, or perhaps petty criminals not sentenced to prison time. Since the Prison Bureau did not conceive of fingerprinting as a substitute for anthropometry in the realm of criminal identification, it sought other outlets for the new technology. In May 1903 Parke wrote to the U.S. Bureau of Immigration and the Navy suggesting that fingerprinting would be useful for "identifying immigrants, particularly the Chinese whose features present to American eyes so little variation." The Immigration Bureau turned down Parke's offer, however, because it had already begun implementing the Bertillon system "in the Chinese Service."[45]

Thus even the Immigration Bureau, which might have been expected to prefer fingerprinting to identify Chinese immigrants, actually preferred the more tested Bertillon system. Nonetheless, the idea that fingerprinting was particularly well suited for the identification of members of "other" races persisted well into the 1910s. American proponents like Harris Wilder continued to advocate the use of fingerprinting for the "identification of Chinese Coolies, or of Undesirable Immigrants." "Chinese are proverbially difficult of identification by the ordinary facial recognition," Wilder noted, "and even the use of photographs does not always prove conclusive." Wilder's view of fingerprinting as an identifier for "other" races would play a crucial role in the struggle for supremacy between anthropometry and fingerprinting in the United States.[46]

But, surely finger impressions are not enough, unaided by any other means of identification. For indifferent Hindus and wandering Arabs it might answer. The English regime has not been considered too particular in the matter of identity of native suspects. We, in America, however, demand something scientifically reliable.

—F. H. DePue, *The DePue System of Identification* (1902)

CHAPTER 6

From Anthropometry to Dactyloscopy

For many years, visitors to the Federal Bureau of Investigation's public tour at its headquarters in Washington, D.C., were shown a display about the famous "Will West case." It was this case, tourists were told, that made fingerprinting the leading method of criminal identification in the United States, proving its value and demonstrating its superiority to its predecessor identification technique, an anthropometric system based on bodily measurements and descriptions of ears. On May 1, 1903, the story went, an African-American man named Will West entered the United States Penitentiary at Leavenworth. Like any other new prisoner, West was subjected to the standard admission procedure: prison clerks took photographs, a physical description, and eleven anthropometric measurements. Using West's measurements and description, identification clerks matched him to the record of a William West, who had a previous conviction for murder.

Not surprisingly, in the clerks' view, West denied that he was this man. The discovery of Will West's past conviction must have seemed routine to the Leavenworth clerks: once again, the world-famous Bertillon system of identification had prevented a criminal from escaping his past. Once again, science had exposed a criminal's lies and evasions. The incident suddenly deviated from the usual, however, when the clerks discovered to their amazement that this same William West

(above) Will West
(below) William West

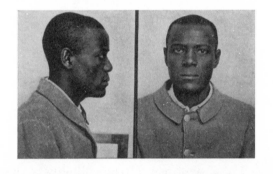

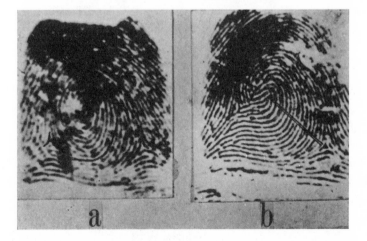

15. Mug shots and fingerprints of "the two Will Wests." The comparison was meant to illustrate that fingerprints could distinguish even two individuals who look "as alike as twin brothers."

was *already* incarcerated at Leavenworth! The second West was summoned, and he looked startlingly like the first. Their faith in anthropometry shaken, the clerks fingerprinted the two men, and their fingerprints were completely different, thus conclusively demonstrating the greater individualizing resolution of fingerprinting—its ability to discern difference where Bertillonage and photography saw none. The warden, R. W. McClaughry, according to legend, declared, "This is the death of Bertillonage!" and discontinued anthropometry at Leavenworth "the very next day."[1]

The West story portrays the conversion from anthropometry to fingerprinting as the outcome of a "crucial test," a single, decisive experiment, which suddenly and conclusively kills a scientific theory or a technological system. Indeed, it almost seemed as if the West incident had been designed to test the relative merits of photography, anthropometry, and fingerprinting (and also of using names as the basis for identification). As the FBI's official history concludes:

> It would be hard to conceive a more nearly perfect case for refuting the claims of rival systems of identification. Although the two Wests denied being related, there was a facial resemblance like that of twin brothers. The formulas derived from their Bertillon measurements were nearly identical . . . and, finally, there was the crowning coincidence of the similarity of names. The fallibility of three systems of personal identification—names, photographs, and Bertillon measurements—were demonstrated by this one case. On the other hand, the value of fingerprints as a positive means of identifying people was dramatically shown.[2]

Upon closer examination, most "crucial tests" in the history of science turn out not to be quite so crucial after all. The Will West case was no exception. The historical record demonstrates that the West incident *was* indeed designed to make precisely this point. In fact it was fabricated, since it could not have happened as FBI officials—and many historians and scholars as well—say it did. There are several holes in the story. First, Leavenworth's Warden McClaughry learned about fingerprinting from Scotland Yard's John Ferrier at the St. Louis Exposition in 1904, a year after the supposed West incident. In October 1904 Ferrier accompanied McClaughry and his son William to Leavenworth, where they fingerprinted the entire inmate population. It may have been at this time that McClaughry decided to compare the fingerprints of the two Will Wests or it may have been later, but it could not have been in 1903. Second, since the purpose of Bertillonage was to determine identity even when the suspect employed an alias, the names the prisoners were using should have been irrelevant to the identification process. But apparently the prison clerks were allowing the names on the cards to influence their judgment. This point is given added force by the fact that the two Will Wests had apparently overlapped at Leavenworth once before, in 1901, without being detected. At that time Will West had successfully used the alias "Johnson Williams."[3]

Finally, if the West case had so decisively debunked the world-famous Bertillon system, we would expect it to have merited some mention in the press or the scientific literature. But the Kansas fingerprint examiner and historian Robert Olsen found no mention of the West case in the Leavenworth records or in the press from 1903 through 1910. It would seem, then, that although the Wests may have had their fingerprints taken as early as 1904, their case was not turned into a significant event until some later date. The earliest mention of the story appears in a book published in 1918, Harris Hawthorne Wilder and Bert Wentworth's *Personal Identification*. Wilder and Wentworth, however, use the Wests solely to demonstrate that there are pairs of individuals who might be distinguishable through fingerprinting but not through anthropometry. They never state that the Wests' fingerprints were taken in 1903, or that the incident was responsible for the discontinuance of anthropometry at Leavenworth. In fact, we know that anthropometric measurement continued at Leavenworth in conjunction with fingerprinting until at least 1919. Olsen was probably correct in concluding that in the 1930s Wentworth and A. J. Renoe, head of the Leavenworth Identification Bureau, dropped these subtleties in order to provide a tidy, appealing creation story for what was by then the FBI's prized, unrivaled identification technique.[4]

But perhaps the most important flaw in the Will West story is that, even had the incident occurred in 1903 as stated, it need not have conclusively debunked Bertillonage. Most important, Bertillon had set strict limits on the "maximum tolerable deviation" between two measurements of the same person. The left foot measurements of the two Wests exceeded these deviations. The measurement for Will West was 28.2 cm., while that of William West was 27.5 cm., a difference of 7 mm., well outside the 3 mm. allowable margin of error for the foot measurement mandated by Bertillon (Table 6). Strict adherence to the tenets of Bertillonage would then have precluded the operator from mistaking the two men. Determined advocates of anthropometry could have convincingly salvaged Bertillonage by arguing that it had been improperly applied in the West case and attributing the error to the Leavenworth clerks rather than the system itself.[5]

The West story tells us more about the state of identification in 1918 than about 1903, and it tells us more about Wilder, Wentworth, and Renoe than it does about McClaughry or his turn-of-the-century clerks. In *Personal Identification* Wilder asserted that "Chinese are proverbially difficult of identification by the ordinary facial recognition" and offered fingerprinting as a way to tear away the veil of homogeneity from any unfamiliar population: "The same is true of negroes, and of all peoples of a race unlike that of the examiner, where the racial characters stand out so sharply as to obscure the finer details upon which recognition largely depends." In this context, it is significant that Wilder and Wentworth used two Negroes, the Will Wests, to illustrate the hazards of anthropometric identification. They shamelessly exploited the prejudice common among Americans that, as Wilder had put it in 1902, "peoples of a race unlike that of the examiner . . . offer hardly sufficient individuality to be at all times trustworthy." At the same time, they glossed over evidence of the individuality of the Will Wests, such as the 7 mm. difference in foot lengths, despite the fact that their own book calls a difference of this magnitude a "discrepanc[y] beyond which one is *justified in declaring non-identity.*"[6]

The portrayal of the two Will Wests—who may, in fact, have been twins, brothers, distant cousins, or unrelated—as having "a facial resemblance like that of twin brothers" evokes eerie echoes of Mark Twain's exploration of twins, race, and identity in *Pudd'nhead Wilson* through the identical twins Angelo and Luigi Capello and the nearly identical babies Tom Driscoll and Chambers, one born free, the other a "pure-white" slave. Similarly, the construction of the West story around two African Americans with identical names unmistakably evokes the complex circumstances surrounding the naming of African Americans during and after slavery. Legally, slaves could not possess surnames, and their given names were fleeting expressions of the master's whim, although many enslaved people did adopt secret names as a means of cultural resistance. After the Civil War, freed slaves adopted new surnames. Though some deliberately refused to assume their former masters' surnames, many others did so. In the case of large planta-

TABLE 6

Anthropometric measurements of Will West and William West taken at the United States Federal Penitentiary at Leavenworth, Kansas, on May 1, 1903 (note the difference in foot lengths)

Measurement	Head length	Head breadth	Middle finger	Foot length	Forearm length	Height	Little finger	Trunk	Arm span	Ear length	Cheek width
Will West	19.7	15.8	12.3	28.2	50.2	178.5	9.7	91.3	187.0	6.6	14.8
William West	19.8	15.9	12.2	27.5	50.3	177.5	9.6	91.3	188.0	6.6	14.8

Source: Harris H. Wilder and Bert Wentworth, *Personal Identification: Methods for the Identification of Individuals, Living or Dead* (Boston, 1918), 33.

tions, a large number of related and unrelated persons would end up with the same surname. From the point of view of white government officials, therefore, names had even less value for distinguishing African Americans than for whites, and this perspective is discernable in the Will West story.[7]

Despite all these logical and historical flaws, Wentworth and Renoe succeeded in turning the Will West case into an appealing origin myth for fingerprinting. Over the years, popular true crime authors and professional scholars alike have repeated the Will West story as if it really happened and as if it explained the replacement of anthropometric identification by fingerprinting. More important than the simple problem of historical inaccuracy, however, is that fact that the story incorrectly implies that fingerprinting smote anthropometry with a single devastating blow, a "crucial test" that conclusively demonstrated its superiority. History seldom works this way. In fact, the shift of allegiance from anthropometry to dactyloscopy among American law enforcement agencies, including Leavenworth itself, was a gradual process that had more to do with competing models of science and the social construction of race in America than with a single decisive case.[8]

When the Henry system of fingerprint identification first washed up on American shores, it was anthropometry, not fingerprinting, that was generally viewed as more scientific. Wilder himself had declared anthropometry more scientific in 1902. The sole advantages of fingerprinting were that it required less time and money and, of course, that it could be used to identify people of "other" races, who were difficult to distinguish through anthropometry. Fifteen years later Wilder had changed his mind, calling fingerprinting a "method which furnish[es] absolute identification." Anthropometry, in contrast, provided only "partial identification." Although Wilder by this time believed in the superiority of fingerprinting for identifying everyone, he was still not above exploiting the perception of racial homogeneity. Even as late as 1918, after all, the conversion of prisons and police departments to fingerprinting remained an uphill battle, and Wilder needed all the ammunition he could muster to convince skeptical identification bureau chiefs to adopt the "more scientific" system.[9]

Despite being false, the story of the mistaking of the two Will Wests does provide important clues regarding the practice of anthropometric identification in the United States. Most American operators learned Bertillonage from translations of Bertillon's books. (Warden Mc-Claughry himself had recently completed an English translation of one of Bertillon's manuals.) This kind of training did not instill the same discipline in operators that the exacting Bertillon achieved by training them personally. Hence anthropometric practice was not nearly as precise in America as it was in France. American complaints about the accuracy of Bertillonage had surfaced as early as 1891 at the International Congress of Demography in London, when Lt. Col. Charles Greenleaf complained that a military court had found "Bertillon's anthropometric method insufficient before courts-martial, because of possible inaccuracies in measurement, and because of allowable errors." Jacques Bertillon, Alphonse's brother, retorted that the problem lay not with the system but with its application in the United States, and he expressed doubt about "whether the anthropometric method had received a fair trial in America, the measurements being made by persons not specially trained, whereas in France the establishments, though small, are thoroughly efficient."[10]

The idea of anthropometric identification had disseminated faster and more successfully than Bertillonage itself. Many institutions, vaguely aware of anthropometry, simply measured prisoners, without troubling themselves with the niceties of Bertillon's rules or notation. While identification bureaus colloquially referred to these procedures as "the Bertillon system," most would have been described more accurately as anthropometric identification systems inspired by the French system. Others could not even be called anthropometric. The U.S. Army, for example, classified enlistees by eye color, subclassified them by height, and sub-subclassified them by the presence or absence of a tattoo. This scheme clearly showed the influence of Bertillon, but it bore scant resemblance to Bertillon's actual system.[11]

Even when identification bureaus did attempt to implement the Bertillon system intact, operators tended to be lax about such details as learning Bertillon's elaborate morphological vocabulary, assuming incorrectly that bodily measurements formed the whole of the identification system. The "Bertillon records" kept by Sing Sing Prison in New York, for example, would have given Bertillon himself apoplexy. After the New York State Bureau of Prisons instituted anthropometric identification in 1896, the Sing Sing admission registers were changed to include entries, not for measurements of the head or foot, but for hat and shoe size! Apparently prison officials had ignored Bertillon's caveat that "the aim . . . is not to make a pair of shoes, but to obtain a constant length that will be unalterable and that may at any time be taken over again with as much precision as at the time and place of the operation."[12]

The Sing Sing register also provided spaces to describe the prisoner's complexion, eye color, hair color, stature, weight, ears, nose, lips, forehead, eyebrows, mouth, teeth, and general features. Prison clerks filled in these spaces, not with the standardized morphological terms enumerated in Bertillon's instruction manuals, but with arbitrary, colloquial terms drawn from everyday language. Ears might be "medium and flaring," "small and well shaped," "good size good shape," or "unusual and irregular." Noses might be "medium straight," "rather short," "medium rather thick," "short thick," "large thick crooked," "small and sharp," or "medium crooked and slight Roman." General features might be "fair small face," "fairly good chin short," "good bald head," "coarse," or, by far the most common description, simply "regular." From an identification standpoint, such information was almost meaningless for two reasons. First, there was no manual that defined what was meant by "medium" ears, a "small" nose, a "good chin," or a "good head." The second problem was the prevalence of generic terms like "medium" and "regular," which conveyed hardly any descriptive information at all. The registers also included a large space for "scars and identification marks." Here again, the clerks did not follow Bertillon's procedure of recording the precise locations, dimensions, and descriptions of scars, but relied instead on vague, meandering descriptions. These records indicate an awareness of the general idea of Bertillonage without any familiarity with its actual rules of practice. The prison had added more descriptive categories to its printed forms, but it had not trained its clerks in Bertillon's procedures. It was of little use to have prison clerks write detailed descriptions of each prisoner without training them in Bertillon's morphological vocabulary. The result was a litany of "regulars," and "mediums."[13]

Loose practice also applied to the taking of measurements. Inconsistency between operators was a major drawback of anthropometry in the United States, as in India. Unlike France, where Bertillon himself loomed as a formidable presence over the whole criminal identification bureaucracy, in the United States no one was overseeing the operation of the overall system or disciplining the operators. By 1899 delegates to the annual meeting of the International Association of Chiefs of Police (the IACP, despite the name, was a primarily American organization) were complaining about poor measurements taken by Bertillon operators in the United States. One American police chief remarked that the system was perfect but the operators were not. Implementing anthropometry was neither easy nor cheap, and the temptation to cut corners on instrumentation, procedure, or training must have been overwhelming. In California, for example, the Folsom penitentiary discontinued anthropometry by 1902 "because of its unreliability," even before fingerprinting came along to replace it, and the chief Bertillon operator at San Quentin prison declared, "No two men will measure a subject alike by the Bertillon system." Thus in America, as in India and Britain, a potential advantage of fingerprinting was that it required less skill from the operator.[14]

But anthropometry retained the crucial advantage of being viewed as a more scientific technique. The scene at the St. Louis World's Fair, where John Ferrier and James Parke introduced the Henry system to the United States, makes the differences between the rival identification techniques clear. Criminal identification was merely one of many scientific applications of anthropometry on display at the fair. Perhaps the most prominent site of anthropometric activity was the anthropology exhibit, considered by many to be the central exhibit at the fair. For the St. Louis Exposition the Smithsonian Institution put together the most extensive anthropology exhibit yet seen at any world's fair. Such anthropological luminaries as Franz Boas and Aleš Hrdlička participated in its preparation. The Anthropology Building attracted a million and a half visitors. Anthropometry played a prominent role in the exhibit's "representation . . . of the world's least known ethnic types, races or sub-races." Scientific measurements were needed to fulfill the exhibit's aim "to represent human progress from the dark prime to the highest enlightenment." Anthropometry and psychometry (the quantitative measurement of mental ability, states, and processes through a variety of psychological tests) laboratories provided such measurements, demonstrating, in the words of W. J. McGee, the head of the Anthropology Department, "so far as measurements may—the relative physiological value of the different races of the peoples involved in the fair."[15]

If anything at the fair overshadowed the Anthropology Department, it was the enormous Philippine Reservation. Forty-seven acres in size, the Philippine Reservation was "an exposition within an exposition." The exhibit housed 1,200 Filipinos representing more than fifty tribal groups found in the newly acquired American territory. Ninety-nine percent of fair visitors—more than four million people—reportedly saw the Philippine exhibit, and many called it "the most impressive exhibit" in the whole exposition. The Philippine Reservation was intended to display, *in vivo,* the range of human evolution: from the more primitive tribes, such as the "savage" Bagobos and "monkey-like" Negritos, on through the "picturesque" Igorats and Islamic Moros, up through the "high and more intelligent class of native," such as the Visayans, and culminating in the, mostly Caucasian, fair visitors themselves, a cultural hierarchy that, not surprisingly, corresponded neatly with skin color, with darker-skinned ethnic groups at the bottom and whites at the apex. In short, the reservation was meant to be viewed as a living diorama of human evolution.[16]

The presence of living representatives of some of the most "primitive" tribal groups known offered a golden opportunity for, in the words of the Exposition's director, David Francis, "observing and comparing the human types assembled on the grounds." Again, "the methods and appliances used in anthropometry and psychometry in measuring the physical and mental characters of men" were harnessed in the effort to lend quantitative scientific rigor to the argument that visitors were also expected to be able to see for themselves: that Western civilization was the culmination of human evolution. The combined effect of "the exhibits in the Anthropology Department and on the Philippine Reservation provided fair goers with an anthropologically calibrated yardstick for measuring the world's progress." Anthropometry was a crucial part of that yardstick.[17]

Though the use of anthropometry and psychometry to measure the evolutionary state of human beings has long since been discredited, at the time it was seen as solid science, the fulfillment of the Darwinian vision. The psychologist Hugo Münsterberg "believed the results obtained from the laboratories 'will be a real contribution to science.'" The anthropologist Clark Wissler concluded that the anthropology exhibit had conclusively demonstrated that "racial differences exist," and that "most fairgoers left the laboratories with the same idea firmly ingrained in their minds." Even Boas, a relatively enlightened anthro-

pologist by today's standards of political correctness, "regarded the Anthropology Department . . . as a valuable source for field research."[18]

Small wonder, then, that anthropometric identification was viewed
as more scientific than dactyloscopy. While some of the world's most
eminent scientists, from major universities and museums, were using
anthropometry in the Anthropology Department, a Scotland Yard detective and a prison clerk were demonstrating fingerprinting over in
the State Exhibits Building. Whereas anthropometry seemed like a scientific method of identification, dactyloscopy was perceived as a mere
novelty, a hokey, unproven upstart. In 1904 the burden of proof was
clearly on dactyloscopy, not on anthropometry, to validate its scientific credentials. Hence, in Arthur Conan Doyle's 1902 novel *The
Hound of the Baskervilles*, a visitor to Sherlock Holmes insults his
host by calling Bertillon, not Holmes, Europe's highest expert in criminalistics. But he assuages Holmes by favorably contrasting his "practical nature" to Bertillon's "scientific nature." Though Holmes, and
fingerprinting, may have been more "practical," Bertillon, and anthropometry, were seen as more "scientific."

Proponents of anthropometry also denigrated fingerprinting for its
Eastern origins, as in Bertillon's disparaging reference to it as "the Chinese method." Moreover, fingerprinting was associated with colonial
governance and the social control of native peoples, while anthropometry was associated with the higher-status governance of European
nation-states. Alluding to dactyloscopy's colonial origins, San Francisco Police Chief F. H. DePue dismissed it as good enough only "for
indifferent Hindus and wandering Arabs. Thus dactyloscopy was perceived as useful as an emergency measure for physically homogeneous
nonwhites who could not be adequately distinguished through a "scientifically reliable" technique like anthropometry.[19]

This view of the two systems was backed by the weight of scientific
opinion. In December 1904, just after Ferrier had introduced dactyloscopy to the United States, *Scientific American* echoed Bertillon's assertion that "thumb prints in themselves do not present elements of
variability sufficiently well defined to serve as the basis of classification in a file of several hundred thousand prints." The magazine lik-
ened fingerprinting to other nonstandard methods, such as "the taking of plaster casts of the jaw, the making of minute drawings of the
aureola of the eye, the taking of a photograph of the ear, the notation of

all peculiar characteristics, such as beauty spots and scars," and concluded that anthropometry was clearly the best system. It repeated this endorsement a year later.[20]

Those agencies which did adopt fingerprinting during the first decade of the twentieth century treated it as a supplement to anthropometry. This was the case at the New York State Prison Bureau, which introduced fingerprinting in 1903, the Chicago Police Department and the Federal Bureau of Criminal Identification at Leavenworth, which instituted fingerprinting in 1904, and the New York Police Department, which adopted fingerprinting in 1906. At this point American officials had no good reason to expect that fingerprinting, rather than anthropometry, would become the standard technique, but they did find it easier to implement, requiring less training, time, and expertise in making and accessing criminal records. Above all, it was by far the cheaper method in terms of time, personnel, and necessary training.

In 1907 a French Academy of Sciences survey found the world fairly evenly divided between the two identification methods. Dactyloscopy had taken root mostly in the British Empire and South America, places with a direct connection to either the Henry or the Vucetich system: England, the British Indies, Egypt, Argentina, Brazil, Uruguay, and Chile. Anthropometric systems of identification were used in France, Russia, Belgium, Switzerland, Romania, Spain, and Mexico. Germany, Austria, and Portugal used combined systems that classified prisoners according to fingerprints but included anthropometric data. Reluctantly, the French Academy report did concede that dactyloscopy appeared to be the technique of the future: "We are now in a transition period, but there doesn't seem to be any doubt that events are leading toward the progressive substitution of dactyloscopy for Bertillon measurements."[21]

Even this verdict was insufficient to convince wary American law enforcement officials to commit to fingerprinting. To understand identification bureau chiefs' concerns, it is necessary to recall the importance of indexing to criminal records. The method of indexing—whether fingerprint patterns, anthropometric measurements, or names—is the means by which all records are accessed. (This was why Bertillon did not object to including fingerprints on French identification cards but insisted that records be indexed according to anthropometric measurements.) If the method of indexing becomes obsolete, then existing records become inaccessible and almost useless. The decision that bureau chiefs faced, therefore, was similar to the practically irreversible choices faced by a librarian trying to decide whether to catalogue according to the Dewey Decimal, Library of Congress, or Richardson system or a consumer trying to decide whether to collect movies on Betamax, VHS tapes, laserdisk, or DVD. The very fact that there *was* a rivalry between anthropometry and fingerprinting only heightened the chiefs' uncertainty. If fingerprinting was threatening to replace anthropometry after only twenty years, then how long could fingerprinting be expected to last before it too would be rendered obsolete by some new, superior system? Nervous bureau chiefs' fears would have been heightened, for example, if they had read a 1910 article in *Scientific American* entitled "A New Method of Identifying Persons: The Veins on the Back of the Hand."[22]

In light of all this confusion, it is not surprising that most chiefs hedged their bets. In 1906 Richard Sylvester, chief of police of the District of Columbia and president of the IACP, advised his constituents to maintain dual identification systems. "There is and will continue to be a difference of opinion as to the worth of the two prevailing means of identification now in use," he said, "but all will agree that two are better than one."[23]

For the first decade of the twentieth century, fingerprinting enjoyed its greatest success in the United States in civilian identification, where lives and liberty were not at stake. In addition to DeForest's civil service file, the U.S. Army began fingerprinting recruits, instead of taking measurements and descriptions, in 1906 because "the labor and time involved in the operation became excessive." The Army used fingerprints to detect "repeaters," deserters or men dishonorably discharged who sought to reenlist. It would later propose using fingerprints to identify the dead and—returning to the technique's original application—to control pension disbursement. The Navy followed a year later. Criminal identification, however, was considered too sensitive to entrust to fingerprinting. Identification bureaus remained wedded to using anthropometry to identify convicts. It was not until 1910 that fingerprinting found a useful application in the criminal justice system.[24]

In 1910 the Inferior Criminal Courts Act mandated the taking of prostitutes' fingerprints in New York City magistrates' courts. Prostitutes made an ideal target population for the new identification technique for several reasons. Although female convicts had sometimes been subjected to anthropometric measurements, identification experts often lamented the difficulties of using anthropometry to identify women. The chief difficulty was that anthropometry, with its emphasis on applying calipers and rulers tightly, required a physical intimacy between the operator and the prisoner's body that was not deemed appropriate for female prisoners. Vienna Police Chief Camillo Windt probably had this in mind when he complained about the lack of "feminine" Bertillon instruments in 1903. Similarly, the notation of peculiar marks presented difficulty because "in women the marks are not infrequently in such a position as to practically preclude comparison." It was also said that Bertillonage did not work on women because their bouffant hairstyles threw off the height measurement and because of unspecified "recurring pathological disturbances," perhaps a reference to slight changes in the size of the female body over the course of the menstrual cycle. Once again, fingerprinting could compete with anthropometry only when applied to bodies in which difference and distinction were thought to be invisible to anthropometry. Just as fingerprinting had made it possible to distinguish the bodies of colonial natives, immigrants, and African Americans, it also turned women into suitable objects of the gaze of the state. If the problem with racially "other" bodies was an appearance of homogeneity, the problem with female bodies was their general inaccessibility to instruments of measurement.[25]

Prostitution was perceived as an especially "habitual" crime in the Progressive era. Progressive reformers cast women convicted of prostitution as "female defective delinquents," driven inexorably to sex crimes by a combination of biological and environmental factors. In 1908 the progressive Women's Prison Association had secured passage of a bill establishing a work farm for habitual female offenders. The new law, the Association's annual report noted, "is the expression of a conviction which is gaining ground among all who have to deal with persistent offenders of either sex that the only rational way to deal with habitual offenders of any class is to segregate them in a farm or industrial colony under an indeterminate sentence for a prolonged period." The Association had identified 800 women in the city and 1,000 in the state who had been arrested between 20 and 200 times. In 1903, it found, 1,400 sentences had been passed on a mere 100 women. In the 1910s, intelligence testing at the reformatories found high rates of "feeble-mindedness" among prostitutes. This finding supported the reformers' belief that there was a hereditary "predisposition" to prostitution caused by some biological flaw. In 1912 New York passed a law allowing the sterilization of criminals and persons deemed "feeble-minded, insane, or epileptic." Since keeping track of these women was considered important to the social welfare, reformers looked for an identification system that would be appropriate for female subjects.[26]

Prostitution was a common, petty crime that seldom merited prison time (unless habitual criminality warranted commitment to a House of Refuge). The definition of prostitution was broader than it is today, encompassing a wide range of sexual behavior by women in various states of financial deprivation. From a public hygiene point of view, it was thought all the more necessary to distinguish occasional from professional prostitutes. The population of New York City was quite large, and the time and expense of subjecting every woman arrested for prostitution in the city to anthropometric identification would have been prohibitive. Fingerprinting offered a cheap means of rapid identification. If fingerprinting was less reliable than anthropometry, the consequences of an error in a prostitution case was not all that dire. (In Argentina as well, around the same time, officials deployed dactyloscopy in the battle against prostitution and syphilis.)[27]

For all these reasons, New York City prostitutes offered an ideal target group upon which fingerprinting could prove its reliability in criminal identification. Fingerprinting offered a way to separate "female defective delinquents" from women who might have only recently fallen into crime. Defective delinquents could then be subjected to special penal regimes, such as reformatories or houses of refuge, designed to "cure" their criminality. The new fingerprint system proved quite successful at identifying "habitual criminals" among women arrested for prostitution. Between 1910 and 1913 the magistrates' courts recorded the fingerprints of more than 12,000 women arrested for prostitution. The magistrates tended to "regard the third print as a strong presumption of incorrigibility" or "positive recidivation." Fingerprinting told the magistrates what they wanted to know: that a large portion of crimes were committed by "incorrigible habitual offenders." The fingerprint system, commented one magistrate, "tell[s] us that approximately 629 recidivous women are constantly walking our streets for victims and furnishing a large proportion of the business in the Woman's Night Court." Like anthropometry before it, fingerprinting made the recidivist real, by providing the criminal justice system with increasing numbers of flesh-and-blood recidivists. Yet fingerprinting, with its higher speed and lower cost, extended the penological mechanisms directed at recidivists to more, and pettier, criminals. Fingerprinting also allowed the criminological notion of recidivism to leap the gender barrier and include female habitual criminals as well as male.[28]

While this hesitant experiment in fingerprinting petty criminals progressed in New York City, concern about crime persisted across the nation, fueled by continuing heavy immigration and increasing urbanization. Just as it did in Argentina, the influx of immigrants perceived as racially inferior and prone to criminal behavior put a strain on anthropometric identification systems and invited the faster, less expensive alternative of fingerprinting. As the demands on prisons grew and it became impossible to imprison petty offenders like drunks and vagrants, the burden of dealing with crime shifted increasingly from prisons to police departments and courts. In contrast to prisons, which could measure their inmates at their leisure, these institutions emphasized the rapid and efficient processing of criminal bodies. Police departments, moreover, were increasingly expected to fight the crime problem as opposed to merely maintaining order and suppressing political unrest. Police departments and courts, therefore, embraced fingerprinting as a stand-alone identification system for dealing with large numbers of petty offenders while prisons still conceived of it as a supplement to anthropometry.[29]

Having established the usefulness of fingerprinting in identifying female petty criminals, the New York magistrates' court extended its use to men. In 1913 the magistrates' courts began fingerprinting men arrested for intoxication and vagrancy. Six months later resolutions by the Board of Magistrates added men arrested for disorderly conduct, jostlers (pickpockets), mashers ("persistent insulters of women in public places," a group that remains well represented in New York City), and "degenerates." Prints taken at all the magistrates' courts throughout the city were forwarded to a central office at 300 Mulberry Street in lower Manhattan. Copies were distributed to the district courts and police headquarters. Magistrates were obligated by law to have these district files searched before passing sentence. "By this means," the magistrates opined, "it will no longer be possible for a defendant to plead sympathy on the ground that he is a first offender when as a matter of fact he has been convicted previously." By 1915 the magistrates' court files held more than 80,000 sets of fingerprints.[30]

A 1916 amendment to the law extended the reach of fingerprinting to even more petty crimes. This broad measure apparently inflamed "an existing prejudice among many citizens against using the process as an aid in the imposition of sentence in the magistrates' courts." These citizens were concerned that "the individual thus printed is thereby permanently branded as a criminal," a punishment deemed too harsh for some of the most minor offenses, like vagrancy. This was the first time the American public objected to fingerprinting, signifying that the taking of fingerprints, no longer a novelty, was clearly understood to brand someone a criminal. The recording of fingerprints for "disorderly conduct cases involving only trifling infractions of the public peace" provoked enough public hostility to force a hasty change in policy. The rules were amended to include "only" jostling, rowdyism on public conveyances, mashing, riotous conduct, and offenses involving considerable injury to persons or property, along with degenerates, beggars, and confidence men. In 1919 the New York City Health Commissioner also proposed fingerprinting drug addicts.[31]

Again, the magistrates extolled fingerprinting as an effective crime-fighting tool, on the basis of its ability to identify petty recidivists. "This city is the first to print for minor offences and disturbances," boasted City Magistrate Joseph Deuel in 1917, "and from present information she still stands unique in that respect. The primary object was, and is, to accomplish what was unsuccessfully attempted by the cumulative sentence law of 1895: crush out the 'regulars,' or 'repeaters,' or 'professionals' by successively lengthened sentences, thereby serving as a deterrent for others to drift into that class." As examples Deuel cited two particular offenders, one male, one female: "Under seven different names the woman appeared before thirteen different magistrates and in five different courts; the man, under nine different names, was convicted by fourteen different magistrates and in two different courts. In no instance was either arrested twice by the same policeman. The man was found intoxicated in seven different police precincts; the woman in four." Fingerprinting prevented recidivists from assuming a fresh identity each time they appeared in court. In this way it solved a problem engendered by the sheer size and complexity of New York

City's municipal justice system. Fingerprinting, according to Deuel, restored order to the urban jungle. "We are enjoying better order and decorum in the city than ever before, and much of the credit is due to the finger-print process."[32]

Fingerprints allowed magistrates to base sentences on what Bonneville had called, three-quarters of a century earlier, the "state of recidivism," rather than merely on the specific offense. Even if petty offenses could not be severely punished, magistrates could now punish recidivism itself, arguing that recidivists could be expected to offend again and should be segregated. At the same time, petty offenders like "perverts," violent alcoholics, professional thieves, "feeble-minded prostitutes," drunkards, vagrants, unemployables, and "born tireds" were figuring more prominently in criminological discussions of recidivism. Thus penology, criminology, and criminal identification all worked together to target the petty recidivist.[33]

Fingerprinting helped turn recidivism into the fulcrum of criminal justice system. Aside from the offense itself, recidivism became the most important factor in discretionary sentencing. This completed the overthrow of classical jurisprudence. Instead of the criminal anthropologists' long-deferred dream of being able to diagnose "born criminals" and separate them from redeemable offenders, the anthropologists' less prestigious rivals, fingerprint clerks, offered a reliable method of measuring recidivism. In essence, the recidivist became the born criminal, and legislators and jurists hoped to combat the crime problem by cracking down on recidivists. Progressives across the country introduced new measures aimed at giving judges, magistrates, and wardens the discretion they needed, not only to sentence redeemable offenders to probation and parole but also to sentence recidivists to longer terms. By providing reliable information about criminal histories, fingerprinting transformed recidivism into the primary measure of a convict's worth and potential for rehabilitation and ultimately helped decide the convict's punishment.

The tendency toward individualized punishment, begun during the heyday of Bertillonage, accelerated during the Progressive era. The trend, beginning around 1900, was to build more discretion into the system—for magistrates, judges, wardens, and a variety of criminological experts. Probation became popular in the United States between 1900 and 1920, and indeterminate sentences (in which the prisoner's sentence was given as a range, with the specific release date left to the discretion of the warden or judge) became more common. The Parole Commission Law of 1915 introduced parole to New York, mandating indeterminate sentences of up to two years for persons convicted of minor offenses like disorderly conduct, vagrancy, breach of the peace, or prostitution thrice in a two-year period or four times in a lifetime. Fingerprinting enabled progressive reformers to introduce discretionary tools, like probation, parole, and indeterminate sentencing, that were based on individualized criminal histories. New York's Parole Commission, for example, "was specifically founded on the fingerprint process."[34]

Fingerprinting, then, emerged not as a method of criminal identification superior to anthropometry but rather as a quick and cheap, supposedly less scientific way of identifying those whose crimes did not justify the expense of anthropometry. Only the low-level magistrates' courts were willing to gamble on an identification system based on fingerprints alone. Over the course of the 1910s the magistrates' courts— and a handful of police departments across the country—amassed large numbers of fingerprint records without any egregious cases of error, and this made other identification bureaus less apprehensive about the technique. Fingerprinting thus routinized criminal identification and democratized the notion of recidivism, extending it down to the pettiest echelons of crime.

Through its success in identifying habitual criminals in the New York City magistrates' courts, fingerprinting got its foot in the door of the criminal justice system. In 1910, the year fingerprinting began in the magistrates' courts, the tide of scientific and public opinion began to turn in its favor. *Scientific American* reversed its position, arguing that fingerprinting was preferable to Bertillonage because it saved on the cost of instruments and required less skill and training of the operator. In 1912 the *New York Times* shifted its support from anthropometry to fingerprinting. The following year the New York legislature ordered the fingerprinting of all prisoners. Nonetheless, anthropometry remained in place for the more serious offenders: felons were both measured and fingerprinted, while petty offenders could merely be fingerprinted.[35]

The earliest uses of fingerprinting for forensic identification in the United States came in two criminal trials in 1910 and 1911: *People v.*

Jennings, a Chicago murder trial, and *People v. Crispi,* a New York City burglary case. The first case resulted in a conviction that was upheld by the Illinois Supreme Court, and the second resulted in a confession, with the burglar admitting to having touched the glass where his fingerprint was found. These two trials helped enhance the national reputation of the new technique. But while fingerprinting offered the side benefit of forensic identification, Bertillonage still offered the side benefit of the *portrait parlé,* "by means of which, in a few words, a face may be described by a trained man with such accuracy as to enable another to identify the subject in a large crowd, although he has never seen him." Although the *portrait parlé* sounds fanciful today, it was taken quite seriously at the time. Shortly after helping secure the country's first criminal conviction based on fingerprint evidence alone in *People v. Crispi,* NYPD Lieutenant Joseph Faurot set sail for France—to meet with Bertillon and undergo further instruction in the *portrait parlé.*[36]

And so in American police departments the two systems coexisted through the 1910s. By 1915, however, progressive police reformers such as Raymond Fosdick were campaigning for a wholesale switch to fingerprinting. Fosdick had been influenced by developments in Europe, where he had been doing research for his book *European Police Systems* (1915). At the meeting of the International Police Congress in Monaco in 1914, shortly after the death of the obstreperous Bertillon, Fosdick reported, it was "freely predicted" that all European criminal identification files would soon be *classified* according to fingerprint patterns. Word of anthropometry's demise was slow to reach the United States, though. "Accustomed as we are to the notorious backwardness of our cities in adopting improvements which promote efficiency," Fosdick sighed, "it is nevertheless painful to contemplate the fact that at the very time that European cities were discarding their Bertillon cabinets as superfluous, many of our police departments were busy installing them. The writer has recently been in three cities of size and importance that are this year inaugurating a Bertillon system under the impression that it represents the latest word in the scientific detection of criminals!"

Progressive reformers like Fosdick, acutely sensitive to America's reputation as backward compared to Europe, wanted the United States to embrace the latest technology, and that meant fingerprinting. Wary

American identification bureaus, however, continued to maintain dual systems. "In some American cities an identification method seems to be looked upon by the police officials as a sort of charm or talisman," Fosdick ruefully observed in 1915, "and in more than one department visited by the writer the boast was made that it had *two* identification systems." In Fosdick's view this redundancy reflected most identification chiefs' woeful ignorance of the identification techniques they employed. "The heads of these so-called bureaus of identification gloried in their possessions, even when they did not know how to hold a pair of calipers or how to classify fingerprints!" Another American observer grumbled in 1917: "In the hurry to be in the fashion and in the rage of extravagance which is so natural to us, we have been installing Bureaus based on the Anthropometric System without knowing how to manage them at all, and without knowing the consequences of installation. The fingerprint system should be the only system adopted in America."[37]

In 1916, at the second meeting of the International Association for Criminal Identification (IACI), the professional organization of North American police and prison identification bureau chiefs, Superintendent Nickelson of the Washington State Penitentiary suggested that the association go "on record as favoring the finger-print system over the Bertillon as a standard of identification, and read a telegram he had received from the Secretary of the Sheriff's Association of Washington asking him to use his efforts at the convention for the abolition of the Bertillon system." This motion was opposed by identification bureau chiefs who had already invested substantial resources in collecting criminal records indexed according to anthropometric measurements and were not convinced that fingerprints would be the last word in criminal identification. The more records a bureau had indexed according to an anthropometric system, the less inclined it was to undertake the task of recataloging those records according to the Henry system. The meeting adjourned without endorsing either system. The ambiguity was visible in the IACI's logo, which depicted a pair of anthropometric calipers surrounding a fingerprint. The calipers remain in the logo of the International Association for Identification (IAI, the descendant organization of the IACI) even today, symbolizing its original role as an organization of Bertillon operators.[38]

One reason for the resistance to fingerprinting was discomfort with the abstractness of fingerprint patterns. Anthropometric identification codes, no matter how arcane they were, focused on the body and the face, which most people think of as the natural way to identify individuals. Fingerprinting took identification to a new level of abstraction, in which the identifier did not even resemble the body or the face. This move toward abstraction, which would later be taken even further with DNA, took some getting used to. Many identification chiefs agreed with F. H. DePue's view of fingerprinting as a transitional technology between anthropometry and some higher-tech method of facial identification. In other words, they expected—or hoped—that identification would return to the face. DePue's system, for example, projected stereoscopic images onto a large ruled screen. Other new facial identification systems, elaborate techniques for dividing the face into fine-grained "zones" and noting the appearance of features in each zone, appeared in the 1920s, testaments to the natural preference for identifying people by the familiar contours of the face rather than the abstract whorls of fingerprint patterns.[39]

It was in this context that Wilder and Wentworth published their book *Personal Identification* in 1918. Their outspoken advocacy of fingerprinting over anthropometry was part of the efforts by progressive identification experts to persuade the more conservative police bureaucrats who ran the major identification bureaus to switch to fingerprinting. These efforts did have an effect on what was by then the nation's largest identification bureau, the NYPD, which ceased recording anthropometric measurements in 1920. The following year Joseph Faurot told the delegates to the National Police Conference: "I think that every police department should drop the Bertillon system. The fingerprint system has been in vogue now five or six years." According to Faurot, not only the *recording* of identification information but also its *retrieval* was faster with fingerprinting: four minutes per search versus twenty minutes for anthropometry. But many American law enforcement agencies were reluctant to give up anthropometry. In 1922 a proposal to abandon Bertillonage provoked a heated debate at the annual convention of the IACP. Everett Van Buskirk, superintendent of the IACP's National Bureau of Criminal Identification, attested that operator errors occurred as frequently with fingerprints as with anthropometry. Michael Evans of Chicago called abandoning Bertillonage "a mistake—a great mistake. Any city that wants to be up to date has got to have both systems." He argued that fingerprint files were so new that they did not cover many older convicts and that Bertillonage served as a check against poor impressions taken by fingerprint operators.[40]

Only slowly, over the course of the 1920s, did fingerprinting become the preferred criminal identification technique in the United States. Bertillonage retained some of its scientific luster, in part because the instruments made it *look* scientific. Captain John Golden of the NYPD conveyed this in his remarks at the 1925 meeting of the IAI: "The Bertillon system today really cannot be compared with finger prints as to efficiency, and never could be. Therefore it is really an extra burden on the office." Nonetheless, he added, "It is a very great thing to walk into a bureau and see the calipers lying around, and the measuring box, and the stretch-off instruments—it is a wonderful moving picture scene; but when you figure out all the work that it entails . . . it really is a waste of time."[41]

Still, many U.S. police departments kept Bertillon records well into the 1920s. The New York State Division of Identification only fully ceased recording Bertillon measurements in 1931. Even then, Clara Parsons, director of the Division, predicted that "the Bertillon description and photograph will in all probability always remain a part of every identification system." And indeed, for reasons that are unclear, the New York State Prison at Auburn took Bertillon measurements of all prisoners through 1930 and completed some Bertillon cards as late as 1938. Even in Argentina, the cradle of dactyloscopy, prison officials continued to record anthropometric measurements and physical descriptions until 1926.[42]

Proponents of fingerprint identification like Wilder and Wentworth exploited identification bureau chiefs' fears that anthropometry was not sensitive enough to individualize people of "other" races, principally African and Asian Americans. Fingerprint identification offered a way of individualizing people, who, it was feared, would all look the same. But even if the fingerprint system of identification traced its origins in part to racist thinking, wouldn't the individualizing technology of fingerprinting itself tend to militate against racial typing? Paradoxically, fingerprinting actually reified the very crude racial categories that had helped produce it. Although the fingerprint system, unlike anthropometric systems, did not use either skin tone or facial features for individualized identification, it was possible to superimpose crude skin-based racial identification onto the fingerprint system.

In 1922, for example, the New York Police Department Identification Bureau inaugurated a separate "yellow file" for fingerprints to go along with its "black" and "white" files. "In New York City we have quite a number of Chinese who are residents of the city, and quite a number of visiting Chinese from Boston and Newark," Captain Golden remarked at an annual meeting of the IAI, "and I found out that it would be very well for us to have a yellow file in addition to a black file. You identification men know a Chinaman when you see one, or a Japanese; you will not make a mistake in that, and, therefore, when a Chinaman or a Japanese is brought into your bureau, you can simply mark on the front of the card, 'Yellow,' the same as you would mark it 'Black' for a negro, and file that file in a separate file." Thus crude subdivisions based on race and gender made smaller files that were easier to search. With the "yellow file," Golden pointed out, "it is an easy matter to look up a Chinaman when he is brought in; instead of going through our entire collection, we merely go through the yellow collection."[43]

So the triumph of fingerprint identification over anthropometry did not banish the specter of racism from the realm of criminal identification. Instead, fingerprinting enabled law enforcement officials to have individualized identification while maintaining a simple, physiognomically based, tripartite (white, black, yellow) system of racial classification. An anthropometric identification system, in contrast, by exposing the existence of mulattos and other racial "hybrids" and forcing identification officials to name and recognize intraracial physiognomic variation, would have been incompatible with such crude racial classification. Fingerprinting did not discredit racial classification; it turned it into a simpler, skin-tone-based means of categorization.

Fingerprint identification allowed law enforcement officials to ignore the reality of human variation: that the "races" were arbitrary categories that masked both the enormous breadth of intraracial variation and the existence of individuals who blurred racial boundaries. Instead, the widespread adoption of the fingerprint system allowed the mythical tripartite categorization of all people into "black," "white," and "yellow" to persist. This crude categorization has, of course, had profound consequences in the exigencies of policing in the United States. The recent furor over "racial profiling" is only one example of the problem of police using crude skin-tone-based categories to guide their assessments of the dangerousness of individuals.

The Will West legend suggests that the choice of fingerprinting over anthropometry was made on narrow technical grounds. In fact, the two techniques had different strengths and weaknesses and drew upon different resources for legitimacy. Anthropometry was a "scientific" tool familiar to anthropologists, ethnologists, and anatomists, which rested upon the reliability of trained, skilled observers. While most identification experts associated this emphasis on observation with science, some criticized the reliance on human observation. These critics saw anthropometry as a step backwards from the mechanical reproduction that had characterized photography. DePue expressed this view in 1902: "Nature has furnished us with so much material of fixed or rigid character and mechanism has such a peculiar power for accuracy that it would seem we ought in time be released from the nightmares of horror caused by our too well grounded fears of the alarming possibilities of human fallibility. Nature has given to man in mechanism his best, because safest hand; therefore, by mechanism we hope to properly fix identity."[44]

Although DePue himself was no advocate of dactyloscopy (he favored facial identification), fingerprinting did possess this mechanical quality. It drew upon a different model of science, which the historians of science Lorraine Daston and Peter Gallison have labeled "mechanical objectivity," in which the supposedly objective gaze of mechanism replaced the subjective gaze of the human observer. Advocates of fingerprinting tapped this rhetoric to suggest that mechanical reproduction made fingerprint records more objective than anthropometric measurements. "The print of a finger," one journalist noted in 1909, "is a document complete in itself." Similarly, the Boston Police Department justified its switch from Bertillonage to fingerprinting in 1910 by claiming that "as the digits *record themselves* there are no inaccuracies."[45]

At the same time, supporters of fingerprinting could capitalize on the emerging rhetoric of industrialization. Machines were performing ever more tasks in modern society. By emphasizing the mechanical nature of fingerprint identification, dactyloscopers could portray fingerprinting as fashionably modern. Police officials compared the process of recording fingerprints to emerging technologies of duplication, such as the letter press, carbon paper, "the message-recording machine, the machine that sets type and the press that prints thousands of copies to the hour." Like these technologies, fingerprinting promised to provide more accurate, and faster, representation by eliminating the human element from copy work. In short, fingerprinting seemed like part and parcel of the new, rationalized bureaucracies, scientific management, mass production, Progressive era technocracy, and, as DePue put it, "the general systematization of trade and industry and methodization of government." "The fingerprint system," Joseph Faurot said in 1921, "reduced identification to a method of bookkeeping."[46]

Anthropometry looked like science; fingerprinting looked like technology. Anthropometry was observational; fingerprinting was mechanical. Anthropometry evoked the rigors of scientific observation; fingerprinting evoked the efficiencies of mass production. Anthropometry was performed by skilled workers, trained through apprenticeship; the recording of fingerprints was performed by unskilled hastily trained workers (though skilled workers performed the classification). Advocates of anthropometry emphasized quality, measuring identification in scientific terms, according to the accuracy and consistency of the data; dactyloscopers emphasized quantity, measuring identification in the language of industrial production, in terms of processing speed, cost, and the size of their bureaus. Anthropometry placed its trust in the conscientious, meticulous, properly trained, disciplined operator; fingerprinting placed its faith in a mechanical process that transferred a bodily inscription onto a paper record. Whereas anthropometry tended to identify people who were like those doing the identifying, white men of European descent, fingerprinting established itself as the means by which "others"—colonial populations, immigrants, people of color, and women—could be drawn into the web of state-sponsored identification. Only later did fingerprinting become a universal identification technique, regardless of gender, race, and social status.

A final perceived advantage of fingerprinting was its evasion of the distorting lens of language. By representing identity as a visual image, fingerprinting avoided Bertillon's translation of the body into numbers and coded abbreviations. Instead, the fingerprint was a language unto itself, a "truly universal language," as Vucetich put it. "'God's fingerprint language,'" Frederic Brayley, author of one of the earliest American fingerprint manuals, called the new technique in 1909, "the voiceless speech, and the indelible writing imprinted on the fingers, hand palms, and foot soles of humanity by the Allwise Creator for some good and useful purpose in the structure, regulation, and well being of the human body."[47]

The rise of fingerprinting represented an important rupture in the visual culture of identification techniques. The photograph, despite all its ambiguities and deceptions and its inability to offer any reference point for classifying, had at least represented the individual human body as a visual image, rather than as a sequence of words and numbers. Bertillon had abstracted human identity, transforming it from a representative, if not necessarily accurate or complete, visual image, such as the photograph, into an alphanumeric expression. But for all the linguistic tricks of Bertillonage, identification, in all three phases of Bertillon's tripartite system, remained a visual act, dependent on the perceptions of human operators. The *portrait parlé*, in which a visual image of the criminal was reconstructed from fractured words and numbers, reveals Bertillon's continuing need to return to the visual. Human identity was still *seen*. In fingerprinting, identity was represented by an abstract image. Mechanical reproduction disciplined the unruly vision of human observers. Fingerprinting signaled a return to the belief that language was too ambiguous to convey with confidence the subtle differences between human forms.

Fingerprinting, therefore, brought identification back to visual imagery, utilizing an image that, though it bore no topographic resemblance to the body it represented, nonetheless was a relatively unmediated visual image of at least a portion of that body. Fingerprint records actually touched the body of the criminal, whereas anthropometric records were mediated by a human observer. A person's fingerprint, John Henry Wigmore, the leading U.S. scholar on legal evidence, famously asserted in 1923, "is not testimony about his body, but his body itself."[48]

I at first had little faith in this expert evidence, but after the experiment conducted by Lieutenant Faurot in the court-room, in the presence of the Court and jury . . . when he was able to designate the person who made the imprint on the glass, I became satisfied that there is something to this science.

—Judge Otto A. Rosalsky, sentencing hearing, *People of the State of New York v. Carlo Crispi* (1911)

CHAPTER 7

Bloody Fingerprints and Brazen Experts

Early dactyloscopers did not conceive of fingerprint identification as a forensic technique, for solving crimes by linking criminals to evidence left at crime scenes. Instead, they viewed fingerprinting as a record-keeping technology, a way of linking bodies in custody to their criminal records. Forensic use of fingerprinting developed later, and it was considered only a fringe benefit of the fingerprint system of criminal identification. Forensic fingerprint identification was a more delicate task than recordkeeping. It required establishing the uniqueness of every *single* fingerprint in the world, rather than the uniqueness of every person's *set of ten* fingerprints. In most cases, moreover, it required establishing the uniqueness even of *partial* single fingerprints, small fragments of ridge detail. Furthermore, forensic identification could actually decide a defendant's guilt or innocence, rather than merely determine whether or not a defendant had been arrested before. Besides the uniqueness of all single fingerprints in the world and all partial fingerprint fragments, it required establishing that fingerprint examiners could reliably match crime-scene fingerprints to one and only one source finger.

In early-twentieth-century criminal trials the status of forensic fingerprint evidence was similar to that of DNA evidence today. Scientists, prosecutors, and the police touted it as a miraculous demonstration of the power of science to find the truth. They suggested that fingerprinting could transform criminal justice by basing it on a stronger form of truth. Defendants, defense attorneys, some judges, and a handful of skeptics, meanwhile, contended that fingerprinting was dangerous because it rested on a shaky scientific foundation (anthropometry was still viewed as more scientific than fingerprinting) and yet it was prone to mislead juries with its exaggerated claims to scientific certainty. Even more serious was the charge that it was vulnerable to misuse and abuse by the police because of lack of training, sloppy or rushed procedures, and desire to convict the accused. As with DNA today, the general public was somewhere in the middle, swayed by the authority of "science" but still wary of entrusting it with weighty legal decisions.

The history of forensic fingerprint identification began with the Albany, New York, detective John Maloy, who performed the earliest known forensic fingerprint identification sometime around 1856. The idea of using bloody fingerprints to investigate crimes also occurred to Thomas Taylor, Henry Faulds, and Mark Twain in the late nineteenth century. Faulds solved a small mystery in the embassy compound in Tokyo in the 1870s, and Twain used a bloody fingerprint as a plot device in *Life on the Mississippi* in 1883. These cases all involved visible fingerprints left in blood. In 1888, however, a Prussian veterinarian, Wilhelm Eber, suggested using what would later be called "latent" prints: invisible fingerprints left on "doorhandles, glasses or other objects suitable for picking up and leaving behind a handprint," which are developed using a dusting powder to expose traces left by the oily secretions of the fingertip. In 1892 the French legal physician René Forgeot reported experiments on the development of latent prints. Forgeot compared latent and inked prints by enlarging them and enhancing the ridge lines, resulting in a "plate and exhibit" which would be "palpable and explanatory for a jury." In that same year Francis Galton proposed that fingerprints might be matched by comparing corresponding "minutiae," or ridge characteristics.[1]

The earliest forensic identification in Europe occurred in 1902, when the Paris police found a bloody fingerprint at the scene of the strangling of a valet in a dentist's office on the Rue du Faubourg Saint Honoré. Alphonse Bertillon, in addition to running the Department of Judicial Identity, was the Paris prefecture's resident expert on all matters of criminalistics, including crime-scene investigation, and he photographed the bloody fingerprint. Since Bertillon had recently added a space for fingerprints to his identification cards, it was possible to search for a matching fingerprint in his card file. The fingerprint matched that of a recently released convict named Scheffer, whom neighbors then identified as having been a frequent visitor to the victim. Some commentators have found it ironic that it was Bertillon, the founder and leading proponent of the anthropometric identification system which would eventually be displaced by fingerprinting, who made this identification, but in fact it is not at all surprising. Bertillon was never opposed to using fingerprints for forensics, he only opposed *classifying* criminal records according to fingerprints. As in the Rojas case in Argentina in 1892, a trial was avoided, because Scheffer, faced with the fingerprint evidence and eyewitness identification, confessed.[2]

Francis Galton originally believed that fingerprint evidence could be evaluated by untrained laypersons, and that "expert opinions will be required for blurred fingerprints" only "until everybody becomes familiar with fingerprints." Galton was not alone in this belief, as was evident in *Emperor v. Abdul Hamid*, a 1905 impersonation case in India. An expert witness testified that two fingerprints matched, which implied a guilty verdict—but the jury acquitted the defendant. Questioning the jurors, the trial judge learned that they had simply not accepted the opinion of the expert. Finding this verdict "perverse," he referred the case to a higher court. The appeals court, however, sided with the jury. Even more ominously for fingerprint examiners, the appellate justices fancied themselves just as competent as the expert at comparing the two prints. One of them, Justice Henderson, reported having "myself subjected the impressions to a careful study both with the naked eye and a magnifying glass" and professed himself "unable to say more, than that in some respects a distinct similarity can be traced." "Under these circumstances," he concluded, "I should hesitate to say that the jury was wrong in not accepting the evidence of the expert." Henderson assumed that similarities which were "far from clear" to him must also be indistinct to the expert. A second appeals judge, Justice Geidt, conceded that "the classification of finger impressions is a science requiring study" and that "it may require an expert in the first instance to say whether any two finger impressions are identical." "Yet," he cautioned, "the reasons which guide him to this conclusion are such as may be weighed by any intelligent person with good power of eyesight." "I have examined these impressions for myself with the aid of a magnifying glass," he added, "and endeavored to test the subinspector's reasons. Considering the difficulty I have in perceiving the marks, I can not say that the jury were wrong in declining to regard him as an expert."[3]

In *Abdul Hamid* there was no expertise. Each actor was considered just as competent as any other to interpret fingerprint evidence. In a sense this lived up to Galton's original vision of fingerprinting. The future of the technique turned out to be just the opposite. After a brief period in which jurors and judges felt they had the epistemological authority to question the judgments of experts, the interpretation of fingerprint evidence became the exclusive domain of experts. In part this came about because identification bureau clerks sought professional jurisdiction over the interpretation of latent fingerprint evidence and jealously guarded it against all rivals. In part, however, it came about because latent fingerprint identification is not as easy as it looks. There is a world of difference between a clean inked fingerprint, taken carefully and methodically at a police station, and a latent fingerprint, left by accidental contact on some surface at the scene of a crime. Latent prints are blurred, smudged, overlaid upon one another, incomplete, and distorted by foreign particles and dirt. The analysis of latent fingerprints requires a great deal of interpretation and inference as to how the evidence took on the appearance that it has. Did the perpetrator touch the object only once, or twice, a "double tap"? The latent print examiner must also distinguish between "signal" and "noise," to use modern terminology: which lines are impressions of ridges and which are caused by background, dirt, or some other foreign particle? The ability to interpret latent fingerprints is a skill that requires both a certain knack and extensive training, including a lot of time spent looking at fingerprint patterns acquiring an intimate knowledge of how papillary ridges flow and how latent prints appear on different surfaces. Fingerprint evidence is in some sense visually accessible to everyone, but people with experience looking at latent and inked fingerprints can see things that lay observers cannot.

Shortly after fingerprint identification had been established at Scotland Yard in 1901, police officers there began performing forensic identifications. Chief among those officers was Inspector Charles Stockley Collins, who made his first forensic fingerprint identification in a burglary case in 1902. Although "up till then a fair amount of scepticism had been displayed by the public, and even some of the magistrates and judges, surprisingly, there was no strong attack on the fingerprint evidence by the defence." The print was accepted as proof of the accused's physical presence at the scene of the crime and was sufficient to convict him.[4]

Collins next presented fingerprint evidence later that same year in the prosecution of Harry Jackson for the burglary of some billiard balls. Collins matched a print found on a recently painted windowsill with Jackson's inked left thumbprint. Collins testified: "In my opinion it is impossible for any two persons to have any one of the peculiarities I have selected and described." Photographs of the matching prints were displayed to the jury and "examined with much interest." The defense contested the lifelong permanence of the ridges but not the fundamental uniqueness of fingerprints.[5]

In a 1903 burglary case in Windsor, however, the defendant himself offered a somewhat stronger defense, a "spirited protest against a modern innovation": "I must challenge this evidence," he declared. "It is fallacious." Referring to the Scheffer case or perhaps confusing fingerprinting with anthropometry, the defendant inaccurately denounced fingerprinting as "an importation from France," which, he predicted, "will cause as much mischief here as it has done there, where many innocent men have been convicted because of it." "It is not English," he proclaimed patriotically. "It is not evidence." "There are too many decimals," he went on, perhaps referring to the Henry system of classification with its complicated numerical formulas. "It is too hazy. English people do not like it."[6]

That defendant's view was vindicated somewhat in early 1905, when a skeptical jury acquitted another defendant who had fingerprint evidence against him. Such evidence was still unfamiliar enough that the jury was hesitant to use it as a basis for conviction. The frustrated magistrate could do little more than "rebuke" the jury, warning the accused that "the jury, fortunately for you, did not know, as I now do, the absolute identification of your fingerprints possessed by Scotland Yard, where they are remarkably well known."[7]

It took a murder trial, the famous "Deptford Murder Trial," to air many of the legal issues surrounding fingerprint evidence. Two brothers, Alfred and Albert Stratton, were accused of murdering a Deptford couple who managed an art supply shop, Thomas and Ann Farrow, during a robbery on the night of March 26, 1905. Scotland Yard detectives matched a bloody fingerprint found on a cash box at the scene to that of Alfred Stratton. The Yard dispatched Inspector Collins to make the identification and to testify for the Crown at the Old Bailey. Collins showed the jury the two prints and pointed out eleven matching ridge characteristics which led him to conclude that the bloody fingerprint on the cash box must have been left by Alfred Stratton.[8]

Collins's method of latent fingerprint identification consisted of finding and labeling matching ridge characteristics, or "points of similarity," between the questioned and the known print. For example, a ridge ending or bifurcation in the latent print would be labeled (1), and the corresponding ridge ending or bifurcation in the inked print would also be labeled (1). In this case, Collins then proceeded through ten more matching "points." This method had been inspired by Galton's idea of matching minutiae. There was nothing magical about the number eleven. Precisely how much matching ridge detail was enough to warrant concluding that the latent print must come from Stratton to the exclusion of all others had not been clearly articulated. When asked this question, however, Collins answered that four matching characteristics would be sufficient to declare an identification. His basis for this number was that, in his experience examining fingerprints at Scotland Yard, he had seen different fingerprints with three matching ridge characteristics but none with four.

To oppose Collins, the defense retained Henry Faulds as an advisor and John Garson to testify. Faulds had been one of the pioneers of the British system of fingerprint identification. Garson had headed Scotland Yard's Anthropometric Office in the 1890s and had opposed the Yard's switchover to fingerprinting in 1901. At the trial Garson employed a shrewd strategy: he conceded the efficacy of fingerprinting as a forensic technique in theory while imputing sloppy practice to the Yard's detectives in this particular case. Garson testified that dactyloscopy "was a splendid means of identification when properly used, but that it required careful use, that he had no hesitation in saying *that the way in which it was being used by the police was just that which would bring it into disrepute.*" This was the same strategy employed almost a century later in the O. J. Simpson trial: Simpson's defense largely conceded the validity of DNA typing in principle but claimed that its application by the Los Angeles Police Department had been incompetent and prejudicial. Garson, however, was discovered to have offered his services to both sides in the case, and this was highly damaging to his credibility. Collins's testimony won over the jury, although not the judge. Judge Channell was not yet ready to make the leap from the validity of using inked sets of ten prints for recordkeeping to using partial, latent prints for forensic identification. The judge noted that "when proper impressions are taken, the system is extremely reliable, but it is a different thing to apply it to a casual mark made through the perspiration of a thumb." Judge Channell felt he had to abide by the jury's verdict, though, and he "almost apologetically" sentenced the Stratton brothers to hang.[9]

Henry Faulds sat through the trial without saying a word. It is not clear what impelled him to hold his tongue. But after the trial Faulds launched an attack on the validity of forensic fingerprint identification. Faulds was no opponent of fingerprint identification; he had even performed one of the world's earliest forensic identifications in Tokyo. But while he was enthusiastic about using fingerprints for criminal recordkeeping, he urged extreme caution in using *latent* fingerprints to secure convictions. Like Garson, Faulds sounded a note of scientific caution about what he saw as the haphazard use of the technique by detectives without proper scientific training.

Faulds published a diatribe decrying "the faulty use of this new way of finger-prints" in his *Guide to Finger-Print Identification* (1905). He pointedly contrasted his own scientific background with Collins's lack of scientific training, complaining that dactyloscopy had been taken over by ignorant bureaucrats. In his own career Faulds had witnessed the transformation of dactyloscopy from "a mere curiosity of science too fine for the everyday world" to a widely known bureaucratic technique. Initially those who dealt with fingerprints were scientists like himself and Francis Galton; by 1905 they were police officers like Collins. Whereas dactyloscopy had once been a subject fit only for scientists to study, Faulds complained, "Officials are now becoming rather disposed to . . . treat the matter as one which can be dealt with by subordinate officials untrained in scientific observation. In this current misapprehension lurks some danger to the community." Faulds was concerned that the group of people who were rapidly assuming the mantle of "fingerprint experts" were not only untrained in science but also all employed by the police. Such a community of experts was inevitably biased toward the legitimation of fingerprint evidence and the conviction of those accused of crimes. Faulds believed both traits revealed themselves when Collins testified that four matching ridges characteristics would be sufficient to convict. In Faulds's view, "those who use such language . . . either . . . are unacquainted with the elements of dactylography or have a strong and unwholesome bias toward the reconviction of old criminals whatever the nature of the evidence may be which is alleged in the case."[10]

Just as the idea that experts should have authority over fingerprint evidence was becoming established, Faulds raised the question of who the fingerprint expert should be. Should it be a scientist like Faulds himself or Garson, or a detective like Collins? How much scientific knowledge was necessary to interpret fingerprint evidence? It required no scientific training at all to gain the visual acuity to analyze, interpret, compare, and testify about fingerprint evidence. Actually studying the question of how much matching ridge detail would be necessary to confidently link a latent print to one person to the exclusion of all others, in contrast, would have required a great deal of scientific training, and no one was undertaking this kind of inquiry.

But Faulds's critique did not end there. He went on to challenge the fundamental premise of dactyloscopy: "The imaginative journalist may contend that the popular,—once philosophic, fiction, that no two fingers can be alike (for purposes of identification) is a sober fact of the highest scientific certainty, but the only proof of it is seemingly the same 'fact' repeated in other words—that Scotland Yard by its system of classification has never been able *to find* two fingers alike; or rather, when looked into, that the system does not permit them to be found even supposing them to be there." Faulds was alluding to the fact that the Yard used the Henry system, which classified fingerprint cards according to the aggregate patterns of all ten fingers. If two people *did* have identical patterns in single fingers but the other nine fingers showed different patterns, the Henry system would not expose the two identical prints. Real research on whether any two single fingerprints were alike would have required a "single-print" classification system, which did not yet exist. The Yard's inability to find duplicates only suggested that, according to the data gathered thus far, there were no two *complete sets* of ten fingerprints alike. This argument was fine for criminal recordkeeping, but it was less useful for legitimating forensic matches, which were often based on a single print and usually a partial print at that.[11]

Therefore, while Faulds strongly favored the use of inked ten-prints for criminal recordkeeping, he was extremely skeptical of the use of latent fingerprints, which he insisted on calling "smudges," for forensic identification. "There is no miraculous efficacy in the single smudge which need lead us to sneer at old and well-tested rules of evidence or methods of procedure," he wrote.

> The ordinary rules of evidence require to be even more diligently and methodically employed in the case of so delicate a method, which officials not scientifically trained are apt to misunderstand or overstrain, in their natural eagerness to secure convictions. "Repeat patterns" in single fingers are often found which come so near, the one to the other, that the least smudginess in the printing of them might easily veil important divergences in one or two lineations, with appalling results. I can hardly emphasize this point too strongly.[12]

In the absence of a single-print filing system designed to find any like prints, proponents of forensic fingerprint identification had little evidence to answer Faulds's argument. Anatomists, meanwhile, could only hypothesize that environmental influences were so numerous and so varied that all fingerprint patterns must be unique. In 1904 Inez Whipple, probably the world's foremost expert in the morphology of fingerprint patterns, attributed individual fingerprint patterns to a combination of "germinal selection" and the effects of pressure on the embryo. Thus the basic pattern was genetic, but the details were environmentally influenced. Hence identical twins had similar, yet different, fingerprints—one of the chief arguments marshaled in support of the uniqueness of all human fingerprints. But the knowledge that identical twins had different fingerprints did not answer the question of how likely it was that two different fingers might produce similar-looking latent fingerprint impressions, with the "appalling results" Faulds mentioned, or the question of how small a latent fingerprint could be without raising the risk of such a misidentification too high.[13]

Meanwhile, the French medico-legalist Balthazard refined Galton's statistical argument for the uniqueness of fingerprints. Around 1910 Balthazard calculated that the odds of finding a duplicate of a print with 17 ridge characteristics would be 1 in 17 billion, enough to ensure positive identification among the current population of the world. The popular press presented Balthazard's calculation in even more dramatic terms. The probability of two fingerprints being alike, *Scientific Amer-*

ican reported, was 1 in 10^{60} or once in every 2×10^{48} years. *Harper's* announced: "Only Once during the Existence of Our Solar System Will Two Human Beings Be Born with Similar Finger Markings." Balthazard's estimate would become a favorite of fingerprint examiners presenting evidence in court.[14]

Probabilistic arguments like Balthazard's, however, were aimed at determining the likelihood of *whole* single fingerprints matching exactly in every particular. They completely overlooked the question relevant to forensic identification, which entailed matching partial fingerprint fragments. This was perhaps too subtle an argument for defense barristers to mount at the time. In *Rex v. Castleton,* a 1909 burglary case, Thomas Castleton's fingerprint was matched to a print found on a candle at the crime scene, the only evidence against him. In Britain's Court of Criminal Appeal, the justice demanded of the defense barrister, "Can the prisoner find anybody whose finger-prints are exactly like his?" The defense, rather than arguing that the print on the candle and Castleton's print were not exactly alike either or asking how likely it might be that the partial print found on the candle would match some other person, merely contended that the defendant "was an associate of thieves, and it may have been that the finger-prints were put there by someone else." The appeals court upheld Castleton's conviction, establishing in law that defendants may be convicted on fingerprint evidence alone. Soon this principle would be established in the United States as well. On February 16, 1912, the State of Illinois hanged a man named Thomas Jennings, who had been convicted for the murder of Clarence Hiller in Chicago. The Jennings case, which was tried in 1910, represented not only the trial of an individual but also a public trial of fingerprinting.[15]

Shortly after midnight on the morning of September 19, 1910, Clarence Halsted was awakened by a man entering his ground-floor bedroom window on Church Street in the Englewood section of Chicago. The man sat on the windowsill and lit a match. When Halsted rose from his bed and grabbed at the intruder, he swung back out the window and fled, but Halsted caught hold of the man's coat pocket, tearing it. At 2:00 A.M. that same night, someone entered the McNabb house, around the corner from Halsted's. The man, described as "tall, broad shouldered, and very dark," approached Mrs. McNabb in bed and "put his hand under her clothes against her bare body." After Mrs. McNabb pushed his hand away and cried out, he fled down the stairs. A few minutes later, the Hillers, neighbors of the McNabbs, also discovered an intruder. Fifteen-year-old Clarice Hiller was awakened by a man holding a lighted match in her bedroom doorway. The man then entered thirteen-year-old Florence's bedroom and pushed up her nightgown and touched her bare body. He then left the room and met the girls' father, Clarence Hiller, in the hall. The two men grappled and rolled down the stairs. At the bottom of the stairs, the intruder shot Hiller once in the neck and once in the chest, killing him almost instantly.

Thomas Jennings, an ex-convict, a Negro "laboring man," was apprehended three-quarters of a mile from the Hillers' house thirteen minutes after the shooting by four off-duty police officers who, unaware of the murder, saw blood on his shirt and found a .38 caliber revolver in his pocket. The revolver contained cartridges which matched those found at the crime scene and bore chemical traces of recent firing, Jennings's coat pocket was torn in a manner consistent with that described by Halsted, and Jennings had fresh cuts that may have been defensive wounds. Jennings contended that he had torn his coat at work, had injured his hand by falling off a streetcar, and had never fired his revolver. None of the witnesses had seen the intruder's face in the dark; they could only describe his build and say he was "a colored man." Nonetheless, Clarence Halsted, Mrs. McNabb, and her daughter Jessie all testified that Jennings looked like the man who had broken into their houses that night. In a manner reminiscent of the West case, then, the Chicago Police Department called in its fingerprint examiners to individualize a "colored" man, whom witnesses could not identify except to say that he was colored. William Evans, who worked for his father Michael Evans at the Chicago Police Department's Bureau of Identification, found finger impressions in the recently dried paint on Hiller's porch railing, and he matched these prints to inked prints taken from Jennings.[16]

Fingerprinting was new enough to warrant an extended debate over its validity as a forensic technique at the trial. Five fingerprint examiners testified as expert witnesses: Michael and William Evans; another Evans son, Edward, formerly of the Bureau of Identification, who had taken prints from Jennings upon an earlier arrest; Edward Foster, chief of the Bureau of Identification of the Canada Dominion Police; and

Mary Holland, head of the U.S. Navy Bureau of Identification. All five had been trained in fingerprint identification by Detective John Ferrier of Scotland Yard at the St. Louis World's Fair. Foster and Holland testified that they had subsequently traveled to London for further instruction and that they had passed proficiency tests at the Yard. All five agreed that the print found in the paint of the porch railing matched Jennings's prints—both those taken on previous arrests and those taken after his most recent arrest. Foster testified that he had never seen two fingerprints with ridge characteristics so "exactly alike." He portrayed the identity of the two prints as a matter of fact rather than interpretation:

Q: In comparing these fingers it is your opinion that the lines in those photographs were made by the same person?
A: I am positive. It is not my opinion.[17]

Although it was reported in the press that one unnamed fingerprint examiner "stated after examining the photographs that the Chicago po-· lice had the wrong man," this examiner was never called to testify by the defense. Instead, the defense tried to undermine the very notion of expertise in fingerprint analysis, along the lines taken in *Abdul Hamid*, contending that "the only benefit that the state can derive from the introduction of the finger prints is for the jury to compare these finger prints without the aid of the opinion of any expert." The defense suggested that "the jury can take the magnifying glass and then come to a conclusion as to whether or not these photographs are identical." Citing "great progress in scientific research and inquiry upon these matters," the judge overruled the defense's objections, concluding that "it is now an established fact that . . . the lines upon one's fingers are different from that of the fingers of any other human being." The court supported its conclusion by analogy: "Just as ones face never resembles quite the face of any other human being."[18]

The Supreme Court of Illinois agreed that "the classification of finger print impressions and their method of identification is a science requiring study" and that, therefore, expert opinion was warranted. Reversing the reasoning followed in *Abdul Hamid*, the court wrote: "While some of the reasons which guide an expert to his conclusions are such as may be weighed by any intelligent person with good eyesight from such exhibits as we have here in the record, after being pointed out to him by one versed in the study of finger prints, the evidence in question does not come within the common experience of all men of common education in the ordinary walks of life, and therefore the court and jury were properly aided by witnesses of peculiar and special experience on this subject."

The court contrasted fingerprint evidence, which required expert interpretation, with footprint evidence, which could be interpreted by jurors: "In view of the knowledge and experience of men in identifying by footprints as compared with their knowledge and experience in identifying finger prints, it is manifest that opinions by experts might be entirely proper as to the latter class of testimony when they would not be with reference to footprints. The jury, if the facts were all stated would be able to draw conclusions as to footprints as well as could expert witnesses."[19]

Though the members of the jury were encouraged to see fingerprint matches "for themselves," fingerprint evidence was not transparent; it required expert interpretation. In the legal literature, the principle was quickly understood: fingerprint evidence was so powerful that it had to be funneled through an expert. "From the scientific standpoint, therefore," one legal commentator noted, "finger prints offer strong evidence of identity, though only properly available in trials through expert testimony." Thus the Jennings case established both the admissibility of fingerprint evidence and the exclusive authority of "experts" to testify for it.

The court relied on the general agreement among authorities, such as legal textbooks and encyclopedias, that fingerprinting was a reliable system of identification. At the time the standard test in American law for whether expert evidence should be admitted was whether the proposed expert had engaged in "greater study respecting certain subjects." The courts did not ask the kinds of questions about the technique's scientific validity that they might ask today. The absence of any credible scientific expert with a skeptical view of fingerprint evidence—Henry Faulds, the most informed potential critic, had squandered his credibility in his self-serving priority dispute with William Herschel—allowed the courts to admit it on the basis of general agreement and anecdotal evidence and discouraged them from subjecting it to the level of scrutiny it merited. Instead, the court simply noted that in England the system had been used "in thousands of cases without error," not realizing that if there had been an error—a innocent person falsely convicted because of faulty fingerprint evidence—there would be no way of knowing it had occurred unless other circumstances exposed the false conviction. The court concluded that "this method of identification is in such general and common use that the courts cannot refuse to take judicial cognizance of it."[20]

Although several jurors told the *Chicago Examiner* that "the fingerprints, and the finger-prints alone, convinced us that Jennings was the slayer of Hiller," other circumstantial evidence had pointed to Jennings as the killer.[21] A more spectacular demonstration of the power of fingerprint evidence took place a few months later in New York City. On the morning of February 22, 1911, the owner of M. M. Bernstein and Brothers, a textile loft at 171 Wooster Street in Manhattan, arrived to find that the premises had been burglarized. The investigating officers noticed a fingerprint on a pane of glass that had been removed during the burglary, and they delivered the pane to the New York Police Department's (NYPD) fingerprint expert, Lieutenant Joseph Faurot. He checked the print against "between 50 and 200" prints in his file of known "loft burglars," and the print matched that of one Carlo Crispi, alias Charles Cella, who had been fingerprinted and photographed in 1907 following an arrest on another burglary charge.

Crispi was a tougher trial for dactyloscopy than *Jennings* because the fingerprint was the sole evidence against the defendant. A number of Crispi's relatives, including his wife, gave him an alibi. As the prosecutor, Isidor Wasservogel, noted in a pretrial memorandum, "this case depends entirely on finger print identification." The prosecution began by trying to "show that the lines upon the hand never change." It introduced as exhibits photographic reproductions of two fingerprints: one taken in 1907 when Crispi was arrested for the previous burglary, the second taken in 1911 when he was arrested for the Wooster Street burglary. On the photographs Faurot labeled sixteen matching ridge characteristics between the two prints.[22]

As in *Jennings*, Crispi's attorney, Robert Moore, objected to the need for expert interpretation of the evidence, contending that the fingerprint impressions "are in evidence and speak for themselves." He suggested that the jury examine the exhibits instead. The prosecution, despite its confidence that fingerprint evidence could "speak for itself," still insisted on having an expert speak for the evidence. Judge Otto Rosalsky allowed Faurot to give expert testimony, noting explicitly that dactyloscopy—unlike handwriting analysis, which by that time had acquired a thoroughly unsavory reputation—required expert interpretation: "It would be idle ceremony simply to put that before this jury without an expert enlightening them. If it were handwriting it would be different. This is a new science. I shall allow it." Faurot testified that "when two clear prints are brought together and are made by the same hand, these characteristics, there is no chance of error, no margin of error." Between Crispi's inked prints and the prints found on the glass, he said, "there are sixteen points of comparison, very marked comparisons, which correspond identically."[23]

The prosecution next tried to introduce into evidence the photographs, anthropometric measurements, and fingerprints of Charles and Frank Terry, a pair of identical twin vaudeville actors the NYPD had enlisted to demonstrate the uniqueness of fingerprints. Moore strenuously objected to this evidence "as incompetent, immaterial, irrelevant and inadmissible in this case," but Rosalsky overruled the objection, reasoning that the evidence would help validate the scientific

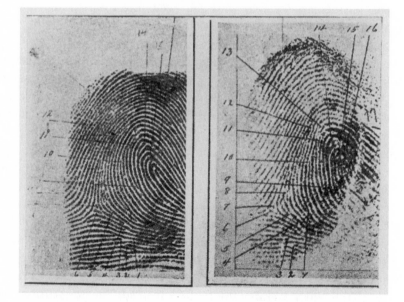

16. Fingerprint "chart" used by Lieutenant Joseph Faurot in *People of the State of New York v. Carlo Crispi*, 1911, comparing an inked print (left) with a latent print taken from a window pane (right).

basis of the new identification technique. "Mr. Moore," he declared, "this is a new science. In our country our law cannot be like a pool, permitted to become stagnant. It has to become flexible and we have to advance in accordance with the times." Not yet beaten, Moore contrasted the new "science" with established identification methods: "I could come here with half a dozen photographs and introduce those in evidence and say that the photographic identification was a stronger one than this. Then I could go a little further and I could bring any man's handwriting into court and say that is the best means of identification and then show them to the jury." He continued, "There might be two other men whose faces would be as unlike as dark and daylight, and their fingerprints might yet be as like as two peas."[24]

Rosalsky, however, allowed the prosecution to exhibit the twins' photographs. "They are two pictures very, very similar," Faurot testified. He then reported the twins' anthropometric measurements: "I measured them from height, that is identical. Their outstretched arms are identical. Their head lengths, that is from the root of the nose to the greatest head length is identical. The head width was two millimeters different. That is very small. It is so small that that is what we allow in error for measurement in deviation between our operators . . . These measurements alone would deceive a Bertillon operator in his research." In contrast, he went on, "The finger prints are different in the two twins. You can readily see, where I take one finger only . . . one is an ulnar loop, and the other is radial loop. In the ulnar loop the ridge lines run one way and in the other man on the same finger they run the opposite way. That one finger alone, that peculiarity will differentiate them." Both the jury and the press gallery apparently found this evidence impressive. The *New York World* reported: "the face and profiles of the twins were identical, as were their Bertillon measurements. The measurements and photographs were passed around to the jurors and they all admitted that they could not tell which was which. Lieutenant Faurot then produced the finger prints of the twins and demonstrated to the jury how simple it was to tell the two apart."[25]

The Terry twins were strongly reminiscent of the fictional identical twins Angelo and Luigi Cappello whose different prints demonstrated the power of fingerprinting in Mark Twain's *Pudd'nhead Wilson*. And Faurot's borrowing from Twain did not end there. He went on to perform a demonstration very much like the one in the climactic trial scene of the novella. Faurot left the room and William Haley, his assistant, took inked fingerprints from a dozen jurors and courtroom personnel. The prosecution then asked one of the dozen to grasp the windowpane from the loft that had been admitted into evidence. Again Moore objected, "for the reason that it is impossible to produce this experiment under the circumstances similar to the case at bar." The prints taken from the crime scene, Moore pointed out, "are crossed over and superimposed, one upon the other, and it does not make a complete and perfect hand." He suggested that the court was creating pristine experimental conditions unlike the messy state of the crime scene. In the end, the judge instructed the subject to pick up the pane of glass several different times and let it slip from his hands in order to emulate the superimposed effect visible in the evidence. Over Moore's heated objections, Faurot successfully completed his demonstration. He returned and correctly matched a single print with its owner.[26]

Despite having established his expertise in such dramatic fashion, Faurot invited the jury to share in the process of matching the fingerprints. Not wishing to squander a powerful visual image, he distributed enlargements of the evidence to the jurors so that "they can readily see for themselves." Thus jurors were encouraged to feel not only that they had witnessed the expert making the identification but also that they had witnessed the match.[27]

After hearing Faurot's evidence, Crispi decided to change his plea to guilty. Judge Rosalsky, not wanting to squander an opportunity to test the persuasiveness of fingerprint evidence, polled the jury as to whether they would have convicted Crispi on the basis of the fingerprint evidence offered. Several jurors indicated that they would not have convicted Crispi on fingerprint evidence alone. Rosalsky then asked Crispi to testify as to whether he had really committed the burglary.

THE COURT: Crispi, I want you to make a full confession. I can assure you that no indictment will be found against you or against any witnesses for perjury which may have been committed in the course of your trial, but I want you to make honest and truthful statements. It is important to the cause of justice that you do so. It is important to the cause of science to know whether or not the expert testimony is valuable or valueless. Finger-print experts are of the opinion that this science is more exact than photography, and that experts are able to identify persons by finger prints with a greater degree of ac-

curacy than under any other system of identification. Did you re-
move the pane of glass which was offered in evidence here?

THE DEFENDANT: Yes, sir.[28]

Rosalsky thus turned the trial into a test of the validity of fingerprinting, but in order to do so he had to rely on the honesty of a convicted criminal. He thus put the defendant in the curious position of
testing the expert witness. More convincing even than Faurot's dramatic demonstration was Crispi's confession. "Crispi," the judge told
the defendant, "the fact that you pleaded guilty demonstrates beyond
any doubt that Lieutenant Faurot was right in his conclusions." Satisfied that he had validated an exciting new science, Rosalsky scolded
the jurors who had been loath to convict. He told them: "Out of one
hundred and fifty thousand finger prints examined by these experts,
they find no two similar. Now, in handwriting we find similar characteristics, and also in photography, but in this science, the experts agree
that there are no two persons whose finger prints are alike, and that is
certainly marvelous." Rosalsky, citing Crispi's "great service to the
cause of justice and science," handed down a rather light sentence of
six months.[29]

Rosalsky's enthusiasm was somewhat premature, though, as indicated
by the unwillingness of some jurors to convict Crispi on fingerprint evidence alone. A few months later Faurot's testimony failed to sway a
jury in a Jersey City burglary case. Lay opinion remained divided, even
after the Jennings and Crispi cases. Crispi's attorney was one convert
to the new science. Several months after the trial Robert Moore told
the *New York World:* "Fingerprint evidence is absolutely conclusive. It
is the most sure, deadly evidence that has ever been found. In time lawyers and courts will be educated up to this belief . . . It is a much surer
method of identification than the photograph or even the Bertillon
measurement system."[30]

Other defense attorneys were less credulous than Moore. John
McIntyre, defense counsel for a murder suspect in New York City later
that year, denounced fingerprint evidence as "conjectural and speculative." He told the *World:* There is nothing certain about the method.
Atmospheric changes play an important part. They can either contract or expand the marks left by the finger . . . Finger-prints are most

dangerous and unreliable. The lines in fingers and hands are too closely alike for any one to assert that he can positively identify the impress of one man's finger from those of all the other fingers in the world. It is absurd. To introduce finger-prints as evidence means simply juggling with the lives and liberty of human beings. I do not believe any American jury would think of condemning a man on such evidence.[31]

Although latent fingerprints degrade fairly quickly when exposed to open air, McIntyre's suggestion that atmospheric changes might actually alter a latent fingerprint's appearance was unfounded. His point that partial fingerprint fragments might be mistaken for one another had merit, though. But defense attorneys like McIntyre and Moore did not even attempt to articulate this argument in court. It is clear that they would have benefited from the advice of a defense expert familiar with the technical aspects of dactyloscopy. But almost the only people with such expertise at that time were law enforcement officials who were hardly likely to work for the defense. Fingerprint evidence won acceptance without being subjected to the kind of organized skepticism and careful scrutiny that is supposed to be inflicted upon scientific and legal facts. The lone expert with a skeptical attitude remained Henry Faulds, who had published books full of inflammatory statements about the reliability of latent fingerprinting. Faulds did offer a critique that might have given support to a defense attorney striving to impeach the credibility of fingerprint evidence.

One of the few cases on record in which the defense drew upon Faulds's critique was the 1915 Albany murder trial *People v. Roach*. In Palatine Bridge, New York, a farmer named John Barrett was shot and bludgeoned to death on the night of December 20, 1913. The police arrested a farmhand named Lewis Roach. Adding to the mystery of the case was the fact that Roach's attorney, Andrew Nellis, was the father-in-law of one George Potter, who was originally implicated in the murder with Roach. Nellis appears to have convinced Roach to recant his story implicating Potter and then taken over his defense. It is possible that Nellis's goal was to see his own client, Roach, convicted and hanged before he could again implicate his son-in-law. However, this is not apparent from the trial transcript, which shows that Nellis mounted a vigorous defense. Some blurry, bloody fingerprints and a handprint were found at the scene. The local authorities delivered these items to Edward Parke, son of James Parke, who had introduced fingerprinting to American penal institutions at the New York State Identification Bureau. Parke, unable to match the fingerprints, unwisely attempted to link the suspect to the crime using the *size* of his hand. Because of the speculative nature of this method of identification, plus his bombastic claims to be the leading fingerprint expert in America, Parke found himself subjected to a severe and humiliating grilling on cross-examination.[32]

The prosecution then called a better-qualified forensic expert, Albert Hamilton. Nellis's cross-examination of Hamilton illustrates the kind of questioning that might have produced reasonable doubt and ultimately tempered the credibility of forensic fingerprint evidence. Nellis introduced Faulds's *Guide to Finger-Print Identification* as an authority on the subject. Taking his cue from Faulds, Nellis referred to the latent print as a "smudge" when cross-examining Hamilton:

Q: Now, is it a fact that even that smudge K, or that you call it a finger print K, I will call it so too in my questions to you,—is it not a fact that that finger print K is limited in area and is hazy and blurred in some parts?

A: Some parts, yes.

Q: It certainly is limited in area, isn't it?

A: Right.[33]

In this exchange Nellis begins to scratch around some of the crucial problems with latent fingerprint identification, problems that were usually ignored in the obsession over the rather less relevant question of whether any two complete, inked fingerprints are exactly alike: the poor quality and fragmentary nature of latent prints.

Although the jury found Roach guilty of murder, Nellis had managed to introduce a voice of skepticism that might have led a jury to find reasonable doubt. Why didn't more defense attorneys try to use Faulds's critique in this way? Faulds certainly made himself a resource for such arguments. In 1923 he again acknowledged that *ten-print* identification had "immense evidential strength," but he insisted that *single-print* identifications rested upon an unproven premise: "It is useless to tell us that no two fingers can ever be found alike. This is pure dogma, based on fictitious experience, and cannot be a true deduction from evidence, especially when we take into account the ambiguity of some patterns due to imperfect printing." The last point reflected Faulds's deep distrust of the Yard's techniques for developing and interpreting latent prints, which, throughout his life, he continued to call "dactyloids" or "smudges."[34]

By this time, however, Faulds's dispute with William Herschel and Scotland Yard over his role in the history of fingerprinting had become so vituperative that it was relatively easy to portray him as an embittered old crank. Faulds himself played into this role by linking the two issues in an exchange with Herschel in the journal *Nature* in 1917. While Herschel gracefully acknowledged Faulds's contribution to fingerprint history, Faulds displayed no such tact. "A most curious confusion has arisen from an original police blunder that no two single finger print patterns are ever alike," he wrote, "for which, I think, Sir William himself is mainly responsible. I am quite sure that there is no scientific basis for such an assertion." The priority dispute, which—carried on by a protégé on behalf of Faulds's daughters—would last into the 1950s, made Faulds seem like nothing more than a self-aggrandizing egomaniac and distracted attention from the more valid points he raised. While mainstream fingerprint examiners were speaking effectively on behalf of the assertion that "no two fingerprints are alike," Faulds, for all his fiery rhetoric, was proving a singularly ineffective spokesman for skepticism.[35]

Faulds's criticisms were not answered so much as successfully ignored. He failed to rally the scientific community to his cause. Scientists were losing interest in fingerprinting and moving on to other areas of research, and police examiners quickly filled the void. There were a few opponents of fingerprinting, including the radical journalist John Beffel, who, along with the fingerprint "forger" Albert Wehde, launched a scathing attack on the methodology of fingerprinting in a 1924 tract entitled *Finger-Prints Can Be Forged*. Besides raising the issue of forgery, Beffel dismissed the "doctrine of infallibility" as "dogma" based on mere rote repetition of Galton and Balthazard's statistics. He portrayed fingerprint examiners as self-interested, obligated, by interest in preserving their own livelihood, to defend the validity of fingerprint identification against all challenges. Beffel and Wehde, however, were unabashed political radicals and, like Faulds, easy to dismiss as marginal critics. Yet their forgotten objections would remain relevant in cases where police motives and actions became suspect.[36]

By the end of the 1920s the moment for challenging forensic fingerprint identification had been lost. The fundamental premises of latent fingerprint identification had been largely established in the absence of any organized, credible scientific challenge. Also established was the exclusive authority of a self-anointed group of professional fingerprint examiners to interpret fingerprint evidence. Even with its premises widely accepted, however, the technique was still only as good as the fallible human examiners who performed the latent print analysis and comparisons. In coming years, debates about latent fingerprint identification would focus less on its fundamental premises and more on the examiners themselves. Issues of competence, and even malfeasance, on the part of fingerprint examiners would become the center of attention.

It might well be that until a juryman witnessed this demonstration he would never believe that a plain porcelain slab would reveal the incriminating finger print, but having seen their own finger prints developed from invisible impressions on sheets of paper, it was no longer a question of speculation; it was to the jurymen a fact as commonplace as radium or wireless or flying in the air.

—R. N. French, Counsel for the State,
Charles Moon v. State of Arizona (1921)

CHAPTER 8

Dazzling Demonstrations and Easy Assumptions

On the morning of September 7, 1919, John Treu arrived at his butcher shop in Bisbee, Arizona, to discover that his safe and cash register had been burglarized overnight. The sheriff, who "had previous experience with finger printing," found the prints of four fingers on a porcelain slab in front of the cash register. Though some of the prints were illegible, one, which by its position appeared to come from the ring finger of a right hand, was "exceptionally perfect." The sheriff also found a bloody piece of what appeared to be human skin "adhering to a closet door situated alongside the safe which had been broken open." Searching the town, the sheriff's officers arrested a man with an injured hand. The man, Charles Moon, agreed to be fingerprinted, and fingerprint examiners matched his print with a photograph of the print found at the crime scene.

At Moon's trial, which took place on November 20–25, five expert witnesses testified. All five agreed that the "finger print impressions of the defendant corresponded exactly with the finger print impressions appearing upon the porcelain slab of the cash register." They asserted that "never in the world were there two sets that exactly corresponded." They also described a fingerprint as "an unforgeable signature," and, quoting the author Frederick Brayley, as "part of the plan of the Creator for the ultimate elimination of crime . . . in the discovering and identification of lawbreakers."

The prosecution, not sure that this testimony would convince the jury, petitioned the court to allow one of its expert witnesses, the Los Angeles fingerprint examiner E. N. Sanders, to perform a demonstration like the one in the Crispi case. Unlike Joseph Faurot in that case, who matched jurors' inked fingerprints, Sanders matched twenty-four *latent* fingerprints, which he developed, using fingerprint powder, after jurors pressed their fingertips on cardboard. Sanders correctly identified all but one, which he deemed illegible. A juror later admitted to making the illegible print intentionally "for the purpose of convincing himself if" the fingerprint expert "knew [his] business." The jury convicted Moon of burglary.

On appeal, Moon argued that the judge should not have allowed this demonstration. The state countered that the demonstration had convinced the jury, in a way that words never could, that latent fingerprint identification was possible. "To a layman," the state argued, "unsophisticated and incredulous, the idea that a finger laid on a clean sheet of paper, leaving no visible trace, thereby leaves a signature upon that paper, absolutely and positively is a fact startling enough, but to see that finger print developed under the finger print powder is a demonstration impressive and convincing." The state was not confident that the testimony of experts alone could convince a jury: "It might well be that until a juryman witnessed this demonstration he would never believe that a plain porcelain slab would reveal the incriminating finger print, but having seen their own finger prints developed from invisible impressions on sheets of paper, it was no longer a question of speculation." The state compared fingerprinting to other recent technological advances that at first had seemed wildly fantastic but had soon become familiar. After the demonstration, the state contended, fingerprinting "was to the jurymen a fact as commonplace as radium or wireless or flying in the air."

The Supreme Court of Arizona agreed that the fundamental premise of latent fingerprint identification—the uniqueness of all human fingerprints—was questionable enough to warrant a visual demonstration of its truth. "To most of us," the justices reasoned, "it is very hard to conceive that there cannot be two fingers that are exactly alike." The Court also agreed that the mere words of expert witnesses were unlikely to convince the skeptical: "The evidentiary value of the abstract explanation of the methods of the system of developing finger print impressions given by the expert witnesses was probably difficult for the jury to grasp." A demonstration, however, might "illustrate the methods of the system of finger print identification and the truth of the claim that invisible finger prints can be developed and identity of the maker revealed by simple process to positive certainty."[1]

In *Moon* yet another court had upheld fingerprint examiners' right to perform courtroom demonstrations. The fingerprint community hailed Sanders's demonstration as a heroic achievement. The editors of the newly founded *Finger Print and Identification Magazine*—fingerprint examiners' first trade journal, which symbolized the growth of the profession—dubbed the trial The Great Cochise County Finger-Print Trial. "Nothing like it has ever been attempted before in or out of court," they crowed. "Mr. Sanders deserves great credit for the cool way in which he went about his work and successfully accomplished what might be considered by finger-print experts as being 'impossible.'" At the same time, another consideration tempered the editors' enthusiasm. They complained that such demonstrations should no longer be necessary; they argued that the reliability of forensic fingerprint evidence should no longer be *demonstrated*, but *assumed*. "We call this test unfair, because there have been enough finger-print cases successfully prosecuted to have thoroughly proven the reliability of finger-print evidence," they declared, and they expressed hope that such a demonstration "may never occur again." In making this argument, professional fingerprint examiners were seeking to shift the locus of credibility from the specific, demonstrated competence of the individual examiner to the general reliability of the technique of latent fingerprint identification.[2]

The reliability of the technique, however, depended on the competence of individual examiners, as illustrated by the Loomis case, which occurred shortly after The Great Cochise County Finger-Print Trial. Robert Loomis was accused of murdering Bertha Myers while burglarizing her home in Easton, Pennsylvania, in 1918. At trial, in 1920, two expert witnesses for the prosecution testified that a fingerprint found on a tin jewelry box matched Loomis's inked print. The defense, "being without knowledge of the district attorney's intention to introduce such evidence, produced no expert testimony in reply." Still, the defense managed to impeach the testimony of at least one of the expert witnesses, an employee of the Scranton office of the American Express Company named Goff. An observer reported that Goff's "knowledge of the science of classifying finger-prints was ridiculed and discarded, and later investigation proved that he was putting over a fraud, and Goff was declared a fraud, by men who know the science of reading finger-prints." The jury convicted Loomis anyway, but the Pennsylvania Supreme Court ordered a new trial on the grounds that the trial judge's instructions to the jury had been biased against the defendant.

By the time of Loomis's second trial the following year, the prosecution had changed its mind about the fingerprint evidence, "admitting that the mark was not that of Loomis." Following this turn of events, it was the defense that sought to introduce fingerprint evidence at the second trial—with the aim of showing that someone else had handled the box. Although the defense was allowed to demonstrate that the fingerprint did *not* match that of Loomis, the trial judge again tainted the jury in his instruction, by stressing that the fingerprint evidence could be used only to impeach the credibility of an eyewitness (an alleged co-conspirator), not to establish reasonable doubt. The Pennsylvania Supreme Court again determined that the judge's instructions had prejudiced the jury (which had again convicted Loomis), and again reversed the conviction. The Court pointed out that if fingerprint evidence can establish guilt it must also be able to establish reasonable doubt: "If weight is to be given finger-print testimony, then the jury, in passing upon the guilt of Loomis, would be justified in taking into consideration the fact that someone else handled the box either at or about the time of the murder." The record does not explain what convinced the prosecution that the fingerprint did not belong to Loomis, but both Goff and the other expert had clearly overstepped the bounds of certainty by declaring a match—a match that had helped secure a conviction—which could not be sustained under closer scrutiny.[3]

The Loomis case demonstrated the need for some sort of policing of latent fingerprint identification. In order to maintain the credibility of the technique, it would be necessary to protect it against both the kind of marginal match declared in the Loomis trial and the marginal "experts," like the hapless Goff, who made them. How much corresponding ridge detail was necessary to warrant a declaration of a match between a latent and an inked print had still not been clearly defined. If the area of corresponding detail was small enough, the examiner would clearly be venturing out of the realm of certainty and into the realm of conjecture. But there was neither a set of rules for defining the boundary between certainty and conjecture nor an institutional mechanism for policing examiners. The courts, which were becoming increasingly trusting of fingerprint evidence, were loath to provide the necessary scrutiny of fingerprint examiners or their conclusions. The policing of fingerprint identification would have to come from within the field itself.

The people who first took up fingerprinting in the United States were mostly "Bertillon clerks" who oversaw the taking of anthropometric measurements and the completing and filing of Bertillon cards. Some were police officers, others were civilian employees of police departments, prisons, or courts. They presided over vast archives of criminal records, the exotic and impressive-looking anthropometric measuring instruments, and, in large agencies, a handful of subordinates. As knowledge of the Henry system began to disseminate through American police departments and prisons, police chiefs and wardens naturally put these Bertillon clerks in charge of testing or implementing fingerprint classification systems. Learning to record inked fingerprints required very little training. Any law enforcement agency that wanted to index its own archive of criminal records according to the Henry system, however, needed at least one person trained in the Henry system of classification.

This was a far more difficult undertaking, especially if the novice examiner was learning entirely from a manual with no personal instruction at all. Learning to classify fingerprints required, first, that the novice spend a great deal of time looking at fingerprints, so as to become visually oriented around fingerprint patterns, and, second, careful study of Henry's intricate rules of classification. As they had been with anthropometry, the clerks were mostly self-taught, learning from books like Henry's *Classification and Uses of Finger Prints* or a host of new American instruction manuals that began to appear during the 1910s, such as *Brayley's Arrangement of Finger Prints* (1909), Lee Seymour's *Finger Print Classification* (1913), and Frederick Kuhne's *The Finger Print Instructor* (1917). Even police departments were primarily interested in using fingerprints to index criminal records; latent fingerprint identification was a mere sideline to the real work of maintaining a criminal record archive. Only the most zealous identification clerks trained themselves in latent fingerprint identification, and only those in the largest cities gained enough experience looking at and working with latent prints to become really expert in the subject. Years of training and experience were necessary before an identification clerk could properly be considered a "fingerprint expert."

In 1916 Thomas G. Cooke founded a correspondence school for fingerprint instruction, the University of Applied Science (UAS), in Chicago. The UAS taught fingerprint classification, answered students' questions, and administered tests by mail. Law enforcement agencies soon came to rely on the UAS to supplement their own training efforts or even to provide the primary instruction. Again, the emphasis was on the Henry system of classification; analysis of latent fingerprints was an added topic for advanced students. The UAS, soon renamed the Institute for Applied Science (IAS), portrayed fingerprinting as an easy avenue to professional status for young people without a college education. A diploma from the IAS, it claimed, "is to the finger-print man what a Johns Hopkins diploma is to the physician; what a Harvard Law School diploma is to the lawyer." The IAS used the prestige of the professions in the Progressive era to promote fingerprinting. Here is what a 1920 promotional brochure had to say:

> This is the age of the man who knows—the trained expert. There are many fields in which after long years of preparation, and a big outlay of money, you can become a professional and begin to climb to the top, where there are waiting for you $2,500–$10,000 Incomes. But in what profession is it possible for you to step right out of college prepared to accept a position that places you in the chair of authority, that gives you at one stroke all the privileges and advantages of the respected specialist? Not Medicine. Not the Law. Not the Church. Not Engineering. Not Teaching. Not Finance. Not any profession—except the Profession of Identification, or Finger Print Expert.[4]

But the IAS did not just appeal to "the *man* who knows." Dactyloscopy offered a way to overcome the inequalities imposed by gender as well as by education. "Women can enter this profession with equal chance of making a brilliant success," the Institute's advertisements promised. Ever since Mary Holland had joined John Ferrier's first cadre of fingerprint examiners trained in the United States in 1904, women had had a significant presence in the professional fingerprint community. Although some dactyloscopers, such as Henry DeForest, claimed that women had better aptitude for the work owing to their "brains" and "attention to detail," the appearance of women in identification bureaus probably had as much to do with the more general feminization of clerical work at the time. Holland had introduced fingerprinting to the U.S. Navy, and she became the foremost fingerprint trainer in the country. Clara Parsons became chief of the Identification Division of the New York State Bureau of Prisons in 1914, and she was "not the only woman to occupy the position of head of an identification bureau." Parsons, calling men "gay deceivers," maintained an all-female division until her death in 1936. Mary Hamilton became the first female fingerprint examiner for the New York Police Department in 1917. During the manpower shortage of World War I, IAS-trained Marie S. Dahm outscored all candidates on a U.S. Navy fingerprint classification examination given in 1917. Dahm "startled the authorities in Washington with her ability," the IAS crowed, "and now Chief [John] Taylor says she is one of the best in her line, in the Government service." By the war's end, 95 percent of the 115 identification clerks employed by the Navy were female.[5]

Calls for establishing a professional association of identification clerks had been heard at the annual meetings of the International Association of Chiefs of Police (IACP) since 1899. It was not until 1915, however, that Harry Caldwell, an inspector in the Oakland Police Department, established such an organization. The modest first meeting, held at the Poodle Dog Cafe in Oakland, included only clerks from the Bay Area, but it resulted in the formation of the International Association of Criminal Identification (IACI), which at that point was still mainly an organization of Bertillon operators.[6]

Around the end of World War I fingerprint identification finally began to gain ground upon its rival, anthropometry, and emerge as the dominant criminal recordkeeping system in the United States. After the war professional identification institutions expanded rapidly. In 1919 the IACI became the International Association for Identification (IAI), and it issued 160 certificates and 325 "credential cards." The IAI's official goals were to gather identification personnel "so that the business in all its branches may be standardized and more efficiently and scientifically administered"; to disseminate information on identification work and methods; "to use the full power of the Association to induce all Bureaus of Identification and Investigation to adopt modern methods"; and to "inspire a just pride in the work" of identification.

Unable to ignore the influx of female fingerprint examiners during the war, the IAI began admitting women in 1918, though it still restricted membership to "white persons."[7]

The association's new name had been adopted at the prompting of the dactyloscopers Henry DeForest, G. Tyler Mairs, and Patrick Ryan, who convinced the membership of the IACI to drop the word "criminal" in an attempt to erase the "criminal stigma" from fingerprint identification. The IAI, however, remained oriented toward law enforcement, and in 1919 DeForest, Mairs, and others formed a new organization, the International Society for Personal Identification (ISPI) with a broader vision for dactyloscopy. The ISPI looked toward an era of "universal fingerprinting" in which the fingerprint would be a civilian identifier used in all aspects of daily life and social interaction. Identification would become a natural part of citizenship. Universal fingerprinting reflected progressivist, technocratic efforts to bring about a more orderly, and hence more efficient, more just, and more prosperous, society. Knowing precisely who everyone was, being able to keep track of all citizens, was an important part of the technocratic vision. The ISPI's official mission was "to influence public opinion to the end that the protection of every law abiding citizen may be maintained and safe-guarded by means of Personal Identification." ISPI meetings often ended with requests that members of the audience volunteer their fingerprints, which were deposited in the organization's private file. Appropriately, DeForest, who had pioneered the use of fingerprinting for verifying the identity, not of criminals, but of civil service applicants, was elected the ISPI's first president.[8]

During the 1910s enthusiasm grew for civilian applications such as fingerprinting schoolchildren. "What a valuable file the police could control," Frederick Kuhne, a fingerprint examiner for the New York Police Department, mused in 1916, "if the public would only realize the latitude of finger print possibilities and benefits to be derived therefrom not only by themselves, but their families and relatives, if the police were equipped (by reason of having their prints) to identify all persons coming within their jurisdiction, irrespective of circumstances; whether it be a criminal, a person who was murdered or killed accidentally, an unconscious person, or one suffering from aphasia." In arguing for universal fingerprint identification, Kuhne referred to the Slocum Disaster of 1904, a deadly ship fire on a pleasure cruise in New York City's East River in which hundreds of unidentified women and children died—the most deadly American maritime tragedy of the twentieth century, taking a larger toll even than the sinking of the Titanic. With universal fingerprint identification of civilians, Kuhne declared, much of the suffering of relatives after the Slocum Disaster might have been averted.[9]

Kidnapping and amnesia were additional justifications for civilian fingerprinting, rather thin pretexts for convincing all Americans to voluntarily submit to fingerprinting. Nonetheless, numerous entrepreneurs and public officials thought it could happen. In 1919 New York City Deputy Police Commissioner Joseph Faurot, claiming that the wealthy already fingerprinted their children as a provision against kidnapping, urged middle-class citizens to be fingerprinted. At the 1921 IAI convention in Washington, D.C., President Harding had his fingerprints publicly taken. That same year Edward and James Murphy convinced Governor Alex J. Groesbeck to be publicly fingerprinted in order to "convey to the people of Michigan his approval of Universal Finger Printing." The Murphy brothers operated a private bureau that charged citizens $2 to register their fingerprints, $3 for a pocket identification card with leather case, and, for children, $2.50 for a souvenir fingerprint record suitable for framing. "Should you decide to come in and have the registration made at the bureau," the Murphys suggested, "bring the kiddies with you. We will be pleased to show you what their own pudgy prints, magnified over 2,000 diameters, look like on a moving picture screen." In 1925 New York Police Chief Richard Enright called for the mandatory fingerprinting of all New York City residents. Rising crime and political and economic discontent led to broader calls for identifying all residents in order to better control them and keep the peace.[10]

The two rival professional organizations represented different interest groups among dactyloscopers. While the IAI was composed largely of identification bureau chiefs and clerks who worked in law enforcement, the ISPI was the forum for more philosophically minded dactyloscopers, or "dactyloscophers," as they called themselves, like DeForest and Mairs, who were still interested in "scientific" questions about fingerprints: the evolutionary basis of fingerprint patterns, the fingerprints of primates, predicting character traits from fingerprint patterns, and so on. ISPI members appeared to have a genuine aesthetic fascination with fingerprints: they often signed their letters with their own fingerprints. IAI members, in contrast, had neither the inclination nor the scientific background to delve deeply into the nature of fingerprint patterns. In their view, fingerprints offered a means of positive identification, no more, no less. Thus the ISPI had the appearance of an amateur scientific society, while the IAI looked like a law enforcement organization. The IAI grew in strength, while the ISPI became moribund by the mid-1920s. Of the four potential applications of fingerprinting— an index to criminal records, a forensic technique, a universal civilian identifier, and a means for tracing heredity and evolutionary history— only the former two thrived. The success of the IAI symbolized the triumph of a vision of fingerprinting oriented toward law enforcement. Its primacy contributed to the marginalization of the morphological research program spawned by Francis Galton. Fingerprint examiners became a professional community overwhelmingly dominated by law enforcement clerks.

Sociologists of technology use the term "black-boxing" to describe the process of taking a technical process for granted—of declining to inquire further into its inner workings. Over the period roughly between the two world wars, fingerprint examiners would gradually "blackbox" latent fingerprint identification. The skill of the fingerprint examiners would be vouched for by their credentials—the title "FPE" (fingerprint examiner)—and their membership in a recognized professional community rather than demonstrated to the jury in each particular case. The mysterious truism "no two fingerprints are exactly alike" would become an accepted piece of popular wisdom, which no longer needed to be "proved" to juries through statistical or metaphorical gymnastics. In this way, The Great Cochise County Finger Print Trial marked the zenith of the era of the virtuoso fingerprint examiner, with his dramatic courtroom demonstrations. Over the next two decades the public's trust in the reliability of fingerprint identification shifted from the individual examiner, whose skill was demonstrated before their eyes in the courtroom, to the reliability of the technique itself, as vouched for by the collective experience of the professional community. Fingerprint identification became routine.[11]

In part this was due to the growing acceptance of fingerprint identification in criminal identification bureaus. In part it was also due to the emerging professionalism of police. The police were increasingly perceived more like impartial scientists and less like political thugs in the employ of party machines. The "scientific policing" movement, led by Berkeley Police Chief August Vollmer and his "college cops," enhanced the credibility of the kind of police science of which fingerprinting was a prime example. Finally, fingerprint identification began to seep into popular culture, appearing in detective novels like R. Austin Freeman's *The Red Thumb Mark* (1907) and in silent films like *The Adventure of the Thumb Print* (1911), *Thumb Prints and Diamonds* (1914), and *Fingerprints on the Safe* (1920). Films and novels made fingerprinting more familiar to the jurors who were asked to trust it in criminal trials.[12]

Graphologists, or handwriting experts, had been giving evidence in court about identity since at least the eighteenth century. Graphologists, however, could not agree on the proper method of analyzing handwriting, nor was there any control over who could call themselves handwriting experts. It was easy for an attorney to find a graphologist willing to counter the testimony of another graphologist. Cases involving handwriting evidence tended to feature "dueling experts"—drawing on the same body of knowledge yet reaching opposite conclusions. In the late nineteenth century the world's leading graphologist, Jean-Hippolyte Michon, attempted to unify the field under a single method. He proposed that all attempts to match handwriting samples should yield only two results, an indisputable match or "inconclusive." This effort ultimately failed, and by the twentieth century the field of graphology was bitterly divided as to method. Handwriting experts had an unsavory, mercenary reputation, and their opinions carried little weight in court. The Dreyfus affair, in which numerous experts (Alphonse Bertillon among them) came to contradictory conclusions about the authenticity of the document known as the *bordereau*, particularly damaged the reputation of handwriting analysis. Graphologists were an extreme case, but even physicians and psychiatrists, or "alienists," tended to fall into the "dueling experts" pattern, a pattern that did little to foster the appearance of scientific objectivity.[13]

Fingerprint examiners learned from the examples of other presumed experts. They deliberately sought the kind of strict control over method and opinion that Michon had tried to exert over graphology. They saw forensic fingerprint analysis as a discipline in which consensus, rather than discord, should rule. "It is believed that in all of the cases in which [fingerprint] evidence has so far been made use of," a legal expert commented in 1913, "in no instance has there been that conflict of opinion between the experts which is a disgusting feature of the testimony of the so-called 'alienists.'" This had not been true of the Deptford trial, but none of the other early cases involved defense witnesses. Instead there was consensus among the many experts called: four in *Jennings* and five in *Moon*, for example.[14]

Newly professionalized fingerprint examiners made this possible by articulating norms of method and conduct that would *preclude* disagreement between experts. Around the end of World War I, leading dactyloscopers began describing latent fingerprint identification as so unambiguous that every qualified examiner would reach the same conclusion. The key to such assertions was the "point counting" method of matching corresponding ridge characteristics between the latent and inked prints. Although experts could, and occasionally did, disagree as to whether a corresponding point matched, the point counting method generated relatively little disagreement. If an examiner confined his or her identifications to prints showing a large number of matching points, the chances of having another expert dispute his or her conclusions would be greatly reduced.

Precisely how many matching points were necessary to achieve this margin of safety was not clear. The great French criminalist Edmond Locard proposed the earliest minimum standard, twelve points of similarity, in 1911. The following year Alphonse Bertillon challenged this standard in what may have been a last-ditch effort to strike back at the technique that was threatening to displace his anthropometric system of identification. Bertillon published two *different* fingerprints which ostensibly showed sixteen matching points of similarity. In fact, his illustrations were crude collages of fragments of different fingerprints that no trained examiner would mistake for actual fingerprints. Moreover, as dactyloscopers responded, some of Bertillon's "points of similarity" were not really identical at all, but clearly distinguishable from one another. Nonetheless, Bertillon's argument had been made: it was conceivable that two different prints showing sixteen points of similarity could exist—in artifice, if not in nature.[15]

Neither Locard's nor Bertillon's standards were binding, but over the next several decades many law enforcement agencies did adopt minimum standards, ranging from seven to twelve points. Oddly enough, it was only Britain, the nation most committed to dactyloscopy—and therefore perhaps the most protective of its integrity—that took Bertillon seriously, imposing a sixteen-point minimum standard in 1920. Fifteen years earlier Britain's leading forensic fingerprint expert, Charles Collins, had declared that only four matching points were necessary for certain identification, but now a latent print comparison resulting in fewer than sixteen points of similarity would be declared inconclusive automatically. In contrast, the United States, with its fragmented legal jurisdictions, never set a national minimum standard, although many individual state and local law enforcement agencies set their own informal minimum standards. In general, however, examiners everywhere began limiting themselves to matches showing relatively large numbers of matching points, in the neighborhood of eight to twelve, in order to provide a safe margin against any unseemly disagreement between experts. Such disagreement was especially undesirable because fingerprint examiners were phrasing their identifications as matters of fact, rather than as opinions. Of course, fingerprint matches *were* opinions—they did not exist outside the subjective perceptions of human fingerprint examiners—but the *unanimity* of opinion among fingerprint examiners allowed them to present identifications in court as matters of fact. Thus Frederick Kuhne asserted in 1917:

> The testimony of a finger print expert is not subject to contradiction by another finger print expert, for the reason . . . that the print is from the person; while in cases of testimony by handwriting experts there is always a possibility of contradiction, because the identification of handwriting is merely the opinion of a person who has made a study of detecting similarities in the formation of letters; and another expert, who is just as competent, might not agree with the conclusions of the first expert, thus giving cause for doubt.[16]

Dactyloscopers presented fingerprints as a new kind of evidence, never before seen in courts of law. They distinguished it from both medical evidence and other types of identification evidence such as graphology. It claimed to be thoroughly "scientific," yet, unlike other types of scientific or medical evidence, it was presented not as opinion but as error-free fact. In a 1919 article entitled "How the Finger Print Expert Presents His Case in Court," the fingerprint examiner A. A. Gribben distinguished fingerprinting from both pseudo-sciences like palmistry and other types of evidence:

The identification of a person by his finger prints or their impression
. . . must not be confused with "palmistry," that pretended art by
which the charlatan and faker for a consideration pretends that he can
foretell future events. Nor is it to be confounded with the operations of
the Handwriting Expert, who is only able at the best to give AN OPIN-
ION as to the possibility of two writings having been made by the
same person. It has no connection with the Bertillon System of identification, which depends upon the measurements taken from certain
members and portions of the human body, relying especially upon the
lengths of certain bones. Any or all of these methods are subject to error, and there is always an element of doubt in their findings that
makes their conclusions unreliable . . . The finger print expert has only
facts to consider; he reports simply what he finds . . . If two prints are
identical in every particular, they were made by the same person. If
they are different, they were not made by the same person. No matter
how many finger print experts may be engaged in the labor of comparing two prints, their verdict *must* be the same.[17]

"Their verdict *must* be the same." Gribben's statement was both descriptive and normative. At this early stage in the development of the
profession, it was directed at other fingerprint examiners as much as at
judges.

A correct fingerprint interpretation was one that everyone with similar training also could see. Fingerprint examiners voluntarily restricted their own vision by insisting that anything their colleagues
could not see was by definition invisible. This principle was crucial
in sustaining the extraordinarily high degree of certainty claimed by
latent fingerprint evidence. Thus dactyloscopers gradually coalesced
from individual practitioners, whose skill and reputation stood alone,
to a professional community with a collective set of skills and reputation. The emphasis on consensus required that dactyloscopers exhibit
a new kind of skill, which lay less in the spectacular ability to match
fingerprints before the jury than in the ability to conform to the judgments of one's peers. This was a skill of consistency (the ability of examiners everywhere to render identical judgments) and of restraint
(not overreaching, as Goff apparently had in the Loomis case, not
breaching the limits of common visibility, no longer performing mira-
cles).

This attitude was reflected in the debate over whether the E in FPE stood for "expert" or "examiner." Perhaps not surprisingly, it was the "most professional," nationally recognized FPEs who favored the humble term "examiner," while it was the FPEs with more suspect qualifications who adopted the more grandiose title of "expert." For those examiners who were trying to articulate an ethic of self-restraint, the "examiner/expert" debate went to the heart of the conservative methodology of latent fingerprint identification. The essence of their vision of identification practice lay precisely in discouraging examiners from thinking of themselves as "experts." IAI founder Harry Caldwell linked the two issues at the 1927 IAI meeting:

> Now while on the subject of ethics, I wish to call your particular attention to the fact that a number of instances have come up wherein members of the profession, namely finger-print experts (that is a term I personally do not like, although we have to qualify as experts in finger prints cases) . . . have made extreme efforts to make accidental or latent prints conform to the prints of some man they wished to connect with a crime, and were not warranted in doing so. Now, ever since organization, and long before, I personally, have been strictly against taking, or attempting to place before a court or jury any expert evidence or testimony that was not perfectly clear to myself, and admitted of explanation and demonstration so clearly that any person of ordinary intelligence could be shown everything we, ourselves, were *sure* of. It is better that we let several guilty men escape than to convict one innocent person, and cause him to be punished, his relatives disgraced and his friends humiliated, etc.[18]

Once again, fingerprint examiners sought to preserve the credibility of fingerprint evidence by erring on the side of caution. The conservative ethic that guided latent fingerprint identification echoed Blackstone's maxim that it is better to allow ten guilty people go free than to convict one innocent person.

A related area of concern was the dilution of talent among fingerprint examiners. The advertisements of the IAS and some of its shadier rivals had been all too successful. At its 1927 meeting the IAI condemned the "misleading advertisements and extravagant promises" of correspondence schools, "turning out thousands of so-called 'University' graduates with the degree of F.P.E." These schools had graduated "tens of thousands of country boys and incompetent people," and this "vast horde" threatened not only the livelihood but also the credibility of those already in the profession. The IAI announced that it "vigorously condemns and denounces the widespread and wicked system of increasing the number of identification experts as purely mercenary, unethical and a rank imposition and fraud upon the press and public." It further resolved "to warn the general public that there is actually no demand whatever for the services of the scores of thousands of so-called graduates who have already spent their money for these correspondence courses in the science of Finger Prints." Even the FPE designation became suspect, since correspondence schools conferred it so liberally. "I never signed F.P.E after my name yet, and I don't think I will," declared a Mr. Jones of Minneapolis. "To see the individuals I meet who carry cards with F.P.E. on them, I don't think I want one."[19]

In sum, after World War I dactyloscopers articulated a novel set of occupational norms for their nascent profession. Fingerprint examiners were expected to be more skilled than lay observers, but they were also supposed to exercise restraint. Declared fingerprint matches should be only those matches which would demand agreement from *all* the examiner's colleagues. Uncertain matches should be ruled inconclusive, thus maintaining the appearance of consensus within the profession and the impression that fingerprint matches were unambiguous "facts."

The professional community soon began to see some signs of success in its struggle to be recognized as authoritative and respectable. Defendants and defense attorneys alike were learning not to dispute fingerprint evidence. Based on "hundreds of finger-print clippings that reach our office," *Finger Print and Identification Magazine* reported in 1924, "we are impressed by the large proportion of cases in which criminals confess when they learn that the finger-print system is being used. The criminal classes have learned to fear the system that disproves their lies and shows up their false alibis . . . In one large midwestern city, criminal lawyers refuse to take cases in which finger-print evidence figures. They cannot afford to risk their reputations on cases which will surely find their clients guilty."[20]

Despite its growing credibility and its increasingly prominent role in popular culture as a symbol of "scientific policing," actual uses of latent fingerprint identification remained rare. Patrol officers were still poorly trained, as likely to destroy fingerprint evidence as to secure the crime scene. The number of detectives with the training to dust for latent fingerprints was still small. And most important, unless the police had a particular suspect in mind, searching the files for a match was laborious and a significant drain on manpower. Unless the case was particularly high profile or grisly, police chiefs were unlikely to allocate scarce resources for such "cold searches" of the fingerprint files. This was especially true because "old school" police officers, who remained in control of police departments in many cities, were hostile to scientific policing: at the 1937 IAI convention, J. Edgar Hoover would reminisce fondly about the days when "too many law-enforcement officers were men of low intelligence, some of low morals, and, indeed, of a low opinion for anyone who sought to make science his aid and his standby in the pursuit of a criminal." "During the years which have followed," he would recall, "we, of this organization, have found ourselves laughed at, sneered at, reviled as being 'Boy Wonders,' college boys, or imitation Sherlocks."[21]

As juries, judges, and even defense attorneys showed themselves increasingly inclined to believe fingerprint evidence, its greatest impact lay, as always, in forcing confessions out of accused persons faced with the threat of incontrovertible evidence. If a defendant with fingerprint evidence against him did choose to try his luck with a jury, he faced unfavorable odds, as awareness of fingerprinting and respect for the authority of science seeped deeper into the culture and jurors became more and more ready to take fingerprint evidence on faith, without having seen it with their own eyes through some sort of courtroom demonstration.

Although courtroom demonstrations were still performed in at least two cases in 1927, a 1928 decision by the Supreme Court of Vermont seemed to do away at last with the need for them. On July 5, 1927, the corpse of a farmer named Ivon Burnham was discovered in his home in Calais, Vermont. The crime scene suggested a murder so "vicious and inhuman" that Judge Powers of the Vermont Supreme Court declined to recount "the brutal and distressing details." The evidence against the defendant, Silas Lapan, included latent finger and partial palm prints found on a blood-stained glass lamp at the scene. In this case the defense, not the prosecution, urged that a courtroom experiment be performed. On the theory that there might have been kerosene on the lamp, the defense attorney challenged one of the prosecution experts,

Roscoe C. Hill of the Massachusetts Bureau for the Identification of Criminals, to take a print in kerosene. The trial judge refused to allow this experiment. Upon appeal, the Vermont Supreme Court echoed previous rulings about such demonstrations: "It was within the discretion of the trial court to admit *or exclude it.*" On the principle of not interfering with the trial court, therefore, the appeals court upheld the banning of the demonstration. Although demonstrations had consistently been upheld, when the defense requested a demonstration it was excluded. To add insult to injury, the Supreme Court adopted the very argument that had been used to oppose such a demonstration by the defense in the Crispi trial: "the dissimilarity of conditions justified the rejection of the experiment."

The defense introduced its own expert witness, Corporal Charles H. Baker of the U.S. Army Medical Corps, but he qualified only "as an expert finger print taker, but not as a finger print reader." In other words, Baker could take inked fingerprints, which required minimal skill, but he was not trained for the far more rigorous work of analyzing, interpreting, and comparing latent and inked fingerprints. His opinion as to the quality of the latent print was therefore excluded by the court—an exclusion upheld by the appeals court. This appears to have been a common problem for defendants confronted with fingerprint evidence: a lack of access to qualified expert assistance. Examiners with proper training in latent fingerprint analysis tended, almost invariably, to be employed by law enforcement agencies, and they were not inclined to testify for the defense. Even in this rare instance of the defense introducing its own expert, the expert was not as well qualified as the state's experts.

More noteworthy, however, was Judge Powers's written opinion on the question of whether fingerprinting was properly characterized as "a generally recognized science." In his appeal, Lapan demanded evidence "as to the state of this so-called science." The court held: "No such evidence was required. The subject is one of the things that does not have to be proved." Powers had shifted the legal and epistemological ground significantly from the Moon case. No longer was the idea of fingerprint identification so implausible that it required direct visual proof. Instead it had become so widely accepted and intuitively plausible that it "does not have to be proved." "This knowledge of the courts goes so far as to enable them to say, *without proof,*" Powers went on to write, "that the imprint of the palm side of the human hand, when fairly taken, presents reliable, individual, and unchanging characteristics of the papillary ridges." Fingerprint identification was, therefore, black-boxed. Without any empirical demonstration, fingerprinting had become "science."[22]

The Criminal Court of Appeals of Oklahoma echoed the *Lapan* opinion two years later in *Stacy v. State,* a burglary case, citing "numerous books, monographs, and articles on the subject of finger prints, giving the origin, the history, and the manner of taking and preserving finger prints, and touching the reliable character of this class of evidence." These "authorities" included the *Encyclopaedia Britannica* and *Pudd'nhead Wilson.* The court announced: "we take judicial knowledge that there are no two sets of finger prints exactly alike." Once again, however, the court specified "sets" of the fingerprints. By this time, the large collections of ten-prints held by law enforcement agencies might be taken as evidence—though not definitive proof—that no two people shared identical sets of ten fingerprints. But Henry Faulds's point—that the individuality of all *single* fingerprints had not been proven—remained unanswered, as did the question of the individuality of partial fingerprint fragments.[23]

That same year one Clem Steffen was accused of burglarizing a store in Council Bluffs, Iowa. His fingerprints were matched to latent prints found on plate glass windows that had been broken during the burglary. An unidentified fingerprint examiner testified for the state, over the objections of the defense attorney John J. Hess:

Q: I will ask you to state from the examination you made of them, and the comparison of them, whether or not you are able to state whether the print found on the glass, Exhibit 2, was made by the same finger that made the print which is found to the left on Exhibit 3, the enlarged reproduction; are you able to state if those were made by the same fingers?

A: I am.

Q: What is the fact?

MR. HESS: Objected to as asking for the conclusion of the witness on a matter that the jury must determine, rather than the witness. He isn't asking for his opinion. He is asking for a fact. He doesn't know. It is incompetent, immaterial, irrelevant. (Overruled.)

A: They were made by one and the same finger.

Upon appeal, the defense contended that it was improper to allow the state's experts to testify to the "ultimate fact," rather than as to their opinion. In other words, the fingerprint match was such damning evidence that it was tantamount to declaring the defendant guilty as charged, a job for the jury, not an expert witness. The state countered that "because of the peculiar nature of the science pertaining to finger prints" the expert witnesses "should be allowed to testify to the ultimate fact of the identity of the finger prints on the broken glass with those of the appellant." The court agreed with the defendant, upholding the long-standing principle "that while an expert may be permitted to express his opinion, or even his belief, he cannot testify to the ultimate fact that must be determined by the jury." Therefore, the court took the unusual (in comparison with almost all the other cases I have discussed) step of reversing the conviction.

Three judges disagreed with this decision. In his dissenting opinion, Judge De Graaf declared: "The ultimate fact is whether or not the defendant was guilty of the crime charged, and the evidence relative to finger prints was a mere item of evidence." But De Graaf also argued that fingerprint evidence was both "opinion evidence" *and* "a question of fact for the consideration of the jury." He believed that fingerprinting *was* fact: "Finger printing is based on the law of nature, or upon a universally recognized physical fact . . . All authorities on the subject recognize that the finger prints of no two persons are the same." Therefore, De Graaf concluded, "Finger printing is a science."[24]

In *Steffen* fingerprint examiners had pushed the "factual" nature of fingerprint evidence too far. The court, sensing that the examiners were no longer behaving as expert witnesses but rather were usurping the fact-finding function of the courts themselves, served fingerprint examiners with a warning: if they wanted to remain expert witnesses, they would have to stop talking in terms of "facts." Fingerprint examiners heeded this warning; they pulled back from the "fact" language. This allowed them to remain experts—to continue to interpose themselves between the evidence and the jury, to maintain their recently acquired authority over the interpretation of fingerprint evidence. Fingerprint examiners continued to insist both that fingerprints "spoke for themselves" and that credentialed experts spoke for them.

A year later, in a Pennsylvania burglary case, *Commonwealth v. Albright*, Judge Keller of the Pennsylvania Superior Court declared: "It is well settled that the papillary lines and markings on the fingers of every man, woman and child possess an individual character different from those of any other person and that the chances that the finger prints of two different persons may be identical are infinitesimally remote." Though the defendant cited the Loomis case as evidence that fingerprinting was unreliable, Keller noted that the unfortunate error in the Loomis case "does not tend to show that more than one person has the same finger print. It goes to the care exercised by the expert in comparing the finger prints and the points of identity or similarity between them, and is for the jury." Again, both the court and the defense failed to grasp that the care, and ability, of fingerprint examiners was not known and had never been tested. Knowing how often examiners made errors was just as important as the philosophical proposition that no two people had identical fingerprint patterns.[25]

This suite of cases from 1928 to 1931 shows that courts were increasingly willing to take the reliability of fingerprinting for granted, "without proof." Fingerprint matches were treated as indisputable evidence that contact had occurred between the finger of a particular individual and some surface. Opportunities to dispute fingerprint evidence were limited to claiming "legitimate access"—that the defendant might have left the fingerprint on some occasion other than the commission of the crime. Fingerprint evidence was becoming more tightly black-boxed and more difficult to dispute. Fingerprint matches were "facts," and fingerprinting was "science." Thus fingerprint examiners in 1931 were in an ideal situation: for all practical purposes, judges, jurors, and defense attorneys seemed to treat fingerprint matches as indisputable facts, yet legally they were regarded as expert evidence, subject to expert opinion.

Still, the skills of fingerprint experts—or people presenting themselves as experts—remained a matter of concern into the 1930s. Courts tended to admit anyone who called himself a "fingerprint expert." In a series of letters and articles in *Finger Print and Identification Magazine* in 1935, contributors complained that "persons who are not *qualified* Fingerprint Experts, are now employed in the capacity of Fingerprint Experts." Disturbingly, fingerprint examiners found themselves powerless to prevent such usurpations. The only solution seemed to be some kind of state-run certification program. The magazine's editor T. G. Cooke proposed such a program:

> A vast amount of finger print men strongly favor the idea of having some kind of state legislation to properly protect the *qualified* finger print expert and to thereby protect the interest of the profession to warrant its receiving the recognition this time-honored profession merits . . . Qualified F.P.E.'s in every state should organize to promote a state law in their respective state that will regulate the activities and protect the interests of *qualified* identification men and finger print experts and permit *only* "qualified" men to act as finger print experts.[26]

Cooke called for lobbying state governments to begin licensing fingerprint examiners, but these suggestions came to nothing. Like most professionals, dactyloscopers would be forced to police themselves.

In *Shelton v. Commonwealth* (1939) the Kentucky Court of Appeals reversed a murder conviction because the fingerprint identification had been made by H. G. Coffey, an "expert" of suspect qualifications. Coffey claimed to be a graduate of Cook and Evans University in Chicago, a garbled reference to the IAS. Dactyloscopers eager to legitimate the profession welcomed the distinction the court drew: "If Coffey is expert in the science of finger printing, his testimony is entitled to great weight; but if he is really not an expert and is merely an amateur doing inaccurate and unreliable work, his testimony is entitled to no weight." But they took no comfort in the fact that Coffey had testified in Kentucky without being challenged at least twice previously, both times securing convictions which had passed muster with the Court of Appeals. Clearly, the courts were not performing their gatekeeping function very aggressively. Essentially anyone who called himself a "fingerprint expert" could be admitted to testify as an expert witness; no specific education or certification was required.[27]

In two cases near the beginning of World War II, courts were called upon to decide whether fingerprint evidence could support a conviction in the absence of any other evidence. In the first, a 1937 burglary case in Parish, New York, the appellate court ruled that fingerprint evidence alone could support a conviction. Indeed, Justice Dowling wrote that "the facts and circumstances upon which the jury reached their verdict are of such character as to exclude every reasonable hypothesis other than that of the defendant's guilt and are not only consistent with his guilt but are inconsistent with his innocence and this is all the proof that is required to warrant a conviction in a criminal case."[28]

The second case concerned a pane of glass from the door of a café that had been burglarized in Hamilton, Texas, in 1940. The latent fingerprint was found in a place that had been covered by molding until the pane was removed in the course of the robbery. Therefore the defendant could not claim "legitimate access"—that he had touched the glass while dining at the café. The state's expert witness, J. O. McGuire, matched the fingerprint to a local man, Newton Grice. The defendant, his father, and another relative claimed to have been in Fort Worth at the time of the burglary. At trial, McGuire estimated the odds against accidental duplication of a fingerprint as in the "billions and trillions or something." Grice's attorney, Tom L. Robinson, in what the appellate court would call "a very intelligent cross-examination," pointed out that Galton gave a much smaller probability, 1 in 64 million. McGuire, apparently, "would not agree to a figure that small." (Actually, McGuire was right in that Galton *had* said 1 in 64 *billion*. For reasons that are not clear, the figure was often, as in this case, misquoted as 64 million.)

On this issue, Judge Beauchamp of the Texas Court of Criminal Appeals noted that "the question is one capable of ascertainment to a satisfactory degree at least," something "not always true of scientific deductions." But instead of looking for an empirical test of the reliability of fingerprint identification,Beauchamp merely undertook a literature review. His review of previous decisions revealed a case law almost uniformly supportive of the validity of fingerprint identification. Even the matter at issue—whether the defendant could be convicted on fingerprint evidence alone—had been decided in the affirmative (though outside the United States) as early as 1909 in the British Castleton case and in the 1912 Australian case *Parker v. Rex*. The only significant note of caution had been sounded in a series of Texas cases in which the defendant had legitimate access to the site on which the fingerprint had been found.[29]

The widespread use of fingerprints for both criminal and civil record-keeping had helped support the notion of their uniqueness. By 1941 the weight of this evidence was even greater: the FBI, for example, held 9.5 million fingerprint records. Beauchamp wrote: "In various branches of government activities finger prints are taken by the multiplied thousands. They have been assembled, classified, and indexed systematically and if there are two alike in the great number of which there is authentic record and available to litigants and others interested in the subject, that fact could be definitely proven and the claims of experts successfully contradicted. So far as we have been able to tell, no such contention has ever been so rebutted." Once again, however, this opinion overlooked the difference between the use of complete sets of ten fingerprints for recordkeeping and the comparison of single, partial latent fingerprints for forensics.

Beauchamp, reviewing thirty years of fingerprint litigation, also found that defense attorneys had tended not to challenge fingerprint evidence. And even when they did challenge it, he noted, they had not been able to produce the single disconfirming case that might suggest that there *were* two fingerprints alike: "While the assertion has been insistently made that no two people have identical finger markings, we have found no case of record in which the defense has produced an exception or has attempted to refute such testimony by an example of two or more people with identical finger prints. Generally this assertion is not even challenged."

In light of all this evidence, and minding his (self-imposed) charge to "form a definite and certain policy and rule," Beauchamp decided to reverse the epistemological burden of proof. "It has occurred to us," he wrote, "that instead of the state being called upon longer to offer proof that no two finger prints are alike, it may now be considered in order for those taking the opposite view to assume the burden of proving their position." Notice that Beauchamp had finally dropped the cautious term "sets" from the assertion: no two finger prints were alike. By lack of disproof, the fundamental premise of fingerprint identification had finally been "proven." The 1941 Grice decision may be taken as the moment at which American courts decided that there really were no two fingerprints alike.[30]

This decision was made in the legal, not the scientific, arena. Just after the end of World War II, *Finger Print and Identification Magazine* asked several leading dactyloscopers to address the scientific question of whether it was possible for any two fingerprints to be alike. These authorities still appealed to a vaguely articulated natural law. The uniqueness of fingerprints was supported by reference to observations of seemingly infinite variety elsewhere in the natural world. Perhaps the most familiar analogy was with snowflakes. In 1924, after recording more than four thousand photomicrographs over more than twenty years, the farmer-scientist Wilson Bentley of Jericho, Vermont, asserted "the fact that no two snowflakes are ever alike, or ever can be alike." Just as there were no two snowflakes exactly alike, dactyloscopers reasoned, so there were no two fingerprint patterns exactly alike. "It is common knowledge that Nature never has been known to make any exact duplicates," G. Tyler Mairs wrote in 1945: "No two snow-flakes, no two grains of sand, no two leaves, no two of anything are *exactly* alike, that is, identical down to the most minute detail of form or size or position or combinations of them. Variations are always found in one or more of these factors which are distinctive enough and sufficiently extensive to establish the necessary perceptible differences required to distinguish one object from another in the same category of general likenesses." Mairs also appealed obliquely to embryology: "Duplication is impossible because of the inherent variability of controlling growth factors during fetal development. Even Nature cannot duplicate them as she has no 'master mold' into which all human life can be poured. Each creation represents a master 'blue print,' but exhibits all of the variables inherent in individual workmanship."[31]

"Absolute duplication in finger print patterns, or, for that matter, in *anything*, is a basic natural law, namely: *Nature never repeats*," echoed the Oakland dactyloscoper Burtis Bridges in 1946. "It will be understood that this applies to all things—leaves on the trees, sands on the sea-shore, dust particles in the air, snowflakes, everything including, of course, finger prints." Bridges's generalizations were so sweeping that he boggled his own mind: "No fact known to modern science is more amazing . . . The mind reels from the computation of so vast a multiformity of patterns . . . The physical and temporal principles which resulted in the creation and development of any person's body (including his finger prints), could never find an exact counterpart in the past, present, or future. Everything is in a state of perennial impermanence." Thus fingerprint examiners' own "scientific" validation of the premises of latent fingerprint identification was based on the principle that no two natural objects are exact duplicates of each other. While this may have served to validate that argument that no two complete, single fingerprints would be exactly alike, it did nothing to address the more difficult question of whether a fragmentary, low-quality latent fingerprint might appear to match inked fingerprints from more than one source finger.[32]

By the beginning of World War II fingerprint examiners had transformed fingerprinting from a novel technique that required support from elaborate courtroom theatrics into the most credible and unassailable form of identification evidence around. But this victory did not come without cost. Fingerprint examiners achieved this high degree of credibility by portraying fingerprint identification as a routine process, so routine in fact that the skills and judgments of individual examiners were interchangeable. As the sociologist Steven Shapin has pointed out, interchangeability is one of the principal attributes of the type of scientific worker commonly called a "technician." By routinizing their own work, fingerprint examiners had undermined their own claims to being scientists and had made themselves look to the outside world more like technicians.[33]

Though fingerprint examiners frequently referred to themselves as scientists, and to fingerprinting as a science, both inside and outside the courtroom, they were chagrined to find that they were not necessarily treated accordingly. As early as the 1925 IAI convention the fingerprint examiner Al Dunlap had complained: "The identification profession is the most underpaid profession in the civilized world. In this very town [Detroit], the man at the head of the identification bureau is rated as a sergeant." The convention appointed a committee to report on the matter, and the following year the IAI denounced the "unjust treatment . . . accorded a majority of the members of the identification profession." "In most instances," the committee complained, "their employment, particularly those who are members of municipal police departments, is rated as merely clerical. In other cases they are rated as ordinary patrolmen, no distinction being shown between such technically trained officers and those performing regular police duty." "The work to which identification specialists are assigned," the IAI pointed out, "requires special qualifications, special training and a long period of practical experience," which "usually follows a number of years of successful performance of the normal duties of a police officer." "A qualified identification expert," the IAI argued, needed "at least four years practical experience in the work of finger print identification and its branch studies of photography and court procedure." Although the IAI did not refer to any written, enforceable standard for this requirement, it argued that the identification expert "is, and should be, given the same consideration in a court of law as any expert witness, a physician, alienist or analytical chemist." Like these acknowledged experts, the fingerprint examiner was "repeatedly called upon to exercise judgment and initiative, and his decision in a question of identity must be considered final."[34]

The IAI dispatched Dunlap to convey its concerns at the next meeting of the IACP. In an address bluntly entitled "Identification Chiefs Are Professionals," Dunlap drew the police chiefs' attention to the disturbing fact that "in one of the largest metropolitan departments of the country, the superintendent has spent his life in deep research work and is generally recognized as a scientist of the highest order, yet he still receives the nominal rank and salary of a sergeant of police." "High-class identification experts," he declared, "are about the poorest paid scientists and specialists in the world."[35]

Despite their complaints, fingerprint examiners were not viewed as scientists either within law enforcement bureaucracies or by academic scientists. The conservatives of the IAI won out over the enthusiasts of the ISPI; the "examiners" won out over the "experts"; the "technicians" over the "scientists," methodologically, if not semantically. The only site where fingerprint examiners *were* known as experts was the witness chair, the very site for which they had constructed their professional identity. But most fingerprint examiners appear to have been satisfied with the bargain. In exchange for modest professional status, they testified in criminal trials with almost complete immunity from attack. No other expert witness could make this boast. Eventually, however, this delicate arrangement would begin to collapse, and some fingerprint examiners would seek to renegotiate its terms.

I must Create a System or be enslav'd by another Man's.
—William Blake, *Jerusalem* (1804–1820)

CHAPTER 9

Identification at a Distance

In the 1920s, one by one, American law enforcement agencies either introduced new criminal identification files indexed according to fingerprints or gradually phased out anthropometry in favor of fingerprint-based files. Cheaper, faster, and more widely applied than anthropometry, fingerprinting allowed law enforcement agencies to identify more recidivists than ever before. Their enhanced ability to identify recidivists prompted the passage of new laws that used the number of convictions as a guide to sentencing. These new statutes were known generically as "Baumes laws," after the author of New York's statute, State Senator Caleb Baumes, chairman of the State Crime Commission. New York's Baumes law, passed in 1926, did away with many of the procedural difficulties that had hampered the enforcement of New York's previous habitual-criminals statutes, and it provided for a mandatory life sentence for the fourth felony conviction. By 1931 two hundred four-time offenders had been sentenced to life under the Baumes Law. Other states followed New York's example, and by 1930 twenty-three states had adopted "Baumes laws."[1]

Fingerprint records were vital to make these statutes work. "Of what significance is a severer penalty for a repeater," asked a National Crime Commission report in 1927, "or a life sentence threatening a man who is convicted of his fourth felony if there is no authoritative means of ascertaining how many previous sentences he has served?" Finger-printing provided that means. Criminal justice authorities' increased confidence that they could "know" criminals helped encourage the de-velopment of new progressive measures designed to individualize pun-ishment, providing harsher sentences for repeat offenders and proba-tion or parole for novices in crime who might still be rehabilitated. Parole, formerly a special measure intended to rectify miscarriages of justice, began to be used for recidivists after World War I.[2]

Fingerprinting increased the amount of knowledge police officials, judges, prosecutors, probation and parole officers, and prison wardens could have about an individual criminal. (While many criminologists still dreamed of more sophisticated forms of knowledge, such as under-standing the etiology of each individual's criminality, they also recog-nized that, for the time being at least, knowing the number of each criminal's past offenses was far better than nothing.) Fingerprinting had fulfilled the long-deferred dream of the penal reformer Arnould Bonneville, perhaps the first person to envision a modern criminal identification system: a criminal could no longer escape his past, and judges could pass sentence knowing the criminal's "state of recidi-vism."

Or could they? Surprisingly, the new criminal identification systems had still not managed to close one of the most prominent loopholes mentioned by the mid-nineteenth-century reformers Bonneville and Tocqueville: criminals could often evade detection simply by crossing jurisdictional boundaries. In the United States criminals could often escape their criminal pasts by crossing state lines, just as they had in Tocqueville's time. In Europe criminals could, in some cases, escape detection by moving to a new city or region, and if they went to an-other country they could almost certainly assume a brand-new iden-tity. Governments viewed this mobility as a grievous threat. Suspicion of immigrants, fear of "political criminals" and radicals like anar-chists, and newfound awareness of the phenomenon of "international crime" (a term the German criminologist Franz von Liszt had coined in 1893), all contributed to the perception that it was necessary to curb the mobility of criminals. The authorities were especially alarmed by the anarchist movement, which threatened the destruction of all gov-ernment. The increasing mobility of the world's population, the break-down of traditional communities in which local officials could know the local population, and the development of transportation technologies like the railroad and steamship, it was felt, had internationalized crime. Newly professionalized police forces in the early part of the twentieth century, therefore, felt an acute need to broaden their networks for exchanging information.

Fingerprint identification systems had been developed at the local level, mostly by urban police departments. These municipal agencies were accustomed to operating autonomously, and they had not designed their identification systems with an eye to "networking" them with those of other agencies. This networking would prove extremely difficult. In the years following World War I, fingerprinting was still quite some distance from becoming the hoped-for "international and national system of recording and exchanging finger prints" which would make it "impossible for criminals to move from country to country or city to city and continue their operations." Instead, fingerprint files tended to be only locally applicable. Police could check a suspect's prints against their own files, but making inquiries to neighboring cities, states, or countries proved far more cumbersome. The police might make extra prints, and mail them to neighboring jurisdictions, which was slow and costly. Somewhat more cheaply, they might send the classification, instead of the print itself, to other agencies, but this would not conclusively identify a print. Moreover, neighboring agencies were likely to use a different classification system: the Vucetich system instead of the Henry system, for example, or any of a vast array of regional and national variations of either of the two original systems. What was called "*the* fingerprint system" was in fact a patchwork assortment of local classification systems. Thus fingerprint classifications could not be exchanged between countries or even, in some cases, between localities or different bureaus. Even by the 1920s, American fingerprint examiner Mary Holland's 1908 prediction "that in a few years the police departments and penal institutions of the entire world will be working under one universal system" had not yet come to pass.[3]

In the United States inquiries between different bureaus had to be made one by one. For instance, police in New York City looking for a suspect's criminal record would have to write separately to the police in Newark, Philadelphia, Hartford, Trenton, Boston, Albany, and so on. How many letters the police were willing to write depended upon how badly they wanted the information. There was no comprehensive central agency where they might direct their inquiries. There was a Federal Bureau of Criminal Identification in Leavenworth, Kansas, which took prints of the small number of federal prisoners (around 3 percent of the national total in 1910) and received fingerprints from other agencies on a voluntary basis. There was also a National Bureau of Identification, privately run by the International Association of Chiefs of Police (IACP) in Washington, but submission was again voluntary and therefore extremely spotty. Neither of these was truly a national database. The nation's largest fingerprint files were held by the municipal police departments of New York and Chicago.[4]

"To get information you must write to three or four places before you can secure the record of a criminal," said Police Chief Abbott of Fort Wayne, Indiana, in 1921. "That means that if you write to Washington today, you get a return 'not known,' you write to Leavenworth, and you get a report that he is known. You write to Chicago, and you may find something of him there." Nor were there even central files at the state level, except in a handful of states. "Instead of exchanging information with one central bureau in each of the seven territories and forty-eight states," the New York State Prison Association complained in 1924, "it is necessary to keep in contact with as many of the chiefs of police, sheriffs, wardens of institutions, special agents of railroads, probation and parole officers in each state, who care to cooperate with the National Bureau."[5]

The decentralization of fingerprint information made fingerprinting a somewhat empty promise as a national and international tool of criminal identification. "It is generally known that there is a large number of separate collections of fingerprints in this country and that by far the most of these are in the hands of police departments," commented New York City Police Commissioner Richard Enright in 1924, "but it is not equally appreciated that these collections can never be really effective, nor can any organization now collecting fingerprints be effective, unless some well-designed agency is created, financed, and operated by the Federal Government to collect, file, and make available to all proper authorities all records of criminal identification throughout the country." Nor was there a central agency in Europe where the police of the several nations might pool their information, and few European nations even had centralized national files.[6]

Moreover, fingerprint identification systems were already beginning to buckle under the weight of their own success. Fingerprint files were growing rapidly, and this had the effect of filling up each subclassification—literally overflowing the pigeonholes and file drawers. Further subclassification would have to be devised in order to whittle each category to a manageable size, if the identification bureau was to avoid becoming a "statistical cemetery." Around 1920 the New York Police Department held 400,000 fingerprint cards in its files, the Federal Bureau at Leavenworth and Scotland Yard each held more than 300,000, and Berlin had around a quarter of a million cards. Identification bureaus were, to use the philosopher of technology Bruno Latour's phrase, "drowning in a flood of inscriptions and specimens."[7]

As fingerprint files grew, the original Henry system quickly became "inadequate in its allowance for sub-dividing such an immense collection." In 1919, A. J. Renoe, superintendent of the Federal Bureau at Leavenworth, "excogitated a Modification and Extension of the system," and many American bureaus adopted it. The "Renoe extension," however, could not be forced even upon American bureaus, some of which devised their own extensions of the Henry system, let alone bureaus in Europe, which had no intention of adopting an American modification. The Renoe extension, then, only introduced another incompatibility, sundering even bureaus that used the Henry system from one another.[8]

A related problem emerged with latent fingerprints. Both Henry and Vucetich were *ten*-print systems—that is, the fingerprint classification was based upon a reading of the patterns on all ten fingers in aggregate. This arrangement was consonant with the systems' goal of maintaining a file of known criminals, but it was ill-equipped for solving crimes on the basis of a single latent fingerprint found at the scene of a crime. An investigator could not search a ten-print file with a single latent print because the files were ordered according to the total number of patterns on all ten fingers. An investigator with a single latent print would have no idea what patterns might be on the other nine fingers and therefore no way to even begin searching the ten-print files for a match. In some cases detectives could infer from the position of the latent print which finger it was. Even then the examiner would have to make multiple searches by guessing the patterns of the other nine fingers. Such searches might have been feasible earlier in the century, when files were relatively small, but the rapid growth in the number of fingerprint cards in most agencies' files rendered such "cold searches" prohibitively time-consuming. "Because of the extensive growth of fingerprint identification," Thomas Jaycox, a Wichita police official, concluded in 1931, "the Henry System had outgrown it's usefullness for latent or single fingerprint work."[9]

By the 1920s most suspects arrested in the United States had their fingerprints taken and filed in a local or state file. In general, these ten-print files allowed the police to determine whether a suspect had a criminal record in the locality in which he or she was arrested. Latent fingerprints allowed the police to match a crime-scene print with that of a *known* suspect. More sophisticated uses of fingerprinting were relatively rare. In terms of the goal of a universal system of identification, which would allow everyone's past actions to follow them all over the world, the fingerprint system, despite its triumph over anthropometry, still left a lot to be desired. "If the police are to bring a reasonable proportion of the criminals of this country before the courts of justice and present evidence that will convict," warned the National Crime Commission in 1927, "then there will have to be a great development and expansion in the machinery now used in taking and recording finger prints."[10]

The 1920s and 1930s saw attempts to redress all of these perceived shortcomings and create national and global systems of fingerprint identification, capable of tracking criminal bodies wherever they might roam—to turn fingerprinting into a universal language, like Esperanto, through which police forces from different localities and nations might communicate. Some police officials became what the historian of technology Thomas Hughes calls "system-builders," who struggled "to construct and force unity from diversity, centralization in the face of pluralism, and coherence from chaos."[11]

Progressive reformers sought to introduce this sort of thinking to police work. Raymond Fosdick, who studied police procedures at the behest of the Rockefeller-sponsored Bureau of Social Hygiene, articulated the importance of the idea of "system" in his two influential comparative studies: *European Police Systems* (1915) and *American Police Systems* (1921). For Fosdick, "criminal records and identification devices" should be "but parts of one huge interrelated system." But, Fosdick lamented, although there was occasional international cooperation, "of broad cooperation on a systematic basis there is none." The technocratic idea of "system" and the methods of business administration emerged as potential solutions to both domestic and international problems of identification. "One of the outstanding facts disclosed by an investigation of detective bureaus in America," Fosdick complained in 1920, "is the amazing lack of ordinary business system in the prosecution of the work." "The outstanding fault with the identification bureaus of the police departments of today is the fact that they are not systematized as a whole," echoed New York Police Department (NYPD) Deputy Commissioner Joseph Faurot in 1921. "While their methods as adopted may work out satisfactorily as an individual department, complications arise when exchanging with another department or forwarding to a central bureau." In part, reformers believed they were only mirroring developments in the criminal underground itself, which they increasingly described as "an industry [with] established customs, practices and a recognized technique." Progressive reformers pointed to the increasing mobility of criminals to justify expanding criminal identification networks. "The professional criminal is a cosmopolitan," Fosdick warned. "He knows no national boundaries . . . The problem of the criminal is thus no longer national but international." It was imperative for criminal identification information to be at least as mobile as criminals themselves.[12]

"Mobilizing inscriptions," Bruno Latour has argued, is the central problem of technoscientific systems. Information is useful only to the extent that it can be transmitted across time and space. Latour's phrase is particularly apt for the effort to extend the reach of fingerprint information. Fingerprints were literally inscriptions from the criminal body, which could be archived in the institutional memory of the bureaucracy (transmitted across time) or mobilized for transmission across space. The story of fingerprinting after World War I was the story of attempts to take criminal identification systems to the next level of panoptic surveillance, to allow law enforcement authorities to follow criminals across greater expanses of time and space, to draw more tightly the web of state-sponsored surveillance. The efforts to "mobilize" fingerprints took three forms. One focused on finding more mobile formats—whether physical or taxonomic—for the information. The second focused on establishing what Latour calls "centres of calculation," giant institutional memories where information could be centralized. The third would be harnessing automated data-processing technology in order to provide better access to criminal identification information. These efforts represented, in Latour's words, "the history of all the little inventions made along the networks to accelerate the mobility of traces, or to enhance their faithfulness, combination and cohesion, so as to make action"—or identification—"at a distance possible."[13]

Though knowledge of the Henry and Vucetich systems spread around the world, many identification bureaus did not adopt them intact but rather developed their own systems based on them. By 1925 Italy was using the "Gasti system," Denmark had its "Jørgensen system," Norway used the "Daae system," Austria-Hungary used the "Windt-Kodiek system," French Indochina used the "Pottecher system," and Belgium used a hybrid of the Henry and Vucetich systems. The French, reeling from the collapse of Bertillonage, had "changed their system three times in the past twelve years." Germany did not even have a nationwide system, using the "Klatt system" in some jurisdictions and the "Roscher system" in others.[14]

The United States was even more fragmented. New York, under the stewardship of an identification clerk, James Parke, had been the first state to adopt dactyloscopy. Working only with Henry's poorly written book, Parke and his son Edward had struggled to master the Henry system. When they introduced the system into the Bureau of Prisons, they effected a simple, and seemingly logical, modification. Henry classifications are expressed as fractions with odd-numbered fingers in the numerator and even-numbered in the denominator. Thus the numerator consists of three fingers from the right hand and two from the left. Parke simply put the left hand in the numerator and the right hand in the denominator, which seemed easier to remember. Parke called his system "The American System of Fingerprint Classification," which eventually became quite an egregious misnomer, since his efforts to diffuse the system in the United States failed miserably. Parke, who was concentrating on an ultimately unsuccessful attempt to patent the American system, never even published an explanation of his system. He neglected the two chief means of disseminating a system: published books or pamphlets and personal tutelage. As a result, the "American system" became an oddity, and to this day New York State classifications are incompatible with those of the FBI, the NYPD, and every other law enforcement agency in the country. Most of these used some form of the Henry system, but New York's was not the only maverick bureau. Boston, Newark, Hoboken, and Portland, Maine, all used another type of classification, the "Connolly [or Conlay] system."[15]

Identification experts frequently called for a single international standard, but this only sowed dissension between adherents of the Henry and Vucetich systems. Henry was slightly more popular, owing to its power base in Britain, but there were experts who insisted that the Vucetich system was technically superior. Some proposed institutionalizing the dominant Henry system, others insisted upon a painful but necessary conversion to the superior Vucetich system, while still others suggested a new hybrid combining the best aspects of both. Edmond Locard, probably the world's leading criminalist, advocated establishing a combination of the Henry system and the Daae system as the international standard. By the 1920s, however, identification bureau chiefs already viewed the reclassification of extant fingerprint collections as too costly a job to justify the establishment of an international system, and the situation remained as it was. When fingerprints did have to be exchanged between jurisdictions using different classification systems, the prints had to be copied, forwarded to the neighboring agency, and reclassified. As is often the case with technological systems, incompatibilities and inefficiencies had simply become too entrenched and costly to eliminate. By 1935 a survey counted thirty-five different ten-print systems around the world. All of these were basically variations on Henry or Vucetich, but they differed enough to render their classifications incompatible. Ten years later another survey found similar variety.[16]

Once detectives began using latent fingerprints for identification, they realized that ten-print systems were of little use for searching for crime-scene prints. The earliest "unidigital," or "monodactyl" classification system was published by the Belgian criminalist Eugene Stockis in 1914. That same year, at the First International Police Conference in Monaco, Hakon Jørgensen, head of the Copenhagen Identification Bureau, introduced a system, evocatively named "Distant Identification" (DI), that would allow for both single-print classification and the transmission of fingerprint descriptions by telegraph. Jørgensen envisioned an international system of coding, which could transmit either ten-print or single-print descriptions. Instead of developing a universal ten-print classification system, he suggested, DI could translate between the various local classification systems. DI codes, up to fifty digits in length, were not classified, but simply assembled in numerical order in an annually updated international "lexicon" not unlike a modern telephone book.[17]

A typical DI code might look as follows:

> 33455 44544 2112 18.5.7.3.9 D 8.21.5–31.64 x 073.92.11
> N.B. 7329–5831 73.5 29.4.88 John Doe.

The first ten digits represented the general pattern type of each finger, beginning with the right index finger, through all the fingers of the right hand followed by the right thumb, the left index finger, the fingers of the left hand, and finally the left thumb. In this case the right index and middle fingers have loop patterns sloping to the left (indicated by the numeral 3); the right little finger, right thumb, and left ring finger have whorls (indicated by the numeral 5), and the remaining fingers have loops sloping to the right (indicated by the numeral 4). The numerals 1 and 2 represented arches. As with the Henry and Vucetich systems, further subclassification was achieved through ridge counting and tracing. The next four numerals represented the index and middle fingers of each hand. In the case of loops, (1) represented a low ridge count, (2) represented a high ridge count. In the case of whorls, (1) indicated an "inner" whorl, (2) represented a "meeting" whorl, and (3) indicated an "outer" whorl. Thus in the example above, the right index finger is a high-ridge-count loop (indicated by the numeral 2), the right middle finger is a low-ridge-count loop (indicated by the numeral 1), the left index finger is an inner whorl (indicated by the numeral 1), and the left middle finger is a meeting whorl. The next five numbers represented the ridge counts of each of the fingers of the right hand, which completed the "general formula."

The letter D indicated the beginning of the "detailed formula," which consisted of a numerical description of the single finger that gave the clearest impression. Looking at the print through "a special magnifying and ruled glass," the examiner described each ridge in order. The first numeral indicated a ridge characteristic, if any, that appeared on each ridge, according to the following guidelines:

> 0—a straight or pure ridge
> 1—a ridge with an island, known as an "eye"
> 2—a ridge with a fork [a bifurcation]
> 3—an upturned or contra fork

4—a ridge with a small downward bifurcation or hook

5—a ridge with a small upward bifurcation or hook

6—the beginning of a ridge

7—the ending or stopping of a ridge

8—a delta

9—a small fragment [a short ridge]

The second numeral indicated the length of the characteristic described in millimeters. Each ridge description was then followed by a period.

Next the examiner would record the "Nota Bene Formula." This was a description of the location and appearance of one or two particularly unusual ridge characteristics. The Nota Bene Formula was given as a four-digit number, in which the first digit represented which finger the characteristic appeared on, the second digit represented which sector of the finger the characteristic appeared on, the third digit represented the ridge count from the core to the characteristic, and the fourth digit represented the type of characteristic, according to the descriptions enumerated above. The sector was determined using the ruled magnifying glass which, when placed with its center at the center of the pattern, divided the print into eight equal sectors. Finally, the examiner recorded the subject's height in centimeters, followed by the subject's birth date and name.

Through this system, Jørgensen envisioned the complete reduction of personal identity to coded information which could be wired anywhere in the world. DI also provided codes for Bertillon's *portrait parlé,* which could be appended to the end of the fingerprint code. In this way DI could transmit, not just the coded fingerprint, but the entire criminal body. For instance, a typical *portrait parlé,* such as "stature tall, color of hair light chestnut, arcades [part of the forehead] small, depth of root of nose small, bridge of nose concave and wavy, salient big, height of upper lip small, lower lip pending, mouth small, helix [part of the ear] beginning part small, adherence of ear lobe total, antitragus convex and pluriforked," would be coded as:

$$a(28)1(\tfrac{1}{3}6)7(19) \, b114\tfrac{1}{3}\,\tfrac{2}{6}$$

DI, which enthusiastic officials called "an intensification of the fingerprint system of identification," reduced the criminal body to a code, a unique numeral, which could be transmitted across space. Some semblance of the criminal body, as well as its unique identity, could be reconstructed anywhere in the world. The body could now be fully "captured" by the state, the terms of its exchange governed only by the laws of the state and the limits of international cooperation. DI mobilized the fingerprint, allowing it to cross physical, political, and taxonomic boundaries without compromising its immutability. Criminal identification information could, as San Francisco Police Chief F. H. DePue had predicted in 1902, "laugh at distance and time."[18]

Jørgensen published DI in Danish in 1916, and in 1921 he presented the system at the Congress of Medical Jurisprudence in Brussels. In the spring of 1922 he toured Europe demonstrating DI in the Netherlands, Switzerland, Germany, Poland, and Austria. That fall he crossed the Atlantic and presented DI at the First National Police Conference (NPC) in New York City, where it was received enthusiastically. "There is no doubt, gentlemen, that this is something new in criminal identification," gushed New York Police Commissioner Richard Enright, "and as soon as we can get hold of it in a proper way, we will have it installed in this Bureau, at New York; and, of course, we will be very glad to transmit it to anybody else who desires to obtain it." The conference formed a committee to study the system and report back the following year. After the conference Jørgensen toured the East Coast, training identification clerks from Charleston to Boston in Distant Identification. DI classification, however, was even more complicated and arcane than the Henry and Vucetich systems. Although the identification community initially got very excited about DI, the system proved too rigorous and demanding to win widespread application.[19]

By the early 1920s single-fingerprinting's time had clearly come; single-fingerprint systems multiplied as rapidly as ten-print systems had a decade earlier. In 1921 Charles S. Collins, the leading expert at Scotland Yard's Identification Division, who had seen DI demonstrated in 1920, published his own system. Like DI, the Collins system used a ruled magnifying glass and included a numeric telegraphic code by which a crime-scene print might be circulated to other jurisdictions and even other countries, provided that they maintained a single-print file classified by the same system.[20]

In 1922, even as Jørgensen was demonstrating DI in New York, two domestically bred single-fingerprint systems were presented to the IACP in San Francisco. The first had been devised by John A. Larson, a protégé of the legendary Berkeley police chief August Vollmer. The chiefs were enthusiastic about Larson's system, through which, they hoped, "a full classification of any finger may be sent out, or placed on the wire, and so establish a scientific identity at any distance any time it is wanted without another fingerprint for comparison." However, the chiefs worried about repeating the problem they already had with incompatible ten-print systems, since a second single-print system, the "Crosskey system," was introduced at the same meeting. Walter Crosskey was in charge of fingerprint classification at San Quentin. Like many prison fingerprint clerks, he was an inmate, but, as one of the chiefs remarked, "that is nothing against his system." Crosskey saw a commercial angle to his system: for so-called "civilian" uses of fingerprinting, such as in banks and insurance companies where fingerprints were used only to verify identity, one fingerprint would do as well as ten, and they might be in the market for a single-print system.[21]

In 1923 Jørgensen returned to New York to attend the second meeting of the NPC, now globalized into the International Police Conference (IPC). The conference resolved that DI become "standard police procedure for cooperation between the different police departments." The conference also agreed to compile "a 'One Finger Register' of the fingerprints of burglars and housebreakers, taken at the scene of crime," and that "the Police Department of the City of New York be requested to establish a school of instruction" in Distant Identification. Finally, the conference set up apparatus for transmitting coded fingerprint descriptions by radio in eighteen eastern cities. By 1925 the European International Police Conference held in Vienna had endorsed DI, and an *International Fingerprint Register* containing 5,000 "signalments" based on DI was available for sale at the IPC in New York. DI was still going strong and publishing a *Register* in 1927, but so was the Collins system, updated by Frederick Cherrill, which reportedly made more than 350 identifications in 1928 and 1929. Single-print systems continued to proliferate. Thomas Jaycox of Wichita published a modification of the Larson system in 1931. By 1935 at least thirteen new single-print systems had been added to those already mentioned: Oloriz (Madrid), Borgerhoff (Belgium), Gasti (Italy), Moran (San Diego), Born (Bern), Sagredo, Heindl (Dresden), Neben (Germany), Lyonnese (Lyon), Battley (Britain), Giraud and Henquel (Algiers), and Barlow (Los Angeles). August Rosenfeldt of Seattle devised another system in 1940.[22]

Single-print classification posed a number of confounding technical problems. A true single-print system would require that a bureau hold ten times as many identification cards as with a ten-print system, and, if the examiner did not know from what finger the latent print derived, identification "may necessitate the searching of ten collections." Single-print files were, therefore, usually limited either to especially notorious offenders or separated by *modus operandi* (method of operating). *Modus operandi* filing systems—behavioral rather than somatic systems of identification—proliferated along with fingerprint systems. W. L. Atcherly, chief constable of West Riding in the Yorkshire Constabulary, developed the most elaborate *modus* system in 1913. With Atcherly's system, "habitual or traveling criminals can be traced from community to community by a comparison of their methods of work." Crimes could be classified according to type of person or property attacked, means of entry, objects taken, time of day, "style," accomplices, transport, and "trademark." The last category made provisions for "certain extraordinary acts not associated with the object of the crime, such as 'poisoning the dog,' 'leaving a note behind,' 'changing their clothes,' 'drinking the wine and smoking cigars,' or even 'committing a nuisance on the scene of the crime.'"[23]

Moreover, single-print files required an entirely new method of classification based only upon the information contained in a single print. Single-print classifiers could not simply add up the pattern types in ten fingers. There were two primary strategies to address this problem. The first, adopted by Jørgensen, Collins, Cherrill, Battley, Crosskey, and others, was to define enough different pattern types so that even single fingerprints could be divided into searchable groups. For single fingerprints, it would not be sufficient simply to divide them into arches, loops, and whorls: many more subdivisions would be necessary. Usually this entailed some form of ridge counting. A similar strategy was to derive information from measured distances between given points on the print. Either of these methods required some sort of fine measuring tool, such as a magnifying glass etched with a grid like those used by Jørgensen and Collins. The Swiss "Born system" also used a magnifying glass and a "zone scheme," San Diego Deputy Sheriff Boyd B. Moran's system used a transparent grid, and Cherrill and Battley used a glass etched with concentric circles.[24]

Critics contended that these "counting and glass methods" were "artificial" and "inadequate for the final solution of the problems" of identifying latent prints. The problem with measuring was that differences in pressure during the printing process might alter measured distances by up to two millimeters. Moreover, in order to classify a print these systems required a nearly complete fingerprint, something that criminals were seldom considerate enough to leave at the crime scene, and "one or more points of orientation which may or may not be found in the latent fingerprint." It was not uncommon to find partial latent prints where the examiner could not tell for certain which way was up. In response to these criticisms, Larson, Heindl, Oloriz, Vucetich, and Jaycox adopted what they called a "morphological approach": a very detailed reading of the characteristics of the core and delta, which did not require knowledge of the location or orientation of the area under study. Under the Larson system, for instance, core types might be called "enclosures," "forks," single, double, plain, and eyed "staples," or "rods." Larson classified prints first according to overall pattern type (arch, loop, or whorl), then by the direction of the slant of the ridges, by the core type, the characteristics of the "envelope" (the area surrounding the core), delta characteristics, a description of the first ridge in front of the delta, and then by a ridge count or trace. (Since arches don't have cores, Larson and the others made separate provisions for subdividing arches.) Using these serial subclassifications, morphological single-prints systems could "describe" a print by a lengthy alphanumeric string.[25]

Morphological schemes, however, shared a weakness with "counting and glass methods" in that they engendered such an enormous variety of pattern types that identification clerks could hardly be expected to master them, let alone distinguish them consistently. The greater the number of pattern types, the greater the danger that identification clerks would mistake them. As some critics had said earlier about the Battley system, "it is impossible for the human mind to remember the variations that arise under this system." Even Larson was forced to admit that "the problem thus far has not been satisfactorily solved."[26]

Although single fingerprinting was promising enough to keep the system-builders working, identification bureaus viewed the cumbersome single-fingerprint systems that were available as more trouble than they were worth. Collins's telegraphic code, which was supposed to link the entire British Commonwealth, was actually used only twice:

LOOPS

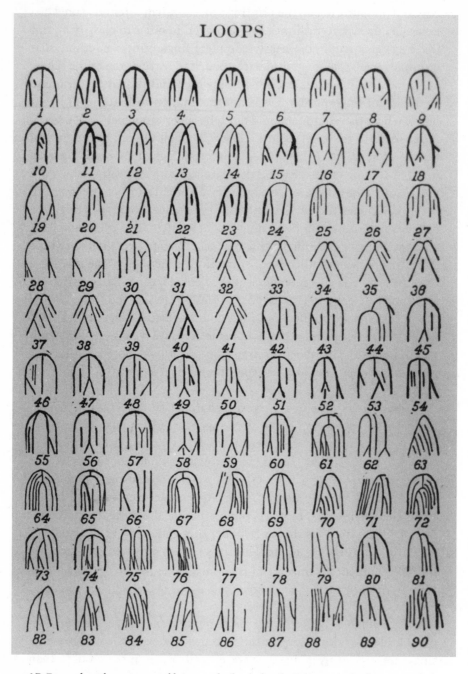

17. Examples of core types of loops and whorls for the Larson single-fingerprint classification system.

once to New Zealand and once to Australia in 1924. The NYPD received the Collins code, but in four years they were not once called upon by Scotland Yard to use it.[27]

An alternative was to transmit the image of the fingerprint itself rather than reducing it to a lengthy telegraphic code. Since the fingerprint was such a magnificently economical packet of information, why bother encoding it at all? The problem was the slow speed of the mail, but a potential solution lay in telephone and telegraph wires and radio waves. Primitive facsimile technology had existed since 1843, and by the 1920s photographs were being transmitted across the Atlantic Ocean by facsimile. As early as 1905 Henry Faulds had suggested that fingerprints "might be photographed to a distance and lead to arrest." As two-dimensional images which required neither color nor even gray scales, fingerprints were ideally suited for early facsimile technology. The Frenchman Eduard Belin's facsimile apparatus, for example, worked far better with pure black-and-white images like fingerprints than with the half-tones of photographs. Belin used a special ink and powder, sometimes applied directly to the fingers of the suspect, to create an embossed fingerprint image. The raising or lowering of a stylus as it passed over the image modulated an electric current, which could be transmitted either by telegraph, telephone, or radio. The receiving apparatus was a sensitive galvanometer, which beamed light onto photographic film according to the current it received. Fingerprints worked well because the stylus did not have to detect varying heights on the image—the images were digital, in the sense that the current was either on or off, either there was a ridge or there wasn't. By 1922 Belin had completed the first transatlantic facsimile transmission of a fingerprint, from Bordeaux to Bar Harbor, Maine, by wireless.[28]

In 1924 Illinois Bell demonstrated a more sophisticated device for transmitting both fingerprint descriptions and images over telephone wires. And in 1925 AT&T Vice President John J. Carty displayed facsimile equipment for fingerprint transmission at the IPC in New York. After wiring a set of fingerprints to Chicago in the morning, Carty telephoned Chicago in front of the delegates to ask whether they could identify the prints. (They could.) Carty boasted that he could wire fingerprints anywhere in the country within eight minutes. AT&T's apparatus was fairly elaborate; it used "specially prepared telephotographs" rather than the relief images employed by Belin. In Rome progress was also reportedly made on a system for "transmitting photographs by numerals over telegraph wires."[29]

Facsimile transmission did not catch on, though. "While it is a beautiful thought to send fingerprints by telegraph, wireless, etc.," commented Chief Bayle of the Paris Bureau of Judicial Identification in 1926, "it is more or less theoretical, and though it has been done successfully in some instances, it will be some years before these methods replace the actual mail." In fact, it turned out to be much longer than that. Facsimile transmissions of fingerprints did not become common until the modern fax machine itself did, in the 1980s. Although AT&T's devices, which cost $30,000 each, were out of the price range of even the largest state and municipal police departments, Belin's were not. But the main problem was that a facsimile device would only be useful to the extent that neighboring identification bureaus adopted the same, or a compatible, device. In other words, facsimile transmission required international, interstate, and interagency cooperation. Lack of cooperation between law enforcement agencies, not technology, was the chief obstacle to extending the criminal identification network and further mobilizing the information it contained. As these agencies began to view fingerprint files as valuable commodities, they would spend as much time vying for control of criminal identification information as they did sharing it.[30]

Glass, light, calculation and electricity—these do the work and laugh at distance and time.

—F. H. DePue, *The DePue System of Identification* (1902)

CHAPTER 10

Digital Digits

If transferring information between law enforcement agencies invited so many technical difficulties, why not simply centralize the information: create a single comprehensive agency, at either the national or the international level, responsible for collecting and filing all information on criminals? This would be what Bruno Latour calls a "centre of calculation," where information, or knowledge, can be accumulated. "Gaining knowledge," Latour argues, requires learning "how to be familiar with things, people and events, which are *distant.*" An effective center of calculation, however, requires accumulating "simultaneously as little and as much" information "as possible." Centers of calculation that heedlessly acquire information are prone to "drowning in a flood of inscriptions and specimens." Hence it is necessary to "simultaneously mobilise elements while keeping them at a distance." Central identification bureaus ultimately settled on this kind of solution. Central bureaus did collect criminal identification information, but local bureaus also retained it. The information thus remained dispersed, kept at a distance, which helped avoid information overload— at least temporarily.[1]

This was not the only reason all criminal identification information was not centralized. As fingerprints became police departments' and courts' preferred medium for storing criminal identities, fingerprint files became valuable commodities. State bureaucracies began to realize that knowledge was power. Large urban—and, in Europe, national—police departments were among the first bureaucracies to realize this, and they were reluctant to give up the information they had collected. By the 1920s urban police departments had amassed the world's largest collections of fingerprints. Some police chiefs resisted relinquishing their fingerprint files to any central agency. They invoked the tradition of policing as a local, rather than federal or national, function. Fingerprinting offered the promise of enhancing the panoptic power of the state, but "the state" was not a monolithic entity. Internecine struggles between arms of the state militated against the construction of a truly all-seeing fingerprint network. Urban police chiefs would emerge as the unlikely, and somewhat unwitting, heroes of the resistance to the centralization of surveillance information by the state.

In the United States policing was constitutionally a function of local government, reflecting the long-standing American sentiment that the federal government could not be trusted with police powers. At the turn of the century the federal role in law enforcement was still minuscule, limited to a few tax and postal inspectors and the Treasury Department's Secret Service. The exponential growth in federal law enforcement would be one of the major developments in policing in the twentieth century. But it did not occur without fierce opposition. Local law enforcement officials, playing David to the federal government's Goliath, nearly succeeded in wresting control of the central fingerprint bureau away from the federal government. These officials almost forestalled the establishment of the institution that today holds the world's largest collection of fingerprints: the Federal Bureau of Investigation (FBI).

In 1893 American police chiefs founded the country's first national police organization, the National Police Chiefs Union, which was aimed at facilitating communication between fragmented local jurisdictions. From the beginning a standardized criminal identification system was a key part of any such integration. At the Union's first meeting, Chief Roger O'Mara of Pittsburgh called upon "the Legislature of each state to pass such laws as may make it imperative upon the chief officer of each prison for felons to adopt the Bertillon system, and that the several police departments of cities, and sheriffs of counties, have reasonable access to official records of such measurements, or that some proper system of exchange of information be adopted and enforced."[2]

In 1895 the Union became the International Association of Chiefs of Police (IACP), although it remained almost exclusively a North American organization. The IACP called on the U.S. Department of Justice to establish a national bureau for the identification of criminals. This proposal faltered for constitutional reasons because it involved turning over what was essentially state information to the federal government. In 1896 Chief Jacob Frey of Baltimore suggested that the IACP establish its own privately run identification bureau, and two years later the National Bureau of Criminal Identification opened for business in Chicago. It moved to Washington, D.C., in 1900.[3]

In 1902 Congress authorized its own National Bureau of Criminal Identification, located at the Federal Penitentiary in Leavenworth, Kansas, to keep Bertillon records, photographs, and "information of a special as well as general criminal nature, concerning persons here as elsewhere." Since federal law enforcement was modest at that time and the number of federal prisoners small, the Federal Bureau did not have a large base upon which to build its fingerprint collection, although it did solicit copies of fingerprints from other bureaus.[4]

Law enforcement, however, was mainly a state matter, and most convicts were in the custody of states, not the federal government. The states, therefore, commanded the largest collections of identifications, and the largest states, in particular the Empire State, thought *they* should serve as the central clearinghouse for identification information. Already state institutions were viewing criminal identification bureaus as sources of prestige and power, rather than as burdens. In 1898, the same year the IACP opened its National Bureau of Identification, Cornelius Collins, the New York superintendent of prisons, suggested that the New York State Prison Bureau, as the largest identification bureau in the country with 24,000 Bertillon cards, be established as a central bureau. In 1900 Collins preemptively announced that he had "arranged to receive cards from nearly every penal institution in the United States and Canada which uses the system, thus making this Bureau the Central Bureau for North America, and affording a system of criminal supervision and record international in its scope." By 1901, a year before the establishment of the Federal Bureau at Leavenworth, New York held Bertillon records contributed from seventeen states and Canada. The next year Collins reported that "the bureau is in constant correspondence with the police of most of the large cities in America and has frequent requests from France, Germany, and Austria for the records of criminals under arrest in those countries, thus proving that its scope has become international." In 1904 Collins boasted that New York's exhibit at the St. Louis Exposition brought "the Albany bureau . . . more clearly to the attention of the chiefs of police and its value as an aid in the supervision and detection of criminals was more fully impressed upon them. The result is that the applications for information have largely increased in number; and the bureau, which is by far the largest on this continent, has thus materially extended it sphere of usefulness."[5]

If states' rights stymied police cooperation in the United States, the problem was even greater among the sovereign nations of Europe. In 1914 Prince Albert I convened the First International Police Conference in Monaco, which was attended by twenty-four countries from Europe, South America, and the Middle East. (The United States took little official interest in the meeting. The sole American representatives were Raymond Fosdick, who reported on the conference for the Bureau of Social Hygiene, and "a judge from Dayton," whose name has not been preserved.) The conference called "for the establishment of centralized international criminal records," but, significantly, "of a kind which have not yet been agreed." The need for standardization had to be balanced against national sovereignty and cultural peculiarities.[6]

In 1922 Hakon Jørgensen announced that until an international identification bureau could be established he would "take upon himself" to operate an international Bureau for Distant Identification in Copenhagen. That year he secured the agreement of the identification bureaus of Switzerland, Amsterdam, Berlin, Stuttgart, Dresden, Munich, Hamburg, Vienna, and Warsaw to contribute to the international lexicon held in Copenhagen. In 1923 the Copenhagen Bureau was named the official fingerprint bureau of the International Criminal Police Congress, a pan-European police organization that would eventually evolve into Interpol.[7]

In the United States, meanwhile, two giant figures in American law enforcement would vie for control of fingerprint files. One, an obscure assistant attorney general, would become a household name synonymous with national policing; the other, commissioner of the nation's largest police force, would be forgotten to history. Their battle pitted the power of the federal government against the American tradition of local control of police powers.

The battle was initiated by New York City Police Commissioner Richard E. Enright, a new "professional" type of policeman who liked to apply business principles to law enforcement. In 1921 Enright convened a mammoth National Police Conference (NPC) in New York City with the backing of the Chamber of Commerce and Baron G. Collier, an eccentric millionaire with an interest in law enforcement issues "who liked to sport a police badge and drive around with a police siren blaring on his motor car." With the NPC, Enright mounted a challenge to the authority of the IACP. Relations between the NYPD and the IACP had always been tense, ever since the 1900 IACP meeting in New York, when New York Police Commissioner William D. Devary lost his bid for the presidency of the IACP to Richard Sylvester of Washington, D.C. New York boycotted the meeting until 1918, when Enright became commissioner, a conspicuous absence that prompted accusations of arrogance and aloofness from the other chiefs. At the same time, many NPC delegates, who were, by design, limited to municipal officials, felt that the IACP was dominated by sheriffs, private detectives like those of the famous Pinkerton Detective Agency, "private interests and private officers of railroad organizations."[8]

In its managerial outlook, its sharp distinction between public and private policing, and its consolidation of the power of municipal law enforcement agencies, the NPC was representative of the growing professionalization and rationalization of municipal government during the Progressive era. The NPC was part of "the general transition of city government in the post-1890s era to a 'functional' model of organization . . . imitating the emerging managerial models of corporations." Enright urged American police to apply the same rational principles that had generated such success in the railroads, big business, finance, and the insurance industry. "There is one great and important business—the Police Business—in this country that is still unorganized," he declared, "that is still, for the most part, at least a generation behind the age." Enright was a police chief who epitomized the Progressive era, who brought a progressive emphasis on rationalization and technocratic management to police work. Progressive chiefs like Enright transformed policing from a political spoil for party hacks into a profession and a "business."[9]

At the NPC the internationalization of crime was high on the list of concerns. Enright cited an anarchist bombing on Wall Street that killed thirty-nine people in September 1920 and warned of an invasion of radicals, anarchists, and criminals, trained in firearms and now adrift in bankrupt postwar Europe. One of the NPC's goals was the "establishment of some efficient method of handling criminal immigration through United States ports, or over borders from Mexico and Canada." Immigrants were pouring into the United States, and the chiefs, like many Americans, suspected that Europe was exporting its "criminal class" across the Atlantic. In contrast to the nation's relatively relaxed immigration policy, the chiefs suggested that "the character, habits and moral tendencies of all persons seeking to enter the United States shall be investigated respecting their purposes and fitness, morally or otherwise, to enter the United States." They called on the federal government "to arrange for a finger-print identification of such persons either at their port of embarkation, or upon their arrival at any port in the United States or the boundaries between the United States and other countries." The police in New York City, which, as the nation's portal for European immigration, bore the brunt of absorbing the new immigrants, were particularly concerned. "If immigrants are not fingerprinted upon their arrival, it is of small use to print them upon their deportation, and if it is necessary to print them upon deportation, then why not upon their arrival?" reasoned Joseph Faurot, now deputy commissioner.[10]

Police officials stoked nativist prejudice by invoking the specter of the "international professional criminal," whom they mythologized as a glamorous jewel and art thief along the lines of Adam Worth, the famous "Napoleon of crime." "The professional crook is a factor which must be reckoned with by the authorities," said Faurot. "There are hundreds of them who do nothing but travel about the world, plying their chosen vocations, which makes it more necessary that a Central Bureau should be maintained." That such high-end criminals bore little resemblance to the typical American immigrant mattered little. Increasing mobility prompted the demand for internationalization, as officials sought to make criminal identification information as mobile as criminals themselves. August Vollmer agreed: "Rapid transportation has changed crime conditions all over the world. Professional criminals no longer confine their operations to a particular locality, but travel from one end of the country to another and from one country to another. If we hope to reduce the extent of their operations, central bureaus must be located in every state, and national clearing houses in each country. Clearing houses for criminal records are no longer an experiment; they are a necessity."[11]

In accordance with the emphasis on international crime, Enright took steps to make the NPC the truly international organization the IACP claimed to be. At its second meeting, in 1922, which Enright touted as "the largest and most representative congress of police officials ever gathered together for the common purpose of devising ways and means for the more efficient prevention of crime, promotion of law and order and the suppression of criminality throughout the world," the NPC metamorphosed into the International Police Conference (IPC) and welcomed delegates from Argentina, Belgium, Brazil, Canada, Denmark, England, France, Germany, and Mexico.[12]

In order to facilitate cooperation between domestic and international identification bureaus, one of the chief items on the agenda of the NPC/IPC was "establishing a Central Police Bureau in Washington, D.C., or elsewhere," which would hold criminal intelligence and information, a goal that had eluded the IACP for two decades. A central fingerprint file and "some efficient method of distributing information regarding the movement of known criminals in and out of prisons" was one object of such an bureau, but Enright also envisioned that the bureau would allow standardization of police procedure and methods, cooperation between police forces, standardized traffic regulation and signals, immigration control, and "establishing some system of controlling and tracing the movements of criminal anarchists and radicals."[13]

"Let the bureau embrace the best fingerprint and criminal record library in the country," urged Colonel Douglas McKay, Enright's predecessor as police commissioner of New York, "with necessary and adequate arrangements for making information promptly available to all proper persons." The use of fingerprints in the United States was growing, Enright was pleased to report, but "when these records are made they should not be hidden under a barrel. The local police authorities should keep a copy, of course, but another copy should be sent to some central depository of information . . . available for the immediate use of any Police Department in this country of high or low degree; indeed it will be available for the information of police authorities at home and abroad."[14]

Enright saw no reason to delay the establishment of a central bureau any longer. "I do not think we ought to await legislative action of Congress or anybody else to do this very necessary work," he announced. "Any city that has extra fingerprints or extra copies of their criminal records will send them to our temporary Clearing House here in New York. We will go to all the pains of cataloging them and take care of the situation until the time comes when we will turn it over to somebody else. You realize, of course, that receiving, indexing, handling and furnishing information of this kind is quite a burden, but we are willing to assume it for the benefit of the organization and for the benefit of all concerned until something else can be done."[15]

The commissioner's offer was, of course, not entirely selfless. In establishing the NYPD as a temporary national fingerprint bureau, Enright sought to seize control of the nascent national fingerprint system. He was already off to a good start. The NYPD fingerprint bureau, which held 400,000 sets of fingerprints, was the country's—and probably the world's—largest, larger even than the Federal Bureau at Leavenworth, which held around 350,000 prints, and far larger than the IACP's National Bureau of Identification in Washington. By fingerprinting petty offenders, police departments were able to expand fingerprint files much faster than penal institutions, which could only print convicts. The NYPD's identification bureau, which began collecting fingerprints in 1905, outstripped the New York State Prison Bureau during the 1910s and began exchanging fingerprints with other cities and countries on its own. In 1915, revealing its aspirations, the NYPD reported that "the New York Bureau is rapidly becoming a national clearing house for information concerning criminals." By 1924 the NYPD's identification operation employed fifty-three people and commanded a budget of $140,000.[16]

In 1921, therefore, New York was fulfilling long-harbored ambitions when the NPC delegates resolved "that until such time as a National Police Bureau is established under Federal laws, Police Headquarters, New York, be designated as the temporary National Police Bureau to receive, file and furnish to the various police departments of the country, upon request and at their expense as to postage, telephone or telegraph charges, any criminal information which may be available." So solicitous were the delegates that they almost scuttled the resolution, for fear of imposing "an undue burden and expense on New York City," a concern Enright deftly allayed, granting, "I think for this year at least we can handle it." Enright was willing to shoulder the expense of maintaining a central bureau in exchange for the power offered by the control of centralized information. Enright recognized that he was sitting on the most valuable cache of fingerprint information in the country, if not the world, and he had no intention of giving it to the IACP, or the federal government, for nothing. Indeed, in 1924 Enright declared that "the New York Police Department will never file a criminal record with any central bureau unless a bureau is organized which is to be under police control."[17]

Enright's enemies suggested that, despite his protestations, he wanted to seize the national bureau for New York. At the 1922 meeting IACP President Joseph M. Quigley, police chief of Rochester, complained: "There seems to be some selfish motive back of the attitude taken by New York City. New York City went down to Washington and attempted to have this Bureau established in New York, and to practically put it under the control of New York. New York has for a number of years been building up a bureau of identification on its own, and they have been a little bit stingy about giving out fingerprints, pictures and measurements, to other departments around the country."[18]

The IACP's embarrassing inability to get the job done had been crucial to Enright's success. "If the Chiefs of Police Association does not accomplish what we are here to accomplish, why should we defer longer in accomplishing something that everyone here knows we need?" asked Police Director Myers of Richmond at the 1921 NPC meeting. "I am for the International Association of Chiefs of Police of the United States if they do something, and if they do not do anything I am for any organization that will do something," added Lee Seymour. After having failed to convince Congress to fund a national bureau since 1895, the chiefs, alarmed by Enright's aggressive actions in New York, had finally conceded that they would be willing to fund the bureau themselves, if Congress would merely authorize it. In 1921 they finally interested Attorney General Harry Daugherty in shepherding the proposal through Congress, but legal complications delayed the process.[19]

In 1923 Daugherty presented Congress with a fait accompli by simply ordering the files of the Leavenworth bureau combined with the

IACP files to form an Identification Division under the auspices of the Justice Department's Bureau of Investigation, an agency that had been founded by Attorney General Charles Bonaparte in 1908. Daugherty hoped to secure congressional approval shortly thereafter, but the Teapot Dome scandal abruptly drove him from office. Thus the Identification Division had been established before acquiring Congress's sanction. In what the historian Donald Dilworth calls "one of the ironies of history," the establishment of the Identification Division "was probably outside the law."[20]

Enright enlisted the help of the New York congressional delegation in a final desperate bid to forestall the federal bureau. In 1924 Representatives John Kindred and Fiorello LaGuardia both introduced bills which would establish a national police bureau without placing it under the control of the Justice Department. At congressional hearings in April, Enright cited states' rights and the severe constitutional limitations on federal law enforcement. "There is not very much friendship between the Department of Justice and most of the police departments of our country," he testified, "and we rather object to becoming an annex to the Department of Justice." When pressed about who should run the proposed bureau, Enright suggested the Department of the Interior. He proposed to shape the new bureau more like an information "clearing house" than an arm of law enforcement. He also tried to stir up opposition to Justice Department sponsorship by appealing to suspicion of the federal government and private interests, calling for "a central bureau for criminal identification that is absolutely free from political influence, a bureau which is controlled by the police of the country and closed absolutely to the convenience of politicians and private detective agencies."[21]

Enright invoked the American traditions of local control of law enforcement and opposition to any sort of federal police power, in contrast to the European model of national police forces:

MR. HERSEY: You have no prejudice against the Department of the Interior?

MR. ENRIGHT: They will not have the control of this information that belongs to the police organizations of America.

MR. HERSEY: Keep it out of the Department of Justice?

MR. ENRIGHT: Yes, sir; we do not want to work into the position of nationalizing the police, and if it goes to the Department of Justice, right along the idea is in the minds of the people that that would eventually lead to a more or less nationalization of the police but if it is in another organization, it is not felt that this nationalization will take place.[22]

The opposition exploited fears that the new bureau would provide a wedge for the Justice Department to begin moving into law enforcement. "A jealous regard for State rights," LaGuardia argued, opposed any inkling of a federal role in law enforcement: "To get the Department of Justice involved in the police duties of the municipalities or cities, I fear would cause friction rather than harmony." Therefore LaGuardia wished to restrict the new bureau to "a clearing house for criminal information. This would simply be a clearing house or central filing bureau for criminal identification records and nothing else." He further noted "that the Department of Justice, under the Attorney General, has no authority in law to collate, collect, and furnish this information in the manner contemplated by this bill. As a matter of practical legislative experience, you will find that there will be great opposition to extending any such powers to the Department of Justice."[23]

The IACP leadership was infuriated, and they denounced Enright at the same hearings. In a telling slip, IACP President William P. Rutledge of Detroit misunderstood the initials of the National Police Conference, referring to it as the "New York Police Conference." This organization, he claimed, "was formed for the purpose of disintegrating and undermining the old organization of the chiefs of police of this country. The New York Police Conference and the New York police officials gained the idea of a national central bureau of criminal identification from the International Association of Chiefs of Police."[24]

On May 8, 1924, Representative George Graham of Pennsylvania introduced a compromise bill. LaGuardia's proposed revisions to the bill indicate his continuing concern that the new bureau not be granted police powers. By June 21, however, the battle was lost. Congress authorized funding for the Identification Division in the Justice Department's Bureau of Investigation, which was temporarily placed under the charge of a young assistant director of the Bureau named John Edgar Hoover.[25]

One might plausibly argue that under Hoover the Bureau of Investigation, soon to be renamed the Federal Bureau of Investigation (FBI), did exactly what Enright had warned it would: become a federal law enforcement agency with police and investigative powers beholden to "the convenience of politicians." One might even argue that over the ensuing half-century the FBI would vividly demonstrate the dangers, as well as the benefits, of federal police powers. Even aside from the assumption of police powers, the Identification Division provided Hoover with an enormous power base founded upon criminal intelligence and information. Hoover acted upon the principle foreseen by Enright: that knowledge, in the form of criminal identification, could be power.

The NYPD continued to hold out against the federal bureau for several years. Captain John Golden justified this by acting as if the FBI were still something other than a national bureau. "Some day," Golden promised in 1925, "when a national bureau is created, we will be very glad to turn over to the bureau, thirty, forty or fifty thousand finger prints for a start, and these finger prints will embrace criminals from all over the country." With legal authority behind him, however, Hoover had won the battle. The FBI had become both the centralized criminal identification clearinghouse and the coordinator of national policing activities that Enright had envisioned. In 1926 George McLaughlin replaced Enright as commissioner, and at that year's IACP meeting Hoover was able to announce "a notable achievement, and one in which I know that each and every one of you gentlemen will be personally as well as officially interested: the securing as regular contributors to our Division of Identification of the cities of New York and Chicago."[26]

The fingerprint file formed the core of the FBI's criminal files, which soon expanded to include surveillance data as well as mere identifying information. Hoover worked quickly to consolidate his position at the center of the American criminal identification network. He put the new combined fingerprint file into order, completing the recataloguing of the entire collection on June 30, 1925. He aggressively lobbied local enforcement officials at all levels to submit copies of prints to the FBI.[27]

With his conception of the FBI as a domestic surveillance agency, Hoover wanted the ability to track as many citizens as possible, not just those convicted of crimes. His vision of fingerprint identification went beyond merely recording the prints of those individuals who happened to pass through the criminal justice system. In a time of political tension and unrest, with war on the horizon, Hoover's conception of fingerprint identification was like a perversion of the International Society for Personal Identification's (ISPI) old Progressive vision of uni-versal civilian fingerprinting as a means to a more civil society. Hoo-ver, in contrast, saw universal fingerprinting as the key to a national web of individualized surveillance, under his personal control.

In order to achieve this goal, Hoover breached the unwritten rule that fingerprinting was for criminals, not law-abiding citizens. He sought to gather the fingerprints of as many civilians as possible, begin-ning with government employees and immigrants. In 1929 the federal government began fingerprinting all civil servants. In 1937 the FBI re-ceived the prints of members of the Civilian Conservation Corps, and in 1939 prints were taken from employees of the Works Progress Ad-ministration (WPA). In 1940 Congress passed the Alien Registration Act, which eventually delivered over a million fingerprints to the FBI. It was this policy that soon enabled the FBI to surpass the NYPD Iden-tification Bureau and the Buenos Aires General Register for the Identi-fication of Persons as the world's largest fingerprint collection. After a brief period in which fingerprinting was restricted to people convicted of crimes, Hoover returned fingerprinting to its origins, as a mecha-nism for state monitoring and surveillance of citizens, especially those deemed foreign, politically radical, or otherwise dangerous. To a cer-tain extent, Hoover did succeed in exploiting fingerprint information for political intimidation and surveillance, just as Enright had warned. With his pervasive, yet hidden, influence over American life for most of the century, Hoover embodied the notion that information was power.[28]

"Formerly disunified and incoherent," by the 1930s, under Hoover's leadership, the universal fingerprinting movement had "taken on dis-tinct shape, become solidified and articulate." "Hoover imparted a new and sinister impetus" to the universal fingerprint campaign, shud-dered the American Civil Liberties Union (ACLU), which actively op-posed universal fingerprinting. "Through his colossal publicity set-up," Hoover was able to promote universal fingerprinting far more adroitly than earlier advocates. Hoover and the organizations support-ing him began to speak of "voluntary" fingerprinting and to urge that all citizens, for their own protection, rush to the nearest police station to have their fingerprints recorded. The national trauma over the kid-napping of the Lindbergh baby in 1932 helped popularize the notion that all citizens should have themselves and their children finger-printed for their own protection. A universal fingerprinting campaign in Massachusetts, led by Boston Police Commissioner Lewis Valentine, collected 500,000 "non-criminal" fingerprint cards between 1928 and 1935. The State of Illinois, meanwhile, collected 100,000 civilian fingerprint records. In the summer of 1935 Hoover announced plans to collect an estimated 1.4 million fingerprint cards from "people other than criminals," and he assigned WPA workers to collect civilian fingerprints. In a 1936 campaign the Berkeley Police Department, under August Vollmer's leadership, set up stations for voluntary fingerprinting, where compliant citizens were rewarded with an "I have been fingerprinted" button. The Merchants' Association offered discounts to participants, prominent citizens had their prints publicly taken, and participating businesses received decals reading "100% fingerprinted." The Berkeley Police Department collected over 50,000 prints during the campaign.[29]

These calls for universal fingerprinting had unmistakable political overtones. The ACLU accused a number of anti-labor forces of being behind universal fingerprinting, including national and local Chambers of Commerce, the National Manufacturers Association, the National Bankers Association, the Daughters of the American Revolution, the American Legion, the Hearst newspaper empire, and the American Coalition, a nativist organization. "What interest has the Manufacturers Association or the American Coalition in our fingerprints?" the ACLU asked rhetorically. The amnesia argument simply wasn't convincing. "It is specious to say that these organizations are humanely interested in seeing that we don't get lost. What are the motives that have inspired this campaign?" The real goal, the ACLU claimed, was police "intimidation, control, restriction upon freedom of movement," and the establishment of a domestic passport system, akin to those with "disastrous effects on freedom" in Europe. "The fingerprint drive is an early—and effective—move in the direction of general regimentation of the population," the ACLU suggested, which "subjects the whole populace to police surveillance" and violates "the freedom of the individual's anonymity."[30]

Despite all the rhetoric, universal fingerprinting never did get very far in the United States. It would seem that Americans were unwilling to submit to what was clearly a surveillance program, no matter how impassioned the appeals to civic duty or hysterical the threats of kidnapping. "Despite their endeavors, despite the acquisition of the capable Mr. Hoover to head their campaign," the ACLU noted in 1938, the proponents of universal fingerprinting "have thus far not been notably successful in fingerprinting the great mass of Americans." Nor were lawmakers, no matter how prejudiced they may have been against criminal and subversive "elements," willing to legislate away the civil rights of their constituents. In 1935 Congress created the first unique bureaucratic identifier to apply to all (or almost all) citizens, the social security number. This would have been an ideal opportunity to implement universal fingerprinting, by requiring that citizens deposit a fingerprint to receive a social security number—and it would have made the social security number a lot more fraud-proof—but Congress declined the opportunity. The criminal stigma associated with fingerprinting remained alive and well, and Congressmen did not want to authorize treating their constituents like criminals. A 1940 bill calling for universal fingerprinting did not get through Congress, nor did the 1943 Citizens Identification Act, which called for identification cards with fingerprints. Though Americans were susceptible to demagoguery aimed at immigrants and political dissidents, they remained steadfastly protective of their own privacy. Americans saw the universal fingerprinting movement for what it was: an effort by the state to establish a comprehensive surveillance system over its own citizens.[31]

Even if Hoover had been able to force Americans to accept universal fingerprinting, it is not clear that the FBI could have handled such an enormous volume of fingerprints. Already the FBI was straining under the weight of its own files. It was fruitless to call for universal fingerprinting, John Golden pointed out in 1925, until the problem of further subdividing the files could be solved. Otherwise agencies were simply inviting disaster, bogging themselves down in unsearchable files. Indeed, as the FBI files grew, searches became extremely slow to execute, often a matter of weeks. As early as 1935 the FBI warned law enforcement officers "that usually it is impossible to identify a latent or single fingerprint with prints in a large collection unless some facts are available to indicate the probable identity of the suspect." Hence, although the FBI eventually amassed the world's largest collection of fingerprints, it paradoxically took the longest time to access its records. Like criminal identification archives before and after it, the FBI became a victim of its own success: the more records it amassed, the less effective it became at accessing those records. Therefore, it relied on local identification bureaus to maintain their own local collections and to do the vast majority of searches internally. The FBI adopted Latour's strategy of "simultaneously mobilising elements while keeping them at a distance." In order to build an even larger collection of fingerprints, the FBI would need a better method of accessing them. For this, even Hoover's ingenuity would be insufficient; they would need to turn to the power of computing.[32]

In the late nineteenth century, when the word "fingerprint" had not yet been coined, dactyloscopers sometimes referred to the impressions of the friction ridge of human fingertips as "digital signatures" or "digital photographs." Today these antiquated terms have a futuristic ring to them, since the word "digital" has come to be more closely associated with binary computing devices than with human fingers. Through the application of the "digital revolution" to the field of criminal identification, the term "digital," when applied to fingerprints, has taken on a double meaning.

As early as the 1920s identification bureaus turned to automated data-processing technologies, such as IBM punch-card sorters, to handle the problem of searching large numbers of criminal identification records. In a sense, the use of punch cards to represent individuals brought identification full circle, since the problem of personal identification had stimulated the development of the punch card. During the late nineteenth century, railroads concerned about people stealing or reselling train tickets had developed a "punch photograph" which consisted of a set of descriptive categories printed on the ticket. "The conductor . . . punched out a description of the individual, as light hair, dark eyes, large nose, etc." The suggestion, offered around 1885 by "a gentleman from Cincinnati," of applying a "thumb-mark" to tickets instead, was never taken up by the railroad companies. The punch photograph, however, inspired Herman Hollerith to use punch cards for his famous tabulating machines used to compile the 1890 U.S. Census. Hollerith's Tabulating Machine Corporation, founded in 1896, merged in 1911 with the Computing Scale Company and the International Time Recording Company to form the Computing-Tabulating-Recording Company (C-T-R). In 1924 C-T-R was renamed International Business Machines (IBM).[33]

In 1919 the California State Bureau of Identification introduced a punch-card system, called the Robinson Findex, for mechanically storing and retrieving *modus operandi* information, similar to the

Atcherly system developed in England several years earlier. Punched holes corresponded to particular *modus operandi* characteristics. The machine could then retrieve the cards containing certain characteristics. This system harnessed the power of emerging information-processing technologies to sort through a welter of criminal intelligence. As Clarence Morrill, superintendent of the Bureau, enthusiastically remarked, "This machine works only with facts."[34]

In 1934 the FBI began using an IBM card-sorter to search coded fingerprint classifications from the most overcrowded categories of the Henry system. In 1937 the New York State Division of Criminal Identification installed an IBM horizontal card-sorter, which could sort 420 cards per minute. The machines could retrieve all fingerprint cards containing a certain classification. The New York State Bureau also used punch-card sorters to search a personal appearance file and a single-print file, in which each finger had its own card, for searching latent prints. In the 1940s and 1950s other identification bureaus also installed punch-card sorters manufactured by IBM and other data-processing companies.[35]

Punch-card sorters offered a fairly awkward solution to the problem of searching large databases. Although sorters reduced the number of cards it was necessary to search, human examiners would still have to scrutinize each of the selected cards. What was wanted was imaging technology that could not only search the database but also produce candidate matches. Experiments with optical recognition of fingerprint images began in the 1960s. In 1963 John Fitzmaurice of Baird-Atomics developed a new classification system, based on a grid superimposed over the fingerprint, which would be compatible with optical recognition technologies. That same year Joseph Wegstein and Raymond Moore began work on an automated fingerprint identification project jointly sponsored by the FBI and the National Bureau of Standards (NBS).[36]

This period also saw some attempts to use holographic images of fingerprints for automated searching. Researchers at General Electric, McDonnell Douglas, Sperry Rand, and the KMS Technology Center all experimented briefly with holographic systems during the late 1960s and early 1970s. Although holography was an attractive technology, these early forays suggested that a holographic identification system would be extremely expensive and would also be excessively sensitive to the inevitable "noise"—that is, the impression of the background surface upon which the print was deposited, dirt and other foreign matter, and printing artifacts—contained even in inked, not to mention latent, fingerprints.[37]

In 1972 the FBI installed a system with a fingerprint scanner built by Cornell Aeronautical Laboratory and a prototype FINgerprint reaDER (FINDER) built by North American Aviation. Money from the Justice Department's Law Enforcement Assistance Administration was crucial, providing around 90 percent of the funding of early automated fingerprint systems. During the 1970s the FBI scanned all the records of persons born after January 1, 1929, from its Criminal Master Fingerprint File. By 1980 it had scanned a total of 14.3 million cards into its computerized database. In 1979 it began testing automated searches, and the system proved "such a resounding success, both from the accuracy achieved and the manpower savings, that it was expanded to all searches in the main fingerprint file at the Identification Division." By 1983, the FBI reported, "the total fingerprint file of all criminals born after 1928 was on-line, and all searches were routinely done in this new system." Automated searches only produced candidate matches; operators could program the computer to determine how many candidate matches they wished to examine. Human examiners still performed the final matching.[38]

While the FBI concentrated on computer imaging and digitizing fingerprint records, in the early 1970s some police departments, including Atlanta, Shreveport, Kansas City, Nassau County in New York, and the Royal Canadian Mounted Police (RCMP), installed systems based on analog technology which stored fingerprint images and classifications on videotape or microfilm. These analog systems were more affordable than holography, ranging between $17,000 and $72,000. If detectives recovered an unidentified latent print from a crime scene, they could search that print against the stored images. The system operator would first encode the print using some classification system. The rolls of microfilm or videotape would then be run through a retrieval/display unit which would scan the codes (not the images of the fingerprints themselves) on the film. If the code matched, the machine would stop the film and store the image of the fingerprint for display. Having scanned all the film, the operator could then call up all the potentially matching images on the display unit screen. A trained examiner could then look at the candidate matches. If, having examined the print on the screen, the examiner thought any of the images might

match the latent, he or she would retrieve the original inked fingerprint card and compare the inked card and the latent print. Some police
departments matched around two unidentified latent prints a month
using these systems. As computing power continued to grow, however,
digital storage won out over analog in criminal identification as in so
many other areas.[39]

In the late 1970s Rockwell, a descendant of North American Aviation, began marketing digital Automated Fingerprint Identification
Systems (AFIS) to local law enforcement agencies under the brand
name Printrak. Printrak systems were purchased by several law enforcement agencies, including the San Jose Police Department, the
RCMP, and the Houston Police Department, as well as shared systems
in the Twin Cities in Minnesota and in Montgomery and Prince Georges Counties in Maryland. In 1983 the Japanese company NEC sold its
first system in the United States to the San Francisco Police Department, and soon afterwards it installed a system for the Alaska State Police. In 1985 NEC scored a key victory by installing California's state-
wide Cal-ID system.[40]

With all these different approaches and vendors competing for attention, most identification bureau chiefs were understandably reluctant to commit to any particular automated system. Just as the initial
choice of a manual classification system in the 1920s had wedded a bureau to that system for life, installing a brand of AFIS was a somewhat
irreversible step. Procurement of an AFIS was expensive, in the range
of $2 million to $10 million, and the conversion of the database—scanning fingerprint cards into digital form—could cost hundreds of thousands of dollars. Bureau chiefs' hesitancy to switch to automated fingerprinting was reminiscent of their reluctance to adopt fingerprinting
itself back in the 1910s and 1920s: the existence of a large database of
records stored and classified in a specific format demanded very per-
suasive reasons to switch to any new format. Most of all, bureau chiefs
wanted to be sure that the new format was indeed the medium of a reasonably distant future and not some temporary flash in the pan. Some
police departments were already confronted by the problem of what to
do with miles of fingerprints stored on videotape or microfilm, which
had been rendered obsolete by the newer digital systems.[41]

By 1986, however, identification bureau chiefs had overcome their
reluctance and embraced digital AFIS. That year saw "a frenzy of Request for Procurements and benchmark tests by many agencies that

managed to obtain funds to buy their fingerprint systems"—most of them city police departments or state criminal justice bureaus. The age of digital digits had arrived. That same year a third major vendor, North American Morpho Systems, further complicated the field, selling its first system to the Tacoma Police Department. It was clear that digital storage had triumphed decisively over analog and that AFIS was the wave of the future, but which brand of AFIS was not clear at all. Rather than being monopolized by a single system, the field was populated by several competing vendors whose systems were incompatible with one another. A 1992 survey found twenty-nine U.S. law enforcement agencies using a Printrak system, twenty-six using NEC, and seven using Morpho. Identification bureaus were repeating with automated systems what had occurred with manual classification systems: allowing incompatible systems to proliferate before establishing a universal standard. Too late, the NBS and the FBI undertook the task of establishing a universal standard that would enable communication between these incompatible systems, a project that is still under way.[42]

Three kinds of AFIS searches are possible. Ten-print to ten-print searches compare the complete set of prints from a suspect in custody against the database of ten-prints. The purpose of such a search is to determine whether the suspect is using an alias or has a previous conviction under some other name. This kind of search can also identify an unidentified corpse. The majority of ten-print to ten-print searches take less than three minutes, although some can take more than ten minutes. Latent print to ten-print searches are performed when evidence technicians recover a latent print from a crime scene and suspects are not immediately apparent or do not match the latent print. The latent print is entered into the system and checked against the entire database. This is equivalent to a manual "cold search" of the entire file. If there is not a hit, the latent is entered into an "unsolved latent" file. When new ten-prints are entered into the system, they are automatically checked against this file: a ten-print to latent print search. A hit in this kind of search reveals that the suspect in custody may be responsible for a previously unsolved crime. Early applications yielded substantial numbers of hits. Catching suspects, through this kind of cold search, became vastly more feasible with AFIS.

Modern AFIS systems are minutiae-based. Like most human examiners, they use "minutiae," or ridge characteristics like ridge endings and bifurcations, to match prints. Unlike human examiners, they also use minutiae in their initial search for matches. When an optical image of the fingerprint is scanned, the AFIS records the location and orientation of minutiae in either Cartesian or polar coordinates. The AFIS then stores both the optical image of the print and the minutiae data "describing" the print. When a new print or set of prints is entered, an AFIS component called a "matcher" compares the digital record "describing" the new print against its database, producing candidate matches. The AFIS retrieves the optical images of the candidate matches and displays them, in descending order of likelihood of matching, on a split screen next to the new print. In the final stage of the process, a human examiner compares the prints to determine whether there is a match. Since the computer executes the comparisons of visual images in more rigid, rule-based manner, it sometimes "sees" things quite differently from human examiners. Therefore it is up to the human examiner to chose the "true" matching print from among the list of candidate matches generated by the computer, a list that it would have taken a human examiner weeks to compile. It is not uncommon for the "true" matching prints not to be rated first by the computer. And, of course, the computer generates many candidate matches that the human examiner can eliminate at a glance. In identification work, as in so many other areas, computers are fast but dumb. AFIS systems are very good at winnowing an enormous database into a small group of candidate matches, but they are relatively poor at picking which, if any, of this small group is the actual match.[43]

For this reason it is currently unthinkable to let a computer make a latent print identification. Only human examiners are trusted to make such determinations. Today citizens do not need to worry about "false positives," about being "convicted by a computer glitch." False negatives, on the other hand, in which persons with long criminal histories were reported as having no previous convictions, have occurred, sometimes with tragic consequences. For example, twice in New York City, in 1994 and 1995, the failure of an AFIS to locate a suspect's fingerprints and reveal his criminal record led to the release of an offender who then committed murder. In the first case a man named Andre Foreman was arrested for petty larceny. Foreman, who was wanted for murder in Pennsylvania, had been arrested twice before in New York and used aliases. The AFIS matched Foreman's prints with those taken on his two previous arrests, but the human examiner who performed the final identification decided—incorrectly, according to a review—that the prints did not match. Because they did not discover Foreman's aliases, the police released him without being aware of the outstanding Pennsylvania warrant. The error was all the more surprising because the examiner was not working with a difficult-to-read latent print; the comparison was between two, presumably clear, sets of ten inked prints.

In Foreman's case the system failed at the final stage in which the human examiner reviews the work of the computer. In the second case, however, state officials blamed the false negative not on a human examiner but on a programming error. Shortly before he allegedly murdered a women in Queens, the police released a man named Hector Roman, because many of his previous convictions had been attributed to an alias, Hector Gonzalez. The two cases demonstrated the fallibility of both human examiners and computerized matching systems and emphasized that errors are always possible in fingerprint identification.[44]

The human fingerprint examiner is the final safeguard for AFIS. At the same time, AFIS takes on many of the identification tasks that used to be performed by human examiners. Today's crop of senior latent fingerprint examiners rose through the ranks at a time when novice examiners spent several years classifying, filing, and retrieving inked ten-print cards according to the Henry system or some other system. Latent fingerprint examiners universally attest that this long period of ten-print work allowed them to develop the visual skills necessary for more advanced fingerprint work: how to orient themselves among the whorls of fingerprinting patterns and how to visually analyze fingerprint patterns. This knowledge of how fingerprint patterns tend to flow is crucial when examiners try to "read" a poor-quality latent print. Essentially, this period of ten-print work taught examiners to see fingerprint patterns in a way that is quite different from the way the rest of us see them.

The rise of AFIS has brought about a profound change in the training of latent fingerprint examiners. Since inked prints are now stored digitally, there is no reason to have human examiners classify, file, and retrieve fingerprint cards. Instead, new cards are simply scanned into the computer database. Ten-print classification, therefore, no longer serves as a training ground for examiners. It is not clear how this aspect of training is going to be replaced or how novice fingerprint examiners are going to acquire the visual skills that their predecessors had. Unless new mechanisms are developed to impart these visual skills to novices, AFIS threatens to erode the skill level of latent fingerprint examiners. If that happens, and computer technology keeps developing, computers may eventually begin to achieve levels of accuracy and reliability that are competitive with those of less well trained human examiners.

While early AFIS applications involved optically scanning inked fingerprint cards, in the late 1980s a new technology became available, "inkless fingerprinting" or "livescan," which enabled police officers to scan an image of a suspect's fingerprints directly into the computer. This created a seamless digital fingerprint system encompassing the entire identification process from recording to storage to searching to identifying in one fell swoop. In 1990 the St. Paul Police Department installed the earliest livescan system. Some departments are now outfitting patrol cars with livescan readers. Using cellular transmission, police can now perform an instant fingerprint check on a suspect on the street.[45]

The new technology has had a profound impact on identification practice in the United States. It is now technically feasible to routinely check the fingerprints of everyone who comes into contact with the police. It is also feasible to perform almost limitless cold searches. The principal limitation on fingerprint checks is now legal, not technical. In New York City, for example, the installation of AFIS/livescan technology occurred in concert with Mayor Rudolph Giuliani's new crackdown on "quality of life" offenses. The mayor's reasoning was that those who committed major, violent crimes, such as murder and rape, were the same people who committed minor, nonviolent crimes, such as subway fare evasion, and thus those apprehended for these lesser crimes should be fingerprinted and entered into the system. The John Royster case, the mayor claimed, vindicated this logic. In 1996 the police attributed a series of rapes and a murder to a single, unidentified perpetrator. A latent print found at the murder scene matched Royster's print, which had been taken after an earlier arrest for jumping a subway turnstile. This led to Royster's conviction for murder, seemingly justifying Giuliani's policy of fingerprinting people for even the pettiest "quality of life" crimes. For some, however, such policies present a debatable moral and public policy issue.[46]

Previous advances in identification technology allowed law enforce-ment agencies to create criminal records for ever pettier offenders. The ultimate effect of this shift was to make "recidivists" out of vagrants, drunks, prostitutes, and other repeat offenders who might otherwise have escaped notice because of the relatively minor nature of their crimes. The latest technological advances reach even further, making possible the creation of criminal records for fare evaders, people drink-ing in public, and other minor offenders. If petty crime laws are en-forced selectively—if marginalized people like racial minorities, the poor, and immigrants are arrested with greater frequency for petty crimes such as turnstile jumping and drinking in public—then these marginalized groups are more likely to have arrest records. With AFIS technology, this means that young black people are far more likely to be "in the system" than whites.

The effect of AFIS technology then may be highly prejudicial to those who live in neighborhoods targeted by police or who have an ap-pearance—skin color, dress, and so on—targeted by the police. AFIS technology makes the criminal justice system more sensitive to arrest patterns. If arrest patterns are racist and classist, then the criminal identification databases themselves will contain disproportionate numbers of racial minorities, immigrants, and the poor. Since arrest patterns are inherently affected by the subjective perceptions of police officers, this poses a real danger. Recent reports of "racial profiling" and selective enforcement highlight the hazards of such systems. As technology enables criminal identification networks to become in-creasingly comprehensive and omniscient, the threat to liberty may lie less in the state's ability to see everything and everybody than in its ability to pick and choose whom and what it sees. Individualized iden-tification remains tainted, as it always has been, by group identifica-tion—typing and profiling.[47]

No scientific basis exists for requiring that a pre-determined minimum number of friction ridge features must be present in two impressions in order to establish a positive identification.

—The "Ne'urim Declaration" (1995)

CHAPTER 11

Fraud, Fabrication, and False Positives

In the period after World War II the place of fingerprint identification seemed entirely secure. Central fingerprint databases like the Federal Bureau of Investigation (FBI) and Interpol, as well as countless state, local, and national databases, continued to collect fingerprints, building ever bigger files, and continued to find no two fingerprints alike. Judges, juries, attorneys, and the general public continued to show a high degree of confidence in forensic fingerprint identification, which had become the most trusted form of forensic evidence. In the United States, the Grice decision of 1941 had firmly established the legality of criminal convictions based on fingerprint evidence alone, and other countries had similarly established the legal authority of fingerprint evidence. In short, fingerprint evidence carried an imposing veneer of scientific and legal authority.

Beneath this veneer, however, trouble was brewing. In fact, latent fingerprint identification was still not based on scientific research at all. Instead, it was based on anecdote, experience, and nineteenth-century statistics. The chief evidence in support of latent fingerprint identification remained the simple fact that law enforcement agencies, having now collected hundreds of millions of sets of fingerprints, had never seen any two fingerprints alike. This argument remained vulnerable to Henry Faulds's old rebuttal that these agencies' ten-print classification systems, which were indexed according to the patterns on all ten fingers, were not designed to ferret out identical *single* fingerprints. A second argument remained the appeal to natural law: that biological forms like papillary ridges, or "friction ridges" as they were increasingly called, are inherently unique. But even the contention that no two complete single fingerprint patterns are exactly alike did not address the issue fundamental to forensic identification: how great is the likelihood that a latent fingerprint impression might mistakenly be matched to the wrong source finger.

In addition, new statistical studies, which improved upon the statistical work of Galton and Balthazard, had emerged beginning in the 1930s. One of the chief flaws in Galton and Balthazard's models was that they assumed perfectly legible whole single fingerprints, whereas latent print work usually involved poor-quality partial fingerprints. At least five entirely new statistical approaches, seeking to bring more sophisticated mathematical techniques to bear on the quantitative assessment of the individuality of fingerprint patterns, were proposed between 1946 and 1977, but, according to recent analysis, "none of the models are free from conceptual flaws." Quantitative models, meanwhile, were generated and published within the rarefied world of academic mathematics and statistics. Few rank-and-file examiners were even aware of them, and examiners rarely, if ever, cited these models when they testified in court. The innovative statistical model of fingerprint individuality developed by the Indian statistician Roxburgh in 1933, for example, which used a polar coordinate system in which a radial axis with one terminus at the center of the print swept around the print like a radar screen, was "totally ignored by the forensic science community." Indeed, when examiners did cite a statistical model, even as late as the 1990s they cited Galton or Balthazard rather than one of the more recent, more sophisticated models.[1]

Two different strategies developed during the postwar period for dealing with the uncertainty about how small a partial latent fingerprint fragment could be before the chance of accidental matching with another source finger became too great. The first strategy, which found its most pronounced expression in Britain, was essentially to err on the side of caution by mandating an overly conservative number of matching ridge characteristics, or "points of similarity," as the threshold for an identification. In 1953 the Home Secretary revived the sixteen-point standard that had originally been dictated in 1920 in response to Bertillon's contention that two different fingerprints might show up to sixteen matching ridge characteristics. The sixteen-point standard had gradually fallen into disuse, so the Home Secretary issued regulations insisting that examiners adhere to it strictly, so strictly that fingerprint examiners convinced of a match yet unable to find the requisite six-teen points would have to report a simple finding of "inconclusive" to the investigating officers. The aim was to provide a safe margin of error in order to ensure that fingerprint examiners' worst nightmare, an er-roneous identification—resulting in criminal justice systems' worst nightmare, a false conviction—would never occur. Recall that the cred-ibility of latent fingerprint identification had been built upon finger-print examiners' steadfast insistence that latent fingerprint identifica-tions were absolutely certain and errors were impossible.[2]

The second strategy, which found its most prominent expression in North America, was to do away with point standards altogether and rely instead on the expert judgment of trained, experienced examiners. Owing to its fragmented, overlapping jurisdictions and decentralized law enforcement structure, the United States had never had a national point standard. Over the decades following World War II, American ex-aminers transformed this situation from a historical accident into a scientific principle, insisting that the determination of how much matching detail was enough should be a matter for the expert judg-ment of the examiner. By the early 1950s American examiners were criticizing minimum standards. The number of matching points, they argued, was not always an accurate indication of how similar two fin-gerprint impressions might be. Depending on the nature of the prints, two prints showing only four matching points might be declared an identification in one case; another pair of prints might require fifteen matching points before a conclusion of identification could be reached. Since minimum standards were not based on empirical evidence, but were merely estimates aimed at providing a margin of safety against er-ror, American examiners suggested that they were profoundly unscien-tific and therefore undermined latent fingerprint identification's status as a forensic science. In their place, American examiners proposed what was essentially a floating standard based on the expert judgment of the examiner.[3]

While forensic science had advanced greatly after World War II, the methodology of latent fingerprint comparison had remained relatively stagnant. While British examiners, and many American examiners, considered themselves technicians and remained comfortable in that role, some American examiners began to think of themselves as forensic scientists. As advanced degrees became more common among forensic scientists, however, the gulf widened between them and the many fingerprint examiners who had no scientific background. Eager to join the more prestigious community of forensic scientists, ambitious American examiners found the point-counting system increasingly untenable and a downright embarrassment.

In 1973 the International Association for Identification (IAI), which remained primarily a North American organization, passed a resolution stating that "no valid basis exists for requiring that a pre-determined minimum number of friction ridge characteristics must be present in two impressions in order to establish a positive identification."[4] Instead, the IAI proposed that the standard for a match should be the expert opinion of a trained, experienced examiner: when there was sufficient corresponding detail between an inked and a latent print to convince the examiner that the two prints must come from a common source to the exclusion of all others in the world, then the examiners should declare an identification. This opinion should not be based on a simplistic matching of "points," but rather on a holistic evaluation of all available individualizing ridge detail. Some "points" might count more toward identification than others: a "trifurcation," the splitting of a ridge into three branches, for example, is a rare ridge characteristic and thus should count more toward individualization than a common ridge ending. And some individualizing detail might not be in the form of "points" at all: the location or size of a pore, a sudden change in direction of a ridge, an unusual form along the edge of a ridge, or the shape (rather than merely the location) of a ridge characteristic. With such criteria in mind, it might be possible to match two partial fingerprint fragments showing a very small number of characteristics, perhaps four or five.

The IAI resolution effectively pitted American and British fingerprint examiners against each other in a feud that would simmer for almost three decades. Although every other country in the world had some minimum point standard, the British sixteen-point standard was the most obnoxious to American examiners because it was so excessively high, because it was so unabashedly based on a historical event—Bertillon's collage—rather than scientific analysis, and because British examiners adhered to it so dogmatically. British examiners, meanwhile, thought the IAI policy recklessly invited disaster by allowing individual examiners to operate independently of any shared standard. All it would take was one well-publicized erroneous identification, they warned, to permanently undermine the public's, and the legal system's, faith in latent fingerprint identification and squander the courtroom credibility that examiners had spend nearly a century building. The Americans, charged Gerald Lambourne, a former head of the fingerprint department at Scotland Yard, "would unwittingly sacrifice this integrity for the gratification of one mediocre conviction. Such people find it hard to understand that one established abuse of the fingerprint system anywhere could have disastrous effects on all law enforcement agencies." The benefit of the standard, Lambourne pointed out, was that it "has ensured very little challenge by defence counsels at trials and a willingness of juries to convict on fingerprint evidence alone."[5]

For American examiners, however, the issue was less that the British policy occasionally allowed the guilty to go free—though both sides acknowledged that this did undoubtedly happen—than that the British policy was shamelessly unscientific. Adhering to a standard of practice with no basis in science, they warned, would destroy the credibility of the profession as surely as an erroneous conviction. They were particularly concerned about their colleagues in the forensic sciences. Trained in statistics and scientific methodology, forensic scientists were not likely to look kindly on fingerprint standards based on historical anecdotes.

Britain and the United States represented the extreme poles in the worldwide debate over the future of forensic fingerprint identification. Both sides believed that forensic fingerprint identifications were absolutely certain and reliable, and both wished to ensure that fingerprint examiners continue to testify with ironclad credibility in the courtroom. However, the two sides had very different ways of achieving this. The British viewed latent fingerprint identification as an experience-based practice. They put their faith in rigorous training—they required five years' training before an examiner was permitted to testify in court, while American standards were much looser, varying from agency to agency, and the American courts were free to admit anyone they wished as an expert witness—an extremely conservative methodology that erred on the side of caution, and a long history of trouble-free courtroom testimony. The Americans saw latent fingerprint identification as a branch of the forensic sciences. They put their faith in individual examiners, whose expert judgment should be trusted. Essentially, the British thought of examiners as technicians who followed proven protocols, while the Americans viewed them as scientists who deployed expert knowledge and judgment.

If American examiners wanted to vest the credibility of latent fingerprint identification in the individual examiner, they needed to find a better way of ensuring the competence of those examiners. The problem of incompetence, raised as early as the 1920s, had not yet been solved. The states had rebuffed calls to certify latent fingerprint examiners. The courts, meanwhile, still admitted fingerprint experts at the judge's discretion. Since judges knew little about fingerprinting, they had little way of distinguishing a competent examiner from an incompetent one. Anecdotal evidence suggested that incompetent examiners were being admitted to testify as experts. In the mid-1970s the IAI finally decided to follow the example of other professional groups and establish its own certification program.[6]

The proposal generated a great deal of controversy. Opponents of certification worried about handing judges a tool with which to exclude some examiners. In a profession where training had traditionally occurred in an informal apprentice system at the local level, they resisted bestowing the authority to certify on a national body. Others debated whether current senior examiners could be "grandfathered." Eventually the IAI settled on a compromise. It instituted a certification program, but it explicitly disavowed any claim either that certification rendered an expert qualified to testify or that lack of certification rendered an expert unqualified. Although certification became a useful qualification to put before the court, judges retained the power to decide whom to admit as an expert witness and uncertified examiners still regularly testified as expert witnesses in American courts.[7]

British examiners insisted that even the certification program did not provide total protection against error. As evidence they pointed to the American case *State v. Caldwell*. In 1982 the Minnesota Supreme Court reversed a 1977 murder conviction largely because it decided that the identification by the prosecution's fingerprint expert, Steven Sedlacek, was erroneous. The Court based this conclusion on the testimony of other examiners who reviewed the disputed impression after the trial and deemed it an illegible or inconclusive print. Sedlacek, who was IAI-certified, could not be dismissed as a meddling amateur. Nonetheless, to admit that qualified examiners might reasonably disagree about the legibility of a latent print would have undermined the painstakingly achieved aura of certainty that by then surrounded fingerprinting. Consequently the IAI had little choice but to attribute the dispute, not to reasonable disagreement over a difficult identification, but to outright misconduct on the part of Sedlacek, to sacrifice the individual examiner for the good of both the profession and the technique.[8]

In 1981 the IAI revoked Sedlacek's certification for making an erroneous identification and also revoked the certification of two other latent fingerprint examiners: Claude Cook for submitting "a communication in support of the erroneous identification made by Mr. Sedlacek" and Ronald Welbaum, who had been retained by the defense, for confirming Sedlacek's erroneous identification. The fact that the defense's own expert confirmed the mistaken identification suggested that some defense experts did not review evidence very carefully and merely "rubber-stamped" the opinions of the state's experts. It also suggested that even providing defendants with their own experts would not fully protect defendants against false identification. Significantly, the IAI attributed the error to the practitioner rather than the method. It determined that Sedlacek had recklessly attempted to push the method too far by identifying an "illegible" print. The print identified by Sedlacek properly should have been termed "inconclusive" precisely because it eventually yielded different interpretations from different experts. Any print that yields different interpretations by qualified experts is *by definition* an inconclusive print. In this way, the IAI successfully maintained the principle that there are no disputed prints—only inconclusive ones.[9]

For American fingerprint examiners the Caldwell case demonstrated the need for further measures to ensure the competence of examiners and adherence to agreed-upon procedures. "We must identify and eliminate the incompetent and exalt the goal of excellence BEFORE discredit is brought upon our profession by the unqualified," the examiner Robert Olsen urged in 1982. "We already know of several cases of wrong identifications and mishandled testimony, some of which gained wide-spread publicity. If we do not strengthen our requirements, there could be more such cases. Once lost, it would be difficult to regain the credibility fingerprint identification now enjoys."[10]

British examiners, however, contended that the Caldwell case demonstrated that the American lack of a minimum standard invited disaster. "Due to the frank and open policies of our American counterparts we do know that since early 1981 five members of the International Association for Identification have had their certification revoked because of erroneous identifications," wrote Gerald Lambourne. "The people concerned did not appear to be short of expertise, in fact, two of them had previously been supervisors of fingerprint bureaus. If it was not experience at fault, could it possibly have been the lack of an effective fingerprint standard?" The credibility of fingerprinting, British examiners claimed, rested on the assertion that—aside from deliberate fabrication or misconduct—errors were impossible. "This fingerprint system has gained a world-wide reputation for practical infallibility," Lambourne wrote, "and this deserved reputation must always be protected by placing the standard of identification beyond the realms of assumption and doubt." The difference of opinion over the Caldwell case suggests that different communities of examiners had different goals. North American examiners were preoccupied with being perceived as scientists, while British examiners were more concerned about maintaining their impregnability in the witness box.[11]

American examiners still did not have their own fully developed methodology to propose as an alternative to the old point-counting method. Although they were convinced that point counting was unscientific, the published literature still described fingerprint comparison in terms of counting points. And indeed, in court most American examiners continued to vouch for their identifications by citing a certain number of matching "points" that exceeded some minimum standard, whether that standard was attributed to an agency, the professional community as a whole, or the individual examiner's experience and expert judgment. In 1983, however, David Ashbaugh, a constable in the Royal Canadian Mounted Police, published a slim pamphlet entitled *Ridgeology*. Although the pamphlet was little noticed at the time and even today is not widely known among fingerprint examiners, it has been hailed by some leading examiners as "perhaps the most . . . significant treatise on fingerprint comparison and identification in the twentieth century." Experienced examiners described *Ridgeology* as "a bolt out of the blue" and claimed they had not truly understood the process of individualization through friction ridges "until being enlightened by ridgeology." *Ridgeology*, at last, provided the philosophy of latent fingerprint identification that ambitious, scientifically minded examiners had been looking for.[12]

In *Ridgeology* and a subsequent series of articles, Ashbaugh declared that "it is unacceptable to use the simplistic point philosophy in modern day forensic science." There are no natural objects called "points," he argued, there is only ridge detail. Matches are not established by the accumulation of "points of similarity," but rather by trained and informed visual processing of the two prints: "When all friction ridge formations present are in agreement and the examiner is of the opinion that there are sufficient unique details present to eliminate anyone else as a possible donor, the examiner has formed an opinion of identification." In place of point counting he proposed a new method that, for lack of a better term, he called "ridgeology." The term was meant to convey the idea that the properly trained examiner should look at ridge detail in its totality, not merely at points of similarity. Such detail includes not just the location of points but also the size and orientation of the points themselves, the location of pores along ridges (poroscopy), and the characteristics of the ridges themselves between points, such as "dog-legs," abrupt changes of direction. The practical rationale behind ridgeology is that point counting underutilizes the identifying information available in a latent print. We might liken the difference to that between analog and digital reproduction: by characterizing an area of ridge detail simply as a "point," counting loses some of the available richness of detail. Ashbaugh likens point counting to describing a person only according to the top of his head and his feet. Ridgeology, in contrast, would also derive information along the ridge between the points, from the whole body. By making correlations in characteristics like pore structure, Ashbaugh argued, ridgeology often made it possible to effect identification with fewer points than most agencies required, as few as three or four.[13]

The uniqueness of all human fingerprints, Ashbaugh wrote, citing the work of anatomists like Wilder, Whipple, Bonnevie, and Cummins, had a scientific basis in anatomy, embryology, and histology, not merely the anecdotal basis that the world's examiners had never seen two different fingerprints showing more than three, or four, or five points of similarity. Instead, uniqueness was based on the enormous variability of the environmental factors—like temperature and pressure—that influenced the embryonic formation of friction ridges. Ashbaugh revived the forgotten anatomical research into the formation of friction ridges, which had been ignored by the profession with the exception of a few scientifically minded examiners like G. Tyler Mairs, and he brought it to the attention of fingerprint examiners. For many fingerprint examiners the existence of this scientific literature came as a revelation: "It seemed that a whole new world was out there to be learned about," one wrote. In Ashbaugh's view, it was no longer tenable for fingerprint examiners to testify as expert witnesses and profess almost total ignorance about the anatomical and histological basis of the formation of friction ridges, relying instead on the unscientific assertion that no one had ever seen any two fingerprints alike. Ashbaugh envisioned the transformation of the fingerprint examiner into a very different kind of expert, one more trained in anatomy, embryology, and histology, who never mentioned "points" on the witness stand and who based his or her conclusions of identification, not on a certain number of matching points, but on a holistic evaluation of all available ridge detail.[14]

Nonetheless, Ashbaugh's turn to biology did not solve the fundamental quandary of forensic identification. After all, knowing how ridges are formed does not actually prove they are unique, nor, if we simply assume they are unique in some absolute sense, does it measure *how similar* different friction ridge arrangements might be. Moreover, the theory remains hazy on critical details. It is argued only that the environmental factors influencing friction ridge development are so numerous that all friction ridges must be unique, without actually specifying exactly how numerous they actually are. Most important, however, ridgeology does not propose any definition of a "match" to replace the old point standards. How much matching ridge detail is enough to warrant an opinion that two fingerprints must come from a common source to exclusion of all other possible sources in the world? Having done away with point standards, Ashbaugh falls back on the expert judgment of the examiner. But even he cannot satisfactorily articulate where the threshold between sufficient and insufficient matching ridge detail lies. When it comes to corresponding ridge detail, Ashbaugh acknowledges, a crucial question is: "How much is enough?" But his answer is unabashedly subjective: "Finding adequate friction ridge formations in sequence, that one knows are specific details of the friction ridge skin, and *in the opinion* of the friction ridge identification specialist there are sufficient uniqueness within those details to eliminate all other possible donors in the world, is considered enough. At that point individualization has occurred and the print has been identified."[15]

Ashbaugh's reliance on the subjective judgment of the examiner may in some sense be more scientific than the bogus objectivity of point standards. But with point standards, at least, there is a check on the individual fingerprint examiner. A defendant whose identification was based on four matching points of similarity would have good reason to question the identification. When the threshold for certainty resides only in the mind of the examiner, then neither judges, juries, nor attorneys have any way to challenge the examiner's conclusion, or to measure how strong the evidence of identity really is. In this way, ridgeology may leave defendants more helpless in the face of expert authority. Ashbaugh answers this criticism by—quite rightly—insisting that every declared identification should be *independently* verified by another qualified examiner. (Independent verification means that the verifying examiner should not know what conclusion the first examiner reached. In theory, even under point-counting methodology, all identifications should be independently verified. In practice, it depends upon the country and agency how rigorously this practice is adhered to—if at all.) Since the verifying examiner is sure to be another law enforcement officer, usually from the same agency, however, the new method still leaves defendants vulnerable to unconscious bias or deliberate malfeasance by the police.

Although Ashbaugh was extremely critical of the old methods in general and the point-counting philosophy in particular, he was careful to emphasize that the old methodology was not false—it was merely unscientific. Indeed, Ashbaugh argued that even fingerprint examiners who thought they were counting points were unconsciously doing precisely the kind of holistic analysis of all available ridge detail that he advocated. It was only on the witness stand, in the explanation of the latent fingerprint identification process, that the two methods really differed. Pressed to explain their identifications to juries, most examiners had fallen back on the simplistic matching of points to explain matches they had actually made through a much more complex process that they had not yet learned to articulate, even to themselves. Ridgeology, therefore, was intended to give examiners the proper terminology and scientific foundation on which to base the method they already used. Ridgeology, rather than being a revolutionary change in method, was merely a new way of articulating the existing method. This allowed fingerprint examiners to modernize their practice without undermining the credibility of all the fingerprint matches they had made over the past century. It also provided a way to heal the rift between point counters and their critics, between European protectors of the old standards and North American firebrands who opposed minimum standards of any kind.

British examiners, however, did not accept Ashbaugh's peace offering. They continued to insist that the sixteen-point standard provided a safe margin of error and had "worked" flawlessly for nearly a century. In 1978 the British National Conference of Fingerprint Experts had voted overwhelmingly to retain the sixteen-point standard. The opinion of the rank-and-file examiners, however, was not shared by the Home Office, which was increasingly frustrated by potential convictions sacrificed to the sixteen-point standard. In 1988 the Home Office commissioned a statistician, Ian Evett, and a forensic scientist, Raymond Williams, to conduct a scientific review of the standard. Evett and Williams completed their report within a year, but the subject proved so controversial that it was not made public until 1995, when Evett presented their findings at the International Symposium on Fingerprint Detection and Identification at Ne'urim, Israel. Evett and Williams were not impressed by point standards, which they found had neither logical nor statistical justification. Faced with this characterization of the British standard as unscientific, the Ne'urim delegates, including even the British ones, had little choice but to embrace the American philosophy. The Ne'urim Declaration, which the delegates passed unanimously, repeated the IAI's 1973 resolution almost verbatim, except that it substituted the word "scientific" for the word "valid" in deference to examiners who worked in countries with legally mandated point standards. This represented a decisive repudiation of the point-counting methodology that had dominated the practice of fingerprint identification for almost a century. In effect, leading fingerprint examiners were declaring unscientific one of the fundamental rules of practice that had helped them establish the enormous credibility they enjoyed.[16]

Evett and Williams's report was published simultaneously in the British professional journal *Fingerprint Whorld* and in the American *Jour-*

nal of Forensic Identification, and the response generally divided along national lines. Many British examiners decried the hasty dismissal of a procedure that had won them unparalleled credibility. North American examiners claimed that the report vindicated what they had been arguing all along: that minimum standards (and, for some, point counting itself) were not "scientific." The editor of the *Journal of Forensic Identification*, David Grieve, portrayed the interlocking notions of point counting, minimum standards, and the phrasing of fingerprint identification as a matter of absolute certainty (rather than a probabilistic inference) as dogma:

> The argument that any forensic science, particularly the identification process utilized in latent print comparison, is based solely on deductive logic cannot be substantiated in the face of overwhelming evidence to the contrary. Thus, imposing deductive conclusions of absolute certainty upon the results of an essentially inductive process is a futile attempt to force the square peg into the round hole . . . Once begun, the assumption of absolute certainty as the only possible conclusion has been maintained by a system of societal indoctrination, not reason, and has achieved such a ritualistic sanctity that even mild suggestions that its premise should be re-examined are instantly regarded as acts of blasphemy. Whatever this may be, it is not science.[17]

Despite the increasing venom of the denunciations of point standards by leading American examiners, at the level of the rank and file, even in the United States, "points" were still very much alive. In hundreds of cases, in jurisdictions large and small across the country, examiners continued to testify about points and to vouch for identifications by citing a given number of matching points, a number greater than some minimum standard to which they, or their agencies, adhered. Ridgeology was not yet being practiced in the United States except among a small number of converts. Indeed, few American examiners seemed to know the term "ridgeology" or the name of Ashbaugh. The idea that there was no fixed standard, that the standard was the expert judgment of the examiner, however, had disseminated quite broadly. American fingerprint examiners were in the awkward position of using numbers of points to support their identifications while at the same time contending that there was no minimum number of points because the identification in the end relied on the expert judgment of the examiner. The fluidity of the American standard for a match, although it had persisted without opposition for many decades, remained an invitation to disaster if it encountered a skeptical judge.

This was precisely what happened in a little-noticed California bank robbery trial, *U.S. v. Parks*, in 1991. The prosecution initially introduced the fingerprint examiner Diane Castro to testify that latent finger and palm prints taken from the bank matched the inked prints of the defendant, Kenneth Parks. Castro, though an experienced crime-scene technician, was not very experienced in latent fingerprint analysis, nor was she certified by the IAI. This did not prevent her from being admitted as an expert in court. Upon being asked whether she adhered to a minimum number of points, Castro answered eight. Judge Spencer Letts found this figure suspicious since, it turned out, the crucial latent print in the case showed exactly ten matching ridge characteristics. Letts had seen fingerprint evidence presented in his courtroom before, and the minimum standard number of points always seemed to be fewer than the prints showed in a particular case: "If you only have ten points, you're comfortable with eight; if you have twelve, you're comfortable with ten; if you have fifty, you're comfortable with twenty." Letts found this "sliding scale" extremely suspicious and wondered why there wasn't some standard number of points in the published literature: "I think there are—there must be—some scholarly works . . . There are some studies; there have to be. If there aren't, then this is not a science and there are no experts in it. This woman has not testified that she is aware of any such thing. All she is aware of is department policy, and so far as I can tell, department policy is to be comfortable with whatever you have to be in order to get below the number comparisons available."[18]

The prosecution, sensing trouble, put another fingerprint examiner, Darnell Carter, on the stand. But Carter further exasperated Letts:

THE WITNESS: The thing you have there is that each department has their own goals or their own rules as far as the number of points being a make [an identification]. I think the Sheriff—if I'm not mistaken, theirs is a lot more than 10. I think theirs is 12 or 15, if I'm not mistaken. Scotland Yard uses 18 [*sic*] in order to have a comparison make, so that number really just varies from department to department.

THE COURT: I don't think I'm ever going to use fingerprint testimony again; that simply won't do . . .

THE WITNESS: That just may be one of the problems of the field, but I think if there was survey taken, you would probably get a different number from every department that has a fingerprint section as to their lowest number of points for a comparison and make.

THE COURT: That's the most incredible thing I've ever heard of.

Fingerprint examiners' common practice of using a minimum standard on the stand in order to avoid giving an in-depth explanation of the philosophy behind having no minimum standard had confused Letts. This shortcut backfired because Letts, rather than automatically assuming that fingerprint examiners knew what they were talking about, scrutinized their claims.[19]

The prosecution then called Stephen Kasarsky, an IAI-certified latent fingerprint supervisor for the Los Angeles Police Department, to the stand to "resuscitate" their evidence. Kasarsky tried again to explain the North American no-minimum-standard philosophy:

THE WITNESS: Personally, I'm glad that there is no minimum standard in our country to speak of in fingerprint identification. And I hope there never is a standard. Because as I mentioned earlier about uniqueness, if uniqueness can be found with some unusual points in the print, say four or five that are very unusual, very uncommon points that you hardly ever see, and they fit in unique relationship . . .

THE COURT: All standards have exceptions. You don't have any standards. As far as I can tell, you have no standard. It's just an *ipse dixit.* "This is unique, this is very unusual." "How do you know it's unusual?" "Because I never saw it before." Where is the standard, where is the study, where is the statistical base that's been studied? The FBI has zillions of these things; where is a study of the entire computer bank?

Letts excluded the evidence. The judge appears to have been genuinely surprised by the lack of standards and scientific studies of the individuality of human fingerprints. "I've had my faith shaken in the commonality of the training and the commonality of the standards, the standards of analysis," he declared. "I will say, based on what I've heard today, the expertise is as fragile as [for] any group I've ever heard hold themselves out as experts."[20]

Over the course of nearly a century since the introduction of fin-

gerprint evidence into American courtrooms, science had been transformed from a fledgling field practiced by a few dedicated practitioners into a mammoth enterprise, funded by government and industry,
sprouting a plethora of specialized journals and subdisciplines, and
boasting enormously expensive and precise instruments. Judges had
become accustomed to seeing scientists, including forensic scientists,
testify in court, using sophisticated methodologies, complex statistical
reasoning, and peer-reviewed data. Yet the methodology of latent fingerprint analysis, at the level of the rank and file, had changed little
over this period. Rank-and-file examiners continued to testify—and, in
all likelihood, to practice—as if it were still the early twentieth century. Indeed, even Kasarsky, the super-expert brought in to resuscitate
the prosecution, when asked the likelihood of two different fingerprints' matching, cited Francis Galton's nineteenth-century statistics,
not any of the more recent statistical models. It was as if the judge and
the examiners had both awoken suddenly in 1991 to find that the
definition of science had changed and that what had once been considered a model of scientific evidence and knowledge now had difficulty
fitting that definition.[21]

In the early 1990s attention began to be drawn to yet another chink in
the credibility of forensic fingerprint evidence: not only were even
certified latent fingerprint examiners sometimes incompetent, but
sometimes they were corrupt. On May 26, 1992, the U.S. Department
of Justice reported to the New York State Police that it had uncovered
fingerprint fabrication by state troopers. The information came from
a polygraph interview, conducted by the Central Intelligence Agency
(CIA), with the New York State Police investigator David Harding,
who admitted forging fingerprints on numerous occasions. A four-year
investigation turned up widespread fingerprint fabrication by New
York state troopers: approximately forty cases over eight years. Five
troopers pleaded guilty to charges of perjury, evidence tampering, and
official misconduct. Two of the five were IAI-certified latent fingerprint examiners. One trooper was acquitted but dismissed from the
State Police.[22]

Fingerprint fabrications were nothing new. The earliest forgeries
were by proponents of rival identification methods like Alphonse Bertillon with his sixteen-point collage in 1912. Handwriting experts also

fabricated latent fingerprints in order to impugn the reliability of fingerprint identification. As early as 1913 the San Francisco handwriting expert Theodore Kytka reported that he had discovered a method for transferring fingerprints between objects. In this way a latent fingerprint might be "lifted" from an object that someone had touched innocently and planted on an incriminating object. In 1920 another handwriting expert, Milton Carlson, claimed to have transferred a fingerprint from a newspaper photograph to a knife. With Carlson's method, the forger did not even have to lift an actual latent fingerprint; using an inked impression, or even a photograph of an inked impression, he could engrave a mold that would allow him to plant a fingerprint on an incriminating object.

Carlson challenged fingerprint examiners to answer the "vital question: Can you prove, Mr. Finger-print Expert, that that particular finger-print is NOT forged? If it can be proved beyond a doubt that the finger-print in question is the impression made from the hand and by *contact* of the hand of the defendant, then finger-print testimony is of some value. If the expert on finger-prints cannot *prove* its genuineness or falsity, his testimony is of no value." Carlson claimed that fingerprint evidence suffered from a crucial weakness: it was more fungible than handwriting. The "mechanical" or "manufactured" nature of fingerprint evidence, the very quality that vouched for its authenticity, rendered it vulnerable to imposture: "The form of a finger-print is mechanical in appearance. Mind, will, emotions, conditions, training, etc., do not control, modify or alter the lines of the finger . . . If this be true, to complete a *perfect forgery* of a finger-print in *the exact form* is as easy to make as any steel ruler, surveyor's tape, or a wheel within a wheel." In contrast, Carlson argued, handwriting, as a volitional act, could not be imitated as easily. In 1923 E. O. Brown, a former Secret Service agent, reportedly demonstrated his method of forging fingerprint evidence by planting the fingerprint of the venerable Berkeley police chief August Vollmer at the scene of a burglary. Vollmer was not amused. "It will take much more than the mere discovery of means of transferring the mark left by a criminal to tear down the great fingerprint system which, even though young, has assumed immense proportions," he retorted.[23]

The most sustained attempt to assert the forgeability of fingerprints was mounted by Albert Wehde, an engraver, photographer, and former self-described political prisoner, and John Beffel, a radical journalist.

Wehde had served nine months at Leavenworth in 1921 on the charge of having supplied arms to Indian revolutionaries seeking to overthrow British rule. As an experienced photographer and engraver, Wehde had been assigned to the identification bureau at Leavenworth, where he worked for A. J. Renoe. (It was common practice to employ prison inmates as fingerprint clerks.) The idea of forging a fingerprint, Wehde reported in his book *Finger-Prints Can Be Forged*, had been suggested by the suspicious actions of an identification clerk from the Oklahoma City Police Department. This clerk, Wehde charged, used the Leavenworth facilities to doctor a photograph of a latent fingerprint, apparently with the intention of securing a $33,000 reward. Thus inspired, Wehde set about devising a way of forging latent fingerprints himself. Wehde's training as an engraver came in handy for his method: he left a fingerprint impression in grease on a piece of black tin. He then dusted the print with white powder and photographed it. Finally, he made a copper etching after the negative. The copper plate could then be used to "forge" latent prints.

Wehde's co-workers at the identification bureau were unable to distinguish genuine latent prints from his forgeries. Renoe refused to respond to Wehde's challenge to detect the forged print. After his release from prison, Wehde wrote to Al Dunlap, president of the Illinois chapter of the IAI, requesting permission to demonstrate his method before the chapter's annual convention in Champaign. Dunlap arranged a private demonstration in Chicago instead. The test was attended by Wehde; Gustave Carus, a witness on Wehde's behalf; Dunlap; Emmett and William Evans; Charles Kersting, a photographer for the Chicago Police Department; Ragnar Hedenvall, a Chicago fingerprint examiner; and Charles Carmody, president of the IAI. Wehde mixed authentic and forged prints and challenged the examiners to identify the forged ones. The IAI observers, according to Wehde, "retired to a corner and examined them, debating earnestly in low tones." They then "departed without offering any opinion concerning the merits of my claim." Two days later Dunlap wrote to Wehde:

The method you used is old and crude and known familiarly to every one who was present at the demonstration. It was actually invented years ago in Germany and exposed in England after showing up a few times in Stockholm. The results of your experiment, given under the most favorable conditions for you, were in the judgement of the committee less plausible than a forgery made by rubber stamp . . . In the circumstances, I regret that it will be impossible for me to grant you the floor in order to exploit your preposterous and fraudulent claims at the forthcoming convention of our organization at Champaign, Illinois.

But Dunlap did exhibit enlarged photographs of Wehde's forgeries at the meeting in Champaign without Wehde present. "Then," Dunlap reported, "Mr. Kersting and Emmet [sic] Evans proceeded to blast Wehde's claims to smithereens." In *The Detective*, a magazine he edited, Dunlap announced that "the pretentious claim of one Albert Wehde that he could successfully forge a finger-print so that it could not be detected by a competent expert" had been "properly disposed of." Characterizing Wehde's forgery as a "hellish design," Dunlap declared "the results of his efforts at the official test proved him to be a fakir [sic] of the crudest variety." Since our information about Wehde's forgery comes only from Wehde and Dunlap, neither of whom is a particularly unbiased source, it is impossible to know how realistic it really was. Today's fingerprint examiners insist that no fingerprint forgery is ultimately undetectable. The absence of background "noise" from the surface upon which the fingerprint was deposited, for example, can often give away a forgery. But the real question is whether Wehde's or someone else's forgeries could result in a false conviction. Clearly, they could: renegade New York state troopers secured convictions for serious crimes using fabricated fingerprint evidence. As to whether rank-and-file fingerprint examiners would be fooled by a fabricated latent fingerprint, the question has never been studied.[24]

Dunlap reported on Wehde's test at the national meeting of the IAI in 1927. The IAI Ethics Committee "was unanimous," he noted, "that the alleged forgery by this process is easy to detect." Wehde's forgeries could be identified by the absence of sweat pores. Moreover, the sharp outline, due to copper plate engraving, "would instantly cause suspicion on the part of the expert." The forgery, he concluded, was crude in appearance, resembled "a smear rather than a well-defined fingerprint," and probably didn't even show enough ridge characteristics to be identified. Nonetheless, the committee recognized the danger that Wehde's allegations posed to the profession. "The Committee recommends," Dunlap concluded,

that every possible effort should be made to checkmate these activities insofar as they may prejudice the public against latent fingerprints found at the scene of crime as competent evidence in a criminal trial; that all prosecuting attorneys and fingerprint experts of the country should be cautioned as to the extravagant claims made by this man and any others who advance theories about forged fingerprints that will not stand a scientific test and be advised of the best means of combating such claims when such cases come to trial and fingerprints evidence may be challenged on the alleged grounds that fingerprints can be successfully forged.[25]

Whether or not Wehde's forgery was as crude as Dunlap contended, it was clear from Dunlap's response that he viewed forgery as a threat to the whole edifice of fingerprint evidence in criminal trials. To the extent that police officials did admit that forgery was possible, they emphasized the threat of diabolical criminals planting fingerprints to mislead the police. Responding to E. O. Brown's forgery, August Vollmer said: "The greatest trouble to result from this discovery will no doubt be that a criminal who knows the method employed, and who wished to cover up his crime, will be able to leave the finger-print of another person around the place he worked, and then in some way throw suspicion on the innocent man . . . Fortunately, however, the method is not known to more than half a dozen men at present, and all efforts will be made to keep it a secret of trusted police officials." For Vollmer, knowledge of how to fabricate a fingerprint was to be kept safely in the hands of the police. His assurances ring particularly hollow, though, because every single documented case of fabrication—other than the "staged" forgeries I have described—has been attributed to a law enforcement officer. There are no known instances of criminals planting fabricated fingerprints. Instead, in all known cases police have used fabrications to strengthen their evidence against suspects.[26]

The FBI first identified a forgery by a law enforcement officer in 1925, little more than a year after it opened for business. More were soon reported. At the 1929 IAI meeting Edward Parker reported a fabrication from a Kansas burglary case. Parker's breach of silence on this issue moved a Mr. Axtell to report a similar case in New Mexico, which in turn prompted a Mr. Jones of Minneapolis to report yet another forgery. There is no telling how numerous these incidents really were, but we do know that between 1930 and 1960 "the FBI exposed at least 15 cases of fabrication of latent prints from 13 different states in all regions of the country." The fingerprint examiner Pat Wertheim, who performed a historical survey of reported cases of fabrication, "reasonably believes these cases number in the hundreds or even thousands during the twentieth century. To keep that in perspective, honest identifications probably number in many millions. Still, fabrications occur far too often. A disturbing percentage of experienced examiners polled . . . described personal exposure to at least one of these cases during their careers."[27]

Fingerprint examiners claim that no forgery can withstand expert scrutiny and that highly experienced examiners can always detect traces of the fabrication process. The problem is that few declared fingerprint matches are subjected to such rigorous scrutiny. "We don't really know" how often fabrications or errors occur, says the law professor André Moenssens, because the "documented cases have come to light only by accident or after a particularly tenacious investigator revealed them." This was certainly true of the New York scandal, which was only revealed by the CIA's probing interrogation of David Harding.[28]

It is difficult to gauge the extent of fingerprint forgery because it is difficult to understand the motives behind it. Wertheim attributes fabrications to a desire for quick advancement, resentment against one's employer for some professional slight, or the belief that the suspect is guilty and therefore fabrication of evidence is morally justifiable. The New York scandal, however, contradicted the stereotypical image of the fabricator as motivated by the desire to convict people of whose guilt he is firmly convinced. "Vigilantism," the special prosecutor reported, "does not appear to be a major factor." Instead, it seems investigators fabricated fingerprints "on an almost routine basis," even when doing so was not necessary to secure a conviction, almost as a competition between investigators. "Ego, laziness, craving for publicity and advancement, and gamesmanship appear to be likely explanations" for fabrication, the special prosecutor concluded.[29]

Perhaps the most shocking thing about the State Police scandal was that the rogue investigators operated with impunity for so long: "Some members of the Identification Unit were so careless with their fabrications they left . . . 'practice' fabrications behind in the actual case files in which evidence had been fabricated and used in criminal prosecutions . . . This indifference, in itself, strongly suggests that the individuals fabricating evidence on a routine basis had no fear of discovery and, except with a noted exception, apparently took few steps to cover their tracks."[30]

It is also shocking that the forgeries so easily escaped detection. They ranged from sophisticated, such as lifting a print from an inked fingerprint card and doctoring it to look like a latent print, to extremely crude, such as simply photocopying an inked print and calling it a latent print. According to the outside fingerprint examiners employed by the special prosecutor, the fraudulence of many of the fingerprints offered in these cases should have been blatantly obvious to anyone trained in fingerprint identification. One fabricated print even "contained perpendicular lines lifted from the fingerprint card, lines which were part of the printed box in which the original ink impression was placed." Yet in more than forty criminal cases, some involving homicide, over eight years, the evidence was not once challenged by the defense: "In most if not all of the cases where fingerprint evidence was significant, the defense attorneys were surprisingly complacent about the fingerprint evidence and did little, if anything, to challenge it. In at least one case, the circumstances cried out for an independent evaluation by a defense fingerprint expert. No such expert was hired. Indeed, it does not appear that a latent fingerprint expert participated on behalf of the defense in any of the tainted cases."[31]

This is not to blame defense attorneys. As the special prosecutor noted, "This may be explained, in part, by the fact that in most of the cases, other evidence of guilt was overwhelming, and by the fact that courts are reluctant to authorize the expenditure of public funds for defense experts where other facets of the case indicate that the expenditure may be a waste of time." Nevertheless, the scandal revealed the extent of the trust extended to fingerprint examiners, how little defense attorneys scrutinize fingerprint evidence, and how rare is the retention of an expert by the defense. In their confessions, the troopers themselves acknowledged that they chose to fabricate fingerprint evidence because they knew it would go unquestioned, because it was so thoroughly trusted.[32]

The New York State Police scandal suggested that fabrication might be far more widespread than previously imagined. It showed that rank-and-file fingerprint examiners often operate without oversight from any outside authority, and without any verification of their declared identifications. It also showed that the adversarial process was inadequate to function as a check on the power of fingerprint examiners. At the same time, the scandal strengthened the proposition that all forgeries are ultimately detectable, in that the external reviewers had little difficulty identifying forgeries and inferring the process by which they had been fabricated. And conscientious fingerprint examiners, who devoted enormous time and effort to reevaluating the contested evidence and exposing the forgeries in this and other cases, demonstrated that they considered it part of their professional responsibility to root out fabrication, corruption, and incompetence. But overall the scandal cast yet another ray of doubt on fingerprint evidence in the 1990s. If the examiners who did the identifying could not be trusted, then the whole technique was suspect.

In addition to concerns about corrupt fingerprint examiners, concerns about incompetence resurfaced in 1995, when the IAI helped the Collaborative Testing Service (CTS) perform the first external proficiency tests on American police fingerprint laboratories. The results were astonishing. Only 44 percent of the tested examiners scored perfectly. Six of the 156 examiners reported false negatives—that is, they failed to identify matching prints. But the consequences of a false negative— possibly allowing a guilty suspect to escape conviction—paled in comparison with the consequences of a false positive, in which an innocent person could (and, given the power of fingerprint evidence, probably would) be falsely convicted of a crime. Thirty-four examiners, 22 percent of the total, reported false positives. This was startlingly high for a forensic technique that claimed "practical infallibility." David Grieve noted: "Reaction to the results of the CTS 1995 Latent Print Proficiency Test within the forensic science community has ranged from shock to disbelief . . . As tempting as it might be to dismiss such error as substandard performance, the repeatability of this error exceeds any reasonably normal expectations. If one in five latent print examiners truly possesses a knowledge, skill, or ability level below an acceptable and understood base line, then the entire profession is in jeopardy." The 1996 test yielded somewhat better news. Only 3 percent of the laboratories reported false positives. In the 1997 test 16 of 204 examiners reported false positives, and in the 1998 test 14 of 91 participants (around 15 percent) reported false positives. These rates were still far too high for the comfort of the fingerprint community or to support the long-standing contention that errors in latent fingerprint identification were impossible.[33]

These successive crises might have been thought to strengthen the British hand in the transatlantic struggle for control of the methodology of latent fingerprint analysis. The error in the Caldwell case had exposed three incompetent IAI-certified examiners; the New York State Police scandal had exposed two corrupt ones. A federal judge was questioning the scientific expertise of the entire professional community, and proficiency tests revealed startlingly high error rates. Perhaps the IAI's faith in the individual examiner was misplaced.

Soon, however, it was American examiners' turn to point out that they did not have a monopoly on incompetence or malfeasance. In April 1997 Scotland Yard admitted that its examiners had erroneously matched a latent print from the scene of a burglary at the London home of the writer Miriam Stoppard (ex-wife of the playwright Tom Stoppard) with that of a suspect, Andrew Chiory. Two separate comparisons, both triple-checked, supposedly led to the misidentification. The Chiory case provoked a flurry of publicity with headlines like "Fingerprint Proof 'Flawed.'" The Scotland Yard fingerprint bureau's "first mistake since it was founded in 1901," the press reported, "could throw into doubt the reputation of fingerprints as irrefutable evidence." External examiners from the South Yorkshire Police were called in to investigate, and the Yard expected more than fifty other convictions to be challenged. Reports of the demise of latent fingerprint identification, however, proved to be premature. As in the Caldwell case, the Yard was able to "explain" the error by attributing it to misconduct on the part of the individual examiners. The Yard found that "triple-checking" consisted, not of independently verifying the initial examiner's identification, but rather of simply taking the initial examiner's word for it. Thus the error was attributed not to the technique, nor even to procedures, but to a failure to follow procedures.[34]

In December 1998 the British courts freed Danny McNamee, who had been convicted of building a nail bomb for the Irish Republican Army that killed four cavalrymen and seven horses in 1982. McNamee's fingerprints had been matched with latent prints found on tape and a battery used in the bomb, but, on appeal, fourteen expert witnesses disagreed as to the value of the prints. Two experts, Peter Swann and Martin Leadbetter, contended that the latent prints were too poor to be used for identification. Even the examiners who favored a match could not find the requisite sixteen "points of similarity"; the most they found was eleven. Once more, overzealous police, in this case under heavy political pressure, had claimed a level of certainty that was subsequently found to be exaggerated.[35]

Perhaps most damning of all was the Shirley McKie case. In the spring of 1999 Detective Constable Shirley McKie of the Strathclyde Police in Scotland was tried in Glasgow for allegedly tampering with evidence in a murder investigation. The murder suspect, David Asbury, had been linked to the crime by a latent fingerprint found in the home of the victim and by the victim's print found on a tin in his home. Fingerprint technicians also matched a latent fingerprint from the suspect's home with Shirley McKie. (It is common practice to check all latent prints at a crime scene against those of the police officers who have been at the scene and may have inadvertently left prints.) The problem was that McKie insisted that she had never entered the suspect's house. This inconsistency created a potential defense argument that McKie had somehow framed Asbury by planting the incriminating print. Since McKie steadfastly denied that she had set foot inside the house, and the fingerprint examiners insisted that the print was hers, the authorities felt they had no choice but to try McKie for perjury.

In desperation, McKie contacted the American fingerprint examiner Pat Wertheim, who examined the prints and concluded they did not match. Wertheim and David Grieve testified for the defense. Examiners from the Scottish Criminal Records Office (SCRO) insisted that the match was good. A jury acquitted McKie of the charges. Numerous experts from Britain, the United States, and elsewhere have agreed with Wertheim and Grieve's conclusion. The SCRO, however, remains convinced that the print is McKie's. More than any other case, the McKie case brought the Anglo-American divide over methodology into sharp relief, especially since the Scottish examiners had labeled sixteen "points of similarity" between two prints that the American examiners insisted did not match.[36]

Although many of these events were reported in the media, they did not garner much attention and they did little to sully the reputation of fingerprint evidence. Judge, juries, and the general public, only dimly aware of these potential problems, continued to demonstrate boundless faith in fingerprint evidence and enormous trust in latent fingerprint examiners. In each case the professional community had managed to contain the damage by laying the blame on incompetent or unscrupulous individuals, preserving the reputation of the technique in general. This strategy, however, was not going to work with the fundamental problem of the scientific foundation of latent fingerprint evidence, especially in the United States, where in a 1993 case, *Daubert v. Merrell Dow*, the Supreme Court had handed down a landmark decision on the admissibility of scientific evidence.

Much had changed since forensic fingerprint evidence had first won admission to the courtroom in the Jennings case in 1911. In place of the old, rather loose, standard for scientific evidence—that it enjoy "general acceptance" in its field—*Daubert* posed new standards for judging whether or not evidence should properly be considered scientific. The Court articulated five criteria: peer review and sound methodology, a known error rate, testable hypotheses, application outside of legal proceedings, and, again, general acceptance. The Court noted that these were merely guidelines; none was an indispensable characteristic of science. Latent fingerprint evidence had never been subjected to any legal review under these criteria. Legal scholars and forensic scientists suggested, astonishingly, that fingerprint evidence might not be able to meet the *Daubert* criteria. In a 1997 legal practice guide, the forensic scientist David Stoney concluded that "the criteria for absolute identification in fingerprint work are subjective and ill-defined. They are the products of probabilistic intuitions widely shared among fingerprint examiners, not of scientific research." "Fingerprint evidence," the legal scholar Michael Saks noted, "may present courts applying *Daubert* with their most extreme dilemma . . . When and if a court agrees to revisit the admissibility of fingerprint identification evidence under *Daubert*, the *Daubert* approach . . . is likely to meet its most demanding test: A vote to admit fingerprints is a rejection of conventional science as the criterion for admission. A vote for science is a vote to exclude fingerprint expert opinions." "Woe to fingerprint practice were such criteria applied!" warned Stoney.[37]

Stoney's words came as some surprise to attorneys for a man named Byron Mitchell, who was charged with armed robbery in Philadelphia. It so happened that two latent fingerprints formed the principal evidence against Mitchell. His attorneys sought to have Stoney, along with James Starrs, a law professor and forensic scientist at the George Washington University, testify as expert witnesses at his trial. Since the prosecution objected, the court decided to hold a *Daubert* hearing on the scientific validity of fingerprint evidence in July 1999. The FBI, whose agent had made the identification in the case, took the challenge seriously, as did the whole North American fingerprint community. The credibility of latent fingerprint identification was being threatened, not, as the British had predicted, by an erroneous identification facilitated by the lack of a minimum standard in the United States, but rather, as the Americans had foreseen, by its lack of a well-articulated scientific argument. And so it came to pass that, on the eve of the twenty-first century, ten witnesses spent five days in a federal courtroom debating whether or not latent fingerprint evidence was scientific. Bruce Badler, a professor of anatomy, Ashbaugh, Wertheim, Bruce Budowle, a geneticist who handled DNA analysis for the FBI, and Stephen Meagher, an FBI fingerprint examiner, were among the prosecution's witnesses. Stoney, Starrs, and I testified for the defense.[38]

The prosecution's witnesses argued that the aggregate collective experience of fingerprint examiners over the past century was more than sufficient to establish the fundamental premises of latent fingerprint identification: that "human friction ridge skin arrangements are unique and permanent," and that "positive identification can result from comparisons of friction ridge skin or impressions containing sufficient quality (clarity) and quantity of unique friction ridge detail." The defense witnesses contended that these premises had not been scientifically tested.[39]

The court ruled in favor of the prosecution that latent fingerprint evidence is reliable. The defense witnesses were not permitted to testify at trial. But the court sidestepped the prosecution's request that it take judicial notice that fingerprint evidence is scientific, deeming this question irrelevant to the matter at hand (because evidence need not be scientific to be admissible—it could be based on technical expert knowledge, such as the knowledge of automobile mechanics). The vexing question of whether fingerprint identification should properly be considered science remained unanswered, but it will surely be revisited in the near future. Already the Mitchell case has inspired numerous other *Daubert* challenges to fingerprint evidence.[40]

The most significant effect of the *Daubert* hearing may have been felt within the fingerprint profession itself. If fingerprint examiners were going to articulate a scientific foundation that satisfied *Daubert*, point counting, clearly, would not do. The prosecution's presentation at the hearing, therefore, with Ashbaugh himself appearing as the star witness, emphasized Ashbaugh's ridgeology (or "quantitative-qualitative evaluation," as he now calls it), even to the point of denying that any American fingerprint examiners count points anymore. The fact that the FBI agent at Mitchell's original trial had labeled and discussed corresponding "points" during his testimony was explained as a demonstrative argument for the benefit of the jury rather than a reflection of the actual process by which the identification had been made. The hearing served notice to the fingerprint community that point counting was vulnerable to attack on scientific grounds. And, as perhaps the final straw, Britain abandoned the sixteen-point standard on January 1, 2001. But the triumph of ridgeology is far from complete. Advocates of point counting continue to criticize ridgeology even after the Mitchell hearing.[41]

It may be that ridgeology appeared in the nick of time to rescue latent fingerprint identification from being hurled onto the junk-heap of pseudo-science. Or perhaps something is about to happen that only a few years ago would have seemed unthinkable. Could the credibility of fingerprint identification actually crumble? If so, it would be just in time for a new technology, which accords better with the notion of science promoted in the Daubert decision, to save the day. This new technology is of course DNA typing. It now seems at least possible, if not likely, that a variety of forces—the internal divisions within the fingerprint profession itself, the changing notion of science promoted by the *Daubert* decision, and the far more statistically and methodologically sophisticated example being set by DNA evidence—may conspire to have fingerprint identification declared legally unscientific. If this does occur, history will repeat yet again: a new identification technique, by discrediting the old, will strengthen its own claims to provide credible, reliable, and trustworthy identification.

If we had called this "idiosyncratic Southern blot profiling," nobody would have taken a blind bit of notice. Call it "DNA fingerprinting," and the penny dropped.

—Alec Jeffreys (1996)

CHAPTER 12

The Genetic Age

On the morning of November 22, 1983, a resident of the sleepy English village of Narborough found the body of fifteen-year-old Lynda Mann in a field outside of town. The girl had been raped and strangled. The murder shocked the village, where violent crime was rare, and the villagers demanded that the killer be found and brought to justice. The police had few clues to work with. As in many cases, the crime scene did not yield latent fingerprints. But the killer, like most rapists, had left another trace at the crime scene: his semen. The standard blood tests available at the time revealed only that the assailant was a PGM1+ Group A secretor, meaning his blood contained a particular antigen present in the blood of only 10 percent of the male population of England. This information was enough to eliminate suspects, but not discriminating enough to provide convincing evidence of guilt.

The Mann murder was a heinous crime, the sex murder of an adolescent. Such crimes are increasingly perceived as taking on epidemic proportions these days. Since the 1980s both the United States and Europe have been in the throes of a full-fledged "moral panic" over sexual abuse of children, of which sex murder of children was the ultimate representation. Sex crime, indeed, is thought by many to define all that was going awry in late-twentieth-century culture and society.[1]

The murder of Lynda Mann went unsolved for three years until the police discovered the body of another fifteen-year-old rape-murder victim, Dawn Ashworth. Again, there was little trace evidence of identity, but there were sufficient similarities, including the same rare blood group recovered from a semen sample, to conclude that it was probably the same killer. Villagers and police alike came to the sickening conclusion that there was a serial murderer at large in their town. The police's failure to solve the Mann murder had resulted in the brutal murder of yet another child, and no one felt this more acutely than the police themselves.

Now the Narborough killer was not only a sex-murderer of children but also a serial killer. Serial killers, like sex criminals, have become a preoccupation of our age. The popular image of serial sex killers holds that they roam at will, shielded by the anonymity of modern society and the inadequacy of criminal recordkeeping and surveillance, committing multiple offenses. The failure of the Leicester police to apprehend Lynda Mann's killer before he killed again symbolized the failure of the existing methods of criminal identification to protect society against mobile, anonymous, repetitive sex killers.[2]

New techniques of criminal identification prove their value by identifying a specific group of people who have somehow eluded older methods. Fingerprinting, for example, was able to identify people of "other" races, and women, who were thought to defy anthropometric description. Because of its low cost, it also allowed the identification of pettier criminals. And, in its forensic application, fingerprinting could identify those relatively rare criminals who left legible fingerprints at crime scenes. But forensic fingerprint identification could do nothing to solve the Narborough murders. Measures for tracking and monitoring released sex offenders, meanwhile, were haphazard and passive, relying on the convict to fulfill his legal obligation to keep the authorities apprised of his whereabouts. Media reporting of sex crimes suggested "that *if only* adequate records could be maintained, women and children could be protected. New sexual offences committed by convicted offenders are blamed on failures in record-keeping." Not only did fingerprinting fail to provide forensic evidence against sex offenders except in a few, rare cases, but criminal identification systems were proving inadequate for monitoring the convicted sex offenders at large in the community. Any identification technique that promised to address these problems might be able to break fingerprinting's monopoly on criminal identification.[3]

Suspicion in the Ashworth investigation quickly fell on Richard Buckland, a seventeen-year-old porter at a nearby hospital, who had been seen lurking around the crime scene and who had a history of molesting younger girls. Buckland, a confused outcast, was no match for a long interrogation. He soon confessed to the murder of Dawn Ashworth. But, try as they might, the detectives could not entice him to confess to the murder of Lynda Mann. Buckland's father claims it was he who asked the police to contact the geneticist Dr. Alec Jeffreys, a researcher at the nearby University of Leicester, who had been written up in local papers for inventing a new identification method called "genetic fingerprinting." The police insist that Chief Superintendent David Baker approached Jeffreys in the hope of using genetic fingerprinting to connect Buckland to the Mann murder.[4]

Jeffreys had been investigating ways of using genetic variants as markers for tracing familial lineages, much the same purpose for which Francis Galton had tried to use fingerprint patterns a century earlier. Like Galton, Jeffreys initially had little interest in identification; he was pursuing a far loftier goal—the ability to render inheritance visible, using the late-twentieth-century biological marker of choice, DNA, instead of the late-nineteenth-century marker, the fingerprint. And like Galton, Jeffreys, in his pursuit of hereditary markers, had almost accidentally stumbled across a new identification technique.

A gene is placed on a chromosome at a site called a "locus." Each individual's genes may assume one of two (one for each parent) of a variety of inherited forms, called "alleles." Jeffreys had discovered Variable Number Tandem Repeats (VNTRs), loci where the genetic code, the sequence of proteins that forms the "blueprint" for every organism, "catches" and "stutters," repeating a sequence of DNA base pairs— pairs of two proteins bonded together that compose the double helix strands of DNA—over and over. The length of the stutter varies widely among individuals (hence "variable number"). One individual's genome might repeat a certain VNTR thirty times; another might repeat it hundreds of times. Individuals could be distinguished, Jeffreys realized, according to the length of their VNTRs. He devised a way of physically cutting specific VNTRs from the DNA coil, and he inferred the relative length of VNTRs through a process called "gel electrophoresis." When he passed an electrical current across a gel, the VNTRs migrated across the gel, and the shorter, lighter VNTRs traveled farther than the longer, heavier ones. The double-stranded DNA was then broken into single strands and transferred to a nylon sheet, a process called "Southern blotting" (after a scientist named Ed Southern). Using a radioactive probe that attached to the separated VNTRs, Jeffreys was able to create an X-ray photograph, called an "autoradiograph" or "autorad," that displayed the placement—and thus the relative length —of the different VNTR fragments as dark bands whose location on the autorad corresponded to their length: the first "DNA fingerprint."

No one claims that alleles, or the bands that represent them, are unique. Jeffreys merely claimed that they were highly variable. In order to achieve individualized identification through genetic analysis, it would be necessary to use Jeffreys's method to visualize an individual's alleles at *several different* loci. Then it would be necessary to calculate the frequency with which each allele appears in the general population. By multiplying these frequencies together, one could come up with very high probabilities against two different people having the same alleles at several different loci.

It is important to note that, unlike dactyloscopers, geneticists were not making a claim of absolute uniqueness. Rather they were making probabilistic claims, albeit ones with extremely high probabilities, ranging from 1 in 100,000 to 1 in 100 million. In this way genetic identification is more like the other forensic sciences, which frame their conclusions in terms of probabilities, than like fingerprinting, which frames its arguments in terms of uniqueness and absolute certainty. Hence, after the initial flush of publicity wore off, geneticists quietly dropped the name "DNA fingerprinting," which they thought produced the misleading impression that the genetic information they were dealing with was unique, in favor of the more measured terms "DNA typing" and "DNA profiling," which convey that genetic information is merely meant to be a very rare type or profile, *not* a unique marker. Theoretically, if it were possible to visualize an individual's entire gene sequence, one might be able to claim that DNA typing produces a unique genetic "fingerprint." Current methods of DNA typing, however, do not look at the entire DNA sequence. In fact, they visualize only a few loci, a minute fraction of all the information available on the entire human gene sequence.

It is also important to note that VNTRs are considered noncoding or "junk" DNA. A substantial portion of human DNA does not perform any function; it is just filler. VNTRs fall into this category. That means that the loci used for identification are not the loci that determine an individual's hair, eye, or skin color, intelligence, criminal propensity, vulnerability to disease, or any other personal characteristic. This is an important point because DNA databases can be constructed so that they contain only noncoding information and nothing about personal characteristics.

On September 15, 1984, Jeffreys created his first image of a "DNA fingerprint." Although he had not been thinking about identification, he realized that the process could function as an identification technique. That night Jeffreys and his wife sat down and tried to dream up potential applications for the new technique. The first thing they thought of was not identification of criminals. Like the fingerprint pioneers on the West Coast of the United States—Morse, Lawton, and Taber—almost exactly a century earlier, the Jeffreys first thought of using the new identification technique for controlling immigration. British immigration law allowed children to rejoin parents living in Britain, but many children were denied entry at the border because they could not prove their biological relationship with their parents. Immigration officials suspected that the identities of native-born children were being sold on black markets or transferred to distant relatives in third-world countries, much in the way that U.S. customs officials a century earlier had believed that the identities of returning merchants were being sold in China. In 1985 Jeffreys applied the new technology for the first time in an immigration dispute over a Ghanaian boy who claimed he had been born in Britain. Officials believed that the woman purporting to be the boy's mother was actually his aunt. Jeffreys used his DNA test to show that the boy's parents were indeed who he claimed they were, and the boy was granted British residency.[5]

The murders in nearby Narborough offered Jeffreys his first chance to use the technique for criminal identification. The police had recovered semen samples from the bodies of both of the victims, and they took a blood sample from the suspect, Richard Buckland. Jeffreys's results were startling. DNA typing showed that the semen from both bodies came from the same man, and that man was definitely *not* Richard Buckland. The police were dumfounded. Forensic DNA experts agree that while an "inclusion" (the conclusion that an individual may have been the "donor" of a DNA sample) is merely a statistical likelihood, an "exclusion" (the conclusion that an individual cannot have been the donor) like that of Buckland is a virtual certainty. Reluctantly, the police released Buckland.

Now the police had a genetic profile of the killer, but what could they do with it? There was no genetic database to search. The DNA profile could not be used to generate a sketch of the killer. The authorities came up with a radical solution. Convinced the killer lived in the area, they resolved to take blood samples from every male between the ages of seventeen and thirty-four living or working in Narborough or the surrounding area. Police requested that citizens give samples voluntarily, but those who refused were subject to intensive police scrutiny. The project, which became known locally as "the blooding," would eventually entail taking blood samples from more than 4,000 men.[6]

Despite this massive undertaking, a baker named Colin Pitchfork, by claiming to be terrified of needles, managed to convince a co-worker to give a blood sample in his name. The deceit might never have been detected had the co-worker, troubled by what he had done, not blurted it out to colleagues at lunch. One of these colleagues was disturbed enough to notify the police. Upon arrest, Pitchfork confessed to both murders, and his DNA profile matched the semen samples taken from the two victims. Although mass screening did not identify the killer, it did, as the police had hoped, flush him out. Since then, British authorities have authorized more "bloodings" in response to unsolved rural murders from which DNA samples have been recovered.[7]

Thus began the era of DNA typing, which has been widely hailed as "perhaps the greatest advance in forensic science since the development of ordinary fingerprints." Ever since fingerprinting achieved widespread recognition, new biometric identification techniques have arisen purporting to improve on it. As early as 1927 two American physicians, calling fingerprinting "a method of only relative reliability, since the cutaneous ridges can be accidentally or willfully spoiled by various scarrings," proposed identifying persons by X-rays of the skull. Not only were bones of the skull less accessible for intentional alteration than fingerprints, but, the method's proponents pointed out, the skull had the macabre advantage of staying with the corpse more often than the hands. Others suggested identification by voice or breathing patterns. Using the branching of the blood vessels in the retina, which, like the bones of the skull, could not "be altered nor effaced," was proposed as early as 1935. Today there is renewed interest in alternative biometric identifiers like retina scanning, voice spectrometry, hand geometry, and computerized facial recognition. These technologies are being targeted primarily at civilian applications, which require authenticating a declared identity, rather than criminal applications, which require identifying an unknown person who may be employing an alias. Chief among these civilian applications are the disbursement of welfare and other entitlements, immigration control, banking, workplace security, and access to "smart" credit, bank, or identification cards. Of these biometric identifiers, only DNA typing has the potential to be a formidable rival to fingerprinting in the area of criminal identification.[8]

Identification methods do not flourish and become widely accepted solely on technical grounds. The acceptance of a new identifier as useful and reliable occurs within a particular social, cultural, and historical context. Jeffreys's new technique emerged as useful precisely for solving hitherto unsolvable sex crimes. In the early years around 80 percent of cases involving DNA were sexual assault cases, and this is still the principal application of forensic DNA typing. Although not all sexual assailants leave semen samples at the scene of the crime, a great many of them do. Genetic identification is, therefore, particularly well suited to solving sexual assault crimes. Although improved genetic probes now allow DNA samples to be recovered in some cases from saliva, hair, sweat, or even skin cells, the earliest methods could only generate usable forensic samples from blood or semen. Forensic DNA identification was initially confined to rape cases and those occasional homicides or assaults (like the O. J. Simpson case) in which either the blood of the assailant had been spilled or the blood of the victim had been found on the assailant's clothing or possessions.

In addition, there are technical reasons that genetic identification is particularly reliable in rape cases: the victim's DNA is invariably mixed in with that of the perpetrator. The victim's DNA can be tested against the crime scene sample along with that of the suspect. This provides a built-in control to be sure that the sample has not been degraded by exposure to the environment. Forensic scientists can obtain a known DNA sample from the victim and check it against the crime-scene sample. If the victim's DNA does not show up in the crime-scene sample, then they know the sample has been degraded and is useless. Investigators can ensure the authenticity of the "rape kit" by checking that it matches the DNA of the victim.[9]

Around 1994 the first states began establishing genetic identification databases, and eventually all fifty states followed suit. The laws mandated the taking of DNA samples from "designated offenders." Initially this meant sex offenders and murderers. A blood or hair follicle sample is taken from the prisoner, usually upon release from prison. In some states the sample itself is stored; in others a genetic profile is taken from the sample, which is then destroyed. These samples or genetic profiles make up the states' genetic databases. Forensic scientists with a DNA sample recovered from a crime scene, but without a readily apparent suspect, can test the DNA evidence against the database. In rare, but increasingly common, cases called "hits," the DNA evidence matches a sample in the database and identifies the perpetrator. The police can also use DNA databases to try to solve old, unsolved, or cold cases, if DNA evidence is still available. For example, in March 2000 the New York State database solved its first cold case by linking a 1979 murder to a man named Walter Gill, who was serving time at Sing Sing for robbery. Gill's DNA profile had been entered into the state database as part of an expansion of the database to crimes other than murder and rape. By testing the twenty-year-old evidence against the database, investigators matched the crime-scene samples to Gill's genetic profile.[10]

By 1997 a quarter of a million DNA samples had been collected across the nation. The Federal Bureau of Investigation (FBI) recently announced that all fifty states had connected to its Combined DNA Identification System (CODIS), creating a National DNA Index System (NDIS). As it did with fingerprinting, the FBI is positioning itself less as the keeper of a national database than as a coordinator and facilitator for the communication of criminal identification information between states. Nonetheless, CODIS does have the potential to be something akin to a national genetic criminal identification database overseen by the FBI. Advances in computer technology should make the collection and maintenance of genetic databases increasingly cheap and easy. Similarly, it should become cheaper and easier to access genetic identification information and to transfer such information between agencies, states, and even nations.[11]

The first databases were limited to sex offenders and murderers, but they are gradually being expanded. For instance, the scope of New York State's DNA database was extended in 1999 to include around half of all convicted felons, about 25,000 people each year. The law also mandated collecting DNA samples from everyone in prison or on parole or probation for any of the designated felonies, a total of around 100,000 people. In this way DNA databases are following the pattern set by fingerprinting. Fingerprinting first proved its value for identifying specific groups—immigrants, people of color, prostitutes, and petty criminals—then broadened its domain to other groups of offenders. DNA established itself as a technique for identifying and tracking sex offenders, but it is rapidly expanding to include other convicts. Owing to improvements in the sensitivity of DNA testing, samples are now recoverable not only from blood and semen but also from hair and skin cells, saliva, and sweat. This suggests that it will be possible to use forensic DNA typing to investigate pettier crimes like burglary and auto theft in addition to murder and rape. Already, however, DNA databases are encountering a familiar problem: it is not clear that criminal identification bureaus have the budgetary and technical capacity to collect and store the vast amount of genetic information necessary to maintain a useful database.[12]

Nonetheless, the expansion will probably continue. Beginning in 1995 Britain, retaining its leadership in DNA typing, took DNA samples from anyone arrested for a felony or a misdemeanor. As of this writing the British have amassed a database of more than 500,000 samples. Former New York City Police Chief Howard Safir, Governor George Pataki, and the International Association of Chiefs of Police recently called for taking DNA samples from everyone who is arrested. Others, including New York City Mayor Rudolph Giuliani, are calling for universal identification through DNA typing at birth. And, harking again back to the history of fingerprinting, at least one state has arranged for the voluntary registration of children's DNA by parents worried about the threat of kidnapping.[13]

Whereas fingerprinting is routinely performed upon arrest, DNA database samples are still usually taken only when a convict enters or is released from prison. The database sample consists of a blood sample or, increasingly, a less invasive cheek swab. Forensic technicians process the sample to determine its alleles at several loci. The bands for each locus are recorded by a computer. This yields a genetic profile that can be stored in the computer database. At this point the original biological sample can be destroyed—and is in most states—or it can be retained by the state for possible future testing.[14]

After the Pitchfork case, DNA typing was widely hailed as a revolutionary breakthrough in forensic science, the most significant development since fingerprinting—and in the late 1980s a number of private companies sprang up to take advantage of Jeffreys's new technique. These companies expected the bulk of their business to be in paternity testing—a civil application for which genetic identification was particularly well suited—alongside a smaller but significant volume of forensic work. These private laboratories got a head start on most police laboratories, which were not geared up for the sophisticated molecular biological techniques required for forensic DNA testing. In addition, private laboratories could offer an aura of neutrality: as private entities they could argue that they were not biased in favor of law enforcement the way a police crime laboratory might be. At the same time, private laboratories could be viewed as having a financial interest in finding whatever results their paying client wished to hear.[15]

When forensic DNA typing was new, it was performed by research scientists, who were the only people competent to do the work. Once the problems had been ironed out and the basic protocols set up, however, DNA typing became fairly routine. Those doing genetic identification work now range from Ph.D. scientists to technicians with hands-on experience and high school educations. The recovery of DNA evidence from crime scenes requires somewhat less training: how to locate, preserve, lift, store, and transport biological samples.[16]

In most cases judges and juries alike, awed by the power of science, welcomed and trusted DNA evidence. Defense attorneys, meanwhile, hardly knew enough science to dispute the claims of forensic scientists and rarely could afford to hire experts. In a 1988 murder case, however, prosecutors encountered two young public defenders who were not intimidated by DNA evidence, Barry Scheck and Peter Neufeld. Their client, a building superintendent named José Castro, had been accused of murdering Vilma Ponce and her two-year-old daughter, Natasha, in their apartment in the Bronx in New York City. When detectives questioned Castro, they found blood on his wristwatch. They sent the blood sample to Lifecodes, a privately run DNA laboratory, for testing, and the laboratory reported a match between the blood on the watch and Vilma Ponce. Scheck and Neufeld persuaded several prominent molecular biologists, including Eric Lander of the prestigious Whitehead Institute for Biomedical Research, to examine the evidence for the defense. These experts found several disturbing problems with the laboratory's handling and analysis of the evidence. First, one of the autorads presented as evidence by Lifecodes showed three matching bands between the DNA found on the watch and the known DNA of Vilma Ponce. But the watch sample also clearly showed two additional bands. These bands were not mentioned at all in the Lifecodes report; they had simply been dismissed as either laboratory artifacts or nonhuman contamination. The same laboratory report also cited three matching bands between Natasha and the watch. But the autorad showed only one matching band. On the witness stand, none of the Lifecodes technicians could find the missing bands that their report claimed were there. These two errors suggested that Lifecodes technicians were looking at the evidence *expecting* to see matches, rather than evaluating it dispassionately.

In order to define "matching" bands, Lifecodes had set up quantitative standards for how far apart two bands could appear and still be considered "matching." But supposedly "matching" bands on two other autorads actually fell outside the laboratory's own standards for a match (much as the Will Wests' foot measurements had fallen outside the specified deviation for a match under the Bertillon system). This suggested that Lifecodes technicians were declaring matches by visual comparison rather than by quantitative measurement. Finally, Lifecodes witnesses were unable to specify who had donated the control DNA for a sex test they had performed on the blood from the watch. All these blunders and discrepancies made the way Lifecodes had handled sensitive scientific evidence in a homicide case appear cavalier, amateurish, and careless.

In a highly unusual move, Lander and Richard Roberts, a geneticist at Cold Spring Harbor Laboratory who was testifying for the prosecution, arranged to convene the experts from both sides without lawyers present. In this meeting the defense and prosecution scientists reached common ground: DNA typing was a promising forensic technique, scientifically reliable when properly used, but its application by Lifecodes in this case had been unacceptably sloppy. In short, the prosecution experts agreed to sacrifice the evidence in the Castro case for the long-term good of the technique. Presented with this consensus, the judge ruled that DNA evidence was admissible in principle but excluded the evidence from the Castro trial.[17]

Although José Castro subsequently pleaded guilty to the murders, the Castro decision gave defense attorneys an opening: they could try to convince judges to exclude DNA evidence by showing that its handling had been sloppy. Defense attorneys initially focused on the kind of obvious laboratory contamination or incompetence that Lifecodes had displayed in the Castro case. In 1990 a test conducted by the California Association of Crime Laboratory Directors found a 2 percent error rate at another prominent privately run DNA laboratory, Cellmark, fueling accusations of incompetence. Cellmark's error was apparently due to an inadvertent mix-up of samples in the laboratory, just the kind of error that might, defense attorneys contended, lead to a false conviction.[18]

Just as the issue of incompetence in laboratories began to die down, population geneticists such as Richard Lewontin and Daniel Hartl criticized the statistical probabilities of genetic matches cited by DNA experts on the witness stand. Early advocates of DNA typing had simply multiplied together the frequency of each allele at each locus tested, resulting in extremely high odds against two different people sharing the same genetic profile. But this calculation relied on the assumption that allele frequencies on different loci were statistically independent. This was akin to assuming that the entire population of the Earth mated randomly. Population geneticists argued that the existence of geographic and racial "subpopulations"—groups of people who tended to mate with one another—was well established. Thus people of similar racial and ethnic backgrounds were more likely to share alleles than people of different backgrounds. The earliest statistical probabilities cited in court had failed to take this fact into account. In 1992 a committee convened by the National Research Council acknowledged this problem and sought to address it by articulating a "ceiling principle," which directed that geneticists err on the side of caution when calculating probabilities of accidental matches. Statistical estimates calculated according to the ceiling principle are supposed to be so conservative that there is no risk of misleading the jury, somewhat akin to the old British sixteen-point fingerprint standard.

The population genetics controversy injected the issue of race into the debate over DNA typing. The accusation was that the VNTRs used to individualize people appeared with different frequencies in different racial populations and, therefore, might be used as racial markers. DNA typing, perhaps, did not individualize strongly enough within racial and ethnic subpopulations. Genetically, members of a given ethnic group might tend to "look alike." Critics also worried about potential "genetic profiling": that, on the basis of DNA samples recovered from crime scenes, forensic technicians might be able to make educated guesses about the race, ethnicity, and appearance of perpetrators. Jeffreys himself had suggested that in the future it might be possible to create police sketches of a suspect from genetic evidence alone, although he quickly qualified this by pointing out that genes probably do not code for appearance that accurately. Critics of DNA typing, such as the anthropologist Paul Rabinow, complained that genetic identification relied too heavily on genetic markers that vary directly with race. Rabinow contrasted DNA typing unfavorably with fingerprinting because, he argued, fingerprints "revealed nothing about individual character or group affiliation."[19]

The questions surrounding race and DNA typing attracted global attention in 1994, when detectives investigating the murder of Nicole Brown Simpson and Ronald Goldman found traces of blood on O. J. Simpson's clothing, car, and home. DNA analysis by Cellmark matched these traces to the victims and also matched blood found at the crime scene to O. J. Simpson. The trial quickly acquired racial overtones stemming from the Simpsons' interracial marriage and white Americans' long history of using both violence and the justice system to punish such breaches of the color barrier, as well as from the persistent history of racism in the Los Angeles Police Department (LAPD) and the recent videotaped beating of a black motorist, Rodney King, and the subsequent riot. These factors contributed, however indirectly, to the undercurrent of suspicion that DNA typing, the forensic technique that provided so much of the evidence against Simpson, might be tainted by racist judgments.[20]

Scheck and Neufeld joined Simpson's "dream team" of defense attorneys, and the two sides geared up for a hearing on whether the DNA evidence should be admitted. In the meantime, Eric Lander, the geneticist who had orchestrated the exclusion of DNA evidence in the Castro case, wrote an article with Bruce Budowle, the FBI's leading DNA expert, that was published in *Nature*. Lander and Budowle recounted the various criticisms of DNA evidence that had been raised over the years—some of them by Lander himself—and concluded that virtually all the problems with DNA evidence had been adequately addressed. Since Lander, because of his role in *Castro*, was considered a critic of DNA typing and Budowle, who worked for the FBI, was considered a proponent, the article had the appearance of a bipartisan compromise. Stauncher critics of DNA evidence, however, noting the fortuitous timing of the article, viewed it as a transparent, eleventh-hour attempt to defuse any scientific criticism of genetic identification just in time for the internationally televised Simpson trial.[21]

Judge Lance Ito, who presided over the Simpson trial, admitted the DNA evidence. But Scheck and Neufeld still had ample resources with which to implement the strategy they had employed in *Castro:* to accept the validity of DNA evidence in principle but criticize its application in the Simpson case by the LAPD and Cellmark. They attacked the weakest link in the processing of the DNA evidence, the work of the LAPD's forensic technicians Dennis Fung and Andrea Mazzola, who had committed numerous procedural errors in recovering, storing, and transporting the evidence to the LAPD crime laboratory. Fung and Mazzola made ideal targets because the LAPD already had an untrustworthy reputation, especially when dealing with African Americans, and because they had deviated from procedure and demonstrated incompetence. The subsequent revelations of a history of racist comments and bragging about fabricating evidence by Mark Fuhrman, one of the detectives on the case, only strengthened this argument. In withering cross-examinations, Scheck and Neufeld forced Fung and Mazzola to admit that they had overlooked crucial evidence, improperly stored DNA samples, thus allowing them to degrade, and otherwise deviated from standard procedure. In his closing argument Scheck compared the hygiene of the LAPD forensic evidence truck to a New York City restaurant in which cockroaches are visible, and he suggested that the evidence implicating Simpson had been contaminated or, worse, planted by the police themselves.

The jury acquitted Simpson after only two hours of deliberation. Many commentators could not understand how the jury could ignore the "overwhelming" DNA evidence, and some thought Scheck's deconstruction of that evidence had won the trial for Simpson. At bottom, the Simpson case demonstrates how difficult it is to sustain claims of truth—even the truth of supposedly "ironclad" scientific evidence—against determined, well-funded, highly skilled opposition operating in a highly charged emotional atmosphere. But Simpson's defense was exceptional, and, despite the Simpson verdict, DNA evidence continues to convict defendants who do not have access to Simpson's extraordinary legal resources. Recent trials that turned on

DNA evidence give some indication of both how difficult and—in the vast majority of cases, where the defense is neither well funded nor particularly skilled—how easy is the task of convincing a jury that an identification technique is absolutely trustworthy.[22]

After the Simpson trial, Scheck and Neufeld went back to work at the Innocence Project, an organization they founded which uses DNA evidence to exonerate people who were convicted before DNA testing was widely available. The Innocence Project petitions courts to order the testing of evidence from old cases for DNA. As of this writing, the Innocence Project and others have used DNA evidence to clear seventy-six men imprisoned for rape or murder in the United States, several of them on death row. In all these cases genetic testing showed that blood or semen found on the evidence did *not* belong to the convicted men. The Innocence Project illustrates another important use of DNA evidence: it can exculpate the innocent as well as implicate the guilty.[23]

Today both the construction of genetic databases for criminal identification and the forensic use of DNA are expanding rapidly. Unlike the many pretenders that have arisen over the past century, DNA typing will certainly have a prominent place in the field of identification for years to come. The principal advantage of DNA is its greater potential for forensic application. Detectives can hope to recover DNA traces from many more crime scenes, much more often, than they recover latent fingerprints. This ability to find the perpetrator of particularly reviled crimes makes DNA all the more attractive to the public. This advantage in the realm of forensics, in turn, makes genetic criminal identification databases valuable because they make it possible to solve cold cases.

At the same time, DNA remains complicated and costly compared to fingerprinting, although the gap is narrowing rapidly. In addition, the potential risks of police abuse or incompetent handling of DNA typing have drawn a lot of attention, in large measure because of the Simpson trial. Although DNA typing can be powerful forensic evidence, it should never be treated as a routine or magical method for generating truth. It will always be important for defense attorneys— and, preferably, independent defense experts—to scrutinize all aspects DNA evidence carefully, including the recovery of evidence, laboratory procedures and proficiency, and statistical arguments.

The technical challenges to the credibility of DNA typing have forced its advocates to improve their methods, revise their statistical calculations, articulate their laboratory protocols, and measure their own proficiency. All of these are things that dactyloscopers, who were treated comparatively leniently by the courts, were never forced to do. The scrutiny focused on DNA evidence, however, has had a certain rebound effect on forensic fingerprint evidence. DNA typing has generated a renewed awareness of the problems of laboratory proficiency and the statistical basis of individualized identification, and this awareness has filtered down to defense attorneys confronted with latent fingerprint evidence. To a certain extent the rise of DNA typing may have been responsible for the recent controversies, discussed earlier, surrounding the reliability and scientific basis of latent fingerprint evidence. Paradoxically, "DNA fingerprinting," which initially derived much of its credibility by way of analogy with fingerprinting, may now be undermining its role model. In terms of scientific foundation and reliability, the new technique may be surpassing the old.

Our genetic differences are at the heart of one of the most fascinating paradoxes of the human condition: that *we are all different, yet we are all the same.*

—Geneticist Mary-Claire King (1993)

Bodily Identities

From the laboratory of some cloistered scientist engaged in arcane research, an amazing new method of identifying criminals suddenly emerges. The new technique puts cutting-edge science to work in the service of justice by identifying perpetrators from the bodily traces they leave at the scenes of their crimes, stripping them of their aliases and exposing their past deeds, and perhaps even allowing scientists to discern their character traits. Government and law enforcement officials are jubilant. Enthusiasts proclaim the dawn of a new era, one in which institutions of criminal justice—from the police to the courts to the prisons—will make their decisions based on scientific knowledge rather than guesswork, prejudice, or intuition. Although an occasional spirited defense attorney, skeptical judge, or stubborn jury expresses some reservations about the new technique, by and large the trial courts embrace the new technology with enthusiasm, and it sails through the procedural obstacles the courts have set up for new forms of evidence. The media and the general public are enthusiastic as well. Here at last is a promising solution to the problem of crime: hard science that stands in marked contrast to the usual hollow promises of politicians. We need no longer search for difficult social cures for the conditions that breed crime. Instead, we can attack crime at its supposed root cause: the criminals themselves.

After a period of initial hesitancy, police departments, courts, and prisons race to implement the new technology. Politicians, police officials, and pundits demand that laws be rewritten to subject more criminals to the new identification technique; some demand that all criminals, even those guilty of the most petty misdemeanors, be identified; and still others demand that immigrants be identified before being permitted to enter the country. The boldest suggest identifying everyone in the population. To this end, parents are urged to have their children identified and registered, as protection against their worst nightmare, the abduction of a child. Even adults are urged to register their identities with civil authorities in case of civil disaster or amnesia. The innocent, it is argued, have nothing to fear from the new identification technology; only the guilty need worry.

With a new technique of identification in its arsenal, the criminal justice system turns its gaze upon repeat offenders with renewed focus. Criminologists confidently assert that the crime problem may be traced not to social conditions but to a small number of habitual criminals. Politicians proclaim that "crime is caused by criminals" and propose new measures for removing these dangerous persons from society: new laws targeting recidivists, laws that mandate life sentences for repeat offenders.

And behind all this an even more ambitious strain of thought emerges. Biological theories of criminality come into vogue. Although some experts urge caution, others allow their hopes to run away with them and predict that the new technology might make it possible to diagnose a propensity for criminal behavior even before someone commits a crime. Using the new technique, the authorities might be able to discern potential criminality in the physical structure of the body itself. Here, then, might be the ultimate solution to the problem of crime—either breeding potential criminals out of the species (positive eugenics) or actually executing, sterilizing, or incarcerating for life those stigmatized as inherently criminal (negative eugenics).

This scenario, which fits equally well the beginning of the twentieth century (the age of dactyloscopy) and its end (the genetic age), conveys some of the continuities in the history of criminal identification, even as the technology changes. The most salient continuity is the persistent interlinking of three related modes of inquiry that fall under the general rubric of criminal identification, which we might call forensic, archival, and diagnostic.

- *Forensic identification* seeks to link a specific criminal act to a specific criminal body. Using a physical trace of a body, an impression or an actual body part or remnant, it attempts to establish the presence of a body at the scene of a crime and hence establish authorship of a crime.
- *Archival identification* seeks to link a particular criminal body to itself across space and time. In conjunction with a paper or electronic record, it aims to establish a history of past criminal activities that can be ascribed with confidence to a single body.
- *Diagnostic identification* seeks to read the signs of past or potential criminal behavior in the body itself. On the basis of some biological theory of the etiology of criminality, it endeavors to prevent crimes before they occur by identifying and stigmatizing potentially criminal bodies.

Historically these three modes of inquiry have been strongly intertwined; to gain acceptance as a "criminal identification technique," a new technology must provide at least a gesture toward all three. Modern societies perceive crime-fighting as occurring on all three levels: identifying the perpetrator of a given crime; assessing the "state of recidivism"—to use the nineteenth-century phrase—of the individual criminal; and perhaps someday eradicating crime, or criminals, altogether.

It comes as little surprise, therefore, that forensic and archival uses of DNA typing have been accompanied by renewed popular, scientific, and political interest in genetic explanations of criminality. New forensic and archival criminal identification techniques—photography, anthropometry, fingerprinting—have always stimulated biological theories of criminality, and DNA typing is no different. Moreover, these ideas have always been closely associated with either explicitly or implicitly eugenic criminology and penology. In the early nineteenth century the United States and many ostensibly liberal and enlightened European nations (not to mention Nazi Germany) forcibly sterilized large numbers of people on the basis of "scientific" evidence of irredeemably "bad" heredity. While no one has yet advocated sterilizing anyone on the basis of a supposed crime gene, policymakers and the public are so apt to be dazzled by the authority of "scientific" knowledge that we must remain vigilant against the application of genetics to the fields of criminology and penology.[1]

In the past, diagnostic identification always foundered eventually, and law enforcement institutions settled for forensic and archival applications of the technology. The debate over the expansion of DNA databases, however, has been conducted largely in ignorance of this history. Amid the widespread popular and political enthusiasm for increasing the use of DNA typing in law enforcement, the sole notes of caution have been sounded by civil libertarians concerned about privacy rights. For example, Norman Siegel, head of the New York Civil Liberties Union, has denounced the plans of New York's police chief, mayor, and governor to broaden the scope of DNA typing as "Big Brother" and ushering in a "brave new world"—invoking the familiar cultural icons of the totalitarian state and the eugenic future. Other critics have raised the issue of race. Since DNA typing is based on alleles that appear with different frequencies among different races, it has been suggested that law enforcement officials, in their construction of criminal identification databases, may be inadvertently creating racial databases that—however remote the possibility—might potentially be used to identify all members of a certain racial or ethnic group.[2]

Both of these critiques assert that DNA typing is fundamentally different from fingerprinting. "It is a mistake to equate DNA samples to fingerprints," says Siegel. "Fingerprints are representations of the physical attributes of the tips of our fingers; they are used only for identification purposes. DNA is that plus much more." The anthropologist Paul Rabinow, similarly, concludes that Francis Galton's "regret"—his failure to find a convincing link between fingerprint patterns and ethnic groups—demonstrated once and for all that fingerprint patterns "revealed nothing about individual character or group affiliation . . . Fingerprints were individual, yet bore no trace of character, society, or evolution." Rabinow, therefore, believes DNA typing represents a step backward from fingerprinting, which was solely an individualized identifier. Unlike fingerprint patterns, he argues, DNA contains accurate information about individuals' racial and ethnic origin and heredity. Unlike fingerprint patterns, DNA undoubtedly contains valuable medical information about individuals' propensity for contracting certain diseases. The implication is that, in a social climate in which eugenics attains renewed legitimacy, all this information has the potential to guide a determination of each individual's overall "fitness" and hence usher in a "brave new world" governed by eugenics.[3]

These assumptions about fingerprinting, however, are neither biologically nor historically accurate. For all we know, gross fingerprint patterns—arches, loops, and whorls—like gene alleles, do appear with differing frequency among different ethnic groups. It is entirely possible that a research program with a fraction of the resources currently devoted to genetic research might come up with a way of making even more discriminating determinations of racial and ethnic origin from a closer examination of fingerprint patterns. Similarly, a well-funded research program might well be able to find a way to link some inherited diseases to some aspect of fingerprint patterns. Indeed, "dermatoglyphics" is still being used by respectable scientists to investigate schizophrenia, although fingerprint patterns are not used to diagnose the disease but only to help determine whether or not identical twins shared a placenta.[4]

More to the point, while using fingerprint patterns to gauge susceptibility to disease, propensity for crime, or ethnic origin may seem silly to us today, it seemed entirely plausible to scientifically literate people less than a century ago. Our assumptions about the power of identification techniques are guided by the scientific culture of our time. At the dawn of the twentieth century, anthropology, the comparative study of both physical and cultural attributes of the various races and cultures of humankind, was thought to have important insights into vexing questions of individual and group abilities and tendencies. Were some races inherently more intelligent than others? Could selective breeding improve the human race? Were certain cultures threatened by low birth rates among their upper classes? Were criminals born or made? What was the cause of insanity? Of epilepsy? These were questions to which anthropology was thought to have answers, much in the way we today think DNA holds the answers to these questions. In nineteenth-century scientific culture the human body, which anthropologists, armed with cameras and calipers and rulers, subjected to exacting scrutiny, was thought to hold the key to the question of who we are. In this milieu it made perfect sense that the body, minutely measured and observed, would also be the way individuals could be uniquely identified. At that time the "biometricians," such as Francis Galton, who used anthropometric measurements or fingerprint patterns to study heredity, were at the cutting edge of science.

Today we live in what can appropriately be called the "genetic age." Since the discovery of the double helix structure of DNA in 1953, the sciences of genetics and molecular biology have exploded, overtaking nearly every other scientific discipline in terms of prestige and funding. Molecular biology has replaced theoretical physics as queen of the sciences; the Human Genome Project has replaced particle accelerators as the biggest of the world's "big science" endeavors; and biotechnology has emerged as one of the hot new industries. If the twentieth century was the century of physics, it is widely anticipated that the twenty-first will be the century of biology. Physics had a profound impact on the twentieth century, with its harnessing of the power of the atom, its development of the transistor and the computer chip, and its theoretical advances which reshaped our conceptions of our place in the universe. The science of genetics is likely to have a similarly profound impact on the twenty-first century by developing new cures for diseases, spawning an enormous biotechnology industry, and allowing us to re-engineer the human body, enhance human abilities, and tinker with the building blocks of life itself.

All this has generated an enormous amount of excitement around the science of genetics and the icon of DNA. Ideas about DNA and genetics now pervade our popular culture. Most profoundly, however, we have come to conceive of ourselves as essentially genetic beings, whose abilities, character traits, behavior, and even emotions are all encoded within the intertwined strands of DNA. It is almost impossible to pick up a newspaper these days without reading about the attribution of some human characteristic to genes: homosexuality, shyness, altruism, or propensity for violence or criminal behavior. The trendy new field of evolutionary psychology now purports to explain all of human psychology by reference to our genetic inheritance. Human behaviors that were once thought to be matters of free will and individual choice, such as adultery and even rape, are now "explained," if not always excused, by reference to the impact of natural selection on our DNA.[5]

In our cultural milieu DNA is thought to be the explanation for what we are both individually and collectively. The 99 percent of our DNA that we share with other species makes us living organisms; the somewhat larger portion that we share with all other people makes us human; the still greater portion we share with some other people gives us our ethnic, racial, or cultural identity; and the tiny remaining bit we share only with ourselves is what makes each of us a unique individual. DNA, therefore, serves as a symbol of both group and individual identity. It contains both our ethnic heritage and our individuality.

In such a culture it is scarcely possible *not* to believe that genes cause—or are at least markers of—race, ethnicity, susceptibility to a wide variety of medical conditions, as well as a host of behavioral tendencies and character traits. Those few voices of caution which remind us that genes are likely to exert their effects only in strong conjunction with environmental factors are being drowned out by the din of genetic determinism. In such a culture even libertarians like Siegel display no doubt that a wealth of important and useful medical information is in fact encoded in our genes, and even postmodernists like Rabinow accept that our racial and ethnic background can indeed be inferred from our genes. In order for these critics to demonize the spread of DNA typing and the growth of DNA databases, they believe, and even fuel, the hype surrounding genetic determinism and attribute to DNA a power that it does not necessarily have.

This is all the more unfortunate because civil libertarians and postmodernists should be prominent among the voices debunking the overblown claims of genetic determinism. They should be joining those who insist that the vast preponderance of criminal behavior and violence is surely caused by social conditions, not by genetic inheritance, that many diseases are caused or triggered by environmental factors, and that race and ethnicity are social constructs, not biological realities. In focusing on the immediate enemy, genetic identification, these critics ignore and inadvertently strengthen a more insidious one: a creeping genetic determinism that is being embraced by increasing numbers of people swept up in the enthusiasm for the latest in a long line of biological markers purporting to "explain" human nature. The growing social and cultural acceptance of genetic determinist thought, far more powerfully than the DNA databases themselves, may ultimately make possible what the critics really fear: a eugenic society. As long as people resist the oversimplified notion that genes, or any other biological factors, cause criminality, determine character or ability, or lend biological rigor to the social and political construction of race, DNA databases will be used only to identify individuals, not to lump people into socially constructed categories.[6]

The history of fingerprinting should teach us to heed the difference between a biological *marker* and a *code.* It is still quite possible that "code" is an inappropriate metaphor for our DNA sequences, that genes may turn out to be markers of our inheritance but not "codes" or "blueprints" for our abilities, weaknesses, or destinies. While the history of criminal identification techniques should make us skeptical about likelihood that DNA typing will ever provide a biological explanation for criminal behavior, there is one sense in which DNA typing really is quite different from fingerprinting. The chief difference is that the science that spawned DNA typing, molecular biology, is interventionist. While Galton hoped to achieve his eugenic aims through selective breeding, molecular biology aims to actively re-engineer life itself. Genetic engineering promises to have a profound impact on reproductive technology. The birth of Dolly the cloned sheep demonstrated that cloning, the production of a genetic copy of an individual organism, is feasible. The possibility of human cloning, no matter how remote it may actually be, has profound implications for the science of individualized identification. If individuals can be cloned, then DNA typing will be of as little value in distinguishing them as it now is in distinguishing identical twins. Will we have to return to fingerprinting, with its epigenetic environmental influences, to identify clones?

In stark contrast to previous identification techniques, DNA typing is a product of a technology that may someday undermine the identification technique itself. Genetic engineering threatens our century-and-a-half-old bodily notion of identity. If scientists succeed in replicating individual genotypes, then the individual genotype will no longer be a useful way of distinguishing individuals.

Indeed, the body itself may become a rather antiquated way of defining the individual. A wide variety of new technologies—sex reassignment, cyberspace, artificial intelligence, cosmetic surgery, organ transplantation, and so on—all point toward the demise of the nineteenth-century notion of the body as solid, stable entity and the advent of some new conception of bodies as mutable and flexible. As these technologies come to fruition, we may cease to associate individual identity so closely with the body. As bodies become more malleable and flexible, as more and more of our social and financial interactions take place in cyberspace, where the body is unimportant and cyber-personae can be switched and counterfeited easily, we may develop a new conception of identity. We may cease to think of ourselves, or to identify ourselves, strictly as physically unique bodies and begin to think of ourselves as somewhat more ethereal entities for whom bodies and body parts are merely resources. The equation of identity with a unique body that begins at birth and ends at death is not an eternal notion: it is a product of the nineteenth-century Western imperialist culture. In retrospect, it may turn out to have existed only for a brief period of time before yielding to newer conceptions of what it means to be a unique individual.

1. Impostors and Incorrigible Rogues

1. Natalie Zemon Davis, *The Return of Martin Guerre* (Cambridge, Mass.: Harvard University Press, 1983), 63–68.
2. Norval Morris and David J. Rothman, eds., *The Oxford History of the Prison: The Practice of Punishment in Western Society* (New York: Oxford University Press, 1995).
3. Jane Caplan and John Torpey, eds., *Documenting Individual Identity: The Development of State Practices in the Modern World* (Princeton: Princeton University Press, forthcoming).
4. Michel Foucault, *Discipline and Punish: The Birth of the Prison*, trans. Alan Sheridan (New York: Vintage, 1979).
5. Lawrence M. Friedman, *Crime and Punishment in American History* (New York: Basic Books, 1993), 203, 207; Michael Ignatieff, "State, Civil Society and Total Institutions: A Critique of Recent Social Histories of Punishment," in Stanley Cohen and Andrew Scull, eds., *Social Control of the State: Historical and Comparative Essays* (Oxford: Martin Robertson, 1983), 87.
6. Matt K. Matsuda, *The Memory of the Modern* (New York: Oxford University Press, 1996), 121; David Jones, *Crime, Protest, Community and Police in Nineteenth-Century Britain* (London: Routledge, 1982), 178–209; Friedman, *Crime and Punishment*, 193–210.
7. Andreas Fahrmeir, "Governments and Forgers: Passports in Nineteenth-Century Europe," in Caplan and Torpey, *Documenting Individual Identity*.
8. State Prison of the City of New York, Register of Prisoners Received,

1797–1810, Records of the Department of Correctional Services, New York State Archives, Record Series A0775.

9. Pamela Sankar, "State Power and Record-Keeping: The History of Individualized Surveillance in the United States, 1790–1935" (Ph.D. diss., University of Pennsylvania, 1992), 81–101.

10. Quoted in George E. Harris, *A Treatise on the Law of Identification* (Albany, 1892), 426; Joel Munsell, *Cases of Personal Identity* (Albany, 1854), 35–56, 91–102.

11. Barruel, "Mémoire sur l'existence d'un principe propre a caractériser le sang de l'homme et celui diverses espèces d'animaux," *Annales d'hygiene publique et de médecine legale* 1 (1829), 267–277; Ernest Morillon, "Identité en général et signes professionels en particulier" (M.D. thesis, Faculté de Médecine de Paris, 1865).

12. John Hubback, *A Treatise on the Evidence of Succession to Real and Personal Property and Peerages* (Philadelphia, 1845), 444.

13. The Tichborne case is the subject of a feature film, *The Tichborne Claimant* (1998), dir. David Yates; Harris, *Law of Identification,* 1.

14. Cesare Beccaria, "On Crimes and Punishments" (1764), in John Muncie, Eugene McLaughlin, and Mary Langan, eds., *Criminological Perspectives* (London: Sage, 1996), 7; Norval Morris, *The Habitual Criminal* (London: Longmans Green, 1951), 18.

15. Patricia O'Brien, *The Promise of Punishment: Prisons in Nineteenth-Century France* (Princeton: Princeton University Press, 1982), 288; Leon Radzinowicz and Roger Hood, "Incapacitating the Habitual Criminal: The English Experience," *Michigan Law Review* 78 (1980), 1308; Quetelet quoted in Ian Hacking, *The Taming of Chance* (Cambridge: Cambridge University Press, 1990), 73.

16. Ysabel Rennie, *The Search for Criminal Man: A Conceptual History of the Dangerous Offender* (Lexington, Mass.: Lexington Books, 1978), 61; Nicole H. Rafter, *Creating Born Criminals* (Urbana: University of Illinois Press, 1997), 77; Robert A. Nye, *Crime, Madness, and Politics in Modern France: The Medical Concept of National Decline* (Princeton: Princeton University Press, 1984), 65.

17. *Le grand Robert de la langue française,* 20th ed., vol. 8; *Oxford English Dictionary,* 2nd ed.

18. Arnould Bonneville, *De la récidive* (Paris, 1844), ix–x.

19. Ibid., x; O'Brien, *Promise of Punishment,* 81.

20. Bonneville, *De la récidive,* 44–54.

21. Gustave de Beaumont and Alexis de Tocqueville, *On the Penitentiary System in the United States and its Application in France,* trans. Francis Lieber (Philadelphia, 1833), 55, 101–102.

22. Bonneville, *De la récidive,* 90.

23. Benjamin F. Martin, *Crime and Criminal Justice under the Third Repub-*

lic: The Shame of Marianne (Baton Rouge: Louisiana State University Press, 1990), 79.

24. O'Brien, *Promise of Punishment*, 261–264; Leon Radzinowicz and Roger Hood, *The Emergence of Penal Policy in Victorian and Edwardian Britain* (Oxford: Clarendon Press, 1990), 231–241.

25. T. B. L. Baker, *The Habitual Criminals Act* (Newcastle-upon-Tyne, 1870), 3.

26. James Ram, *A Treatise on Facts as Subjects of Inquiry by a Jury* (New York, 1870), 69.

27. Harris B. Tuttle Sr., "History of Photography in Law Enforcement," *Finger Print and Identification Magazine* 43:4 (Oct. 1961), 3–28; "The Rogue's Gallery," *Albany Atlas and Argus* (Aug. 31, 1860).

28. George W. Walling, *Recollections of a New York Chief of Police* (Denver, 1890), 566.

29. Benjamin P. Eldridge and William B. Watts, *Our Rival the Rascal: A Faithful Portrayal of the Conflict Between the Criminals of this Age and the Defenders of Society—The Police* (Boston, 1897), 318–320.

30. Friedman, *Crime and Punishment*, 195; David R. Johnson, *Illegal Tender: Counterfeiting and the Secret Service in Nineteenth-Century America* (Washington: Smithsonian Institution Press, 1995); Tamara Plakins Thornton, *Handwriting in America: A Cultural History* (New Haven: Yale University Press, 1996), 101–116; Thomas Byrnes, *Professional Criminals of America* (1886; New York: Chelsea House, 1969), 53.

31. Arthur M. Schlesinger Jr., "The Business of Crime," intro. to Byrnes, *Professional Criminals*, xiii-xxvi.

32. Madeline B. Stern, "Matthew Brady and the 'Rationale of Crime': A Discovery in Daguerreotypes," *Quarterly Journal of the Library of Congress* 31 (1974), 127–135.

33. Daniel Pick, *Faces of Degeneration: A European Disorder, c. 1848–c. 1918* (Cambridge: Cambridge University Press, 1989).

34. Cesare Lombroso, *Crime: Its Causes and Remedies*, trans. Henry P. Horton (Montclair, N.J.: Patterson Smith, 1911), 340.

35. Allan Sekula, "The Body and the Archive," *October* 39 (1986), 3–64; Eldridge and Watts, *Our Rival the Rascal*, 353.

36. Eldridge and Watts, *Our Rival the Rascal*, 319–320.

37. Radzinowicz and Hood, *Emergence of Penal Policy*, 261; Charles Edward Troup, Arthur Griffiths, and Melville Leslie Macnaghten, *Report of a Committee Appointed by the Secretary of State to Inquire into the Best Means Available for Identifying Habitual Criminals*, British Sessional Papers, House of Commons, Command Paper, C.-7263 (London, 1894), 7.

38. Troup, Griffiths, and Macnaghten, *Report of a Committee*, 6.

39. Ibid., 14–18.

40. Ibid., 19.

41. Ibid., 10–18; Great Britain Prisons Committee, *Report from the Departmental Committee on Prisons*, British Sessional Papers, House of Commons, Command Paper, C.-7702 (London, 1895), 9–12.

42. Morris, *Habitual Criminal*, 174; Foucault, *Discipline and Punish*, 265; Alexander W. Pisciotta, *Benevolent Repression: Social Control and the American Reformatory-Prison Movement* (New York: New York University Press, 1994).

43. Great Britain Prisons Committee, *Report*, 29.

2. Measuring the Criminal Body

1. Henry T. F. Rhodes, *Alphonse Bertillon: Father of Scientific Detection* (New York: Abelard-Schuman, 1956), 73.

2. Patricia O'Brien, *The Promise of Punishment: Prisons in Nineteenth-Century France* (Princeton: Princeton University Press, 1982), 287; *Lois, décrets, ordonnances, règlements et avis de Conseil d'État* (Paris, 1885), 228–232; Robert A. Nye, *Crime, Madness, and Politics in Modern France: The Medical Concept of National Decline* (Princeton: Princeton University Press, 1984), 38, 58, 173.

3. Alphonse Bertillon, "L'identité des récidivistes et la loi de relégation," *Annales de démographie internationale* 6 (1882), 465–466.

4. Rhodes, *Alphonse Bertillon*, 17.

5. Alphonse Bertillon, *Signaletic Instructions: Including the Theory and Practice of Anthropometrical Identification*, trans. R. W. McClaughry (Chicago, 1896), 118–120.

6. Ibid.; Bertillon, *Instructions for Taking Descriptions for the Identification of Criminals and Others by the Means of Anthropometric Indications*, trans. Gallus Muller (Chicago, 1889), 35.

7. Peter Becker, "The Standardized Gaze: The Standardization of the Search Warrant in the Nineteenth Century," in Jane Caplan and John Torpey, eds., *Documenting Individual Identity: The Development of State Practices in the Modern World* (Princeton: Princeton University Press, forthcoming); Bertillon, *Signaletic Instructions*, 3, 33.

8. Bertillon, *Signaletic Instructions*, 41–47.

9. Ibid., 85–201.

10. Ibid., 45–46.

11. Sing Sing Correctional Facility, Inmate Admissions Registers, 1865–1971, Records of the Department of Correctional Services, New York State Archives, Record Series B0143.

12. Charles Edward Troup, Arthur Griffiths, and Melville Leslie Macnaghten, *Report of a Committee Appointed by the Secretary of State to Inquire into the Best Means Available for Identifying Habitual Criminals*, British Sessional Papers, House of Commons, Command Paper, C.-7263 (London, 1894), 10; Bertillon, *Signaletic Instructions*.

13. Bertillon, *Signaletic Instructions*, 63.

14. Bertillon, "L'identité des récidivistes," 474; *Signaletic Instructions*, 13.

15. Bertillon, *Signaletic Instructions*, 20.

16. Ibid., 23, 63–64.

17. Ibid., 55; Matt K. Matsuda, *The Memory of the Modern* (New York: Oxford University Press, 1996), 138.

18. Harris B. Tuttle Sr., "History of Photography in Law Enforcement," *Finger Print and Identification Magazine* 43:4 (Oct. 1961), 3–28, quotation 12.

19. Bertillon, *Legal Photography*, trans. Paul R. Brown (New York, 1897), 30.

20. Rhodes, *Alphonse Bertillon*, 75–101; newspaper quoted in Frank Smyth, *Cause of Death: The Story of Forensic Science* (New York: Van Nostrand Reinhold, 1980), 118.

21. O'Brien, *Promise of Punishment*, 25, 265–267.

22. Ibid., 289.

23. Richard Bach Jensen, "The International Anti-Anarchist Conference of 1898 and the Origins of Interpol," *Journal of Contemporary History* 16 (1981), 324–341; Bertillon, *Signaletic Instructions*, 78.

24. Bertillon, *Signaletic Instructions*, 19.

25. Bertillon, *Instructions for Taking Descriptions*, 12–13.

26. Edmond de Ryckère quoted in Bertillon, *Signaletic Instructions*, 80.

27. *Oxford English Dictionary*, 2nd ed.; Great Britain Prisons Committee, *Report from the Departmental Committee on Prisons*, British Sessional Papers, House of Commons, Command Paper, C.-7702 (London, 1895), 12.

28. David J. Rothman, *Conscience and Convenience: The Asylum and Its Alternatives in Progressive America* (Boston: Little, Brown, 1980), 43.

29. *International Record of Charities and Correction* 2 (April 1887), 17–18.

30. Ibid.; New York State Prison Bureau, *Annual Report* (1896), 21.

31. *International Record of Charities and Correction* 2 (Oct. 1887), 101; Charles E. Felton, *The Identification of Criminals* (Chicago, 1889), 9–19.

32. Porteus quoted in Donald Dilworth, ed., *Identification Wanted: Development of the American Criminal Identification System, 1893–1943* (Gaithersburg, Md.: International Association of Chiefs of Police, 1977), 5–6.

33. David Garland, *Punishment and Welfare: A History of Penal Strategies* (Aldershot, U.K.: Gower, 1985), 25.

34. Raymond Saleilles, *The Individualization of Punishment*, trans. Rachel Szold Jastrow (1898; Boston: Little, Brown, 1911).

35. Cesare Lombroso, *Crime: Its Causes and Remedies*, trans. Henry P. Horton (Montclair, N.J.: Patterson Smith, 1911), 340.

36. Lombroso quoted in David G. Horn, *Social Bodies: Science, Reproduction, and Italian Modernity* (Princeton: Princeton University Press, 1994), 30; *Year Book of the New York State Reformatory* (Elmira, N.Y.)

17 (1895); 20 (1898), 117–118, in Elmira Correctional and Reception Center, Annual Reports and Handbooks, ca. 1880–1920, Records of the Department of Correctional Services, New York State Archives, Record Series A0636.

37. Ysabel Rennie, *The Search for Criminal Man: A Conceptual History of the Dangerous Offender* (Lexington, Mass.: Lexington Books, 1978), 70; Lombroso, "The Savage Origin of Tattooing," *Appletons' Popular Science Monthly* 48 (1896), 793–803, quotation 793. Robert Fletcher, *The New School of Criminal Anthropology* (Washington, 1891), 24–25; Claire Valier, "True Crime Stories: Scientific Methods of Criminal Investigation, Criminology and Historiography," *British Journal of Criminology* 38 (1998), 88–105.

38. Bertillon, *Signaletic Instructions*, 202.

3. Native Prints

1. Zhao Xiang-Xin and Liu Chun-Ge, "The Historical Application of Hand Prints in Chinese Litigation," *Fingerprint Whorld* 14:55 (Jan. 1989), 84–88; Berthold Laufer, *History of the Finger-Print System* (Washington: Government Printing Office, 1913); Laufer, "Concerning the History of Finger-Prints," *Science* 45 (1917), 504–505.

2. Harold Cummins and Charles Midlo, *Finger Prints, Palms and Soles: An Introduction to Dermatoglyphics* (Philadelphia: Blakiston, 1943), 11; Howard B. Adelman, *Marcello Malpighi and the Evolution of Embryology* (Ithaca: Cornell University Press, 1966), 258–259.

3. Cummins and Midlo, *Finger Prints, Palms and Soles*, 13; John Berry, "The History and Development of Fingerprinting," in Henry C. Lee and R. E. Gaensslen, eds., *Advances in Fingerprint Technology* (New York: Elsevier, 1991), 16–19; Jan Evangelista Purkyně, "A Physiological Examination of the Organ of Vision and the Integumentary System" (1823), trans. Harold Cummins and Rebecca Wright Kennedy, *American Journal of Police Science* 30 (1940), 343–356; Carlo Ginzburg, "Morelli, Freud, and Sherlock Holmes: Clues and Scientific Method," in Umberto Eco and Thomas A. Sebeok, eds., *The Sign of Three: Dupin, Holmes, Peirce* (Bloomington: Indiana University Press, 1983), 81–118.

4. Administrator quoted in Gyan Prakash, "Science 'Gone Native' in Colonial India," *Representations* 40 (1992), 155–160. David Arnold, "Crime and Crime Control in Madras, 1858–1947," in Anand A. Yang, ed., *Crime and Criminality in British India* (Ann Arbor: Association for Asian Studies, 1985), 77.

5. Ronald R. Thomas, *Detective Fiction and Rise of Forensic Science* (Cambridge: Cambridge University Press, 1999), 216–232.

6. William J. Herschel, *The Origin of Finger-Printing* (London: Oxford University Press, 1916), 7–11; William J. Herschel, "Skin Furrows of the

Hand," *Nature* 23 (1880), 76; Staff Corps member quoted in Francis Galton, *Finger Prints* (London, 1892), 150–152.

7. Salil Kumar Chatterjee and Richard V. Hague, *Finger Print or Dactyloscopy and Ridgeoscopy* (Calcutta: Srijib Chatterjee, 1988), 5.

8. Herschel, *Origin of Finger Printing*, 24.

9. Ronald Inden, *Imagining India* (Oxford: Basil Blackwell, 1990), 61; Arnold, "Crime and Crime Control," 84–85; Stephen quoted in Rachel J. Tolen, "Colonizing and Transforming the Criminal Tribesman: The Salvation Army in British India," in Jennifer Terry and Jacqueline Urla, eds., *Deviant Bodies: Critical Perspectives on Difference in Science and Popular Culture* (Bloomington: Indiana University Press, 1995), 82–83.

10. M. Paupa Rao Naidu, *The Criminal Tribes of India: The History of Korawars, Erukulas or Kaikaries*, vol. 2 (Madras: Higginbotham, 1905); Anand A. Yang, "Dangerous Castes and Tribes: The Criminal Tribes Act and the Magahiya Doms of Northeast India," in Yang, *Crime and Criminality*, 108–127, quotation 109; Kavita Philip, "The Role of Science in Colonial Discourses and Practices of Modernity: Anthropology, Forestry, and the Construction of 'Nature's' Resources in Madras Forests, 1858–1930" (Ph.D. diss., Cornell University, 1996), 209–210; Tolen, "Colonizing and Transforming," 84.

11. Yang, "Dangerous Castes," 122; Paupa Rao Naidu, *Criminal Tribes*, 51–52.

12. A. E. Staley to Officiating Under-Secretary to the Government of Bengal, Dec. 28, 1890, 94; R. S. Whiteway to North-West Provinces and Oudh Secretary to Government, July 22, 1890, 137; H. G. Cooke to Chief Secretary to the Government of Bengal, Jan. 6, 1891 (emphasis added); all in India Home Department, "Papers Relating to a Bill to provide for the more Effectual Surveillance and Control of Habitual Offenders in India," *Selections from the Records of the Government of India*, no. 300 (Calcutta, 1893).

13. Ibid.: Staley to Under-Secretary, 94; W. Blennerhassett to Secretary to Government, North-West Punjab, Sept. 8, 1890, 148.

14. Prakash, "Science 'Gone Native,'" 156; Philip, "Role of Science," 179, 206, 207.

15. Edward R. Henry, *Classification and Uses of Finger Prints*, 3rd ed. (1900; London: H. M. Stationery Office, 1905), 70; official quoted in Galton, *Finger Prints*, 150–152; Alphonse Bertillon, *Signaletic Instructions: Including the Theory and Practice of Anthropometrical Identification*, trans. R. W. McClaughry (Chicago, 1896), 41–44.

16. Henry, *Classification and Uses*, 77; Simon Schaffer, "Astronomers Mark Time: Discipline and the Personal Equation," *Science in Context* 2 (1988), 115–145.

17. Bertillon, *Signaletic Instructions*, 23–27.

18. Henry, *Classification and Uses*, 73–74.

19. Ibid., 70; Bertillon, *Signaletic Instructions,* 19.

20. Henry, *Classification and Uses,* 71.

21. Henry Faulds, "On the Skin Furrows of the Hand," *Nature* 22 (1880), 605; Herschel, "Skin Furrows"; Henry Faulds, "On the Identification of Habitual Criminals by Finger-Prints," *Nature* 50 (1894), 548; George Wilton Wilton, *Fingerprints: Fifty Years of Injustice* (Galashiels, U.K.: A. Walker, 1955).

22. Henry Faulds, "The Dawn of Dactylography," *Dactylography* 1:2 (Sept. 1921), 29.

23. Henry Faulds, "The Nature of Finger-Print Evidence," *Dactylography* 1:3 (Nov. 1921), 43–46; Faulds, *A Manual of Practical Dactylography* (London: Police Review, 1923), 34–38; Faulds, *Dactylography, or, The Study of Finger-Prints* (Halifax: Milner, [1912?]), 94–100.

24. Charles Darwin to Henry Faulds, Apr. 7, 1880; Charles Darwin to Francis Galton, April 7, 1880, both in Gerald Lambourne, *The Fingerprint Story* (London: Harrap, 1984), 189; Galton, *Finger Prints,* 60–63.

25. Francis Galton, "Human Variety," *Nature* 39 (1889), 296–300; Galton, *Finger Prints,* 149, 152.

26. Galton, *Finger Prints,* 65–66.

27. Ibid., 65.

28. Faulds, *Manual,* 39.

29. Galton, *Finger Prints,* 100–113.

30. Charles Edward Troup, Arthur Griffiths, and Melville Leslie Macnaghten, *Report of a Committee Appointed by the Secretary of State to Inquire into the Best Means Available for Identifying Habitual Criminals,* British Sessional Papers, House of Commons, Command Paper, C.-7263 (London, 1894), 26–27.

31. Ibid., 26–30.

32. S. E. Haylock, "Khan Bahadur Azizul Haque," *Fingerprint Whorld* 5:17 (July 1979), 28–29; Berry, "History and Development."

33. Henry, *Classification and Uses,* 98–101.

34. C. Strahan and Alexander Pedler, *Report of Committee to Examine into the System of Identification by Finger Impressions* (March 31, 1897), rpt. in Henry, *Classification and Uses,* 109–112.

35. Henry, *Classification and Uses,* 84; Strahan and Pedler, *Report.*

36. Henry, *Classification and Uses,* 5–8.

37. Ibid., 55–59; George Wilton Wilton, "Finger-Prints: The Case of Kangali Charan, 1898," *Juridical Review* 49 (1937), 417–427; Wilton, *Fingerprints: History, Law and Romance* (London: William Hodge, 1938), 94.

38. *Emperor v. Sahdeo,* 3 Nagpur Law Reports 1 (India, 1904), quotations 1, 8–11.

39. Ibid., 10–11.

40. Lord (Henry) Belper, Frederick Albert Bosanquet, Albert De Rutzen, et al., *Report of a Committee Appointed by the Secretary of State to In-*

quire into the Method of Identification of Criminals by Measurements and Finger Prints (London: Wyman and Sons, 1901), 9; Belper, Bosanquet, De Rutzen, et al., *Minutes of Evidence taken before the Departmental Committee on Identification of Criminals* (London: Wyman and Sons, 1901), 11, 28, 39.

41. Belper, *Report*, 10; Belper, *Minutes*, 4, 28–29, 40–42.

42. Belper, *Minutes*, 6.

43. Ibid., 37–38.

44. Belper, *Report*, 11.

45. Convict Supervision Office, Metropolitan Police, *Memorandum on the Working of the Finger Print System of Identification, 1901–4* (London: New Scotland Yard, 1904), 7–11.

46. Leon Radzinowicz and Roger Hood, *The Emergence of Penal Policy in Victorian and Edwardian England* (Oxford: Clarendon Press, 1990), 239; J. B. Thomson, "The Hereditary Nature of Crime," *Journal of Mental Science* 15 (1870), 488–489.

47. Thomson, "Hereditary Nature," 488–489; Sander L. Gilman, *The Case of Sigmund Freud: Medicine and Identity at the Fin de Siècle* (Baltimore: Johns Hopkins University Press, 1993), 181.

48. Gina Lombroso-Ferrero, *Criminal Man: According to the Classification of Cesare Lombroso* (1911; Montclair, N.J.: Patterson Smith, 1972), xxiii, 129–140; Havelock Ellis, *The Criminal* (New York, 1890).

49. Radzinowicz and Hood, *Emergence of Penal Policy*, 269–271.

50. Thomas, *Detective Fiction*, 210–237.

4. Degenerate Fingerprints

1. Henry Faulds, "On the Skin-furrows of the Hand," *Nature* 22 (1880), 605.

2. Henry Faulds, *A Manual of Practical Dactylography* (London: Police Review, 1923), 19–20.

3. Herbert Spencer, "The Factors of Organic Evolution: Concluded," *Nineteenth Century* 19 (1886), 750–762; Francis Galton, "Personal Identification II," *Nature* 38 (1888), 202; Daniel J. Kevles, *In the Name of Eugenics: Genetics and Uses of Human Heredity* (Berkeley: University of California Press, 1985), 3–19.

4. Alec J. Jeffrey, "DNA Typing: Approaches and Applications," *Journal of the Forensic Science Society* 33 (1993), 204–211.

5. Gerald Lambourne, *The Fingerprint Story* (London: Harrap, 1984), 97–98; International Association for Identification, *Proceedings* (1927), 35–37.

6. T. Harster quoted in Harold Cummins and Charles Midlo, *Finger Prints, Palms and Soles: An Introduction to Dermatoglyphics* (Philadelphia: Blakiston, 1943), 210–213.

7. Francis Galton, *Finger Prints* (London, 1892), 2.

8. Jan Evangelista Purkyně, "A Physiological Examination of the Organ of Vision and the Integumentary System" (1823), trans. Henry J. John in *Jan Evangelista Purkyně: Czech Scientist and Patriot, 1787–1869* (Philadelphia: American Philosophical Society, 1959), 54–65; Purkyně, "A Physiological Examination of the Organ of Vision and the Integumentary System" (1823), trans. Harold Cummins and Rebecca Wright Kennedy in *American Journal of Police Science* 30 (1940), 343–356.

9. Alix, "Recherches sur la disposition des lignes papillaires de la main et du pied, précédées de considérations sur la forme et les fonctions de ces deux organes," *Annales des sciences naturelles zoologie et paleontologie* 8 (1867), 295–362; Alix, "Recherches sur la disposition des lignes papillaires de la main et du pied," ibid. 9 (1868), 5–42.

10. Arthur Kollmann, *Der Tastapparat der Hand der menschlichen Rassen und der Affen in seiner Entwickelung und Gliederung* (Hamburg, 1883).

11. Galton, *Finger Prints*, 195; Paul Rabinow, "Galton's Regret: Of Types and Individuals" in Paul R. Billings, ed., *DNA on Trial: Genetic Identification and Criminal Justice* (Plainview, N.Y.: Cold Spring Harbor Laboratory Press, 1992), 5–18.

12. Daniel Pick, *Faces of Degeneration: A European Disorder, c. 1848–c. 1918* (Cambridge: Cambridge University Press, 1989), 31–32.

13. René Forgeot, *Des empreintes digitales étudiées au point de vue medico-judiciaire* (Lyon, 1892), 61–66; Charles Féré, "Les empreintes des doigts et des orteils," *Journal de l'anatomie et de la physiologie normales et pathologiques de l'homme et des animaux* 29 (1893), 232–234; Féré, "Notes sur les mains et les empreintes digitales de quelques singes," ibid. 36 (1900), 255–267.

14. David Hepburn, "The Papillary Ridges on the Hands and Feet of Monkeys and Men," *Scientific Transactions of the Royal Dublin Society* 5 (1895), 532–535.

15. Charles Darwin, *The Origin of Species* (1859; New York: New American Library, 1958), 156; Harris Hawthorne Wilder, "Scientific Palmistry," *Popular Science Monthly* 62 (1902): 46–47.

16. Inez L. Whipple, "The Ventral Surface of Mammalian Chiridium with Special Reference to the Conditions Found in Man," *Zeitschrift für Morphologie und Anthropologie* 7 (1904), 261–368; G. Tyler Mairs, "Random Thoughts Concerning Finger Prints," *Finger Print and Identification Magazine* 36:8 (Feb. 1955), 3–18.

17. Adolf Loos, "Ornament and Crime," trans. Wilfried Wang, in Yehuda Safran and Wilfried Wang, eds., *The Architecture of Adolf Loos* (1908; London: Arts Council of Great Britain, 1987), 100–103.

18. H. Waite, "Association of Finger-Prints," *Biometrika* 10 (1915), 421–478; Ethel M. Elderton, "On the Inheritance of the Finger-Print," *Biometrika* 13 (1920), 57.

19. Elderton, "Inheritance of the Finger-Print," 57–91.

20. L. W. LaChard, "Finger-Print Characteristics," *Journal of the American Institute of Criminal Law and Criminology* 10 (1919), 195–201; *Finger Print and Identification Magazine* 4:3 (Nov. 1922), 16.

21. Kristine Bonnevie, "Studies on Papillary Patterns of Human Fingers," *Journal of Genetics* 15 (1924), 1–112.

22. Rosaleen Love, "'Alice in Eugenics-Land': Feminism and Eugenics in the Scientific Careers of Alice Lee and Ethel Elderton," *Annals of Science* 36 (1979), 145–158; Kevles, *In the Name of Eugenics*, 20–40; Margaret W. Rossiter, *Women Scientists in America: Struggles and Strategies to 1940* (Baltimore: Johns Hopkins University Press, 1982), 51–72.

23. *Fingerprint and Identification Magazine* 7:1 (July 1925), 2.

24. H. Mutrux-Bornoz, *Les troublantes révélations de l'empreinte digitale et palmaire* (Lausanne: F. Roth, 1937), 9–10, 265.

25. Cummins and Midlo, *Finger Prints, Palms and Soles*, 210–281.

26. International Association for Identification, *Proceedings* (1925), 95; G. Tyler Mairs to Henry P. DeForest, July 21, 1938, in Henry P. DeForest Papers, Collection #3214, Department of Manuscripts and University Archives, Cornell University Libraries, Box 6, Folder 8-II; *Fingerprint and Identification Magazine* 7:3 (Sept. 1925), 16–17; G. Tyler Mairs, "Can Two Identical Ridge Patterns Actually Occur—Either on Different Persons or on the Same Person?" *Finger Print and Identification Magazine* 27:5 (Nov. 1945), 3–7; Harriet Ritvo, *The Platypus and the Mermaid, and Other Figments of the Classifying Imagination* (Cambridge, Mass.: Harvard University Press, 1997), 26–28.

27. David J. O'Farrell, "Criminality and Finger Prints," *Finger Print and Identification Magazine* 53:2 (Aug. 1971), 11–23; Ogden L. Glasow, "Can Fingerprint Patterns Predict Criminal Behavior?" *Finger Print and Identification Magazine* 56:2 (Aug. 1974), 3–7; James Hamilton Sr., "Myths, Legends and Half-Truths," *Identification News* 31:11 (Nov. 1981), 8–11.

28. Paul Gabriel Tesla, *Crime and Mental Disease in the Hand: A Proven Guide for the Identification and Pre-Identification of Criminality, Psychosis and Mental Defectiveness* (Lakeland, Fla.: Osiris Press, 1991).

29. C. H. Lin, J. H. Liu, J. W. Osterburg, et al., "Fingerprint Comparison I: Similarity of Fingerprints," *Journal of Forensic Sciences* 27 (1982), 290–304; John Berry, "Race Relationships," *Fingerprint Whorld* (Jan. 1977), 48–50.

5. Fingerprinting Foreigners

1. Gerald Lambourne, *The Fingerprint Story* (London: Harrap, 1984).

2. "Thumbs Down! The Latest Plan for Outwitting the Chinese," *San Francisco Daily Report* (Sept. 19, 1885), 8.

3. *Albany Atlas and Argus* (July 25, Aug. 24, 1857); "Chief of Police Maloy

Dies This Morning from Paralysis," *Albany Evening Journal* (July 22, 1884).

4. "Hand Marks under the Microscope," *American Journal of Microscopy and Popular Science* 2 (July 1877); Duayne J. Dillon, "Finger Print as Evidence First Proposed by Thomas Taylor—1877," *Identification News* (Feb. 1972), 11–12.

5. Roger Daniels, *Coming to America: A History of Immigration and Ethnicity in American Life* (New York: HarperCollins, 1990), 240; Alexander Saxton, *The Indispensable Enemy: Labor and the Anti-Chinese Movement in California* (Berkeley: University of California Press, 1971), 139–156.

6. O. L. Spaulding, "Report to the Secretary of the Treasury," Nov. 2, 1885, *Senate Executive Documents*, 7:103, 2.

7. W. H. Sears to Charles Denby, Aug. 17, 1885, National Archives–Pacific Sierra Region, San Bruno, Calif., Record Group 36, U.S. Bureau of Customs, Port of San Francisco, "General Correspondence from the Office of the Collector," 1869–1931, Box 7.

8. Spaulding, "Report," 2–3.

9. Herbert F. Beecher, Special Agent of the Treasury Department, Port Townsend, Wash., to C. F. Fairchild, Secretary of the Treasury, Sept. 4, 1887; E. E. Penn, Deputy Collector in Charge of Chinese Matters, to Hon. Quincy Brooks, Collector of Customs, Port Townsend, Sept. 2, 1887, both in National Archives, Record Group 85, Custom Case Files no. 3358d, 1877–1891, Box 3; Spaulding, "Report," 7.

10. William W. Morrow, *Chinese Immigration* (Washington, 1886), 4–7.

11. Quincy A. Brooks to Daniel Manning, May 29, 1888, Custom Case Files no. 3358d, Box 1; Beecher to Fairchild, Sept. 4, 1887; Penn to Brooks, Sept. 2, 1887.

12. Ibid.; "Thumbs Down!"

13. William B. Secrest, *Lawmen and Desperadoes: A Compendium of Noted Early California Peace Officers, Badmen and Outlaws, 1885–1900* (Spokane: Arthur H. Clark, 1994), 229–234; Lucie Cheng, "Free, Indentured, Enslaved: Chinese Prostitutes in Nineteenth-Century America," in Lucie Cheng and Edna Bonacich, eds., *Labor Immigration under Capitalism: Asian Workers in the United States before World War II* (Berkeley: University of California Press, 1984), 413.

14. H. N. Morse to J. F. Evans, Feb. 19, 1883; J. F. Evans to Charles J. Folger, Feb. 19, 1883; H. B. James to Judge French, n.d., all in Custom Case Files no. 3358d, Box 43.

15. Spaulding, "Report," 4; Special Committee of the Board of Supervisors, "Chinatown: Startling Report of the Hideous and Disgusting Features of Chinatown," *San Francisco Daily Report*, Supplement (July 21, 1885), 11.

16. "Thumbs Down!"

17. Spaulding, "Report," 5.

18. *Chinese Exclusion Case* (Chae Chan Ping v. United States) 9 S.Ct. 623.

19. Quoted in Gerald T. Lambourne, "Taber—Photographer," *Fingerprint Whorld* 10 (April 1985), 114–115.

20. Walter Hough, "Thumb Marks," *Science* 8 (1886), 167; "Thumbs Down," *Philadelphia Photographer* 22:263 (Nov. 1885), 359–361; *Anthony's Photographic Bulletin* 16 (Oct. 24, 1885), 643; Francis Galton, "Personal Identification and Description II," *Nature* 38 (June 28, 1888), 201; Robert Heindl, "Interesting Finger Print History in the United States," *Finger Print and Identification Magazine* 20:10 (April 1939), 20; Harry Myers II, "History of Identification in the United States," *Finger Print and Identification Magazine* 20:4 (Oct. 1938), 11.

21. Julia E. Rodriguez, "Encoding the Criminal: Criminology and the Science of 'Social Defense' in Modernizing Argentina (1881–1920)" (Ph.D. diss., Columbia University, 2000), 217–220; Carey L. Chapman, "Dr. Juan Vucetich: His Contribution to the Science of Fingerprints," *Journal of Forensic Identification* 42 (1992), 288; Jürgen Thorwald, *The Century of the Detective*, trans. Richard Winston and Clara Winston (New York: Harcourt, Brace and World, 1965), 51–89; Henry T. F. Rhodes, *Alphonse Bertillon: Father of Scientific Detection* (New York: Abelard-Schuman, 1956), 146–148.

22. Chapman, "Dr. Juan Vucetich," 288–291; *Revista de identificación y ciencias penales* 5 (1930), 176–189.

23. Chapman, "Dr. Juan Vucetich," 286–294; Rodriguez, "Encoding the Criminal," 216–217.

24. Rodriguez, "Encoding the Criminal," 225–233; Chapman, "Dr. Juan Vucetich," 288–291; *La Nación*, Dec. 8, 1895, and *La Prensa*, Dec. 8, 1895, courtesy Julia E. Rodriguez.

25. Burtis C. Bridges, *Practical Fingerprinting* (New York: Funk and Wagnalls, 1963), 156–163; Spencer L. Rogers, *The Personal Identification of Living Individuals* (Springfield, Ill.: Charles C. Thomas, 1986), 73–75.

26. Rodriguez, "Encoding the Criminal," 228–243.

27. Nancy Leys Stepan, *"The Hour of Eugenics": Race, Gender, and Nation in Latin America* (Ithaca: Cornell University Press, 1991), 15, 70; Rodriguez, "Encoding the Criminal," 236–237.

28. Aline Helg, "Race in Argentina and Cuba, 1880–1930: Theory, Policies, and Popular Reaction," in Richard Graham, ed., *The Idea of Race in Latin America, 1870–1940* (Austin: University of Texas Press, 1990), 39–43.

29. Ibid., 43–44.

30. Ibid., 64; Julia Kirk Blackwelder and Lyman L. Johnson, "Changing Criminal Patterns in Buenos Aires, 1890–1914," *Journal of Latin Ameri-*

can Studies 14 (1982), 360–364; Samuel L. Baily, "The Adjustment of Italian Immigrants in Buenos Aires and New York, 1870–1914," *American Historical Review* 88 (1983), 284.

31. Helg, "Race in Argentina," 43–44; Herbert S. Klein, "The Integration of Italian Immigrants into the United States and Argentina: A Comparative Analysis," *American Historical Review* 88 (1983), 306–329; Blackwelder and Johnson, "Changing Criminal Patterns," 366; Rodriguez, "Encoding the Criminal," 247–248.

32. Rodriguez, "Encoding the Criminal," 245.

33. Ibid., 228–243.

34. Ibid., 227–242.

35. Samuel Langhorne Clemens, *Pudd'nhead Wilson* (1894; New York: Norton, 1980), 110–113; Susan Gillman, *Dark Twins: Imposture and Identity in Mark Twain's America* (Chicago: University of Chicago Press, 1989), 72.

36. Mark Twain, "A Dying Man's Confession," in *Life on the Mississippi* (Boston, 1883), 340–356; George Wilton Wilton, *Fingerprints: History, Law and Romance* (London: William Hodge, 1938); John Berry and Martin Leadbetter, "The Faulds Legacy Part 6—Inter Alias," *Fingerprint Whorld* (July 1986), 24–26; Robert D. Olsen Sr., "Fingerprints and Mark Twain," *Journal of Forensic Identification* 42 (1992), 282–285.

37. Henry DeForest, "The First Finger Print File in the US," *Finger Print and Identification Magazine* 20 (Aug. 1938), 18.

38. Harris Hawthorne Wilder, "Palms and Soles," *American Journal of Anatomy* 1 (1902), 440.

39. Lawrence M. Friedman, *Crime and Punishment in American History* (New York: Basic Books, 1993), 193–210.

40. David J. Rothman, *Conscience and Convenience: The Asylum and Its Alternatives in Progressive America* (Boston: Little, Brown, 1980), 77.

41. Michael Harling, *Origins of the New York State Bureau of Identification* (Albany: New York State Division of Criminal Justice Services, 1996), 8–12; New York State Prison Department, *Annual Report* (New York, 1903), 11–12.

42. DeLancey M. Ellis, ed., *New York at the Louisiana Purchase Exposition: St. Louis, 1904* (Albany: J. B. Lyon, 1907), 510–511.

43. Harling, *Origins*, 20; David L. Grieve, "The Identification Process: Traditions in Training," *Journal of Forensic Identification* 40 (1990), 195–213; Donald C. Dilworth, ed., *Identification Wanted: Development of the American Criminal Identification System* (Gaithersburg, Md.: International Association of Chiefs of Police, 1977), 64–68.

44. New York Prison Department, *Annual Report* (1903), 11–12.

45. James H. Parke to William P. Potter, Nov. 10, 1903; F. H. Larned to James H. Parke, May 16, 1903, ref. #7250-C, both in historical records of the New York State Division of Criminal Justice Services.

46. Harris Hawthorne Wilder and Bert Wentworth, *Personal Identification: Methods for the Identification of Individuals, Living or Dead* (Boston: Gorham, 1918), 363–364.

6. From Anthropometry to Dactyloscopy

1. Frank Smyth, *Cause of Death: The Story of Forensic Science* (New York: Van Nostrand Reinhold, 1980), 129.
2. *The Identification Division of the FBI: A Brief Outline of the History, Services, and Operating Techniques of the World's Largest Repository of Fingerprints* (Washington: FBI, 1991), 7.
3. Donald C. Dilworth, ed., *Identification Wanted: Development of the American Criminal Identification System, 1893–1943* (Gaithersburg, Md.: International Association of Chiefs of Police, 1977), 66; Joe Nickell, "The Two 'Will Wests': A New Verdict," *Journal of Police Science and Administration* 8 (1980), 406–413.
4. David L. Grieve, "The Identification Process: Traditions in Training," *Journal of Forensic Identification* 40 (1990), 199; Robert D. Olsen Sr., "More about 'The Two Will Wests,'" *Identification News* 32:1 (Jan. 1982), 7; U.S. Justice Department Criminal Identification Bureau, *Annual Report of the Special Agent in Charge* (Leavenworth, Kan.: U.S. Penitentiary Press, 1920); Harris Hawthorne Wilder and Bert Wentworth, *Personal Identification: Methods for the Identification of Individuals, Living or Dead* (Boston: Gorham, 1918), 30–33.
5. Henry T. F. Rhodes, *Alphonse Bertillon: Father of Scientific Detection* (New York: Abelard-Schuman, 1956), 155–156.
6. Harris Hawthorne Wilder, "Palms and Soles," *American Journal of Anatomy* 1 (1902), 440; Wilder and Wentworth, *Personal Identification*, 30–33, 70, 363–364, emphasis added.
7. Nickell, "The Two 'Will Wests'"; Olsen, "More about 'The Two Will Wests,'"; William J. Watling, "Still a Doubter," *Identification News* 32:1 (Jan. 1982), 6; Eugene D. Genovese, *Roll, Jordan, Roll: The World the Slaves Made* (New York: Pantheon, 1974), 443–450.
8. Jürgen Thorwald, *The Century of the Detective*, trans. Richard Winston and Clara Winston (New York: Harcourt, Brace and World, 1965), 94–95; Frederick J. Weihs, *Science against Crime* (New York: Collier, 1964), 39–43; Jack Fincher, "Lifting 'Latents' Is Now Very Much a High-Tech Matter," *Smithsonian* 20 (Oct. 1989), 201–218; Anne Joseph and Alison Winter, "Making the Match: Human Traces, Forensic Experts and the Public Imagination," in Francis Spufford and Jenny Uglow, eds., *Cultural Babbage: Technology, Time and Invention* (London: Faber and Faber, 1996), 193–214; Michael Lynch, Ruth MacNally, and Patrick Daly, "Le tribunal: Fragile espace de la prevue," *La recherche* 300 (July–Aug. 1997), 113–114; Sandra S. Phillips, "Identifying the Criminal," in Sandra S.

Phillips, Mark Haworth-Booth, and Carol Squiers, eds., *Police Pictures: The Photograph as Evidence* (San Francisco: Chronicle, 1997), 20.

9. Wilder, "Palms and Soles," 439; Wilder and Wentworth, *Personal Identification*, 9.

10. Quoted by Francis Galton, *Finger Prints* (London, 1892), 164–165.

11. Charles R. Greenleaf, *The Personal Identity of the Soldier* (Chicago, 1892); J. R. Kean, "The System of Personal Identification by Finger Prints Recently Adopted for the U.S. Army," *Journal of the American Medical Association* 47 (1906), 1175–77.

12. Alphonse Bertillon, *Instructions for Taking Descriptions for the Identification of Criminals and Others by the Means of Anthropometric Indications*, trans. Gallus Muller (Chicago, 1889), 35.

13. Inmate Admission Registers, 1865–1971, Sing Sing Correctional Facility. Record Series B0143, New York State Archives.

14. Quoted in Dilworth, *Identification Wanted*, 97; quoted in F. H. DePue, "The DePue System of Identification" in International Association of Chiefs of Police, *Proceedings* (1902), 98.

15. Robert W. Rydell, *All the World's a Fair: Visions of Empire at American International Expositions, 1876–1916* (Chicago: University of Chicago Press, 1984), 157–164; David R. Francis, *The Universal Exposition of 1904* (St. Louis: Louisiana Purchase Exposition Co., 1913), 524–533.

16. Rydell, *All the World's a Fair*, 162–171; Francis, *Universal Exposition*, 533; Mark Bennitt, ed., *History of the Louisiana Purchase Exposition* (New York: Arno Press, 1905), 673.

17. Rydell, *All the World's a Fair*, 178.

18. Ibid., 162–164.

19. Alphonse Bertillon, *Signaletic Instructions: Including the Theory and Practice of Anthropometrical Identification*, trans. R. W. McClaughry (Chicago, 1896), 13; DePue, "The DePue System," 97.

20. "The Bertillon System of Identification," *Scientific American* 91 (Dec. 17, 1904), 432–434; L. Ramakers, "A New Method of Identifying Criminals," *Scientific American* 93 (Sept. 30, 1905), 264.

21. A. Dastre, "Des empreintes digitales comme procédé d'identification," *Comptes rendus des séances de l'Academie des Sciences* 145 (1907), 32–42.

22. Ciprian Kolb and Leo Gresz, "A New Method of Identifying Persons: The Veins on the Back of the Hand," *Scientific American* 70 (Sept. 3, 1910), 159.

23. Quoted in Dilworth, *Identification Wanted*, 86.

24. Kean, "System of Personal Identification," 1175–77; M. W. McClaughry, "Finger Prints," *Journal of the U.S. Cavalry Association* 17 (1907), 512; John H. Taylor, "The Navy's Identification System," *The Fleet Review* 4 (1913), 5–12.

25. Camillo Windt, "Über Daktyloskopie," *Archive für Kriminal-Anthropologie und Kriminalistic* 12 (1903), 101–123, quotation 121; Galton, *Finger Prints*, 152; Dastre, "Des empreintes digitales," 44; Raymond B. Fosdick, "The Passing of the Bertillon System of Identification," *Journal of American Institute of Criminal Law and Criminology* 6 (1915), 363–369, quotation 364.

26. Nicole H. Rafter, *Creating Born Criminals* (Urbana: University of Illinois Press, 1997), ix, 7–9; Prison Association of New York, *Annual Report* 63 (Albany: J. B. Lyon, 1908), 17; Ruth M. Alexander, *The "Girl Problem": Female Adolescent Delinquents in New York, 1900–1930* (Ithaca: Cornell University Press, 1995), 41.

27. Julia E. Rodriguez, "Encoding the Criminal: Criminology and the Science of 'Social Defense' in Modernizing Argentina (1881–1920)" (Ph.D. diss., Columbia University, 2000), 246–247.

28. Joseph M. Deuel, *Finger-Prints* (New York: M. B. Brown, 1917), 3–6.

29. Eric H. Monkkonen, *Police in Urban America, 1860–1920* (Cambridge: Cambridge University Press, 1981), 157–160.

30. W. Bruce Cobb, "Discussion," in New York State Probation Commission, *Annual Report* (Albany: J. B. Lyon, 1916), 252–253; Board of City Magistrates of the City of New York (First Division), *Annual Report* (New York: M. B. Brown, 1913), 61–63; Alfred A. Hart, "Finger Print Bureau," in New York City Magistrates' Courts, *Annual Report* (New York: Clarence S. Nathan, 1915), 102–105.

31. *Laws of the State of New York* (1916), chap. 287, §3; Deuel, *Finger-Prints*, 9; Cobb, "Discussion," 253; Albert Wehde and John N. Beffel, *Finger-Prints Can Be Forged* (Chicago: Tremonia, 1924), 59.

32. Deuel, *Finger-Prints*, 3–8.

33. J. Francis Sutherland, *Recidivism: Habitual Criminality, and Habitual Petty Delinquency—A Problem in Sociology, Psycho-Pathology and Criminology* (Edinburgh: William Green, 1908), 5–7.

34. David J. Rothman, *Conscience and Convenience: The Asylum and Its Alternatives in Progressive America* (Boston: Little, Brown, 1980), 43–44; Jonathan Simon, *Poor Discipline: Parole and the Social Control of the Underclass, 1890–1990* (Chicago: University of Chicago Press, 1993); *Laws of the State of New York* (1915) chap. 579, §1–10; Deuel, *Finger-Prints*, 21.

35. Harold J. Shepstone, "The Finger-Print System of Identification," *Scientific American* 103 (Oct. 1, 1910), 257; C. K. Talbot, "The Influence of the Popular Press on Criminal Justice Policy (The Competition between the French Bertillon System and the British Fingerprinting System in New York State, 1890–1914)," *International Journal of Comparative and Applied Criminal Justice* 7 (1983), 201–208; Michael Harling, *Origins of the New York State Bureau of Identification* (Albany: New York State Division of Criminal Justice Services, 1996), 24.

36. *New York Times* (July 30, 1911), sec. 5, 12; New York Police Department, *Annual Report* (1911), 5.

37. Fosdick, "Passing," 369. Robert Ferrari, "The Fingerprint Method for the American Police Systems," *Journal of American Institute of Criminal Law and Criminology* 8 (1917), 289–290.

38. "Proceedings of the Second International Association for Criminal Identification Meeting" in *International Identification Outlook* 1:4 (Oct. 1916), 1.

39. DePue, "The DePue System," 98–102; *Revista de identificación y ciencias penales* 3 (Nov./Dec. 1928).

40. National Police Conference (NPC), *Proceedings* (1921), 103–104; Dilworth, *Identification Wanted*, 131–134.

41. International Association for Identification (IAI), *Proceedings* (1925), 66–67.

42. Bertillon Records, New York Police Department, Municipal Archives, City of New York; John Noble, Archivist, City of Rochester, New York, personal communication; Harling, *Origins*, 30; Clara L. Parsons, *Bertillon Measurements Discontinued* (Albany: New York State Division of Identification, 1931), 1; Male Inmate Identification File, 1921–1936, Auburn Correctional Facility, Record Series B0059, New York State Archives; Records in the Archivo Historico, Museo Pentenciario "Antonio Ballvé," Buenos Aires, examined by Julia E. Rodriguez.

43. IAI, *Proceedings* (1925), 60.

44. DePue, "The DePue System," 98–102.

45. Jay Hambridge, "Finger-Prints: Their Use by the Police," *Century* 78 (Oct. 1909), 921; James W. Garner, "Identification of Criminals by Means of Finger Prints," *Journal of the American Institute of Criminal Law and Criminology* 1 (1910), 635, emphasis added; Lorraine Daston and Peter Gallison, "The Image of Objectivity," *Representations* 40 (1992), 81–128.

46. DePue, "The DePue System," 93; NPC, *Proceedings* (1921), 105.

47. Rodriguez, "Encoding the Criminal," 242; Frederic A. Brayley, *Brayley's Arrangement of Finger Prints: Identification and Their Uses* (Boston, 1909), 7.

48. John Henry Wigmore, *A Treatise on the Anglo-American System of Evidence in Trials at Common Law*, vol. 4, 2nd ed. (Boston: Little, Brown, 1923), 874.

7. *Bloody Fingerprints and Brazen Experts*

1. Hans-Joachim Hammer, "On the Contribution Made by German Scientists to the Development of Dactyloscopy," *Fingerprint Whorld* 12:45 (July 1986), 13–15; René Forgeot, *Des empreintes digitales étudiées au point de vue medico-judiciaire* (Lyon, 1892); Francis Galton, *Finger Prints* (London, 1892), 100–113.

2. Henry T. F. Rhodes, *Alphonse Bertillon: Father of Scientific Detection* (New York: Abelard-Schuman, 1968), 116.

3. Francis Galton, *Decipherment of Blurred Finger Prints: Supplementary Chapter to "Finger Prints"* (London, 1893), 15–16; *Emperor v. Abdul Hamid* 32 Indian L. Rep. 759 (Calcutta, 1905); John H. Taylor, *Finger-Print Evidence* (Washington: U.S. Navy Department, 1920), 7–9.

4. Gerald Lambourne, *The Fingerprint Story* (London: Harrap, 1984), 67–68.

5. Anne Joseph, "Anthropometry, the Police Expert, and the Deptford Murders: The Contested Introduction of Fingerprinting for the Identification of Criminals in Late Victorian and Edwardian Britain," in John Torpey and Jane Caplan, eds., *Documenting Individual Identity: The Development of State Practices since the French Revolution* (Princeton: Princeton University Press, forthcoming); Robert D. Olsen Sr., "First Instance of Fingerprint Evidence Presented to a Jury in a Criminal Court in Great Britain," *Fingerprint Whorld* 13:51 (Jan. 1988), 53–55.

6. Quoted in Henry Faulds, *Guide to Finger-Print Identification* (Hanley, U.K.: Wood Mitchell, 1905), 45–46.

7. Lambourne, *Fingerprint Story*, 84.

8. Joseph, "Anthropometry," 17–18.

9. Quoted in George W. Wilton, *Fingerprints: Fifty Years of Injustice* (Galashiels, U.K.: A. Walker, 1955), 13; Martin Leadbetter, "Rex v. Stratton and Stratton," *Fingerprint Whorld* 2:7 (Jan. 1977), 32–38.

10. Faulds, *Guide*, iii-v, 71.

11. Ibid., 52.

12. Ibid., 51.

13. Inez L. Whipple, "The Ventral Surface of Mammalian Chiridium with Special Reference to the Conditions Found in Man," *Zeitschrift für Morphologie und Anthropologie* 7 (1904), 327–328.

14. "No Two Finger Prints Alike," *Scientific American* 105:8 (Aug. 19, 1911); Frank Marshall White, "Crime and Fingerprints," *Harper's* (Winter 1910).

15. *In re Castleton's Case*, 3 Crim. App. 74.

16. *People v. Jennings* (Ill. 1910), trial transcript.

17. Ibid., 137–139.

18. Albert Wehde and John N. Beffel, *Finger-Prints Can Be Forged* (Chicago: Tremonia, 1924), 97–98; *People v. Jennings* transcript, 114–115.

19. *People v. Jennings* 96 N.E. 1077, quotation 1082–83.

20. Michael Saks, "Merlin and Solomon: Lessons from the Law's Formative Encounters with Forensic Identification Science," *Hastings Law Journal* 49 (1998), 1069–1141; Edward Lindsey, "Conviction of Murder on Finger-Print Evidence," *Journal of American Institute of Criminal Law and Criminology* 1 (1911), 848–849; *People v. Jennings*, 1081–82.

21. Quoted in Wehde and Beffel, *Finger-Prints Can Be Forged*, 49–50.

22. Memorandum of the Deputy Assistant District Attorney, Mar. 10, 1911, in *People v. Crispi*, Case File #81943, Municipal Archives of the City of New York.

23. *People v. Crispi* (New York, 1911), trial transcript, Special Collections, Lloyd G. Sealy Library, John Jay College, City University of New York, 41–45.

24. Ibid., 152–154.

25. Ibid., 152–156; *New York World*, May 12, 1911; "Finger Prints of Twins," *New York Times*, May 11, 1911.

26. *People v. Crispi*, transcript, 83–99.

27. *People v. Crispi*, case file.

28. *People v. Crispi*, transcript, 252–255; "Finger Prints Convict," *New York Times* (May 12, 1911), 20.

29. *People v. Crispi*, transcript, 255; case file.

30. Quoted in Wehde and Beffel, *Finger-Prints Can Be Forged*, 39–58.

31. Quoted ibid., 60.

32. Michael Harling, *Origins of the New York State Bureau of Identification* (Albany: New York State Division of Criminal Justice Services, 1996), 26–28; Harling, "Edward Sherman Parke: A Forgotten Fingerprint Pioneer," *Journal of Forensic Identification* 42 (1992), 330–345.

33. *People v. Roche*, trial transcript, in *Court of Appeals* 86 (Amsterdam, N.Y.: Evening Recorder, 1915), 775–777.

34. Henry Faulds, *A Manual of Practical Dactylography* (London: Police Review, 1923), 10, 31.

35. Henry Faulds and William J. Herschel, "The Permanence of Finger-Print Patterns," *Nature* 98 (1917): 388–389; Wilton, *Fingerprints*.

36. Wehde and Beffel, *Finger-Prints Can Be Forged*, 36–48.

8. Dazzling Demonstrations and Easy Assumptions

1. *Moon v. State* 198 P. 288 (Ariz. 1921).

2. "Wonderful Finger-Print Test Successfully Carried Out," *Finger Print and Identification Magazine* 1 (March 1920), 6.

3. Albert Wehde and John N. Beffel, *Finger-Prints Can Be Forged* (Chicago: Tremonia, 1924), 61; *Commonwealth v. Loomis* 267 Pa. 438 (1920); *Commonwealth v. Loomis* 270 Pa. 254 (1921).

4. Wehde and Beffel, *Finger-Prints Can Be Forged*, 70–71; T. Grant Cooke, *Finger Prints* (Chicago: University of Applied Science, 1920), 3.

5. Cooke, *Finger Prints*, 11; David L. Grieve, "The Identification Process: Traditions in Training," *Journal of Forensic Identification* 40 (1990), 195–213; Michael Harling, *Origins of the New York State Bureau of Identification* (Albany: New York State Division of Criminal Justice Services, 1996), 29–39; *Finger Print and Identification Magazine* 2 (Jan. 1921), 4; 6 (Aug. 1924), 6–18; 8 (Nov. 1926), 10; International Association

for Identification (IAI), *Proceedings* (1925), 88–92; Henry P. DeForest to Helen M. Snyder (Nov. 23, 1937), Henry P. DeForest Papers, Collection #3214, Division of Rare and Manuscript Collections, Carl A. Kroch Library, Cornell University, Box 6, Folder 8-II; Sharon Hartman Strom, "'Machines Instead of Clerks': Technology and the Feminization of Bookkeeping, 1910–1950," in Heidi I. Hartmann et al., eds., *Computer Chips and Paper Clips: Technology and Women's Employment* (Washington: National Academy Press, 1986), 63.

6. Donald Dilworth, ed., *Identification Wanted: Development of the American Criminal Identification System, 1893–1943* (Gaithersburg, Md.: International Association of Chiefs of Police, 1977), 29–31, 109.

7. IAI, *Minutes* (1919), 11; IAI, *Proceedings* (1918), 17–18, 34–35.

8. Dilworth, *Identification Wanted*, 109–111; Marion Brooks to ISPI membership, Jan. 9, 1922, DeForest Papers, Box 6, Folder 5.

9. Joseph T. Williams to Edward T. Devine (Nov. 29, 1911), in Committee on Criminal Courts, Community Service Society Papers, Columbia University Libraries Manuscript Collections, Box #111; Harris Hawthorne Wilder and Bert Wentworth, *Personal Identification: Methods for the Identification of Individuals, Living or Dead* (Boston: Gorham, 1918), 366; Frederick Kuhne, "The Origin, Classification and Uses of Finger Prints: An Ideal System of Identification for the General Public," *Scientific American* 114:14 (April 1, 1916), 357–366; Eric Blau, *The Hero of the Slocum Disaster* (Buffalo: Mosaic Press, 1997), 97.

10. Joseph A. Faurot, "Step Up and Be Finger Printed—Everybody," *Finger Print and Identification Magazine* 1:3 (Sept. 1919), 14; Edward H. Murphy and James E. Murphy, *Finger Prints for Commercial and Personal Identification* (Detroit: International Title Recording and Identification Bureau, 1922), 10–11; *Finger Print and Identification Magazine* 6:10 (April 1925), 32.

11. Wiebe E. Bijker, Thomas P. Hughes, and Trevor Pinch, eds., *The Social Construction of Technological Systems* (Cambridge, Mass.: MIT Press, 1987).

12. Samuel Walker, *A Critical History of Police Reform: The Emergence of Professionalism* (Lexington, Mass.: Lexington Books, 1977), 27–73, 156–168; Eric H. Monkkonen, *Police in Urban America, 1860–1920* (Cambridge: Cambridge University Press, 1981), 41; Ronald R. Thomas, *Detective Fiction and the Rise of Forensic Science* (Cambridge: Cambridge University Press, 1999), 217–218.

13. Roxanne Panchasi, "Graphology and the Science of Individual Identity in Modern France," *Configurations* 4 (1996), 1–31; James C. Mohr, *Doctors and the Law: Medical Jurisprudence in Nineteenth-Century America* (New York: Oxford University Press, 1993); Charles E. Rosenberg, *The Trial of the Assassin Guiteau: Psychiatry and Law in the Gilded Age* (Chicago: Chicago University Press, 1968).

14. Edwin R. Keedy, "Finger Prints and Heart Pulsations," *Journal of American Institute of Criminal Law and Criminology* 3 (1913), 952–954.

15. Christophe Champod, C. Lennard, and P. Margot, "Alphonse Bertillon and Dactyloscopy," *Journal of Forensic Identification* 43 (1993), 604–625; Christophe Champod, "Edmond Locard—Numerical Standards and 'Probable' Identifications," *Journal of Forensic Identification* 45 (1995), 136–163.

16. Frederick Kuhne, *The Finger Print Instructor* (New York: Munn, 1917), iv.

17. A. A. Gribben, "How the Finger Print Expert Presents His Case in Court," *Finger Print and Identification Magazine* 1 (1919), 10–14.

18. IAI, *Proceedings* (1927), 39.

19. Ibid., 114–119.

20. *Finger Print and Identification Magazine* 6:3 (Sept. 1924), 2.

21. IAI, *Proceedings* (1937), 72–73.

22. *Hopkins v. State* 295 S.W. 361 (Ark. 1927); *People v. Chimovitz* 211 N.W. 650 (Mich. 1927); *State v. Lapan* 141 A. 685 (Vt. 1928), emphasis added.

23. *Stacy v. State* 292 P. 885 (Ok. 1930).

24. *State v. Steffen* 230 N.W. 536 (Iowa 1930).

25. *Commonwealth v. Albright* 101 Pa. Superior Ct. 318 (1931).

26. *Finger Print and Identification Magazine* 17 (Oct. 1935), 6; (Nov. 1935), 3.

27. *Shelton v. Commonwealth* 134 S.W. 2d 653 (Ky. 1939); *Ingram v. Commonwealth* 96 S.W. 2d 1017 (Ky. 1936); *Green v. Commonwealth*, 105 S.W. 2d 585 (Ky. 1937).

28. *People v. Jones* 12 N.Y.S. 2d 635 (1939).

29. *McGarry v. State* 200 S.W. 527 (Tex. 1918); *Graves v. State* 43 S.W. 2d 953 (Tex. 1931); *Weathered v. State* 46 S.W. 2d 701 (Tex. 1932); *Parker v. Rex* 14 C.L.R. 681 (Australia 1912); *Grice v. State*, 151 S.W. 2d 211 (Tex. 1941).

30. *Grice v. State.*

31. Wilson A. Bentley, "Every Snowflake a Master Design," *Popular Science Monthly* 104:1 (Jan. 1924), 44–45; Bentley and W. J. Humphreys, *Snow Crystals* (1931; New York: Dover, 1962), 15–16; G. Tyler Mairs, "Can Two Identical Ridge Patterns Actually Occur—Either on Different Persons or on the Same Person?" *Finger Print and Identification Magazine* 27 (Nov. 1945), 3–7.

32. Burtis C. Bridges, "No Duplicate Finger Prints," *Finger Print and Identification Magazine* 27 (Mar. 1946), 5–6; Bert Wentworth, "Impossibility of Finger Print Pattern Duplication," 21 (May 1940), 16–17.

33. Steven Shapin, *A Social History of Truth: Civility and Science in Seventeenth-Century England* (Chicago: University of Chicago Press, 1994), 355–408.

34. IAI, *Proceedings* (1925), 121–123; (1926), 125–126.

35. Quoted in Dilworth, *Identification Wanted*, 176.

9. Identification at a Distance

1. George K. Brown, "Recidivism: A Socio-Legal Survey of Its Definition, Incidence and Treatment in the United States," Ph.D. diss., "an essential portion in pamphlet form," University of Pennsylvania (1947), 2–24.

2. Louis N. Robinson, *Criminal Statistics and Identification of Criminals* (New York: National Crime Commission, 1927), 16; Jonathan Simon, *Poor Discipline: Parole and the Social Control of the Underclass, 1890–1990* (Chicago: University of Chicago Press, 1993), 47–48.

3. William J. Kinsley, "Finger Print Identification as Sole Evidence," *Journal of the American Institute of Criminal Law and Criminology* 2 (1911), 407–409; International Association of Chiefs of Police (IACP), *Proceedings* (1908), 117–121.

4. Lawrence M. Friedman, *Crime and Punishment in American History* (New York: Basic Books, 1993), 270.

5. National Police Conference (NPC), *Proceedings* (1921), 41; Prison Association of New York, *Proposing a Bureau for Consolidating Identification, Information and Investigation Records of New York State to Cooperate with the Federal Bureau for the Protection of Society and Justice to the Individual* (1924), 1.

6. *To Create a National Police Bureau/To Create a Bureau of Criminal Identification*, Hearing before the Committee on the Judiciary, U.S. House of Representatives, 68th Cong., 1st Sess., April 17 and 24, 1924, on H.R. 8580 and H.R. 8409, Serial 31 (Washington: Government Printing Office, 1924), 19; Raymond B. Fosdick, *European Police Systems* (1915; Montclair, N.J.: Patterson Smith, 1969), 328–330.

7. NPC, *Proceedings* (1921), 39, 148; (1922), 384–385; U.S. Criminal Identification Bureau, *Annual Report* (Leavenworth, Kan.: U.S. Penitentiary Press, 1919); Bruno Latour, *Science in Action: How to Follow Scientists and Engineers through Society* (Cambridge, Mass.: Harvard University Press, 1987), 233.

8. U.S. Criminal Identification Bureau, *Annual Report*, 7.

9. Thomas H. Jaycox, *Classification of Single Fingerprints* (Wichita: Wichita Police Department, 1931), i.

10. Robinson, *Criminal Statistics*, 14.

11. Thomas P. Hughes, "The Evolution of Large Technological Systems," in Wiebe E. Bijker, Thomas P. Hughes, and Trevor J. Pinch, eds., *The Social Construction of Technological Systems* (Cambridge, Mass.: MIT Press, 1987), 52.

12. Fosdick, *European Police Systems*, 332–333; Raymond B. Fosdick, *Amer-*

ican Police Systems (1920; Montclair, N.J.: Patterson Smith, 1969), 339; NPC, *Proceedings* (1921), 100–103.

13. Latour, *Science in Action*, 233–254.

14. Donald C. Dilworth, ed., *Identification Wanted: Development of the American Criminal Identification System, 1893–1943* (Gaithersburg, Md.: International Association of Chiefs of Police, 1977), 189–190; A. Dastre, "Des empreintes digitales comme procédé d'identification," *Comptes rendus des séances de l'Academie des Sciences* 145 (1907), 34.

15. Michael Harling, *Origins of the New York State Bureau of Identification* (Albany: New York State Division of Criminal Justice Services, 1996), 17–22; Paul D. McCann, *American System of Classification* (Albany: New York State Department of Correction, 1963); International Association for Identification (IAI), *Proceedings* (1925), 72.

16. A. Daae, "Die daktyloskopische Registratur," *Archive für Kriminal-Anthropologie und Kriminalistik* 24 (1906), 26; Dilworth, *Identification Wanted*, 189–190; F. Spirlet, "Méthode de classification des empreintes digitales," *Archives internationales de médecine légale* 1 (1910), 7–34; Paul A. David, "Understanding the Economics of QWERTY: The Necessity of History," in William N. Parker, ed., *Economic History and the Modern Economist* (Oxford: Basil Blackwell, 1986), 30–49; Burtis C. Bridges, *Practical Fingerprinting* (New York: Funk and Wagnalls, 1942), 162–213; Institute of Applied Science, *Directory of Identification Bureaus of the World*, 12th ed. (Chicago, 1945).

17. Eugene Stockis, "One Finger Classification and the Search for Criminals by the Identification of Their Finger Prints," *Archives internationales de médecine légale* (April 1914), 164–185, trans. E. Mead Hudson, in Henry P. DeForest Papers, Collection #3214, Department of Manuscripts and University Archives, Cornell University Libraries, Box 7, Folder 12; Hakon Jørgensen, *Distant Identification* (Copenhagen: Arnold Busck, 1922); Jørgensen, *Distant Identification and One-Finger Registration* (New York: International Police Conference, 1923).

18. New York Police Department (NYPD), *Annual Report* (1922), 94–95; IACP, *Proceedings* (1902), 99.

19. Jørgensen, *Distant Identification* (1922), 1–2; International Police Conference (IPC), *Proceedings* (1921), 381–395; Jørgensen, *Distant Identification* (1923), 6.

20. Charles S. Collins, "A Telegraphic Code for Finger-Print Formulae and a System for Sub-Classification of Single Digital Impressions" (London: Office of the Police Chronicle, 1921), in DeForest Papers, Box 8, Folder 5.

21. J. A. Larson, *Single Fingerprint System* (New York: D. Appleton, 1924), ix; Dilworth, *Identification Wanted*, 181–184; Walter C. S. Crosskey, *The Single Finger Print Identification System: A Practical Work upon the Science of Finger Printing* (San Francisco, 1923).

22. Jørgensen, *Distant Identification* (1923), 7; IPC, *Proceedings* (1923), 301;

Finger Print and Identification Magazine 6:3 (Sept. 1924), 10; IPC, *Proceedings* (1925), 139–140; Dilworth, *Identification Wanted,* 188–189; Gerald Lambourne, *The Fingerprint Story* (London: Harrap, 1984), 99; Jaycox, *Classification;* Bridges, *Practical Fingerprinting;* August C. Rosenfeldt, *Universal Single Print Identification: Complete Instruction* (Seattle, 1940).

23. J. A. Larson, review of Battley, *Single Finger Prints* in *American Journal of Police Science* (July–Aug. 1931), 361–365; Fosdick, *European Police Systems,* 344, 568–569.

24. Bridges, *Practical Fingerprinting;* Harry Battley, *Single Finger Prints: A New and Practical Method of Classifying and Filing Single Finger Prints and Fragmentary Impressions* (London: H. M. Stationery Office, 1931).

25. Larson, review of Battley; Larson, *Single Fingerprint System.*

26. Lawrence V. Harrison to Lawrence B. Dunham, April 21, 1931, Bureau of Social Hygiene Project and Research Files, Lloyd G. Sealy Library, John Jay College, City University of New York, Series III, Reel 17, Box 32, Folder 446; Larson, review of Battley.

27. Lambourne, *Fingerprint Story,* 95; NPC, *Proceedings* (1922), 408.

28. Jonathan Coopersmith, "Facsimile's False Starts," *IEEE Spectrum* 30:2 (Feb. 1993), 46–49; Henry Faulds, *Guide to Finger-Print Identification* (Hanley, U.K.: Wood Mitchell, 1905); Austin C. Lescarboura, "Sending Photographs over Wires: Details of the Belin System to be Tried between St. Louis and New York," *Scientific American* 123:19 (Nov. 6, 1920), 474–484; "Finger-Prints via Radio: Enlisting the Long Arm of Radio in the Search for Europe's Malefactors," *Scientific American* 127 (Dec. 1922), 386; *Dactylography* 1:1 (July 1921), 1–2.

29. *Finger Print and Identification Magazine* 6:3 (Sept. 1924), 10; IPC, *Proceedings* (1925), 176–186; NYPD, *Annual Report* (1924), 42.

30. Quoted in Lawrence B. Dunham, "Identification Methods: French and English," typescript (1926) in Bureau of Social Hygiene Project and Research Files, Series III, Reel 12, Box 23, Folder 341; Jonathan Coopersmith, "The Failure of Fax: When a Vision Is Not Enough," *Business and Economic History* 23 (1994), 272–282.

10. Digital Digits

1. Bruno Latour, *Science in Action: How to Follow Scientists and Engineers through Society* (Cambridge, Mass.: Harvard University Press, 1987), 220–247.

2. Samuel Walker, *A Critical History of Police Reform: The Emergence of Professionalism* (Lexington, Mass.: Lexington Books, 1977), 47; Donald Dilworth, ed., *Identification Wanted: Development of the American Criminal Identification System, 1893–1943* (Gaithersburg, Md.: International Association of Chiefs of Police, 1977), 8.

3. Dilworth, *Identification Wanted*, 11–18.

4. Ibid., 45; United States House of Representatives, "National Bureau of Criminal Identification," Report #429, 57th Cong., 1st Sess. (Feb. 7, 1902).

5. New York State Prison Department, *Annual Report* (1898), 28–29; (1900), 16–17; (1901), 15; (1902), 26; (1904), 24.

6. Richard Bach Jensen, "The International Anti-Anarchist Conference of 1898 and the Origins of Interpol," *Journal of Contemporary History* 16 (1981), 323–347; Fenton Bressler, *Interpol* (London: Sinclair-Stevenson, 1992), 13; Malcolm Anderson, *Policing the World: Interpol and the Politics of International Police Co-operation* (Oxford: Clarendon, 1989), 39; Raymond B. Fosdick, "The Passing of the Bertillon System of Identification," *Journal of the American Institute of Criminal Law and Criminology* 6 (1915), 363–369.

7. Bressler, *Interpol*, 17–22, 99; Hakon Jørgensen, *Distant Identification* (Copenhagen: Arnold Busck, 1922), 2; Anderson, *Policing the World*, 35–41.

8. Bressler, *Interpol*, 21; National Police Conference (NPC), *Proceedings* (1921), 46–47; Dilworth, *Identification Wanted*, 45–46.

9. Eric H. Monkkonen, *Police in Urban America, 1860–1920* (Cambridge: Cambridge University Press, 1981), 160; NPC, *Proceedings* (1921), 12.

10. NPC, *Proceedings* (1921), 60–61, 104, 149–152.

11. Ben Macintyre, *The Napoleon of Crime: The Life and Times of Adam Worth, Master Thief* (New York: Farrar, Straus, Giroux, 1997); August Vollmer, "California State Bureau of Criminal Identification and Investigation," *Journal of the American Institute of Criminal Law and Criminology* 9 (1919), 482.

12. NPC, *Proceedings* (1922), 268; Bressler, *Interpol*, 19.

13. NPC, *Proceedings* (1921), 3.

14. Ibid., 13, 40.

15. Ibid., 93.

16. Ibid., 148; United States Criminal Identification Bureau, *Annual Report* (Leavenworth, Kan.: U.S. Penitentiary Press, 1919); Prison Association of New York, *Proposing a Bureau for Consolidating Identification, Information and Investigation Records of New York State to Cooperate with the Federal Bureau for the Protection of Society and Justice to the Individual* (1924), 2; New York Police Department, *Annual Report* (1915), xxiii.

17. NPC, *Proceedings* (1921), 205–206; "Course of Instruction: Given under Auspices of the International Police Conference," *Journal of Criminal Identification* 1 (1924), 6.

18. Quoted in Dilworth, *Identification Wanted*, 141.

19. NPC, *Proceedings* (1921), 43–44; Dilworth, *Identification Wanted*, 136.

20. Dilworth, *Identification Wanted*, 150–158; Athan G. Theoharis, ed., *The FBI: A Comprehensive Reference Guide* (Phoenix: Oryx Press, 1999), 2–12.

21. *To Create a National Police Bureau/To Create a Bureau of Criminal Identification*, Hearing before the Committee on the Judiciary, U.S. House of Representatives, 68th Cong., 1st Sess., April 17 and 24, 1924, on H.R. 8580 and H.R. 8409, Serial 31 (Washington: Government Printing Office, 1924), 5–6; "Course of Instruction," 6.

22. *To Create a National Police Bureau*, 9.

23. Ibid., 28–31.

24. Ibid., 34, 63.

25. LaGuardia to Graham, May 22, 1924, Congressional Correspondence, Fiorello LaGuardia Papers, Division of Rare Books and Manuscripts, New York Public Library, Reel #7, Boxes 9–10; Dilworth, *Identification Wanted*, 158.

26. IAI, *Proceedings* (1925), 42–75; Dilworth, *Identification Wanted*, 166.

27. Dilworth, *Identification Wanted*, 165–172; Pamela Sankar, "State Power and Record-Keeping: The History of Individualized Surveillance in the United States, 1790–1935" (Ph.D. diss., University of Pennsylvania, 1992), 279–290.

28. United States Civil Service Commission, *Procedure for Fingerprinting Appointees to Positions in the Federal Civil Service*, Form 2828 (Washington, 1931); Theoharis, *The FBI*, 220–221; Sankar, "State Power and Record-Keeping," 292–293; Dilworth, *Identification Wanted*, 223; Walker, *Critical History*, 157–158.

29. American Civil Liberties Union, *Thumbs Down! The Fingerprint Menace to Civil Liberties* (New York, 1938), 4; Dilworth, *Identification Wanted*, 214–221; Richard L. Tobin, "Law-Abiding Americans Find Fingerprinting a Useful Fad Aiding Themselves and Police," *New York Herald Tribune* (May 1, 1935); Walker, *Critical History*, 158.

30. ACLU, *Thumbs Down*, 12–19.

31. Ibid., 12; Dilworth, *Identification Wanted*, 228.

32. IAI, *Proceedings*, 73–74; United States Department of Justice, Division of Investigation, *Fingerprints: Fingerprinting Living and Deceased Individuals, Latent Fingerprints, Court Decisions* (Washington: Government Printing Office, 1934), 17.

33. Joseph F. James, "Thumb-Marks," *Science* 8 (1886), 212; James R. Beniger, *The Control Revolution: Technological and Economic Origins of the Information Society* (Cambridge, Mass.: Harvard University Press, 1986), 412; Martin Campbell-Kelly and William Aspray, *Computer: A History of the Information Machine* (New York: Basic, 1996), 22.

34. International Association for Identification, *Minutes* (1919), 37.

35. Robert M. Stock, "An Historical Overview of Automated Fingerprint

Identification Systems," in International Forensic Symposium on Latent Prints (IFSLP), *Proceedings* (Washington: Government Printing Office, 1987), 51; Michael Harling, *Origins of the New York State Bureau of Identification* (Albany: New York State Division of Criminal Justice Services, 1996), 43; Burtis C. Bridges, *Practical Fingerprinting* (New York: Funk and Wagnalls, 1963), 209–210.

36. Bill Reed, "Automated Fingerprint Identification: From Will West to Minnesota Nine-Fingers and Beyond," *Journal of Police Science and Administration* 9 (1981), 318–319; Stock, "Historical Overview," 51–52.

37. Reed, "Automated Fingerprint," 320–321; Stock, "Historical Overview," 53–54; Vincent V. Horvath, John M. Holeman, and Charles Q. Lemmond, "Holographic Technique Recognizes Fingerprints," *Laser Focus* (June 1967).

38. Stock, "Historical Overview," 52–57; Reed, "Automated Fingerprint," 320–322; Bill Hebenton and Terry Thomas, *Criminal Records: State, Citizen and the Politics of Protection* (Aldershot, UK: Avebury, 1993), 29–30.

39. Reed, "Automated Fingerprint," 322–323; Stock, "Historical Overview," 59; Project SEARCH, *Report on Latent Fingerprint Identification Systems* (Washington: National Institute of Justice, 1974), 84–156.

40. Stock, "Historical Overview," 54–59; Reed, "Automated Fingerprint," 318–324; Gary K. Cooper, "Automated Fingerprint Storage, Retrieval and Sharing in California," in IFSLP, *Proceedings* (1987), 77–81.

41. David J. Klug, Joseph L. Peterson, and David A. Stoney, *Automated Fingerprint Identification Systems: Their Acquisition, Management, Performance, and Organizational Impact* (Washington: National Institute of Justice, 1992), 38.

42. Stock, "Historical Overview," 59; Klug, Peterson, and Stoney, *Automated Fingerprint*, 20–34.

43. SEARCH Group, *Legal and Policy Issues Relating to Biometric Identification Technologies* (Sacramento, 1990), 18–19, 90–97.

44. Klug, Peterson, and Stoney, *Automated Fingerprint*, 41; Dennis Hevesi, "State Says Error by Fingerprint Examiner Was Apparently Fatal," *New York Times* (July 28, 1994), B5; David Stout, "Police Fingerprint System Is Reviewed after Killing," *New York Times* (Nov. 25, 1995), 26.

45. Klug, Peterson, and Stoney, *Automated Fingerprint*, 27; SEARCH Group, *Legal and Policy Issues*, 22–23.

46. David Firestone, "For Giuliani, a Day of Police Praise and Policy Vindication," *New York Times* (June 15, 1996), 25.

47. David Cole, *No Equal Justice: Race and Class in the American Criminal Justice System* (New York: New Press, 1999), 1–62; Fox Butterfield, "Racial Disparities Are Pervasive in Justice System, Report Says," *New York Times* (April 26, 2000).

11. Fraud, Fabrication, and False Positives

1. David A. Stoney and John I. Thornton, "A Critical Analysis of Quantitative Fingerprint Individuality Models," *Journal of Forensic Sciences* 31 (1986), 1187–1216, quotations 1192–1195, 1213.
2. Christophe Champod, "Edmond Locard—Numerical Standards and 'Probable' Identifications," *Journal of Forensic Identification* 45 (1995), 136–163; Gerald Lambourne, *The Fingerprint Story* (London: Harrap, 1984); Graham Hughes, "'Of Cabbages and Kings . . .,'" *Journal of Forensic Identification* 49 (1999), 237–245.
3. G. Tyler Mairs, "Random Thoughts Concerning Finger Prints," *Finger Print and Identification Magazine* 36:8 (Feb. 1955), 3–18.
4. International Association for Identification (IAI), "Standardization Committee Report," *FBI Law Enforcement Bulletin* (Oct. 1973), 7–8.
5. Gerald T. C. Lambourne, "Fingerprint Standards," *Medicine, Science, and the Law* 24 (1984), 227–229.
6. André A. Moenssens, "Testifying as a Fingerprint Witness," *Finger Print and Identification Magazine* 54:6 (1972), 3–18.
7. James R. McConnell, "Certification (To Be or Not to Be)," *Journal of Forensic Identification* 42 (1992), 205–208; Pat A. Wertheim, "re: Certification (To Be or Not to Be)," *Journal of Forensic Identification* 42 (1992), 280–281.
8. *State v. Caldwell*, 322 N.W. 2d 574 (Minnesota 1982); James E. Starrs, "A Miscue in Fingerprint Identification: Causes and Concerns," *Journal of Police Science and Administration* 12 (1984), 287–296.
9. "Certification Revoked," *Identification News* 31 (Feb. 1981), 2; (Sept. 1981), 2; Carol A. G. Jones, *Expert Witnesses: Science, Medicine, and the Practice of Law* (Oxford: Clarendon Press, 1994), 270–271.
10. Robert D. Olsen Sr., "Cult of the Mediocre," *Identification News* 32 (1982), 3–6.
11. Lambourne, "Fingerprint Standards."
12. David R. Ashbaugh, *Ridgeology: Modern Evaluative Friction Ridge Identification* (Royal Canadian Mounted Police, n.d.); Pat A. Wertheim, letter to the editor, *Fingerprint Whorld* (April 1997), 63–64; Hughes, "Cabbages and Kings," 240; John R. Vanderkolk, "Forensic Individualization of Images Using Quality and Quantity of Information," *Journal of Forensic Identification* 49 (1999), 246–256.
13. David R. Ashbaugh, "The Premise of Friction Ridge Identification, Clarity, and the Identification Process," *Journal of Forensic Identification* 44 (1994), 499–516; Ashbaugh, *Quantitative-Qualitative Friction Ridge Analysis: An Introduction to Basic and Advanced Ridgeology* (Boca Raton, Fla.: CRC Press, 1999).
14. Hughes, "Cabbages and Kings," 241.

15. Ashbaugh, *Quantitative-Qualitative*, 70.

16. Ibid., 5; Israel National Police, "International Symposium on Fingerprint Detection and Identification," *Journal of Forensic Identification* 45 (1995), 580–581; I. W. Evett and R. L. Williams, "A Review of the Sixteen Points Fingerprint Standard in England and Wales," *Journal of Forensic Identification* 46 (1996), 49–73.

17. David L. Grieve, "Possession of Truth," *Journal of Forensic Identification* 46 (1996), 521–528.

18. *U.S. v. Parks*, Central District of California, CR-91–358-JSL, trial transcript, vol. 5 (Dec. 11, 1991), 538–556.

19. Ibid., 560–561; Alan L. McRoberts, "Fingerprints: What They Can and Cannot Do!" *The Print* 10:7 (June 1994), 1–3.

20. *U.S. v. Parks*, transcript, 585–607.

21. Ibid., 575–577.

22. Jon Nordheimer, "Trooper's Fall Shakes Both Police and Public," *New York Times* (Nov. 15, 1992), Sec. 1, 41.

23. Albert Wehde and John N. Beffel, *Finger-Prints Can Be Forged* (Chicago: Tremonia, 1924), 74–80; Milton Carlson, "Forging Finger-Prints," *Journal of the American Institute of Criminal Law and Criminology* 11 (1920), 141–143.

24. Wehde and Beffel, *Finger-Prints Can Be Forged*, 107–126.

25. IAI, *Proceedings* (1927), 39–43.

26. Wehde and Beffel, *Finger-Prints Can Be Forged*, 78–80; Pat A. Wertheim, "Detection of Forged and Fabricated Latent Prints: Historical Review and Ethical Implications of the Falsification of Latent Fingerprint Evidence," *Journal of Forensic Identification* 44 (1994), 652–681.

27. IAI, *Proceedings* (1929), 84–91; Wertheim, "Detection," 664–675.

28. Wertheim, "Detection," 667–673; André A. Moenssens, "Novel Scientific Evidence in Criminal Cases: Some Words of Caution," *Journal of Criminal Law and Criminology* 84 (1993), 13.

29. Pat A. Wertheim, "Integrity Assurance: Policies and Procedures to Prevent Fabrication of Latent Print Evidence," *Journal of Forensic Identification* 48 (1998), 431–441; Nelson E. Roth, "The New York State Police Evidence Tampering Investigation," confidential report to the governor of New York (Ithaca, Jan. 20, 1997), 4, 10, 289.

30. Roth, *New York State Police*, 36, 110.

31. Ibid., 110, 312.

32. Ibid., 312.

33. Grieve, "Possession of Truth," 524–526; James E. Starrs, "Forensic Science on the Ropes: Procellous Times in the Citadels of Infallibility," *Scientific Sleuthing Review* 20:4 (Winter 1996), 1–3; Collaborative Testing Services, *Forensic Testing Program: Latent Prints Examination*, Reports no. 9608, 9708, 9808.

34. Stephen Grey, "Yard in Fingerprint Blunder," *London Times* (April 6,

1997); Duncan Campbell, "Fingerprint Proof 'Flawed,'" *The Guardian* (April 7, 1997); Keith Potter, "Error in Fingerprint Identification Could Lead to More Challenges," *Police Review* (April 11, 1997); Graham Hughes, personal communication with author, March 6, 1999.

35. "Expert Evidence in Court Appeal," *Irish Times* (Nov. 24, 1998); "£200,000 Payout: Even Though He Could Be the IRA Hyde Park Bomber," *The Sun* (Dec. 18, 1998); Bob Woffinden, "The Case of the Missing Thumbprint," *New Statesman* 12:537 (Jan. 8, 1999), 28.

36. "Internet Makes Mark in Fingerprint Case," *BBC News* (May 14, 1999).

37. David A. Stoney, "Fingerprint Identification," in David L. Faigman et al., eds., *Modern Scientific Evidence: The Law and Science of Expert Testimony* (St. Paul: West, 1997), 50–78, quotations 70–72; Michael Saks, "Merlin and Solomon: Lessons from the Law's Formative Encounters with Forensic Identification Science," *Hastings Law Journal* 49 (1998), 1069–1141, quotation 1106.

38. David L. Grieve, "Daubert and Fingerprints: The United States of America v. Bryan C. Mitchell," *The Sleuth* 37:1 (April/June 1999), 8–9; Simon Cole, "The Myth of Fingerprints," *Lingua Franca* 10:8 (Nov. 2000), 54–62.

39. Government's Proposed Findings of Fact and Conclusions of Law, *U.S. v. Mitchell*, CR-96–00407, Eastern District of Pennsylvania, 1.

40. Drez Jennings, "Painesville Case Challenges Validity of Fingerprints," *News-Herald* (Mentor, Ohio, Nov. 5, 1999); Robert Selna, "Doctrine of Dactyl Infallibility," *San Francisco Daily Journal* (Aug. 2, 2000), 1, 7; Mike Weiss, "Fact Is, Science Has Never Put Its Finger on Prints," *San Francisco Examiner and Chronicle* (May 28, 2000).

41. *U.S. v. Mitchell*, transcript, Jan. 9, 1997, 30–38; John Thornton, "Setting Standards in the Comparison and Identification," presented at Training Conference of the California State Division of IAI (Laughlin, Nev., May 9, 2000); Stephen Wright, "The Fatal Flaw in Fingerprint Matches," London *Daily Mail* (Oct. 24, 2000), 18.

12. The Genetic Age

1. Philip Jenkins, *Moral Panic: Changing Concepts of the Child Molester in Modern America* (New Haven: Yale University Press, 1998); Jane Caputi, *The Age of Sex Crime* (Bowling Green, Ohio: Bowling Green State University Popular Press, 1987).

2. Mark Seltzer, *Serial Killers: Death and Life in America's Wound Culture* (New York: Routledge, 1998).

3. Bill Hebenton and Terry Thomas, *Keeping Track? Observations on Sex Offender Registers in the U.S.* (London: Police Research Group, 1997); Hebenton and Thomas, "Sexual Offenders in the Community: Reflections on Problems of Law, Community and Risk Management in

the U.S.A., England and Wales," *International Journal of the Sociology of Law* 24 (1996), 427–443, quotation 429.

4. Joseph Wambaugh, *The Blooding* (New York: Bantam, 1989), 187–189.

5. Ibid., 86–95.

6. Ibid., 220–222, 293.

7. "Welsh Police Canvass Men for DNA Tests," *New York Times* (April 15, 1995), A2; Richard W. Stevenson, "Slaying Inquiry in Wales Tests DNA of 150 People," *New York Times* (April 23, 1995), 13.

8. Eric S. Lander and Bruce Budowle, "DNA Fingerprinting Dispute Laid to Rest," *Nature* 371 (1994), 735–738; William Ledlie Culbert and Frederick M. Lau, "Identification by Comparison of Roentgenograms of Nasal Accessory Sinuses and Mastoid Processes," *Journal of the American Medical Association* (1927), 1634–36; Oscar Mueller, *The Expert* (Los Angeles: Saturday Night Pub. Co., 1929), 31; Matt K. Matsuda, *The Memory of the Modern* (New York: Oxford University Press, 1996), 140; Donald Dilworth, ed., *Identification Wanted: Development of the American Criminal Identification System, 1893–1943* (Gaithersburg, Md.: International Association of Chiefs of Police, 1977), 200–202; Irma van der Ploeg, "Written on the Body: Biometrics and Identity," *Computers and Society* 29 (1999), 37–44.

9. Barry Scheck, Peter Neufeld, and Jim Dwyer, *Actual Innocence: Five Days to Execution and Other Dispatches from the Wrongly Convicted* (New York: Doubleday, 2000), 38–39.

10. Carey Goldberg, "DNA Databanks Giving Police a Powerful Weapon, and Critics," *New York Times* (Feb. 19, 1998), A1–12; C. J. Chivers, "DNA Match Implicates Inmate in '79 Murder, Officials Say," *New York Times* (March 13, 2000), B1.

11. Nicholas Wade, "FBI Opens DNA Data Base," *New York Times* (Oct. 18, 1998); Federal Bureau of Investigation, *Press Release* (Oct. 13, 1998); Randall S. Murch and Bruce Budowle, "Are Developments in Forensic Applications of DNA Technology Consistent with Privacy Protections," in Mark A. Rothstein, ed., *Genetic Secrets: Protecting Privacy and Confidentiality in the Genetic Era* (New Haven: Yale University Press, 1997), 212–230.

12. "NY's DNA Database for Crime Expanded," *Associated Press* (Oct. 19, 1999); Richard Pérez-Peña and Jayson Blair, "New York Plan Widely Expands The Sampling of Criminals' DNA," *New York Times* (Aug. 9, 1999), A1; "State Seeks to Expand DNA Database," *Associated Press* (Jan. 5, 1999); Jean E. McEwen, "DNA Data Banks," in Rothstein, *Genetic Secrets*, 231–251.

13. Howard Safir and Peter Reinharz, "DNA Testing: The Next Big Crime-Busting Breakthrough," *City Journal* 10:1 (Winter 2000); Jayson Blair, "Police Chiefs Join in Call for More DNA Sampling," *New York Times*

(Aug. 16, 1999), B5; Richard Pérez-Peña, "Governor to Emphasize Fighting Crime: DNA Fingerprinting and an End to Parole Are Pataki's Priorities," *New York Times* (Jan. 6, 1999), B5; "DNA Test Urged in All Busts," *New York Daily News* (Feb. 19, 1999), 2; Dareh Gregorian, "Morgenthau: DNA Is Key to Solving 12,000 Crimes," *New York Post* (Mar. 5, 1999), 18; Gary Spencer, "Pataki Seeks DNA Testing for All Convicted Felons," *New York Law Journal* (April 14, 1999), 1; "People Constantly Shed DNA, Study Finds," *Associated Press* (June 19, 1997); Bruce Lambert, "Giuliani Backs DNA Testing of Newborns for Identification," *New York Times* (Dec. 17, 1998), B5; Frank Lombardi, "Test Tot DNA, Sez Rudy," *New York Daily News* (Dec. 17, 1998), 33; "Florida Tries DNA Sampling to Protect Children" *New York Times* (Jan. 27, 1999), A14.

14. Murch and Budowle, "Developments"; McEwen, "DNA Data Banks."

15. Arthur Daemmrich, "The Evidence Does Not Speak for Itself: Expert Witnesses and the Organization of DNA-Typing Companies," *Social Studies of Science* 28 (1998), 741–772.

16. Kathleen Jordan and Michael Lynch, "The Dissemination, Standardization and Routinization of a Molecular Biological Technique," *Social Studies of Science* 28 (1998), 773–800.

17. Eric Lander, "DNA Fingerprinting: Science, Law, and the Ultimate Identifier," in Daniel J. Kevles and Leroy Hood, eds., *The Code of Codes: Scientific and Social Issues in the Human Genome Project* (Cambridge, Mass.: Harvard University Press, 1992), 191–210.

18. William C. Thompson and Simon Ford, "DNA Typing: Acceptance and Weight of the New Genetic Identification Tests," *Virginia Law Review* 75 (1989), 126.

19. Alec J. Jeffreys, "DNA Typing: Approaches and Applications," *Journal of the Forensic Science Society* 33 (1993), 204–211; Paul Rabinow, "Galton's Regret: Of Types and Individuals," in Paul R. Billings, ed., *DNA on Trial: Genetic Identification and Criminal Justice* (Plainview, N.Y.: Cold Spring Harbor Laboratory Press, 1992), 5–18.

20. Andrew Ross, "If the Genes Fit, How Do You Acquit?" in Toni Morrison and Claudia Brodsky Lacour, eds., *Birth of a Nation'hood: Gaze, Script, and Spectacle in the O. J. Simpson Case* (New York: Pantheon, 1997), 241–272.

21. Lander and Budowle, "DNA Fingerprinting"; Richard Lewontin and Daniel Hartl, "Letters," *Nature* 372 (1994), 398–399.

22. Jeffrey Toobin, *The Run of His Life: The People v. O. J. Simpson* (New York: Random House, 1996), 334–347.

23. Scheck, Neufeld, and Dwyer, *Actual Innocence;* Edward Connors et al., *Convicted by Juries, Exonerated by Science: Case Studies in the Use of*

DNA Evidence to Establish Innocence after Trial (Washington: National Institute of Justice, 1996).

Epilogue. Bodily Identities

1. Daniel J. Kevles, *In the Name of Eugenics: Genetics and the Uses of Human Heredity* (Berkeley: University of California Press, 1986); Nicole Hahn Rafter, *Creating Born Criminals* (Urbana: University of Illinois Press, 1997).
2. Richard Pérez-Peña and Jayson Blair, "Albany Plan Widely Expands Sampling of Criminals' DNA," *New York Times* (Aug. 7, 1999), A1.
3. Ibid.; Paul Rabinow, "Galton's Regret: Of Types and Individuals," in Paul R. Billings, ed., *DNA on Trial: Genetic Identification and Criminal Justice* (Plainview, N.Y.: Cold Spring Harbor Laboratory Press, 1992), 5–18.
4. James O. Davis, Jeanne Phelps, and H. Stefan Bracha, "Prenatal Development of Monozygotic Twins and Concordance for Schizophrenia," *Schizophrenia Bulletin* 21 (1995), 357–366.
5. Steven Pinker, *How the Mind Works* (New York: Norton, 1997); Randy Thornhill and Craig T. Palmer, *A Natural History of Rape: Biological Bases of Sexual Coercion* (Cambridge, Mass.: MIT Press, 2000).
6. Richard C. Lewontin, *The Triple Helix: Gene, Organism, and Environment* (Cambridge, Mass.: Harvard University Press, 2000).

1. Benjamin P. Eldridge and William B. Watts, *Our Rival the Rascal: A Faithful Portrayal of the Conflict Between the Criminals of this Age and the Defenders of Society—The Police* (Boston, 1897). Courtesy Lloyd G. Sealy Library, John Jay College, City University of New York.

2. Alphonse Bertillon, *Instruction for Taking Descriptions for the Identification of Criminals and Others by the Means of Anthropometric Indications*, trans. Gallus Muller (Chicago, 1889). Courtesy New York Public Library.

3. Collection of Bertillon Records, Municipal Archives, Department of Records and Information Services, City of New York.

4. Alphonse Bertillon, *Signaletic Instructions: Including the Theory and Practice of Anthropometrical Identification*, trans. R. W. McClaughry (Chicago, 1896). Courtesy Lloyd G. Sealy Library.

5. Bertillon, *Signaletic Instructions*. Courtesy Lloyd G. Sealy Library.

6. New York Police Department, *Annual Report* (1911). Courtesy Municipal Library, Department of Records and Information Services, City of New York.

7. Jan Evangelista Purkyně, "A Physiological Examination of the Organ of Vision and the Integumentary System," Habilit. diss., University of Breslau (1823), trans. Harold Cummins and Rebecca Wright Kennedy, *American Journal of Police Science* 30 (1940), 343–356.

8. William Herschel, *The Origin of Finger-Printing* (London, 1916).

9. Property of author.

10. Drawing by John E. Berry. Reproduced by permission of John E. Berry.

11. Drawing by John E. Berry in *Ridge Detail in Nature* 7 (1983), 2. Reproduced by permission of John E. Berry.

12. Henry P. DeForest Papers, #3214, Box 10, Folder 1, Division of Rare and Manuscript Collections, Carl A. Kroch Library, Cornell University.

13. Alix, "Recherches sur la disposition des lignes papillaires de la main et du pied," *Annales des science naturelles zoologie et paleontologie 9* (1868).

14. *Finger Print and Identification Magazine* 7 (Sept. 1925), 16–17.

15. Harris Hawthorne Wilder and Bert Wentworth, *Personal Identification: Methods for the Identification of Individual, Living or Dead* (Boston, 1918), 31–32.

16. Wilder and Wentworth, *Personal Identification*, 287.

17. J. A. Larson, *Single Fingerprint System* (New York, 1924).

ACKNOWLEDGMENTS

Those individuals and institutions whose faith in the project, and in me, helped bring it to completion should share credit for its authorship, though not for its deficiencies. First and foremost, I wish to thank Trevor Pinch, Sheila Jasanoff, Davydd Greenwood, and Ronald Kline for their enthusiasm for the project and for giving me the intellectual freedom to pursue it. Michael Dennis and Vilma Santiago-Irrizary also commented on parts of the manuscript.

The fingerprint examiners John Berry, Carey L. Chapman, and Michael Harling have been instrumental in helping me secure access to hard-to-find primary sources. John Berry also kindly furnished two illustrations. John Kim, Leon Ablon, and Ted Lorsbach provided additional technical assistance with the graphics.

David Ashbaugh, Graham Hughes, Christophe Champod, David Grieve, Ronald Lindell, Donald A. Sollars, Jeremy Johnson, and many other professional fingerprint examiners who wish to remain anonymous spoke candidly with me about the identification process. Robert Epstein and the Defender Association of Philadelphia generously shared voluminous material. I also enjoyed conversations with Mary Jaene Edmonds, who is writing a biography of Mary Holland, the first female fingerprint examiner in the United States.

A Hackman Research Residency enabled me to do research on prison records at the New York State Archives. The New York State Archives Partnership Trust, James Folts, Richard Andress, and other archivists and officials welcomed me to Albany and made my visit there pleasant and stimulating. I also made extensive use of the criminal justice collections held at the Lloyd Sealy Library at John Jay College, City University of New York. Kathy Killoran ably assisted me with my research there. In addition, Julie Johnson-McGrath lent me materials on forensics. During my research trips I was fortunate to be treated to the generous hospitality of Craig Dye and Alex Zapruder and Elizabeth, Aaron, and Dan Coleman.

Portions of my work were funded by a Sage Graduate Fellowship from Cornell University, a Research Training Fellowship from the National Science Foundation (NSF), and an NSF-sponsored research project, "DNA Fingerprinting: The Spectacle of Scientific Controversy" (NSF SBE-9312183). My colleagues on the last of these, Michael Lynch, Saul Halfon, Arthur Daemmrich, and Kathleen Jordan, shared information and insights during the exciting collaborative project that provided the genesis of this book.

A postdoctoral fellowship funded by the National Institute of Mental Health, at the Institute for Health, Health Care Policy, and Aging Research at Rutgers University, supported me while I was completing revisions on the manuscript. I am grateful to David Mechanic and Allan Horwitz for their support and to Gerry Grob for jump-starting the publishing process.

Part of Chapter 5, on the proposed use of thumb printing to identify Chinese immigrants in California, is based on research completed as part of a collaborative project with Mary T. Y. Lui and Arthur Burris. It was a pleasure to work with them, and their contribution to this work has been significant.

My work owes a great deal to numerous discussions with Julia E. Rodriguez and Jennifer Mnookin. I am also grateful to Anne Joseph, Ronald R. Thomas, Irma van der Ploeg, Andreas Fahrmeier, Peter Becker, Charles Steinwedel, John Torpey, David E. Brody, and especially Nicole Hahn Rafter for sharing their writings with me.

In addition to many of those mentioned above, Jill Cooper and Ira Galtman read portions of the manuscript book and gave me valuable criticism. Many others, too numerous to mention, showed great interest and enthusiasm for the project and helped encourage me to bring it to completion. The book benefited enormously from Joyce Seltzer's editorial acumen and guidance. I consider myself lucky to have had the opportunity to work with such an experienced editor. Camille Smith expertly edited the final manuscript.

My family supported my writing of this book through thick and thin. Nancy Kelly provided childcare during the crucial final period of revisions. My partner, Laura Kelly, was, as always, my most patient and most trusted editor. And David, Susan, and Alexa Cole demonstrated a pride and boundless faith in me that I hope this book in some small way recompenses.